SSCP®
Systems Security Certified Practitioner
Study Guide

George B. Murphy

SYBEX®
A Wiley Brand

Development Editor: Tom Cirtin

Technical Editors: Brian D. McCarthy and John Gilleland

Production Editor: Christine O'Connor

Copy Editor: Judy Flynn

Editorial Manager: Mary Beth Wakefield

Production Manager: Kathleen Wisor

Associate Publisher: Jim Minatel

Media Supervising Producer: Richard Graves

Book Designers: Judy Fung and Bill Gibson

Proofreader: Kim Wimpsett

Indexer: Ted Laux

Project Coordinator, Cover: Brent Savage

Cover Designer: Wiley

Cover Image: ©Getty Images Inc./Jeremy Woodhouse

Attacks on organizations' information assets and infrastructure continue to escalate while attackers refine and improve their tactics. The best way to combat these assaults starts with qualified information security staff armed with proven technical skills and practical security knowledge. Practitioners who have proven hands-on technical ability would do well to include the (ISC)² Systems Security Certified Practitioner (SSCP®) credential in their arsenal of tools to competently handle day-to-day responsibilities and secure their organization's data and IT infrastructure.

The SSCP certification affirms the breadth and depth of practical security knowledge expected of those in hands-on operational IT roles. The SSCP provides industry-leading confirmation of a practitioner's ability to implement, monitor and administer policies and procedures that ensure data confidentiality, integrity and availability (CIA).

Reflecting the most relevant topics in our ever-changing field, this new SSCP Study Guide is a learning tool for (ISC)² certification exam candidates. This comprehensive study guide of the seven SSCP domains draws from a global body of knowledge, and prepares you to join thousands of practitioners worldwide who have obtained the (ISC)² SSCP credential. The SSCP Study Guide will help facilitate the practical knowledge you need to assure a strong security posture for your organization's daily operations.

As the information security industry continues to transition, and cybersecurity becomes a global focus, the SSCP Common Body of Knowledge (CBK®) is even more relevant to the challenges faced by today's frontline information security practitioner. While our Official Guides to the CBK are the authoritative references, the new study guides are focused on educating the reader in preparation for exams. As an ANSI accredited certification body under the ISO/IEC 17024 standard, (ISC)² does not teach the SSCP exam. Rather, we strive to generate or endorse content that teaches the SSCP's CBK. Candidates who have a strong understanding of the CBK are best prepared for success with the exam and within the profession.

Advancements in technology bring about the need for updates, and we work to ensure that our content is always relevant to the industry. (ISC)² is breaking new ground by partnering with Wiley, a recognized industry-leading brand. Developing a partnership with renowned content provider Wiley allows (ISC)² to grow its offerings on the scale required to keep our content fresh and aligned with the constantly changing environment. The power of combining the expertise of our two organizations benefits certification candidates and the industry alike.

For more than 26 years, (ISC)² has been recognized worldwide as a leader in the field of information security education and certification. Earning an (ISC)² credential also puts you in great company with a global network of professionals who echo (ISC)²'s focus to inspire a safe a secure cyber world.

Congratulations on taking the first step toward earning your certification. Good luck with your studies!

Regards,

To my beautiful wife, Cathy—thank you for your patience, understanding, and especially your encouragement. You are and always will be my angel. With much love.

Acknowledgments

It's always amazing how many people are involved in the production of a book like this. Everyone involved deserves a world of thanks for all of their hard work and efforts. I especially want to thank Carol Long, who was executive acquisitions editor for Wiley & Sons when we started this project. I genuinely appreciate the opportunity that she afforded me. I also owe so much to many others, especially Tom Cirtin, for keeping everything on track, as well as Christine O'Connor, who tied together all of the production efforts. I want to thank Jim Minatel for herding all of the cats and keeping it all running. Many thanks to Judy Flynn for her tireless efforts in making sure all of the copy worked, as well as the entire team of layout editors, graphic design folks, and others, all of whom provided their expertise to make this project come together. I would like to express a big thanks to Brian McCarthy for his knowledge and his wonderful work as technical editor. I would also like to express my appreciation to both Mike Siok and Willie Williams for their friendship and inspiration through a great many projects over the years. They have always been there to lend an ear and offer encouragement. I want to recognize Chuck Easttom for giving me my break into the world of publishing a few years ago. And, I want to especially thank all of the wonderful folks at $(ISC)^2$ for their ongoing assistance in this and many other projects. Thank you all very much.

About the Author

George (Buzz) Murphy, CISSP, SSCP, CASP, is a public speaker, corporate trainer, author, and cybersecurity evangelist who, over the past three decades, has touched the lives of thousands of adult learners around the world through hundreds of speaking and training events covering a variety of technical and cybersecurity topics. A former Dell technology training executive and U.S. Army IT networking security instructor, he has addressed audiences at national conferences, major corporations, and educational institutions, including Princeton University, and he has trained network and cybersecurity operators for the U.S. military branches, various U.S. government security agencies, and foreign military personnel.

As a military data center manager in Europe, he held a top-secret security clearance in both U.S. and NATO intelligence and through the years has earned 26 IT and cybersecurity certifications from such prestigious organizations as (ISC)^2, CompTIA, PMI, and Microsoft. He is an (ISC)^2 Authorized Instructor specializing in CISSP and Cloud Security certification training. He has authored, coauthored, and contributed to more than a dozen books on a wide range of topics, including network engineering, industrial technology, and IT security, and recently served as technical editor for the *(ISC)^2 CCFP – Certified Cyber Forensics Professional Certification Guide* by Chuck Easttom (McGraw Hill, 2014) as well as for the recent publication *CASP: CompTIA Advanced Security Practitioner Study Guide* by Michael Greg (Sybex, 2014).

About the Technical Editor

Brian D. McCarthy, founder and director of 327 Solutions, Inc., has been involved in placement, consulting, and training since 1992. Brian is an entrepreneur, IT trainer, operations leader, certification expert, recruiter, instructional designer, sales executive, formally trained project manager (PMP), and e-learning guru. He has more than 20 years of talent development expertise, has been working in building technical competency for decades, and has held multiple positions in operations, training facilitation, and sales with increasing responsibility for building a world-class national network of performance experts. Brian has worked hand in hand with the Department of Defense to enable information assurance compliance for cybersecurity workers (8570.1-M / 8140). He also has experience working with cutting-edge e-learning, workshops, immersive environments, gamification/contest design, method-of-action 3D animations, LMS tracking, portal systems, and other learning assets to accelerate world-class corporate teams.

Contents at a Glance

Contents

Introduction

What a wonderful time to be involved with IT security. The role of security practitioner is expanding almost on a daily basis. Challenges abound as we all try to get our arms around not only traditional hardwired networks but also everything involved with wireless communication and the virtualization of everything in the cloud. There is so much to know and understand, and the growth potential seemingly has no bounds. Keeping up with this pace is (ISC)^2, the creators of the Certified Information Systems Security Professional (CISSP) certification, along with several other certifications.

(ISC)^2 is renowned for offering industry-leading cybersecurity and other types of training courses around the world. Achieving the Systems Security Certified Practitioner (SSCP) from (ISC)^2 indicates mastery of a broad-based body of knowledge in IT security. From network engineering to application development and from cybersecurity to physical security, the prestigious SSCP certification indicates that an individual is an accomplished and knowledgeable security practitioner. The certification is not a vendor-specific certification but a comprehensive broad-based certification.

Candidates for this certification will take a 125-question exam over a period of three hours. The exam covers questions from seven separate and distinct areas of knowledge called domains. Upon passing the examination with a score of 700 or better out of a possible 1,000, successful candidates also must agree to adhere to the (ISC)^2 Code of Ethics. Applications must also be endorsed by a current (ISC)^2 member or by the organization. This sets SSCP certification holders apart because they are true accomplished professionals who adhere to a clear set of standards of conduct and are in the forefront of the IT security industry.

This book is intended to thoroughly prepare you for the SSCP examination. It completely covers all of the new material introduced by (ISC)^2 in early 2015. The changes and additional information place increasing importance on subjects such as the cloud, virtualization, big data, and security monitoring and detection as well as the importance of personal privacy protection and its enforcement by new laws and legislation.

Although the requirement for the SSCP certification is one year of employment in the industry, it is assumed that that year of employment will aid in the individual's ability to apply the various concepts covered in this book. The exciting thing about being a security practitioner is the diversity of the assignments and required knowledge of the job. This certification indicates a broad range of knowledge and capabilities and can be a first major step forward in a rewarding career in IT security.

Who Should Read This Book?

Although the Systems Security Certified Practitioner certification has been offered by (ISC)^2 for many years, in 2015 the Common Body of Knowledge (CBK), which forms the foundation for the exam, was substantially modified. To keep the certification relevant with the rapid developments in the industry, the (ISC)^2 organization regularly undertakes a program to ascertain the new skills required by the individuals holding its certification. It has been estimated that as much as 25 to 30 percent of new information has been added to various (ISC)² certifications during this process. As should be expected, the SSCP exam was changed to reflect the additional information and knowledge required of candidates. These changes were announced as recently as the first quarter of 2015. Although other exam preparation sources may contain adequate information for past examinations, they may not offer the complete scope of the new information as contained in this book.

The *SSCP: Systems Security Certified Practitioner Study Guide* is intended for candidates wishing to achieve the Systems Security Certified Practitioner certification. It is a comprehensive exam preparation guide to assist you in understanding the various concepts that will be included on the exam. Although deep technical knowledge and work experience are not required to pass the examination, it is necessary to have a basic understanding of security technologies such as networking, client/server architecture, and the devices and controls used to reduce risk to organizations. This book covers items such as network telecommunications as well as cryptography in very down-to-earth, easy-to-understand language that makes comprehension and information retention easy and painless.

What Is Covered in This Book

This textbook is a comprehensive review of all of the subjects you should be familiar with prior to taking the SSCP certification exam. It generally follows the exam outline as expressed by the (ISC)² organization. Various learning tools will be used, such as examples and typical applications of many of the concepts. You will also read case studies of successful and sometimes not-so-successful real-world examples. Each chapter will include notes that will elaborate in a little more detail about a concept as well as a number of exam points that serve as detailed reminders of important concepts that are important to remember.

As you will see, this book is not a condensed "exam notes guide" type of book. Instead, it comprehensively covers the different subjects and categories of information that a practicing SSCP should know, not only to pass the certification examination but also to apply in the workplace.

To successfully pass this certification examination as well as any future (ISC)² certification examination, it is important not to just memorize the material but to learn and understand the topics. If you understand the material and how it's applied, you will always be successful on an examination.

Chapter 1: Information Security: The Systems Security Certified Practitioner Certification   This chapter introduces the SSCP examination candidate to the requirements and preparation required to sit for the exam. It familiarizes the you with the (ISC)² organization, the requirements you must meet to take the examination, examination registration procedures, the (ISC)² SSCP endorsement requirements, the continuing education requirements (CEU), and the annual fee.

In this chapter you will learn what to expect at the examination center and how to plan for your examination day. Through the years, many other individuals have taken technical examinations similar to the SSCP certification examination. In this chapter, you will learn many of their successful study techniques so that you may be equally as successful when preparing for the examination.

Chapter 2: Security Basics: A Foundation   The SSCP certification examination consists of 125 multiple-choice questions concerning the (ISC)² organization's SSCP Common Body of Knowledge (CBK). This body of knowledge consist of seven domains, or separate sections of information. Chapter 2 introduces you to the concepts of access control and a large number of related terms and definitions. It begins with a description of the CIA triad, which is the foundation for enterprise IT security. The discussion includes an understanding of security terms and concepts. You will see that some of these concepts have various permutations over time such as the wireless security protocols of WEP, WPA, and eventually WPA2 that we use today.

Chapter 3: Domain 1: Access Controls   Protecting enterprise resources is a major part of the job description of an IT security professional. In this chapter, you will learn in detail how access controls are selected and implemented to protect resources from unauthorized use or entry. You will learn the importance of identification, authentication, authorization, logging, and accountability. You will understand that various access control techniques, such as discretionary access control as well as nondiscretionary access control in the form of mandatory access control and roll-based access control may be implemented in various situations throughout an enterprise.

Chapter 4: Domain 2: Security Operations and Administration   Every enterprise must have policies, standards, procedures, and guidelines that provide documented information that guides the actions of the organization as well as the individuals it employs or interacts with. Chapter 4 will introduce you to the concept of information availability, integrity, and confidentiality as it applies to management personnel, system owners, information managers, and end users throughout an organization. In this chapter, you will come to understand change management as well as applying patches and updates to software and systems and complying with data management policies. This chapter will also cover data classification and the importance of validating that a security control is operating effectively.

Chapter 5: Domain 3: Risk Identification, Monitoring, and Analysis   Potential threats pose risks to every organization. This chapter introduces organized assessment techniques to provide ongoing threat identification and monitoring. You will learn the importance of implementing controls to mitigate or reduce threats or vulnerabilities, which thereby reduces overall risk to the organization.

This chapter includes a discussion of risk management concepts, the assessment of risk, and typical techniques organizations use to address risks, such as buying insurance, reducing risk, and possibly avoiding risk altogether. You will also learn the importance of discovering events and incidents as they are occurring through monitoring and reviewing log files as well as the techniques of participating in both risk reduction and risk response activities.

Chapter 6: Domain 4: Incident Response and Recovery   There are several key tasks that may become the responsibility or assignment of the security practitioner. Some of these tasks can involve actions and activities in response to an incident or emergency situation. In this chapter, you will be introduced to the techniques of incident handling (which include investigations, reporting, and escalation) as well as digital forensic concepts. You will learn the actions required of a first responder, including the requirements concerning protection of an incident scene, evidence acquisition and handling, and restoring the environment to a state prior to the incident.

This chapter will also cover the creation of a business continuity plan as well as a disaster recovery plan, both of which are required by an enterprise to be used during a disaster event. And finally, the importance of testing the plans and providing exercises and drills for the participants will be discussed.

Chapter 7: Domain 5: Cryptography   Confidentiality, as a leg of the CIA triad, is a major responsibility of all of the individuals in IT security as well as the SSCP. This chapter will introduce you to the concepts and requirements of confidentiality and how to provide it using cryptographic methods. Cryptographic algorithms, the use of keys, and the types of cryptographic systems will be discussed in detail, but in a way that will be easy to understand. You will discover that every time an individual logs into an e-commerce website, most of the concepts covered in this chapter, such as public-key infrastructure, will be utilized.

You will gain an understanding of the use of digital certificates, how to provide integrity for data, and what techniques can be used so that data is protected when it is at rest or in transit. Finally, you will learn how authentication can be provided by cryptographic means as well as how to ensure that the sender of a message can't deny that they sent the message, which is referred to as nonrepudiation.

Chapter 8: Domain 6: Networks and Communications   IT networks comprise numerous hardware devices that are assembled using various methods and resulting in network models called topologies. Network devices make use of signaling techniques referred to as telecommunications to transfer data between users and through devices. In Chapter 8, you will be introduced to network models and hardware devices as well as the structure of data that flows over the networks and through these devices.

This chapter will cover wireless and cellular technologies including the concepts of Bring Your Own Device and the connection of personal digital devices to the enterprise network. It will conclude with a discussion of converged network communications such as voice and media over the digital network and the prioritization of information that transverses a network.

Chapter 9: Domain 7: Systems and Application Security   Forming the termination point of a network connection are endpoints such as, for example, host workstations, digital wireless devices, printers, scanners, and devices like point-of-sale equipment. Chapter 9 will introduce you to the importance of securing endpoints against many types of malicious code attacks and how to apply various countermeasures to mitigate the threat of endpoint attacks.

You will also become familiar with cloud security and many of the new requirements concerning data transmission between a user and the cloud and data storage in a cloud environment. The chapter includes a discussion about the importance of virtualization, not only in a local IT data center but also throughout the cloud environment.

The chapter will conclude with a discussion of data warehousing and big data environments, including a description of the use of thousands of processors in parallel to analyze big data and derive usable information, including trend analysis, the analysis of weather, and scientific applications.

Appendix A: Answers to the Written Labs   As an additional learning technique, you will find at the end of each chapter a series of five questions that require you to think through an answer in an essay-type format. You will be asked to define the difference between two techniques, for example, or to explain the use of something covered in the chapter. This is an opportunity for you to write out a brief description of your understanding of the concepts that were covered in the chapter. In Appendix A, you will find brief answers to each of the written lab questions. You can compare your answers with these as a review and to determine if further reading and studying is required.

Appendix B: Answers to Review Questions   In this appendix, you will find the answers to each of the review questions found at the end of each chapter.

Appendix C: Diagnostic Tools   The role of the security practitioner can be that of a hands-on technician who utilizes various tools and techniques to analyze and solve problems. This appendix outlines a number of diagnostic tools that are available to the security practitioner. You can practice using any of these tools to gain a better understanding of their application when used in analysis and problem solving.

How Do I Use This Book?

This book is simple to use and simple to read. It offers straightforward explanations of all of the SSCP exam topics. Along the way, there are many Exam Points, which are tidbits of information that are important to understand and remember while preparing for the exam.

Pre-study Assessment Exam   The pre-study assessment exam is a short 10-question quiz on some basic topics that are contained in the book. This will give you an idea of not only of some of the topics in the book but also your current level of understanding. Don't worry, after reading the book, you'll understand every question on the assessment exam.

Notes and Case Studies   Various notes and case studies are included throughout each chapter to point out relevant, real-world applications of some of the topics. The notes will draw your attention to important issues and changes in the security landscape or specific items of interest concerning the topics in each chapter.

Exam Points   Exam Points are important facts and pieces of information that are important to know for the examination. They are sprinkled throughout this book in every chapter. You should understand the fact or the theory but also consider the application of the technique.

Chapter Review Questions   To test your knowledge as you proceed through the book, there are 20 review questions at the end of each chapter. As you finish each chapter, answer the review questions and then check your answers. Should you get a question wrong, you can go back to reread the section that deals with the subject to ensure that you answer correctly the next time.

Electronic Flashcards   Flashcards are excellent for memory and information retention. They may be used to rapidly test your memory and recall of various topics, terms, and definitions. These are similar to the flashcards you might have used when you were in school. You can answer them on your PC or download them onto a personal device for convenient reviewing.

Test Engine   The website also contains the Sybex Test Engine. Using the sample exam and this custom test engine, you can identify areas in which you might require additional study. You'll notice that the practice examination is worded a little differently than the questions at the end of the chapters. The SSCP examination might give you a short scenario and require you to think about the application of the concept rather than just provide a term and ask you to define it.

An examination question quite often will ask you to apply the concept. For example, a question might be worded, "Bill is in the Dallas office of ABC Corporation while Tom is in their sales office in Chicago. Bill needs to send data over an untrusted network to Tom. Which of the following options best describes the technique he should use?"

Glossary of Terms   An extensive glossary of terms is included on the website. You can view these on your PC or easily download them to a personal device for quick and easy reference. I suggest, in the first pass, read the question and respond with the answer. In the next pass, read the answers and determine what the topic is. Remember, exam questions might be phrased by giving you the definition and asking for the term or by giving you the term and asking for the definition. For instance, an exam question may be as follows: When using IPsec, which of the following best describes the services performed by the authentication header (AH)? Or, it may be worded like this: When using IPsec, authentication and integrity is performed by which of the following? Authentication header is the correct answer. Notice that both of these questions refer to the same information.

Assessment Test

1. Jim wants to place a device in the network demilitarized zone that may be broken into by an attacker so that he can evaluate the strategies that hackers are using on his systems. Which of the following *best* describes what he would use?

    A. Honeypot

    B. Decoy system

    C. Honeybucket

    D. Spoofing system

2. Frank calls you from the Los Angeles office to inform you of an attack he has discovered. Due to a vulnerability in an application, an attacker has the ability to intervene in a communications session by inserting a computer between the two participants. To each participant, the attacker appears to be the other participant. Which of the following best describes this type of attack?

    A. Man-in-the-middle attack

    B. DNS hijacking

    C. Trojan worm

    D. Backdoor attack

3. Susan has been alerted that applications on the network are executing very slowly. Which type of attack uses more than one computer to attack network devices with a result of slowing the network down?

    A. DoS

    B. DDoS

    C. Worm

    D. TCP/IP attack

4. Sam has determined that there are social engineering attacks happening in his company. What is the most effective means of protecting against social engineering attacks?

    A. Stateful inspection firewalls

    B. Trusted certificate lists

    C. Rule-based access control

    D. User education

5. Aeroflight Instrument Company has just completed a risk assessment. It has implemented a complete risk management program. What is the primary goal of risk management?

    A. Reduce risk to an acceptable level.

    B. Remove all risks from an environment.

    C. Minimize security cost expenditures.

    D. Assign responsibilities to job roles.

6. Which of the following best describes the use of passwords for access control?

   A. Authentication

   B. Authorization

   C. Auditing

   D. Identification

7. Francine is director of accounting for Infosure Systems Corporation. She is proposing that the company start moving some the accounting applications to a cloud provider. She wants them to be accessible from various client devices through either a thin client interface, such as a web browser, or a program interface. Which cloud service model would best fit this description?

   A. BaaS

   B. IaaS

   C. PaaS

   D. SaaS

8. Ken's boss is asking him what ARO stands for in regard to risk. What should he reply?

   A. Automatic review of operations

   B. Acceptable rate of output

   C. Authorized reduction of options

   D. Annualized rate of occurrence

9. As a defense contractor, Juan's company must comply with strict access control regulations. Juan's supervisor tells him to implement an access control based on the company's users' physical characteristics. Under which type of access security would hand scanning and retina scanning fall?

   A. CHAP

   B. Multi-factor

   C. Biometrics

   D. Token

10. What type of hardware device can be used to filter network traffic based upon an IP address?

   A. Firewall

   B. Bridge

   C. IP gateway

   D. Router

Answers to Assessment Test

1. A. Honeypots are systems that allow investigators to evaluate and analyze the attack strategies used by attackers. A honeypot is a hardened system that is placed in a demilitarized zone and is intended to be sacrificed to gain knowledge or simply to distract attackers. A demilitarized zone is usually created between two firewalls and provides access to servers and other devices from the untrusted external network while protecting the internal enterprise network. Complete networks can be simulated in a single honeypot server, with fake data traffic as well as simulated databases.

2. A. A man-in-the-middle attack attempts to fool both ends of a communications session into believing the system in the middle is actually the other end.

3. B. A distributed denial of service (DDoS) attack uses multiple computer systems to attack a server or host in the network.

4. D. User education is the most effective means of protecting against social engineering attacks.

5. A. The primary goal of risk management is to reduce risk to an acceptable level.

6. A. Passwords are the most common form of authentication.

7. D. With the Software as a Service (SaaS) model, applications are accessible from various client devices through a thin client interface, a web browser, or an API.

8. D. ARO stands for annualized rate of occurrence, which is the number of times an event might occur during the period of a year, drawn on historical data. This is used when calculating the cost of the loss of an asset due to a successful attack.

9. C. A biometric control is any access control method based on a user's physical characteristics.

10. A. A firewall is added to a network to filter traffic and secure the infrastructure. Firewalls are used to protect networks from each other, most specifically an internal trusted network from an external untrusted network such as the Internet. Firewalls filter on a number of traffic attributes, including IP address, destination and source address, and port address.

Chapter

1

Information Security: The Systems Security Certified Practitioner Certification

As a candidate for the Systems Security Certified Practitioner certification from (ISC)², you should be familiar with the (ISC)² organization and the examination requirements, registration procedures, endorsement requirements, and continuing education and annual fee requirements. In addition to introducing you to the requirements, this chapter will help you prepare for the examination. You will learn about various successful study techniques used by other candidates as well as how to register for the exam.

It is important for you to relax and do your best work. By knowing what to expect during your time at the examination center and by being prepared, you will be at ease and will be able to concentrate on the examination subject.

About the (ISC)² Organization

The International Information Systems Security Certification Consortium (ISC)² is a not-for-profit organization formed in 1989 to offer standardized vendor-neutral certification programs for the computer security industry. The first certification offered by the organization was the Certified Information Systems Security Professional (CISSP) certification. It was based upon a Common Body of Knowledge (CBK). The original CBK was intended to be all-encompassing, taking into consideration every aspect of information security from technical networking, information security models, and theory to physical security, such as fire extinguishers, perimeter lighting, and fences. The Systems Security Certified Practitioner (SSCP) credential was launched in 2001. It was intended as a foundational security credential requiring slightly less in-depth knowledge and a much more limited job experience criteria.

A key element central to the foundation of (ISC)² is a Code of Ethics. Every member of the (ISC)² organization, including candidates sitting for any of the certification examinations, must agree to and sign the Code of Ethics. It warrants that the members of the (ISC)² organization adhere to the highest standards of conduct in the performance of their security duties.

Today, (ISC)² is a global entity spanning more than 150 countries worldwide with membership totaling in excess of 100,000 members. The organization has been referred to as the "largest IT security organization in the world."

(ISC)² History

As the stand-alone PC era evolved into an era of networking during the early 1980s, it became evident that there was a need for network security standardization. Security professionals required the ability to describe their problems and solutions with common terminology. Concepts, tools, and techniques had to be shared between individuals on a worldwide basis to solve common problems and take advantage of shared opportunities. Although during this time various vendors coined terms and definitions specific to their products or sector of the industry, a desire arose for a vendor-neutral body of knowledge and a methodology for granting credentials for individuals who exhibited the knowledge and competence required of the IT security industry.

(ISC)² was founded during the summer of 1989 as a nonprofit organization to address the needs of IT security industry. The organization immediately began organizing a collection of topics relevant to the IT security industry. These topics were structured into a framework of concepts and terminology, with contributions from IT professionals around the world. The framework of ideas, terms, and concepts now known as the Common Body of Knowledge (CBK) allowed individuals from security practitioners to those in academia to discuss, create, and improve the IT security industry as it has evolved through the years.

Organizational Structure and Programs

(ISC)² has evolved into a multifaceted organization offering numerous certifications and credential programs. The organization also offers an outreach program where members can use (ISC)² tools and information to educate themselves and others and to increase the awareness of cyber crime in their local communities. Every year, tens of thousands attend an annual (ISC)² Security Congress, which features seminars and exhibits. Central to the organization is the continuous education of its members. During the year, numerous seminars, webinars, and other training sessions are available for (ISC)² members.

Certifications Offered

The award of a CISSP certification is a global recognition that an individual has proven knowledge in the security information field and has attained a high level of information understanding and professional competence. The CISSP certification has met all of the requirements of the ISO/IEC 17024 standard.

CISSP – Certified Information Systems Security Professional   The CISSP certification is recognized around the world as a standard of achievement that recognizes an individual's knowledge in the field of information security. These individuals generally serve in IT management and information assurance and may be employed as managers who assure the security of a business environment.

SSCP – Systems Security Certified Practitioner   The SSCP certification is ideal for individuals with at least one year of experience. These individuals may be employed as security practitioners in a network operations center, security operations center, or data center. The SSCP certification is the perfect starting point for somebody beginning an IT security career.

Additional certifications   (ISC)^2 offers several additional certifications in the area of healthcare, computer forensics, and system authorization professional and a variety of CISSP certifications. Additional information is available on the (ISC)^2 website.

Worldwide Recognition

(ISC)^2 has principal offices in the United States and additional offices in London, Hong Kong, and Tokyo. Major corporations around the world seek out and employ individuals with (ISC)^2 certifications.

With over 93,000 certified IT professionals located in over 135 countries worldwide, the (ISC)^2 organization has set the standard around the world as the leader in IT security certifications.

Industrial and Government Standards

The SSCP certification has been accredited by the American National Standards Institute (ANSI). The certification is in compliance with the International Organization for Standardization and International Electrotechnical Commission (ISO/IEC) 17024 standard.

DoD Directive 8570.1 and DoD Directive 8140

In the aftermath of the September 11, 2001, terrorist attacks and with cybersecurity threats surfacing virtually every day around the world, the United States Department of Defense (DoD) has determined that information security and assurance is of paramount importance to the national security of United States. To provide a basis for enterprise-wide standardization to train, certify, and manage the DoD Information Assurance (IA) workforce, The department issued DoD Directive (DoDD) 8570.1.

DoDD 8570.1, enacted in 2004 and rolled out in 2005, is always evolving. Since 2005, major advancements in technology and cybersecurity have occurred, leading to the newest DoDD, 8140. DoDD 8140 was launched in the first quarter of 2015, retiring 8570.1 in full. DoDD 8140 is based on the National Institute of Standards and Technology (NIST) National Initiative for Cybersecurity Education (NICE) standard. DoDD 8140 will update DoDD 8570.1, adding additional categories and further defining job roles for better training.

The 8140 directive stipulates a much broader scope than the original 8570.1 document by stating that a person that comes in contact with DoD information must abide by 8140 framework standards. The 8140 document does not concentrate on specific job roles as in the 8570.1 but instead lists categories of job tasks that may be performed by any individual throughout the defense industry.

The 8140 directive consists of several main categories that are further broken down into tasks or special areas. Job skills, training, and focus areas are better defined using this category system. There are seven main categories that have tasks or special areas of their own. The main categories are as follows (see Figure 1.1):

- Security Provision
- Operate and Maintain
- Protect and Defend
- Analyze
- Operate and Collect
- Oversight and Development
- Investigate

The SSCP certified individual may be employed at many of these job types but most specifically in the Protect and Defend job category. The jobs and skill requirements in this category center on securing and defending against cyber-related attacks. Computer Network Defense, Computer Network Defense Infrastructure Support, Incident Response, Security Program Management, and Vulnerability Assessment and Management are the special areas in this category.

FIGURE 1.1   The DODD 8140 chart

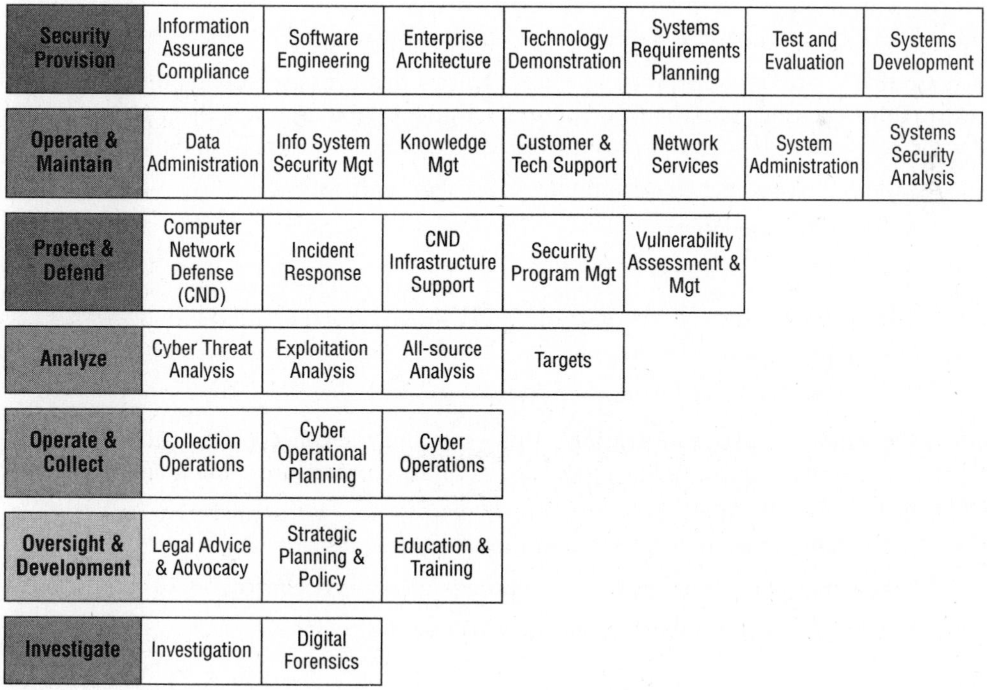

Security Provision	Information Assurance Compliance	Software Engineering	Enterprise Architecture	Technology Demonstration	Systems Requirements Planning	Test and Evaluation	Systems Development
Operate & Maintain	Data Administration	Info System Security Mgt	Knowledge Mgt	Customer & Tech Support	Network Services	System Administration	Systems Security Analysis
Protect & Defend	Computer Network Defense (CND)	Incident Response	CND Infrastructure Support	Security Program Mgt	Vulnerability Assessment & Mgt		
Analyze	Cyber Threat Analysis	Exploitation Analysis	All-source Analysis	Targets			
Operate & Collect	Collection Operations	Cyber Operational Planning	Cyber Operations				
Oversight & Development	Legal Advice & Advocacy	Strategic Planning & Policy	Education & Training				
Investigate	Investigation	Digital Forensics					

Exams, Testing, and Certification

Why certify? Certification represents a mark of achievement and indicates that the individual has attained the required knowledge through personal study, classroom work, or laboratory applications and has passed a requisite examination of sufficient difficulty to thoroughly assess depth of knowledge. To many, the certification represents a milestone in an individual's career. It illustrates diligence, hard work, and a strong desire for self-improvement.

The importance of a certification is a reflection of the esteem and recognition of the institution or organization granting the certification. Hiring officials must recognize the certification as a representation of diligence and hard work on behalf of the individual and also a clear testament to the overall knowledge and skill set as evaluated by an examination. The concept of certifications eliminates the requirement of the hiring official having to "test" the job candidate or having to evaluate their depth of knowledge by some manner.

Certification Qualification: The SSCP Common Body of Knowledge

(ISC)[2] has developed, in association with industry experts, a Common Body of Knowledge (CBK) that the certified SSCP individual must know to adequately perform the typical duties required by the job position for which they were hired. In this body of information are seven general categories referred to as *domains*.

The SSCP CBK consists of the following seven domains:

Access Controls   Access controls include mechanisms that are based upon policies, procedures, and user identification that control or determine what a user or subject may access and what permissions they have to read, write, or modify any information on a system.

- Administrative, technical, and physical access controls
- Methods of authentication
- Administration of access controls
- Trust architectures, Domains, and zones
- Managing identity using automation
- Aspects of cloud computing

Security Operations and Administration   Understanding the concepts of availability, integrity, and confidentiality and how policies, standards, procedures, and guidelines are used to support the AIC Triad.

- Administering security throughout the enterprise
- Managing change, change control mechanisms, change control board
- Baseline security, establishing security criteria

- Culture of security, enterprise security training
- Data and information communication infrastructure
- Host, node and endpoint device security
- Information management policies
- Establishing security practices throughout the enterprise

Monitoring and Analysis   Designing and implementing system monitoring controls used to identify events including a process to escalate events into incidents. Utilizing processes and monitoring technology to collect and analyze data from numerous sources.

- Continuous network monitoring
- Analysis of monitoring of real-time and historical event information

Risk, Response, and Recovery   The procedures used to perform a risk analysis and the calculations used to determine asset value and cost consequences if the asset is lost. Determine the methods by which risk may be mitigated and addressed. Plan for the ability to maintain essential operations and determine a plan for recovery back to normal operations after an adverse event.

- Risk assessment, risk mitigation
- Risk calculations
- Incident response concepts and activities
- Creating business continuity plans (BCP)
- Creating disaster recovery plans (DRP)

Cryptography   The protection of information using techniques that ensure its integrity, confidentiality, authenticity, and non-repudiation, and the recovery of encrypted information in its original form.

The use of encryption methods to protect valuable information from access, ensure data integrity, authenticity, and create non-repudiation and proof of message origin.

- Cryptographic terms and concepts
- Symmetric and asymmetric cryptography
- Non-repudiation, digital signatures and proof or origin
- Certificates

Networks and Communications   The design and implementation of network devices, protocols, and telecommunication services to transport information on both public and private networks.

- Network Design and implementation
- Telecommunication methods
- Remote network access

- Network hardware devices
- Utilizing wireless and cellular network technologies

Malicious Code and Activity   The implementation of controls and countermeasures to detect and prevent malicious code from attacking either the network or the hosts on the network.

- Detecting malicious code
- Countermeasures against malicious code
- Detecting malicious activity
- Coountermeasures against malicious activity

Additional Sources of Information

The complete candidate information bulletin (CIB) is available on the (ISC)^2 website. The CIB provides the basic information about the domains covered in the examination. The CIB outline is only a summary of the topics covered on the examination. It is not specifically a study or review guide. The CIB is subject to change, and it is suggested that the candidate refer back to the (ISC)^2 website from time to time to ensure that the most up-to-date examination information is being studied.

The candidate must also demonstrate at least one year of paid cumulative employment experience in an IT security position. *Cumulative* means that over your working career you spent some time performing the duties within one or more of the seven domains. When listing your experience, combine all of your experiences from any "work" endeavor to obtain a combined amount of experience time. If in doubt, you are invited to call (ISC)^2 and speak with the representatives about meeting your work experience requirements. You will find that they are extremely friendly and helpful.

If you lack the required work experience, you may still take the examination and become an Associate of (ISC)^2 until you have gained the required work experience time on the job.

The endorsement form requires the endorser to complete a number of questions specifically about your employment background and experience. This person then signs the form. If a local endorser is not available, (ISC)^2 may serve as your endorser.

After Passing the Exam

Once you take and pass the exam, you must complete an application and have the application endorsed before you will be awarded the SSCP credential. You may also download the

SSCP Applicant Endorsement Assistance Form from the (ISC)² website for endorsement information. The endorsement form may be completed and signed by an (ISC)² certified professional who is an active member. During the completion of the endorsement form, the certified professional will attest to your professional experience. If you do not have access to an (ISC)² certified professional, you may send all materials to (ISC)², which can act as an endorser for you.

With the endorsement form, you will be asked to send a resume illustrating your total work experience. This type of resume is different from a resume used to gain employment with a firm. (ISC)² specifically wants to know the length of time you spent gaining experience in any of the SSCP domains. To provide this information, include the name of the company, your title, and two to three sentences concerning your job. Below the brief job description, clearly state one or more of the SSCP domains for which this employment position offered experience. Indicate the start date and end date in whole months. For instance, list a date as May 2014 to November 2014, seven months. Remember that (ISC)² requires "cumulative" experience. This may be represented by different periods within the same company, time spent on several different projects, or time employed in a number of different companies.

Although you may have passed the SSCP certification exam, you may not use the SSCP credential or logo until you specifically receive notification with a congratulatory email from (ISC)². It is important when communicating with (ISC)² or anyone else to not use the SSCP logo or the letters behind your name until you have been authorized to do so. Should you include SSCP on the previously mentioned resume, it would be returned to you with removal instructions.

It is important that you do not use the SSCP logo or designation letters on any communications prior to receiving your authorization email from (ISC)². Specifically, do not include a reference to SSCP on your endorsement form or the qualification resume you send to (ISC)².

Certification Maintenance

The (ISC)² certification is valid for three years. Recertification or continued certification requires that the credentials be kept in good standing. Each certified member is required to submit continuing professional education (CPE) credits (referred to as CPEs) annually over the three-year period. A total of 60 CPE credits are required during the three-year period with a minimum of 10 CPE credits to be posted annually. More information on qualifying CPE credits is available on the (ISC)² SSCP website. If you are ever in doubt about whether a CPE qualifies, you can call and talk to the friendly folks at (ISC)².

The concept of requiring continuing professional education is an effort to keep the skill levels of various professionals such as lawyers, doctors, nurses, and IT professionals current and up-to-date with the latest concepts and knowledge in the industry. Individuals may take classes, conduct security courses, write articles or books, attend seminars or workshops, or attend security conventions. All of these activities afford learning experiences to the individual.

As part of certification maintenance, an annual maintenance fee (AMF) of $65 is due each year.

 Do not let your certification expire. If it does, you will be required to retake the examination.

Types of IT Certifications?

There are three general types of IT certifications.

Vendor-Neutral Certification   To earn a vendor-neutral certification, you pass an examination covering general industry concepts, theories, and applications. *Vendor-neutral* means that information specific to a particular vendor's product is not part of the examination. Vendor-neutral certifications are available for PC technicians and network technicians and cover the subject areas of general IT security and other topics such as cloud computing, database management, Information Technology Infrastructure Library (ITIL®) processes, and IT support.

Vendor Certification   Vendor certifications are available from a variety of hardware and software product manufacturers. They represent the attainment of certain level of expertise with the vendor's products. Due to the frequency of vendor product changes, many vendor certifications must be renewed on an annual basis by retaking an examination.

Professional Association Certification   Professional associations offer certifications and credentials to individuals who have validated their competency, work experience level, and knowledge of the job. To become a member and earn a credential, candidates must accomplish various steps, such as complete a rigorous training regime, pass an extensive examination, validate work experience or training experience history, and accomplish routine knowledge maintenance through annual CPE requirements.

Professional association certifications usually have a body of knowledge (BOK) established by the professional association. This body of knowledge is usually quite extensive, encompassing a broad range of topics with which the candidate must be familiar. Professional associations also require members to remain in good standing by paying annual maintenance fees or dues and abide by various rules, bylaws, or codes of conduct.

Typical professional associations include those for IT professionals, accountants, lawyers, medical professionals, project managers, engineers, and many other business, industrial, and service professions. Becoming a member of a professional association is by design a difficult task reserved for those who truly deserve the credential.

Generally, all types of certification organizations award their certification on an all-or-nothing basis. The candidate either passes or fails the examination. There is no such thing as "kind of" a CPA in the accounting profession.

Technical or Managerial

A wide variety of talents are required in the IT security industry. It is not unusual for entry-level positions to be of a technical nature, where individuals learn a wide variety of skills as associates, hardware technicians, help desk analysts, network support associates, and incident responders. Many of these individuals perform the tasks of practitioners. Practitioners generally work in the field and have detailed experience or knowledge of networking devices, situational monitoring, and operational software. The SSCP certification is designed for the IT security professional practitioner.

Those in managerial positions require a greater overview of corporate IT systems and must correlate the goals and mission of the enterprise with the design and security of the IT systems and information. Generally these individuals are less nuts and bolts oriented and much more policy driven in a large-scale environment. The CISSP certification is ideal for IT managers, consultants, and senior staff responsible for information security and assuredness within an organization.

Specialty Certifications

(ISC)² offers a number of specialty certifications for the IT professional.

Certified Authorization Professional (CAP)   The Certified Authorization Professional certification recognizes the skills, knowledge, and abilities of individuals responsible for the process of authorizing and maintaining information systems. The certification is intended for those who regularly assess risk and establish documentation and security requirements for the enterprise. These individuals are responsible for the overall security of information systems and ensure that the system security is commensurate with the level of potential risk.

Certified Cyber Forensics Professional (CCFP)   The Certified Cyber Forensics Professional demonstrates expertise in the area of forensics investigation and procedures, standards and practices, and ethical and legal knowledge to assure the accurate and complete processing of digital evidence so that it may be admissible in a court of law. The certification also establishes a baseline capability in other information security disciplines, such as e-discovery, incident response, and attack and malware analysis.

HealthCare Information Security and Privacy Practitioner (HCISPP)   The HealthCare Information Security and Privacy Practitioner demonstrates knowledge in information governance and risk management, information risk assessment, and third-party risk management within the healthcare industry. These individuals have foundational knowledge and experience throughout the healthcare information security and privacy industry and utilize privacy best practices and techniques to protect organizations and sensitive patient data against breaches, data loss, and organizational threats. They are instrumental in establishing policies, controls, education and training, and risk evaluation throughout an IT organization within an healthcare enterprise.

Certified Secure Software Lifecycle Professional (CSSLP)   The Certified Secure Software Lifecycle Professional is an industry leader in application security. This individual develops application security programs within an enterprise and works to reduce production costs, application vulnerabilities, and delivery delays. This individual works within software production organizations and identifies application vulnerabilities and is knowledgeable of the entire security lifecycle of an application that guides the creation of controls that mitigate risk.

About the Systems Security Certified Practitioner Certification

The Systems Security Certified Practitioner (SSCP) certification is a foundational certification with an emphasis on technical or practical knowledge. For example, it is intended for the person in an active role of systems maintenance, incident detection and response, and other tasks involving equipment support and risk control. The SSCP certification documents the knowledge of an individual and can be displayed on business cards, resumes, and other promotional materials.

What Is the Objective of This Certification?

The SSCP certification demonstrates that the individual has proficiency with IT security knowledge. The certification ensures that the candidate has the requisite knowledge to apply security concepts, tools, and procedures required during security incidents and that the individual can monitor systems and establish safeguards against threats to an organization.

Who Should Take the Certification Exam?

The SSCP certification exam is open to all individuals who are working toward positions like the following within the IT security profession:

- Information assurance technician
- Security architect systems analyst
- Security consultant or specialist
- Database administrator
- Information systems auditor
- Network security engineer
- System administrator
- Network security administrator
- Information systems auditor
- Information systems assuredness specialist
- Security architect
- Information security engineer
- Enterprise security technician

The SSCP certification is an ideal beginning point for those seeking a career in information security technology. It is an ideal introduction to many of the subjects required on future exams, such as the CISSP. (For the knowledge requirements, see the section "Certification Qualification: The SSCP Common Body of Knowledge" earlier in this chapter.)

What If You Are New to IT Security?

The SSCP certification is ideal if you are seeking to improve your information security skills or seeking a position advancement or promotion. The seven SSCP CBK domains cover all of the major topics required by an entry-level IT security professional. These are the same topics covered in greater depth in much more advanced exams.

It is common for an IT security individual to be employed in a position that requires knowledge of only one or two of the domains. It is possible that several of the domains may be quite foreign. Studying for this certification establishes a foundation of knowledge that allows for career advancement, job rotation, management potential, and recognition as a well-rounded IT security professional.

How Much Information Should You Know?

Ideally, the SSCP candidate has at least one year cumulative work experience in one or more of the seven SSCP CBK domains. After the candidate passes the examination, however, this work experience is not necessary to immediately become a member of (ISC)[2]. Individuals may become an Associate of (ISC)[2] until they gain the necessary one year of work experience.

Generally, an interest and a desire to become involved in the fastest-growing segment of the IT industry is all that is necessary to pursue certification. Any prior experience with programming, networking, hardware or software, databases, software applications, or general computer use within an organization is all that is required or desired as a launching point for the SSCP credential.

You will find that the SSCP CBK domains encompass a broad range of topics. What is required is that you have a general understanding of the subject matter and be able to answer examination questions as to the application and definitions of these concepts.

What Do I Have to Do after I Pass the Exam?

The SSCP candidate must complete the endorsement process after successfully completing the examination. The endorsement process has an time limit of nine months after the date of the exam or after the individual becomes an Associate of (ISC)[2]. If you do not obtain an endorsement within the nine-month endorsement time limit, you will be required to retake the exam in order to become certified.

The following steps are required for endorsement:

Create a Resume   This resume should indicate job positions that you have held where you have performed activities supporting any of the SSCP domains. The structure may be simple. This is different than a job-seeking resume. On this type of resume, the (ISC)[2] organization wants to identify the job positions you have held and the number of months in each position. Therefore, list the company name, the job position title, and a very brief description of the job responsibilities. Clearly state the beginning and ending dates of this position. For instance, specify May 2007 to December 2007. (ISC)² will compute this as May 1 to December 31. Also, it is important to list one or more of the SSCP domains used within this period of time.

Complete the Endorsement Form   An SSCP Applicant Endorsement Assistance Form may be downloaded from the (ISC)² website. The form must be completed and signed by an (ISC)² certified professional who is an active member and who can attest to your professional experience. This member may be located through any one of the numerous (ISC)² chapters around the world or possibly through your current employment or a website such as LinkedIn.com. In the event you cannot find an (ISC)² certified individual to act as an endorser, (ISC)² can act as an endorser for you. Please see the endorsement assistant guidelines on the (ISC)² website for additional information about the endorsement requirements.

> The resume that you present to the endorser or (ISC)² should clearly indicate the number of months you were employed in one or more of the SSCP certification domains.

How Do I Maintain My SSCP Certification?

Credentials are maintained in good standing by participating in various activities and gaining professional continuing professional education credits (CPEs). CPEs are obtained through numerous methods such as reading books, attending seminars, writing papers or articles, teaching classes, attending security conventions, and participating in many other qualifying activities. For additional information concerning the definition of CPEs, visit the (ISC)² website.

Individuals are required to post a minimum of 20 CPE credits each year on the (ISC)² member website. Generally, the CPE credit posted will be recognized immediately by the system, but it's also subject to random audit. Please note that any CPEs accomplished prior to being awarded the SSCP certification may not be claimed. If an individual accomplishes more than 20 CPEs during one year, the remainder may be carried forward to the following year. The (ISC)² website describes CPEs as items gained external to your current employment duties.

An annual membership fee (AMF) of US$65 is required each year. The membership time frame is an annual cycle beginning on the member's certification anniversary date.

What Is My Next (ISC)² Certification?

A great many people use the SSCP certification as a stepping stone in their IT security career. In many cases, this may be the first certification obtained. Each of the SSCP CBK domains is foundational information that will show up in greater depth or granularity in many other IT security certifications. Depending upon the current career track, you may pursue vendor-specific certifications or vendor-neutral certifications to further your knowledge and recognition within the IT security industry. After obtaining the requisite years of work experience, you are encouraged to seek the prestigious CISSP credential from (ISC)^2.

How Do I Use My SSCP Knowledge on the Job?

The Systems Security Certified Practitioner will have the knowledge and awareness of many aspects of protecting and defending cyber systems. This will include an awareness of access control, risk mitigation, change control, and network protection as well as many other knowledge areas that may be employed on the job.

It is important for the SSCP to understand the methods of security protection, hardware, and software systems involved and the tasks and procedures that the practioner may be assigned to perform. The use of your SSCP training will provide you with the skills to be able to confidently and competently perform duties in a professional manner.

Display Your Certification with Pride

The (ISC)^2 organization is recognized worldwide as offering the most prestigious IT security certifications. Through the requisite learning process, extensive examination, work history evaluation, subscription to the (ISC)^2 ethics statement, and annual maintenance through continuing education, employers and others throughout the industry recognize and revere the certifications.

Obtaining the SSCP certification is a career milestone. Once awarded, the SSCP letter designation may follow your name on business cards, stationery, and signature lines. You may proudly display the (ISC)^2 SSCP logo and have it associated with your professional work. You will receive a signed, full-color, gold-foil-embossed certificate as illustrated in Figure 1.2, which may be framed and proudly displayed in your office or work area. You will be further identified by an (ISC)^2 member number, which is printed on your certificate. At any time, employers may validate your certifications through the (ISC)^2 organization.

Actively Participate

All (ISC)^2 members are encouraged to actively participate within their organization and throughout their community. (ISC)^2 offers numerous training opportunities such as webinars, magazines, and emails as well as seminars, symposiums, and a security congress. There are think-tank roundtables, local events, and the Global Academic Program (GAP). All of these activities are explained on the (ISC)^2 website.

Demonstrate Your Knowledge at Every Opportunity

As an SSCP, you will be recognized as having attained a certain level of expertise and IT security knowledge. Company managers, supervisors, team leaders, and other individuals may seek you out for insight on how IT security impacts their specific projects or duties in the enterprise as a whole.

FIGURE 1.2   A typical framed SSCP certification

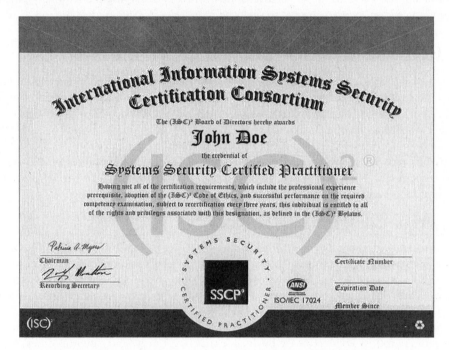

(ISC)^2 members are also encouraged to participate in community programs by spreading the word of IT security. Each member is encouraged to participate in the (ISC)^2 sponsored Safe and Secure Online Program. The Safe and Secure program features a security seminar that can be presented to schoolchildren, churches, organizations, and other general groups of people interested in IT and online security. (ISC)^2 supplies all of the manuals and booklets and facilitator guides required to conduct the seminars.

Join a Local (ISC)^2 Chapter

The (ISC)^2 organization has numerous local chapters around the world. You can locate them by accessing the chapter directory on the (ISC)^2 website. Various chapters may be titled as an (ISC)^2 CISSP chapter, but do not let that deter you. Feel free to contact the chapter manager or membership manager and invite yourself to their meeting. Participating in (ISC)^2 chapter meetings will allow you to meet and network with many of the top IT security professionals in the area. Organization dues are minimal, and usually each chapter offers a speaker or a program at each meeting. You do not have to hold a current credential prior to visiting a chapter meeting. Chapter meetings are a great place to learn about the IT security industry, and many of the individuals within a chapter can be approached for study suggestions, subject questions, or even mentoring or tutoring.

The SSCP Exam

The SSCP exam is a skills and knowledge security exam sponsored by $(ISC)^2$. The exam is focused on understanding key security concepts.

Exam Type   The exam is what's called a proctored examination, which means that an individual will be available in the testing room at all times. In some test centers, each test booth will usually be monitored by closed-circuit TV camera.

Number of Questions   The SSCP exam consists of 125 multiple-choice questions. Only 100 of the questions are graded, and 25 of the questions are evaluated for future tests. The 25 test questions will not be marked. Therefore, you must answer all 125 questions as if they are all graded.

Question Description   Exam questions will have four possible answers. There are no true or false questions. There will be no blanket scenario questions in which a scenario is stated and several following questions refer to the scenario.

You may expect some situation questions, which describe a situation and ask for the action that you would take in this situation. All acronyms will be spelled out, such as, for instance, access control list (ACL). Many questions will ask for the MOST correct or LEAST correct or use logical operators such as NOT, ALWAYS, BEST, TRUE, or FALSE. You should carefully read and understand any questions that contain any qualifier word. In most cases, this word with be in all capital letters, but carefully read any question, whether or not there are capitalized words.

It is important to remember that you are not penalized for wrong answers. Even if it is a guess, make sure every question has a marked answer.

Passing Score   Passing score is 700 out of a possible 1,000. It is reported that the questions are weighted values. This means you may be required to have more or less than 70 correct to pass the exam. The examination is pass/fail.

Preparing for the Exam

You can prepare for the SSCP examination through a variety of activities and techniques:

- Referring to the candidate information bulletin
- Reading this book
- Attending $(ISC)^2$ classroom-based training
- Attending $(ISC)^2$ online training
- Attending $(ISC)^2$ private, onsite training (usually sponsored by a company)

For additional information concerning classroom-based training, online training, or private training, email `education@(ISC)`.org or call 1.866.462.4777 or +1.703.781.6781 outside the United States.

Although it's nice to use the (ISC)^2 training products, please do not think that they are necessary. The majority of individuals who have passed the SSCP exam have done so by self-studying and reading.

Study Time

As you may remember from high school or college, studying for any exam takes time and diligence. Not only must you read through the material, but you must be able to understand the topics and concepts to adequately be able to answer the questions. The challenge on a certification exam such as the SSCP is the broad scope of the information contained in seven domains. While some of the material will seem easy and logical, it may be very easy to become bogged down in other topics.

Finding a location to study is not always easy in our busy lives. The place you select should be private and quiet. This examination is not something that you can study for in a local coffee shop. If you find yourself easily distracted by sounds, many sporting goods stores offer inexpensive earplugs or hearing protection headphones that may reduce the distraction from noise in your study location. If you must select between a location with noise and a location with people coming and going, choose the noisy location with privacy and use earplugs rather than being tempted to look up every time somebody passes by.

Study Techniques, Habits, and Methods

Through our high school and college years, many of us developed a variety of study techniques, habits, and learning methods, some better than others. It is a proven fact that we learn differently. We all have five senses, and some of us make use of these senses in different ways. The following list includes some personal study techniques shared over the years by college students who were studying technical or complex subjects.

Read and Mark   While reading the text, mark, highlight, underline, or make comments in the margin.

Read and Rewrite   While reading the text, rewrite or summarize the concept on a notepad in your own words. Writing things down in our own words reinforces what we are reading.

Read and Draw   While reading the text, draw a rough picture or illustration of the concept. This takes a little more creative thinking, and some of us see concepts as pictures or illustrations. Figure 1.3 illustrates a typical hand-drawn rough sketch of an SSCP topic. This is also a handy memory technique because in some cases, an illustration or picture is easier to recall than text.

FIGURE 1.3   An example of a hand-drawn rough sketch

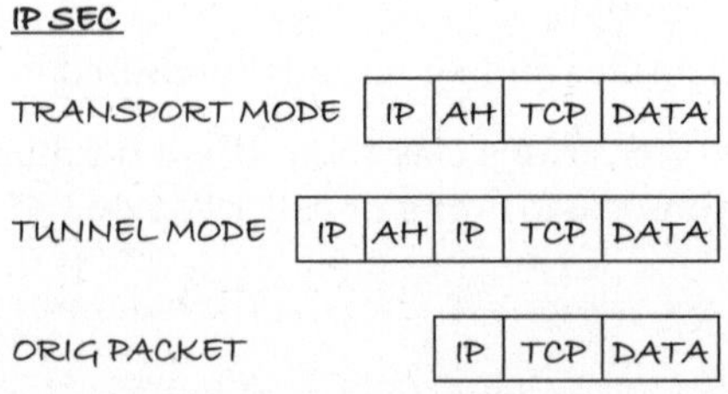

Read and Look Up   Some students like to read different authors' explanations of a concept. In this case, some use two books and refer to the exact same subject in both books, or they utilize an online search, dictionary, or encyclopedia for further research on the subject.

Read and View a Video   Over recent years, video-sharing sites such as YouTube.com have allowed the ability to view a short presentation on a specific subject. These presentations can last from a few minutes to an hour or more. While some presenters are better than others, the ability to view a presentation, especially a short one, has its advantages as a learning technique. A typical YouTube video on IPsec is at www.youtube.com/watch?v=rwu8__GG_rw.

Read and View a Picture   A similar technique to viewing a video is to view a picture or illustration of the subject. Several students utilize the technique of using Google images, Yahoo! images, or other search engines to find pictures or illustrations of concepts. For instance, complex subjects such as Public Key Infrastructure, Kerberos, and IPsec are depicted in dozens of drawings and illustrations gathered from websites around the Internet. Within the search results, you can click an image to be directed to the site containing it. In many cases, there is an explanation of the concept and the image. Figure 1.4 illustrates the results of a Google Images search for images on IPsec.

FIGURE 1.4   An example of a Google Images search on the term *IPsec*

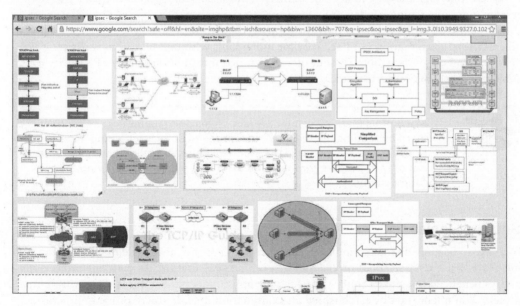

Read, Record, and Listen   Many of us learn by listening. The read-record-listen technique is a method used by some students to study materials while on the go. The student first reads the material in the book out loud in a normal tone of voice while recording it onto their electronic device such as a phone, pad, tablet, or laptop. Then, as time permits, they play back their recording as many times as they wish. Students have expressed that this works great when running or exercising or when driving or commuting.

Read and Explain   A favorite of college graduate students is the read-and-explain study concept. In many universities, some grad students assist professors by stepping in, sometimes at the last minute, and teaching part of an undergraduate class. Using this technique, they read the book material in order to explain it to somebody else.

If you use this technique, envision reading material as if you had to explain the concept to your boss, a committee at work, or even a family member. This allows you to dissect the information and then reform it in your own words so that you can verbally explain it. While you're doing this, jot down some talking points or "lecture notes" on your notepad for your made-up presentation.

Read and Form a Question   Critical thinking has always been part of the learning process. The "read and form a question" concept is a very efficient way of understanding the material. When you read a block of information, stop and ask yourself, "How could I form an examination question based on this information?" In this exercise, place the topic or subject of the information somewhere in your question and create a multiple-choice answer out of the remaining information that refers to or defines the topic or subject. Then switch it around so that the subject is actually one of the answer selections and the description is the question.

When studying, it is easy to become immersed in the subject, especially if you are researching or watching a video. It is important to remember the scope of the SSCP exam subject matter. The exam covers only the terms and definitions of security concepts. This is an entry-level examination in IT security for individuals with one year of experience. It is very easy to find an incredible amount of very detailed information on any IT security subject and become very frustrated.

Many of us learn by using different styles and techniques. Some of us learn by reading, listening, visualizing, and doing something in connection with the subject. Use the study techniques outlined in this chapter not only to prepare for the SSCP exam but also while studying for any future exams.

Setting Goals

It is easy to become distracted in our everyday lives. There are always demands from our jobs, family matters, personal problems, and even procrastination. As with any project, it's always beneficial to create a time frame for accomplishing a project or activities within the project. You might start by establishing an examination date. If you're prone to procrastination, even go so far as to book the exam and pay for the examination voucher. Once you have set the examination date, you have the ability to work backward to schedule your study activities. This may assist you in keeping focused on the task of becoming an SSCP.

Booking the Exam

The SSCP examination may be scheduled and taken at a Pearson VUE professional testing center. To schedule an exam, go to the (ISC)^2 website. You will then be redirected to the Pearson VUE scheduling site. Please note that the (ISC)^2 utilizes the Pearson Professional Centers. The Pearson Professional Centers provide for greater security and candidate authentication. In any metropolitan area, there may be only a few of the Professional Centers compared to many regular Pearson VUE testing centers.

Make sure you read and understand the cancellation, reschedule, and refund policy concerning the examination. Since this is a three-hour examination, exams will begin at only certain times during the day, and in some testing locations, exams may be offered only a few times each month. In the event that you have difficulty finding a Pearson Professional Center, click the Pearson VUE customer service link on the Pearson VUE scheduling website.

While on the Pearson VUE exam scheduling website, you'll see that the SSCP examination is offered in a number of languages. You may select the language of your choice. The examination is available in the following languages:

- English
- Indonesian
- Japanese
- Portuguese – Brazilian

Exam Fees and Payment

An exam voucher may be attained and fees paid during the scheduling process on the Pearson VUE website. Vouchers may be obtained in bulk on the (ISC)^2 website. This is ideal for companies that are scheduling a number of people for various exams. Of course, the more vouchers purchased, the greater the discount.

Exam Reschedule and Cancellation policy

It is very important to understand the Pearson VUE exam reschedule and cancellation policy. This policy is stated on the Pearson VUE website and is reiterated after you have scheduled the exam and purchased the voucher. It's advisable to immediately contact Pearson VUE if you have a conflict with the exam date and/or time.

Reschedule Policy   If you wish to reschedule your exam, you must contact Pearson VUE at least 24 hours prior to your exam appointment. If you reschedule an exam less than 24 hours prior to your appointment, you will be subject to a same-day forfeit exam fee. Exam fees are also forfeited for no-shows. There is a $50 fee to reschedule an exam.

Cancellation Policy   If you wish to cancel your exam, you must contact Pearson VUE 24 hours prior to your scheduled appointment. If you cancel an exam less than 24 hours prior to your appointment or miss your exam, the result may be forfeiting your exam fees. There is a $100 fee for cancellations.

These policies were in effect at the date of publication of this text. You are advised to contact the Pearson VUE website for up-to-date information.

(ISC)² Code of Ethics and NDA

You will be asked to read the (ISC)² Candidate Background Qualifications. The acknowledgement question on the website is as follows:

> *I have read and acknowledge that I am eligible for certification with (ISC)² based on the criteria outlined on https://www.isc2.org/candidate-background.aspx

> ○ I am eligible for certification

(ISC)² requires that the examination candidate agree to and sign the Code of Ethics and a nondisclosure agreement (NDA). The NDA is on the Pearson VUE website at www.pearsonvue.com/isc2/isc2_nda.pdf. It is highly recommended that you read it prior to getting to the exam location. At the very beginning of the exam, you will be presented with the NDA, and you will have 5 minutes to read and accept the agreement. If the 5-minute time limit expires, you will not be able to take the exam and all exam fees will be forfeited.

Taking the Exam

Many of us like to plan ahead. We like to know what to expect. When taking exams, it is important to not create added stress through surprises. In the following sections, you will learn about some best practices and what to expect during your visit to the examination center.

It is often comforting to have a plan for what to do and how to relax the evening before an exam and what to do the morning or afternoon of exam day. For example, you can plan for unusual traffic delays or take into account the time involved locating the exam center in an unfamiliar part of the city.

Evening before the Exam

It may have worked for some people when they were in college, but the SSCP exam is not something that you can cram for the evening before. As mentioned earlier, you should establish a study regime that allows you adequate time to read and reflect on the material. The evening before the exam, you might do a very brief review, have a good dinner, and get plenty of rest. Although you may not need all of the time allotted, it is a three-hour exam.

Day of the Exam

It is important to plan the day of your exam. Here are some best practices to keep in mind:

Scheduling and Arrival   Allow yourself plenty of time. Depending on the testing center location, monitor the distance and traffic so that you arrive in plenty of time. It is highly suggested that you arrive at least a minimum of 30 minutes prior to your scheduled examination time. There are two reasons for this:

- You may have a few forms to complete and various security steps to authenticate your identity.
- The Pearson Professional Centers test a large number of individuals in a wide array of certifications, from pharmacy tech to real estate, and there could easily be a dozen people ahead of you arriving for the same time period.

What to Bring   When you register and pay your examination fee, you'll receive a confirmation email. It is highly suggested that you print this email and bring with you. You also need to bring two pieces of identification, and one must have your picture on it and both must have your signature. There are a number of items that qualify as personal authentication listed on the Pearson VUE website.

What to Expect upon Arrival   Pearson Professional Centers follow thorough procedures prior to allowing someone to sit for an exam. You will be asked to fill out various forms and provide certain information, present your identification, and be subjected to several palm scans or other security identification procedures prior to entrance into the examination room. Lockers will be provided for all of your personal effects. Everything, including cell phones, watches, wallets, and all assorted pocket items, must be placed in the locker.

In the Testing Room   Most of the Pearson Professional Centers feature a large number of 4-foot-wide testing cubicles. Of course, each cubicle contains an individual computer workstation. Most of the testing centers offer noise-reduction headphones at each workstation. If they do not have the headphones, you may request or be offered noise-canceling earplugs. Because other individuals come and go or are being set up on their workstations, it is highly advised that you use the noise-canceling earplugs or headphones to reduce distracting noise.

Plastic Worksheet   Each exam candidate will be issued a plastic worksheet and an erasable marker pen. The worksheets are specifically used during the examination in lieu of scrap paper to make computations or notes.

An ideal use for the plastic worksheet is for a memory dump. Upon beginning the examination, many examination candidates write down on the plastic worksheet information they memorized, including items that might be confusing or detailed, such as the layers of the OSI model, the names of various protocols, cryptography algorithms, and risk formulas. This may be done prior to answering the first test question when the information is fresh in your mind.

In the Testing Room   This is a three-hour examination. You will be instructed to raise your hand if you need assistance from the proctor—for example, if you need to use the restroom, take medications, eat something, or for any other activity. If you need to bring medications or bottled water into the testing room, you are advised to discuss this at the front desk when signing in.

Taking a Break   It is possible for you to take a break during the exam. You are advised to raise your hand to summon the exam proctor. Advise the proctor of your desires, such as, for instance, to take a restroom break or just to leave the room for a little bit. The proctor will make the necessary arrangements. You will not be able to leave the immediate premises to smoke.

Because this is a three-hour exam, you may take a break. This might encompass sitting back in your seat and relaxing for a few minutes, standing at your place and stretching quietly, or taking a few steps. When standing, stretching, or communicating with the proctor, it is important to not create any distraction for other exam takers.

Many exam takers use a break as a stopping point or goal. For instance, you might take a first pass through the exam, answering questions that you recognize and marking those that you wish to return to. At the end of the first pass, you might take a short break. You would then proceed through a second pass, reviewing the questions that were marked during the first pass.

Using the Testing Exam Engine   At the beginning of the examination, you will be asked to read and authorize the (ISC)[2] Code of Ethics and nondisclosure agreement. Remember, you should read this prior to entering the examination room. You will have 5 minutes at the beginning of the exam to do this.

When the exam begins, you will observe a multiple-choice question and four possible answers. In the upper-right portion of your screen, you will see a Mark For Review button. This allows you to return to questions you had a problem with or would like to review at the end of the exam. In the lower section of the screen, you will see forward and back buttons so that you can navigate through the exam. At the end of the exam, you will see a page listing the questions you have marked for review. You can access and review any of the questions prior to submitting your final exam result. At the end of the exam, there will be a Finish And Submit button, which ends the exam.

Stress and Relaxation Techniques   It's a proven fact that lots of oxygen will help your brain cells. During any kind of examination, it's recommended that you breathe deeply from time to time. Feel free at any time to stand up, shake it out, or walk around a little. If you have any difficulties at all, raise your hand and ask for the proctor.

Answering Questions   Wrong answers do not count against you. Therefore, it is important that you mark every question with an answer, even if it is a guess. *Do not leave anything blank*. At the end of this book there is a complete section about the techniques of taking multiple-choice tests.

Upon Exam Completion   Your exam will end either at the end of the allotted time or when you click the finish or submit button. You will not be told immediately if you pass or fail the exam. Raise your hand and the proctor will escort you out of the room. You'll receive a printed copy of your examination report at the front desk. Expect either a "Congratulations; you have passed" or a listing of the domains you must study in more detail for your next examination attempt.

Certifications, (ISC)² Website, and Members Login

(ISC)² is very good about responding to you by email with the expected number of weeks it requires to complete the procedures prior to issuing you a certificate. Upon submission of your resume and endorsement form, you'll receive an email specifying the amount of time required to review the materials. Once your resume and endorsement form have been approved, you'll receive an email congratulating you for having been awarded the SSCP certification. The same email also specifies that you will receive your certification certificate within four to six weeks.

Each member of (ISC)² receives a member number. Once you receive your member number, you may access the (ISC)² website, establish login credentials, and view members-only information. While on the (ISC)² member website, you may also complete your member profile, view open jobs and positions, and subscribe to various periodicals and webinars.

Summary

In this chapter, you became familiar with the (ISC)² organization and its history and the certifications it offers. Various corporate, industrial, and government organizations either require certifications or will state that they prefer candidates for employment to have acquired various certifications.

The SSCP exam is based upon the SSCP Common Body of Knowledge, which has been established as including the knowledge and skills an SSCP should possess. Examination vendors are typically vendor neutral, vendor specific, or a professional association. (ISC)² is a professional association offering premier certifications that are recognized worldwide.

Most successful exam candidates plan their study time and use various methods such as marking the textbook, drawing a concept, or viewing pictures or videos. It is also important to relax and not cram the evening before the exam. Planning for the exam day is also important. The examination centers are busy places. At Pearson Professional Centers, you should register no later than 15 minutes prior to exam time, but it is suggested that you arrive 30 to 45 minutes prior to the exam because other folks will be registering before you. In many centers, expect to "take a number." As an exam taker, you may take a break, call the exam proctor, and make use of a plastic marker sheet and erasable pen during the exam.

I discussed various strategies for taking the exam, such as making an initial pass through the exam and answering questions you recognize first and then returning to those you have marked to review at a later time. All answers count, so do not leave any blank.

Exam Essentials

Common Body of Knowledge The SSCP certification was based upon a Common Body of Knowledge (CBK). The original CBK was intended to be all-encompassing, taking into consideration every aspect of information security, including technical networking, information security models and theory, and physical security such as fire extinguishers, perimeter lighting, and fences.

Department of Defense Directive 8570.1 and Department of Defense Directive 8140 The US Department of Defense Directive 8570.1, signed in August 2004, requires every full- and part-time military service member, defense contractor, civilian, and foreign employee with privileged access to a DoD system, regardless of job series or occupational specialty, to obtain a commercial certification credential that has been accredited by the American National Standards Institute (ANSI).

Department of Defense Directive 8140 replaces 8570.1, which has been retired. DODD 8140 encompasses a much broader scope based upon job tasks rather than position titles.

Work Experience Requirement To qualify for the SSCP certification, a candidate must have at least one year of cumulative paid full-time work experience in one or more of the seven domains.

Endorsement Requirement An endorsement form may be downloaded from the (ISC)^2 website. This form must be completed and signed by an (ISC)^2 certified professional who is an active member and who can attest to your professional experience. In the event that an (ISC)^2 certified professional is not available, (ISC)^2 may act as the endorser.

SSCP Exam Description The SSCP exam consists of 125 questions, of which only 100 are graded. The exam must be completed within 3 hours and features only multiple-choice questions. A passing score of 700/1,000 is required. You either pass or fail the examination; no score is given.

Answering Test Questions Wrong answers do not count against you. Mark every question with an answer, even if it is a guess. Do not leave any answers blank.

Chapter

2

Security Basics:
A Foundation

**THE SSCP EXAM OBJECTIVES THAT WILL
BE COVERED IN THIS CHAPTER:**

✓ **Understanding Access Controls**

 ▪ Access Control Requirements

 ▪ Basic Security Concepts

✓ **Understanding Security Operations and Administration**

 ▪ Security and Administration Concepts

 ▪ Administer Security Awareness Education

The Systems Security Certified Practitioner (SSCP) must understand the (ISC)^2 SSCP Common Body of Knowledge (CBK) in order to pass the (ISC)^2 SSCP exam. In professions such as plumbing, welding, computer programming, and commodities trading, there are fundamental concepts, techniques, and tenets of information that form a basic foundation for all other information and skills to follow. The professions of network security and cybersecurity are no different. Because it is the responsibility of the security practitioner to safeguard the resources and data of an organization, this individual must be able to identify risks, formulate strategies, and apply controls that ultimately reduce the likelihood of a threat exploiting a weakness or vulnerability.

When examining the (ISC)^2 SSCP CBK, it's important to understand what is required to successfully pass the examination. As established by the (ISC)^2 organization, the SSCP CBK contains knowledge a security practitioner with at least one year of IT security experience must have to adequately carry out the tasks assigned to them. What this means is that every concept contained in this book is explained to the depth required.

The Development of Security Techniques

Commercial use of digital computers in business has a history of only about 70 years, with less than half of that featuring any sort of external access or communication with other external entities such as on the Internet. Although data maintained on mainframe computers required security and protection during the 1960s and early 1970s, it would still be a while before hackers would have online access to corporate data and would take delight in attacking machines. During the 1950s and 1960s, various security techniques that originated and migrated through the years were combined with newer security techniques as requirements arose. This is the legacy of the security methodology and techniques we use today.

Following the birth and growth pattern of various industries—such as the automobile, railroad, communications, and even electricity distribution industries, to name a few—several growth concepts and such constants remained the same. One of the primary constants was, "We'll do it our way and let everyone else follow." This led to no one in the industry deciding upon or agreeing on a similar method or standard. Parts were not interchangeable, devices did not work together, and communication between computer systems was impossible.

A second primary constant was of course the "for-profit" enterprise. Even when a firm or company came up with a great idea for solving a problem, the idea was often patented and a license made available at a cost to other firms in the industry. This led to other companies deriving a similar answer to the exact same problem.

During the path to understanding security in general and specifically computer and network security, you will see several instances of both of these constants in practice. This creates the confusion of everybody wanting to do it their way, which in turn results in several tools and devices that all appear to do the same thing. As with just about everything, in a free market economy, competition has driven this industry forward. We are constantly becoming aware of new and better devices, techniques, and methodologies of solving everyday problems. It's the challenge of the security practitioner to understand the problem and know what has come before to be able to understand the new solutions coming down the pike.

Understanding Security Terms and Concepts

The (ISC)² organization requires candidates to have one year of IT security experience prior to receiving the Systems Security Certified Practitioner certification. Although some individuals may have prior educational courses in college or trade schools involving security, there will inevitably be gaps in experience or training. The CBK includes the areas of knowledge that a skilled Systems Security Certified Practitioner should know to perform the typical job tasks expected of them. By taking the practice exams and studying the subjects in this book, you will gain an understanding of the information required to pass the examination and perform as an SSCP.

We will use several learning techniques as we examine the SSCP (ISC)² CBK. In the following sections, I will discuss looking at complex information, understanding its origin, and determining how the security practitioner may use this information on the job. Throughout the book, you will see "exam points," which are specific concepts you should know for the exam. Real-world examples, notes, and other general information sections will assist you in remembering the perspective and application of various security concepts.

The Problem (Opportunity) and the Solution

Although most folks go through life seeking solutions to problems, some folks like to refer to these as "opportunities." For instance, when employees bring their cell phones to work and connect with the company network, it can definitely present a possible problem for the security practitioner. The flip side is that there is a tremendous opportunity to increase productivity and therefore profitability for the firm by allowing these employees rapid access to data and applications. Therefore, both a problem and an opportunity exist in search of a solution.

While learning about the terms (and their definitions) and concepts of security in the SSCP Common Body of Knowledge, picture in your mind the problem or opportunity and the solution. If you can understand this relationship, you will be able to use these techniques in everyday practice and of course ultimately be able to pass the SSCP exam. Throughout this book, strive to understand the concepts behind the solutions to various problems or opportunities. If you thoroughly understand the concepts, the exam answers will come very easy for you.

 It is recommended that you actually draw concepts out on your notepad as an aid to visualizing the solutions. In practicing this learning technique, visualize a situation and relate all of the concepts that provide various solutions to the situation. Once you create this drawing, take a "mental snapshot" so that you may visualize this concept when taking the exam.

⊕ Real World Scenario

Visualizing an End-to-End Process

A remote employee based in Kansas wants to log on to the corporate network based in Dallas. A drawing can help you visualize the relationship between the various techniques that can be used to achieve this.

The following steps might be used as a solution to this situation:

1. The employee accesses their personal computer in Kansas, logs onto the Internet, and clicks a VPN desktop icon.

2. The icon launches the VPN application, which automatically creates an encrypted VPN tunnel through the Internet to a VPN concentrator at the Dallas end of a VPN tunnel across the Internet.

3. Proceeding past various firewalls and border routers, the employee is authenticated by the use of a password forwarded to a remote access server that references information through the use of the RADIUS protocol stored on a RADIUS server.

4. Once authenticated, the employee is directed to an application of their choice on an application server.

In practice, all of the preceding activities support functions such as the use of encryption algorithms, key exchange, certificates, access control, and authorization techniques that all happen virtually at the blink of an eye.

It is not important that you be a great artist. The drawing on your notepad to assist you in learning the relationship between all of the items in this process might look something like the drawing in Figure 2.1.

FIGURE 2.1   This figure illustrates a notepad drawing of a remote user logon

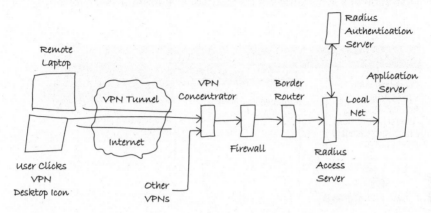

The takeaway from this is that we identified an opportunity, such as giving an employee the ability to log on remotely. We now see the relationship between the VPN concentrator and other devices and the roles they play during this process. We have illustrated where a VPN tunnel exists, and we have seen that remote users might be authenticated by a RADIUS server.

The reason for this scenario is to understand the roles of each item, whether software or hardware, and to draw out or illustrate to the best of our ability the process to assist us in understanding the concepts.

Evolution of Items

Technology continues to evolve, and there always seems to be something new and shiny just around the corner that works better, faster, or cheaper than what we are already using. The unfortunate consequence is that all of this new technology begins stacking up. To anyone just coming into the field, it is sometimes difficult to understand the concepts behind all of these names and acronyms, several of which appear to do the same thing, and discern why they all exist. As mentioned, sometimes it is advantageous to group similar items in a group to which they relate. This may assist in understanding the evolution of the item or concept, how much weight to place on learning about it, and ultimately where we would use it in everyday security protection as a security practitioner.

Real World Scenario

The Use of Different Cryptographic Algorithms over Time

This is an illustration of a symmetric key cryptographic algorithm as it evolved.

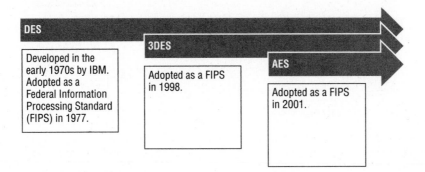

The Data Encryption Standard (DES) was once the predominant symmetric key algorithm used for electronic data encryption. It was originally developed in the early 1970s at IBM, and in 1976, the National Bureau of Standards adopted a modified version for use as a Federal Information Processing Standard (FIPS), after which it was quickly adopted as an international standard.

By 1999 it was proven that the (DES) algorithm could be broken in about 23 hours. As a replacement, Triple Data Encryption (3DES) makes use of three keys and a variety of modes of operation, which was an improvement over DES.

Finally, the Advanced Encryption Standard, AES, is a specification for the encryption of electronic data established by the U.S. National Institute of Standards and Technology (NIST) in 2001. It has now been adopted by the federal government as an official encryption standard.

In Chapter 6, "Domain 4: Incident Response and Recovery," I will discuss each of these encryption algorithms in much more detail. The point here is that there is a progression of algorithms over the years. This is what is meant by putting solutions to a problem in a logical progression.

Group Similar Items into Concept Families

Another memorization technique is to group similar items or terms into a "concept family." For instance, the following list illustrates a family of terms and technology around the single sign-on (SSO) concept:

- Kerberos
- Kerberos authentication server

- Kerberos ticket=granting server
- Tickets
- Ticket-granting ticket
- Federated access
- Sesame
- KryptoKnight
- Centralized authentication
- Decentralized authentication

Should you see any of these terms either in a question or as part of an answer on any exam, you might quickly conclude that the general subject is related to single sign-on or at least user authentication. Of course, seeing one of these terms as an option for a totally unrelated question would mean that the option is most likely a distractor.

Once you create a list of a family or group of similar concepts, I suggest you write at least one or two sentences as a description of each item. Writing the description out in your own words is a significant memorization technique and far surpasses just reading it in a glossary.

Same Item, Different Name

It's not unusual in some industries for the same item to be named differently. In some cases, this might be due to different companies marketing and branding the same item. For instance, a network device called a switch might also be referred to as an L2 switch, a smart switch, an intelligent switch, a NexGen switch, a VLAN switch, or an intelligent hub. You might assume that all of these basically provide a switch function, and the name might be created by the manufacturer and its branding department.

You might also come across devices that provide basically the same functionality but are generically called something different. For example, in the early years of networking there was a device called a passive hub. This simple device featured one Ethernet jack in and usually four Ethernet jacks out, with no amplification of the signals. The device evolved into powered or amplified hubs powered by a wall-wart transformer and then finally switches as we know them today. It is almost impossible to walk into a store and purchase a simple hub.

Throughout your studies, you will find similar acronyms that referred to totally different subjects. Although acronyms will be spelled out on the exam, pay specific attention when learning concepts or answering exam questions. For instance, the acronym *MAC* may refer to both *Media Access Control* and *mandatory access control*. The acronym *RBAC* may refer to *roll-based access control* and *rule-based access control*. It is important to read the question or the answers very carefully to determine the correct context in which these acronyms might be used.

Real World Scenario

Using a Similar Item for a Different Purpose

Sometimes identical or very similar devices may be referred to by different names and used for different purposes. Years ago there was an Ethernet device called a hub. The hub featured one Ethernet signal in and split the signal equally among four different jacks out. There was no processing or logic involved in the device. For all intents and purposes, it just allowed us to connect more devices to an Ethernet cable.

In a completely different realm in the networking industry is a security control device called an intrusion detection system (IDS). An IDS examines packets sent along the Ethernet network, and because it is passive and not placed in the path of the Ethernet signals, such as a switch or router, it requires a different mechanism to attach to an Ethernet network. This device is simply called a tap. A tap is not a sophisticated device and simply features one Ethernet jack in and two Ethernet jacks out similar to a Y connector for your home audio system. Notice the similarity? A tap is simply a passive hub. So by using your imagination and your mind's eye, you can picture both of these devices and recall their applications.

The following illustration shows a hub and tap, two similar devices used in two different contexts.

Ethernet Hub   **Ethernet Tap**

How Do We Agree to Agree?

One of the most difficult aspects of any industry is deciding upon a standard. For instance, most laptop computers feature an SVGA 15-pin D-shaped connector for video out to a projector or monitor (Figure 2.2). In years past, the same connector was located on the rear panel of a desktop computer and was used to connect a video monitor, a keyboard, a mouse, and a scanner, and for serial communications such as a RS-232 serial port, it was used for an external modem.

FIGURE 2.2   A typical 15-pin D-shaped connector

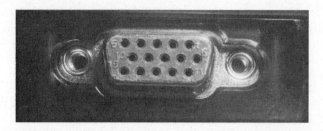

Who decided upon this design and how was it decided that everybody would do it? Industry standards evolve through a number of different means and generally refer to a method or design that is accepted by a majority, or at least a significant group, within the industry. For various reasons, which might include technical disagreement, proprietary patents and licensing fees, or just political reasons, not everyone within an industry accepts the standardization effort.

An industry standard generally means that this is the best practice across the industry of a design or method of achieving a result. In many cases, such as a hardware application (for example, the DIN 15-pin connector), the standard promotes compatibility across many manufacturers.

 Real World Scenario

The Standardization of Compact Discs

During the early 1970s, both Sony and Philips independently developed the compact disc (CD). Later they collaborated and finally released both a CD format and an acceptable CD player by 1982. Based upon this standardization by two major industry participants, hundreds of other companies began producing CD media, CD players/recorders, and content to be placed on CDs.

It is entirely possible that a major industry player might not accept the standard and will ignore or compete directly with the standard. Take, for example, a videotape recording standard called Betamax that was created by Sony. A competing videotape standard created by JVC Corporation called the VHS eventually won out and became the industry standard throughout the videotape industry.

There are a great many reasons one standard wins out over another. In some cases it might be based upon cost or ease of manufacturing. Nikola Tesla's alternating current became an industry standard over Thomas Edison's direct current because of the physical distance electricity could be transmitted and the reduced cost of a single generating station, in the case of alternating current, as opposed to the many generating stations required for direct current.

Within the information technology industry, as with many other industries, there are two types of standards:

Mechanical Standards   Mechanical standards feature specific specifications for the mechanical design, materials, signal paths, waveforms, communication methods, and hardware design.

Standard of Practice, or Procedural Standards   Procedural standards take the form of recommendations or regulatory requirements. Recommendations generally originate with a committee, consortium, or industry organization and take the form of recommended best practices. Regulatory standards, on the other hand, are generally enforced by a governmental regulatory body or a self-regulatory industry organization.

Industry standards or best practices may come from any of the following sources:

Proprietary   This type of manufacturing design or practice is not an industry standard but generally fulfills the needs and requirements within a specific company. For instance, in the early days of PCs, IBM created the Industry Standard Architecture (ISA) bus standard for the personal computers it was creating at the time. Of course these computers became very popular, and many other manufacturers wished to build circuit boards and computers that were compatible with this bus. Several years later, in an effort to be compatible, a group of industry manufacturers known then as the Gang of Nine created an enhanced version of the ISA bus and named it Extended Industry Standard Architecture (EISA) to avoid infringement. This is typical of how a large industry player's proprietary design evolves into an industry standard through slight modifications and renaming.

Standards Organization   Various organizations are chartered with the ability of establishing industry standards or industry recommendations. These may take the form of committee-based or working group organizations that create recommendations, trade groups that create standards to be used in their specific trade, and consortiums that form to create everything from best-practice recommendations to industry regulations.

Government   Various governments around the world create laws, regulations, and statutes that govern the design, manufacture, import, use, or sale of various products and technologies within their control.

Regulatory Agency   An agency may be either created by a government entity or agreed upon by a specific industry group. Generally, an agency may be charged with not only creating a specification but also in enforcing its use.

The security practitioner should be aware of a number of different organizations that are involved in generating standards and specification recommendations throughout the industry. Some of these organizations include the following:

National Institute of Standards and Technology (NIST)   NIST is a non-regulatory agency of the United States Department of Commerce. NIST offers an incredible variety of standards, best practices, research results, and programs for not only the IT industry

but everything from weather reporting to manufacturing. The NIST website is at www
.nist.gov.

Internet Engineering Task Force (IETF)   IETF develops and promotes Internet standards
that may be voluntarily adopted throughout the industry. At one time supported by the
federal government, IETF now performs a standards development function under the
Internet Society. Standards are developed through various committees and the participation
of a large number of interested volunteers. The IETF website is at www.ietf.org.

Institute of Electrical and Electronics Engineers (IEEE)   IEEE (aka I Triple E) is a professional organization for the advancement of computer engineering and computer science,
among other aspects of electronics and communications. As one of the leading standards
organizations, it is responsible for the 802 group of standards, which includes the IEEE
802.3 Ethernet standard and the IEEE 802.11 wireless networking standard. Its website is
located at www.ieee.org.

American National Standards Institute (ANSI)   ANSI is a nonprofit organization that
oversees the development of standards that are approved by consensus and are applied on a
voluntary basis across a given industry. ANSI manages and maintains the ASCII standard.
You can find out more at www.ansi.org.

World Wide Web Consortium (W3C)   W3C is a standards organization in which
members, staff, and the public collaborate to develop web standards. The web technologies
include the recommended implementation of Cascading Style Sheets and XHTML, among
many other recommendations. The W3C website is located at www.w3.org.

International Organization for Standardization (ISO)   ISO is a true standards organization. It tests various products and provides its seal of approval once they pass rigorous tests.
The organization administers over 13,000 standards across many industries. The website is
at www.iso.org.

The Unicode Consortium   The Unicode Consortium is a standards organization that
manages and maintains the Unicode standard. This standard provides a number for every
possible character in every possible language used on the Internet. This allows the development of international versions of websites. Go to www.unicode.org for more information
about the work of the Unicode Consortium.

Telecommunications Industry Association (TIA)   TIA is accredited by the American
National Standards Institute (ANSI) to develop voluntary, consensus-based industry standards for a wide variety of information and communication technologies (ICT) products
and currently represents nearly 400 companies. Its website is at www.tiaonline.org.

SANS Institute   The SANS Institute is a private company formed in 1989 that provides
training to the cyber security industry. SANS is a trade name, short for SysAdmin, Audit,
Networking, and Security. It is also known for industry reports and policy templates. The
website is at www.sans.org.

Security Foundation Concepts

From the beginning of the computer age and throughout the evolution of all the products and concepts we currently use in information security, the fundamental underlying principles and objectives have not changed. These basic principles are referred to as the CIA (or AIC) security triad (Figure 2.3), which consists of *confidentiality*, *integrity*, and *availability*.

FIGURE 2.3   The CIA triad

CIA Triad

Although most textbooks and literature on computer security refer to this as the *CIA triad*, the order of these letters does not matter; it could also be referred to as the *AIC triad*. These three concepts, confidentiality, integrity, and availability, form the basis for security objectives that are the essence of security for all information systems. Security policies, controls, safeguards, countermeasures, and even threats, vulnerabilities, and security processes can and should be considered within the framework of the security objectives.

The security practitioner is constantly weighing every security requirement against one of these three objectives. Generally, the problem or opportunity facing the security practitioner impacts confidentiality, integrity, or availability. Information stored in the Department of Defense computer systems requires confidentiality, whereas credit card transactions in business require information integrity, and of course an e-commerce website owner is concerned with availability. The following represents each leg of the triad:

Confidentiality   The objective of confidentiality applies to both data and system information and is sometimes referred to as the secrecy object. To ensure confidentiality, information must be protected to eliminate the loss or disclosure of the information. The actions taken to protect information from disclosure include numerous controls put in place to create defense in depth. The primary action to encrypt data is to select and use a well-known and unbroken encryption algorithm. The encryption algorithm might be used to protect data when in transit and while it is being stored. Other techniques to ensure confidentiality include hiding data or making it nonaccessible; wiping or erasing data, such as if a cell phone is stolen; and using extremely strong identification and authentication techniques.

Availability   Availability ensures accessibility to all hardware, software applications, and data throughout the system. Availability concepts include hardware and data physical availability, system hardware redundancy, connection and transmission availability, and restoration of services, systems, and data as required. Availability is also ensured through the use of vulnerability mitigation techniques such as the reduction of denial-of-service attacks, scanning systems for malware, and the use of hardware concepts such as automated backups or raid drives.

Integrity   Integrity ensures that the system resources are protected from unauthorized, unanticipated, or unintentional modifications. This objective can apply to both the data and the hardware system. Data integrity is the fundamental concept that data has not been altered by any manner while in storage, during processing, or while in transit unless authorized. Integrity can also refer to system integrity. This is the integrity or quality the system has to perform its intended function in an unimpaired manner free from unauthorized manipulation, design flaws, or intentional or unintentional actions.

Exam Point

It is very important to be able to recognize and explain the three sides of the CIA triad. For exam purposes, remember that the *A* in *CIA* stands for *availability*. There are a number of other words, such as *authentication* and *authorization*, that might distract you.

Primary Security Categories

All the differing roles within the world of security, whether police officer, firefighter, home security alarm company, IT security professional, or a disaster recovery federal agency, are vital to our businesses and our families, neighbors, and community. Each of these individuals or organizations performs a central role in supporting a primary goal of security.

The activities of each one of these individuals or organizations generally fall into three security categories:

Prevention   These are the actions taken or the products purchased and installed in an effort to reduce the likelihood that something bad may happen. In the family home, this might be accomplished by installing a strong front door with a deadlock. Prevention represents the efforts taken to reduce the likelihood of fire, theft, physical harm, intrusion, or other potential undesired or bad occurrences. Although owning a fire extinguisher may reduce the spread of the fire once it has begun, the removal of items such as waste paper or flammable liquids represents the acts of fire prevention.

As a security professional, your responsibility is to design and deploy mechanisms that stand in the way of a potential intruder or other bad actor wishing to do harm to your data or resources. This could be as simple as placing locks on server cabinets, creating a strong identification and authentication system, providing user training, and utilizing strong security rules on firewalls and routers.

Detection   In a home, a typical detection method might be a burglar alarm system, swimming pool alarm, baby monitor, or smoke alarm. In our automobiles, we might notice a check engine light or a low oil indicator. In some instances, we might hear something such as a potential intruder in the backyard, strange noises in the house, or the incessant barking of a dog. Each of these might indicate that something unusual is happening.

As a security professional, you are expected to deploy various methods of detecting unauthorized access to or unauthorized removal of data or resources. You might perform this action by placing detection mechanisms such as an intrusion detection system, automated log monitoring that generates various alerts, or continuous monitoring that utilizes a security operations center to ensure that data and assets are protected 24/7.

Recovery   These are the actions any of us must take after an unwanted occurrence. If you are in an automobile accident, for example, the medical recovery of the individuals involved and physical recovery such as repair or replacement of the assets might both need to be addressed. Or a broken window may need to be replaced after unauthorized access by a burglar.

As a security professional, you are expected to be ready to implement various plans and programs should systems be damaged, databases corrupted, or secrets such as passwords divulged. These plan should be well conceived, practiced, and ready to put into place should any emergency occur.

Exam Point

It's important to remember that the security categories include prevention, detection, and recovery.

Access Control

A responsibility of security professionals is to protect the data and the resources of the organization. The first step in protection is to properly identify and authenticate those individuals or users desiring access to the physical premises, the network, and ultimately the corporate data stored on the network. A series of identity checks and verification steps will be undertaken prior to granting access. The steps include identification, authentication, authorization, and accounting.

Identification

Identification is the first step of the access process. Every user, application, or system begins the access process by providing some form of identification. This identification claim will be compared to data on file, and if it matches, the process will continue.

Each of us is identified by two names, our first name and last name. We may also be identified as being a member of a group, such as an employee of XYZ Corporation, a Boy Scout, a Texan, an American, and, sooner or later, an inhabitant of the planet Earth. As you can see, as the group gets larger, the less integrity a logon system can provide to denote a specific user signing on. This concept might be referred to as granularity of identification.

Authentication

Authentication is the second step of the access process. Where any user or device can make an identification claim, authentication is a request for a second type of identification called a factor. Ideally, this factor should be something unique to the user or the system, providing strong evidence that this individual or system is actually who they claim to be. Numerous authentication mechanisms may be applied in sequence to enhance the reliability of the authentication process.

Authorization

Authorization is the third step of the access process. Upon satisfactory authentication, the user is assigned rights and privileges based upon a profile they have in storage. Various limits may be placed on access to resources or data; the limits are included in an access list, which is based upon the user identity. Other limits may include access to resources or data based upon a label issued to the user who matches the highest label of the resource or data.

Accounting

Accounting refers to tracing and recording the use of network assets and resources by users or intruders. The process of accounting may be performed to achieve a specific purpose, such as monitoring trends or capacity, allocating expenses and costs for the use of resources, and monitoring proper usage of resources. The accounting process as it relates to IT security is involved with monitoring and recording users' access to resources, proper authorization levels of users, changes made to resources (such as changes to a database), and general actions and activities such as creating or deleting files.

Auditing is the act of reviewing or monitoring the data obtained during the accounting process. This may involve reviewing log files or forensic information. Real-time monitoring, also called continuous monitoring, not only creates log files but also can create immediate alerts, emails, and console warning screens for operators and administrators.

Exam Point

People are always the biggest threat to the resources and data within an enterprise. Training is a nontechnical control used with people.

Nonrepudiation

Nonrepudiation is a process whereby a user may be directly identified as the sender of a message. Through the use of nonrepudiation methods, this person may not deny an action that they have taken. For example, Jack wants to send a message to Jill. Jill requests that Jack digitally sign the message, thus providing irrefutable proof that he was the originator of the message. On the other hand, Jack may request that Jill also cannot deny receiving the message. This is achieved through strong identification and authentication of Jill and the use of system logs that provide proof that Jill was the user that actually received the message as sent. In this case, nonrepudiation can be achieved by both parties. This is an application of the integrity rule.

Exam Point

With nonrepudiation, neither the sender nor the receiver (under certain circumstances) may deny their actions. The primary tool used to enforce nonrepudiation of the sender is a digital signature.

Risk

Risk is a chance of damage or loss based upon the exposure to a potential hazard or threat. This sounds like a simple concept. Do I increase risk by leaving my front door unlocked? Do I decrease risk by placing chains on my front door? The responsibilities of a security practitioner are to be aware that there is constant risk. This individual may be placed in a role of identifying risks and selecting various tools and methods that might be used to reduce it. Reducing risk is referred to as mitigating risk. By locking the door, I reduce the risk, and by placing chains around the door, I mitigate the risk even further.

Various components of risk exist:

Threat   This is a general term used to describe any incident or action that, if carried out, could cause harm or loss of data or an asset. For example, there is a threat of fire in the server room.

Threat Vector

A *threat vector* is a path that an attacker might take to take advantage of a vulnerability and do harm. For example, fire is a threat that could do harm to your physical environment or resources.

The threat vector, in this case, represents how the fire might originate. In considering the possible threat vectors of the server room fire, we might simply list the following:

- A component on a circuit board on a server overheats and causes a fire.

- A fuse shorts out and causes a power cable to overheat, causing a fire.

- Air-conditioning in the server room fails, resulting in an extreme amount of heat and causing a fire.

- A room down the hall catches fire and the fire reaches the server room through the ceiling or ventilation.

- The standby power supply batteries overheat and cause a fire.

- The maintenance staff mistakenly leaves a flammable liquid in the room and it catches fire.

- A physical intruder starts a fire in a trash can to cover their tracks.

- A third-shift system administrator is smoking on the premises and inadvertently starts a fire.

- The ballast on the lighting fixture in the ceiling overheats, causing a fire.

- Lightning strikes a power pole and sends a surge into the server room equipment, causing a fire.

Granted, many of these seem fairly far-fetched. It is the responsibility of the security staff to identify that these and other possible threat vectors exist and to determine the likelihood or possibility that any of these could actually occur. As an exercise, think through all the possible vectors that a bad actor represented by an external attacker, an internal employee making a simple mistake, or a disgruntled employee could take to harm a company's customer database. You have three potential bad actor categories, and as a security professional, you need to determine how each might cause harm. After listing these vectors, the next process would be to determine the likelihood that any one of these occurrences could happen and then determine what to do to reduce the likelihood.

Vulnerabilities   These are the weaknesses within a network, host application or database that may be penetrated or exploited by an attacker.

Controls   These items are represented by safeguards, countermeasures, policies, and procedures that may be used to mitigate risk. Controls are grouped into three categories: physical, logical, and administrative.

Exam Point

It is important to remember that vulnerabilities are weaknesses. Controls are used to reduce possibility that a threat will exploit a vulnerability, and these controls may be classified as physical, logical, or administrative.

Prudent Man, Due Diligence, and Due Care

These concepts may together or separately form the basis of actions and provide a measurement for the security professional to ensure that various security controls meet the highest standards possible. The goal of each of these concepts is to reduce risk to a manageable level.

Prudent Man   The *prudent man* concept refers to actions that may be reasonably taken (or are obvious) to safeguard corporate assets and data. This concept may also refer to, as a comparison, the security safeguards similar organizations within the same industry are taking to protect their corporate assets and data. For example, if all banks use a vault to protect the money kept on premises, is it obvious and prudent that your bank requires a vault also?

Due Diligence   Due diligence is verifying that a control or process is performing as intended. This concept may also be referred to as assuredness. For instance, placing an IDS into a network to perform traffic monitoring would be exercising due care, and monitoring the IDS to ensure that it is operating correctly is due diligence.

Due care   Due care refers to taking actions that are prudent and reasonable to protect the assets of the organization, such as installing controls. For instance, exercising due care would be installing an IPS in an effort to protect a network. In summary, due care is taking adequate precautions by installing effective controls to reduce or mitigate risk, while due diligence is performing activities to ensure that the control is functioning to established parameters.

 The term due diligence is also used in the financial industry. Due diligence is the assurance that a complete investigation has been made prior to making an investment.

Exam Point

Due care are the actions that a reasonable and prudent person would make to protect an organization's assets. This would include selecting and installing controls to mitigate risk. Due diligence is ensuring that the controls put into place are functioning adequately.

User Security Management

The security professional's responsibility is to secure and protect the organization's assets, which fall into two general categories:

Resources   Physical *resources* include the general assets of the company, such as computer systems, network hardware, printers, wireless transmission equipment, telephone equipment, and cabling systems. Virtual resources include assets that have been created or are running on hardware devices. This includes virtual servers, virtual networks, cloud-based technology, and the software applications that run the business.

Data   *Data* refers to the content placed on the company network and storage devices. The three states of data are referred to as data at rest, data in process, and data in transit. While a company may own a database, the software database itself is referred to as a relational database management system (RDBMS), and the actual information contained in each row and cell of every table is the content data that requires protection. Data in transit is encapsulated with a header block that contains metadata such as the destination, the length of the data packet, and the various protocols used, among other information. The actual data content in transit is referred to as the *payload*. Data in process is content data that is either being changed or being currently used by a software application. A common security practice is to maintain the most recent version of the content data and work with a copy of the data. If anything goes wrong during the processing of the change transaction, the transaction itself can be "rolled back" to the last known good copy of the data.

Company assets need to be protected and secured against a number of risks. Primary threats to the assets of the company are people. People may be referred to as authorized users, intruders, or attackers. Intruders and attackers intend to do harm or steal from the company. Authorized users may do harm, either by an innocent mistake or intentionally as a disgruntled employee.

Various security controls and user management techniques may be employed by the security professional. These are discussed in the sections that follow.

Least Privilege

The principle of *least privilege* establishes that users, systems, and applications should have only the minimal level of access that is absolutely necessary for them to perform the duties required of them.

Exam Point

Least privilege refers to granting the least amount of access rights and permissions required to perform a task.

AAA

The *three As* of security, also known as *AAA*, are authentication, authorization, and accounting (Figure 2.4). These three processes work together to provide the assurance that access is granted only to authorized users. The implementation can be provided by independent means, such as referring to access control lists (ACLs), using directories such as LDAP or Active Directory, or through a completely unified system that provides all three AAA services.

FIGURE 2.4   An access process illustrating the three AAAs, known as authentication, authorization, and accounting

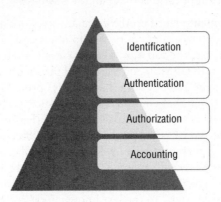

Mandatory Vacation

Requiring *mandatory vacations* is a security technique that allows for the review of employee activities. Most corporate mandatory vacation policies require an individual take at least one vacation each year for a minimum duration of five days. During the employee's absence, various audits may be performed to discover any abnormalities in the employee's work.

Separation of Duties

A *separation of duties* policy ensures that no one person has too much power or control. Duties and responsibilities within an organization should be divided among several individuals, each with assigned responsibilities to complete the task. For instance, authorization and approval of purchase orders, check requests, and payments should be assigned to different individuals or departments within an organization. This eliminates the capability of one individual to commit fraudulent acts against the organization.

M of N Requirement

An *M of N* process requires a certain number of individuals to agree prior to action being taken. *M* represents the minimum number of individuals that must agree on a course of action. *N* represents the total number individuals involved. For instance, a corporate approval policy may require that 3 (M) executives are required to agree on a course of action out of a total group of 10 (N) executives. It is not unusual for an organization to require at least two signatures on a bank check. The policy might also state that four individuals may be authorized to sign checks. This redundancy can act as a safeguard in the event that one of the check signers is on vacation.

Real World Scenario

A Security Procedure in Science Fiction

Through the years, the *Star Trek* movie franchise has featured several movies in which we have seen the M of N requirement in action. The movies *Star Trek III: The Search for Spock* and *Star Trek: First Contact* required the captain to set the self-destruct mechanism on the *Starship Enterprise*. Obviously, he did not have the rights and privileges himself, so he required at least two other bridge officers to assist him in setting the self-destruct mechanism. During this sequence, each would identify themselves by name and rank through voice recognition, and then each officer would state a unique password. Upon completion, the self-destruct mechanism would engage. We might hypothesize, for example, that there are seven possible bridge officers and that any three of them could set the self-destruct mechanism. In terms of the M of N security concept, this would be represented as 3 of 7 where M = 3 and N = 7.

Two-Man Rule

The two-man rule is a procedure popular in very high-security locations and situations. It features two individuals who must agree upon action yet are physically separated and must therefore take action independent of the other. Consider, for example, U.S. Air Force officers stationed in Minuteman Missile silos. The officers had to turn their keys at exactly the same moment. As neither officer could reach the others key and turned both at the same time, this prohibited any one person from being able to initiate a launch sequence.

Real World Scenario

Access to a Highly Secure Environment with Classified Information

The two-man rule has been used when access to cryptographic keys, called *key recovery*, or access to highly classified information is required. Use of the two-man rule, in highly classified security situations, requires the use of separately issued keys, hardware verification, biometrics, and other very formal authentication procedures to access the secure information or take an action. The two-man rule has been in constant use through the Cold War to the present by the military when access to nuclear weapons is involved. Two individuals must be present at all times in the presence of a nuclear weapon.

Job Rotation

A job rotation policy states that an individual in a critical position does not stay in that position for too long (Figure 2.5). Primarily used as a fraud prevention mechanism, rotating individuals between positions provides not only for cross training but also for the capability of cross-checking individuals' work. Job rotation reduces the possibility of fraudulent actions, repetitive mistakes, or position abuse by retaining an individual for a limited length of time in a critical position.

FIGURE 2.5   A typical job rotation scheme

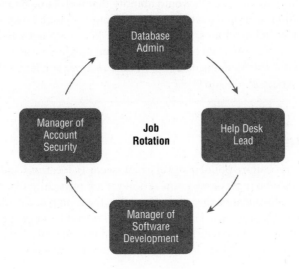

Geographic Access Control

Restrictions may be placed on users based upon where they are currently located. It's not unusual for security policy to state that any network access originating outside the continental United States must be blocked. Additionally, various applications, data, or organization resources may not be available to users logging in remotely. If a specific company resource or certain data is always and accessed only by users in a local office, persons logging in from another location in the country will not be allowed access.

Temporal Access Control, Time of Day Control

Temporal or *time-of-day* restrictions may be placed on various resources. For instance, users within a certain department who are not required to work on weekends may have their account logons restricted to only working hours Monday through Friday.

Privacy

Through the use of the Internet, it is now possible to retrieve an extensive amount of information about individuals, companies, and organizations. Because of this, a number of laws and regulations have been established to protect personal information. Personal health and medical information is protected by the Health Insurance Portability and Accountability Act (HIPAA) of 1996, a federal law that protects the privacy of a person's medical information.

Information security and privacy is the major focus of several European laws that basically state that personal information can be used only for the purpose for which it was collected.

 Real World Scenario

Location Disclosure by Default

"Places" is a Facebook feature that makes public the location of someone on their Facebook page. Users can click their Facebook page "check-in" tab when they visit stores and restaurants or attend events. Unfortunately, many users did not realize that this location tracking is an automatic feature of Facebook and must be turned off manually. Privacy regulatory organizations, including the Federal Trade Commission, have received numerous complaints about Facebook's alleged "unfair and deceptive" trade practices. The claim is that through the use of geolocation services, retailers can target an individual with unsolicited advertising, but more significantly, someone's location could be used in cyberstalking. Numerous techniques are outlined on the Internet concerning disabling the geolocation services on Facebook and other personal information sharing and social networking sites.

Transparency

The principle of transparency is that it allows anyone to access, view, and test hardware or software systems. During testing by the general public or computer specialists, flaws can be found and announced. The operation of all encryption algorithms is completely open and known. This allows anyone to test an algorithm in an attempt to find flaws. Conversely, items that are secret or nontransparent are difficult to test and verify.

 Real World Scenario

Identifying Problems with Cryptographic Algorithms

Transparency can be illustrated with an example of a once popular cryptographic algorithm called WEP, or Wired Equivalent Privacy. Originating in 1999, WEP is an 802.11 wireless network encryption standard designed to offer as strong an encryption as

---

Continues

Continued

found on wired networks of the time. Because the underlying mathematical functions of the most popular cryptographic algorithms are widely known throughout the industry, various individuals attempt to attack or break each one, and if they are successful, the industry in general is made aware of the cracking technique used and the specific vulnerabilities discovered. By 2001, the industry was made aware that there was a problem with WEP, and by 2003, it was replaced by Wi-Fi Protected Access (WPA). By 2005, a group illustrated that WEP could be broken in as little as 3 minutes with commercially available tools. It was this transparency that allowed for groups and individuals to test the algorithm. They proved that if they could attack and break it, others could too.

 The concept of transparency has found its way into a number of other computer fields. From the early days of computers, engineers and technicians have wanted to program and modify software for themselves. Various individuals within the industry took issue with Microsoft being a closed-source or nontransparent software vendor. Various features and functions of Unix, a well-known operating system, were repurposed for personal computers in 1991 as a free and open-source operating system. A large number of other products are available as free and open source.

Implicit Deny

The concept of implicit deny is that access to data or resources is denied unless specific permission has been granted. *Implicit* refers to the fact that no action needs to be taken to restrict access. It will just happen automatically. *Explicit* refers to actions such as writing rules for a firewall or router that specify access that is granted. A simple example is the act of providing two users with a key to a padlock. Providing each user with a key is an explicit action giving permission and granting access. By default, all other users are implicitly denied access because they simply do not have a key.

Exam Point

Implicit deny restricts access to everyone unless they have been explicitly given specific rights to access.

Personal Device (BYOD)

Bring Your Own Device (BYOD) requirements apply to personal cell phones, tablets, pads, and personal laptops. The requirements may be grouped into two main categories:

Administrative Requirements   These take the form of policies, rules, or regulations that may include statements as to where a user may use a cell phone or personal device, whether a cell phone with a camera can be used, and what corporate data can be saved on a device. While some companies allow users to use their personal cell phones to log onto a company network, many provide users with a company phone for company use.

Physical Requirements   Specific attributes or capabilities of a device or software contained on the device fall under the category of physical requirements. For instance, a corporate policy may state that any personal cell phone containing company data must have the capability of being "wiped" or totally erased remotely in the event of theft or loss. Security professionals may enact a security program that restricts various devices, including personal devices, from connecting to a network if they fail to conform to policy. *Network access control (NAC)* is a general term for software or hardware implementations that inspect a device prior to allowing connection. Policies that might be enforced include the device having the latest software updates, up-to-date antivirus protection, or even access to certain types of applications and software. Network Access Protection (NAP) is the Microsoft implementation of network access control.

 Bring Your Own Device (BYOD) was at one time totally restricted by many companies. Many other companies have come to realize that it is difficult to limit the use of personal devices by employees and have come to embrace the increase productivity that portable devices bring to the workplace. Security professionals have been continuously challenged with the requirement of allowing foreign devices access to the organization's network and resources.

Privilege Management, Privilege Life Cycle

During a human resources onboarding event, an individual is granted various rights and privileges to the organization's resources and data. As their employment with the company progresses, users may be promoted, reassigned, or rotated into other positions requiring additional or lesser rights and privileges. Eventually individuals are terminated, resign, or retire from an organization, and thus removal of the rights and privileges granted to them is required. These events may be referred to either as *privilege management* or *privilege life cycle*. There are two important tasks that should be undertaken during the privilege life cycle:

Rights and Privilege Audit   As users progress through their assignments within an organization, they may gather additional rights and privileges. They may also be temporarily escalated and provided with privileges based upon a project or special situation. An audit should be undertaken on all individuals' access accounts to ensure that their existing rights and privileges match the minimum requirement (least privilege) for them to do their existing job.

Account Deactivation   This is the immediate removal of access rights during a termination event. Security professionals should ensure that a program is in place whereby an assigned individual in the IT department is made aware of the event and takes immediate action to withdraw user access to organization resources. Ideally, this action is performed during the exit interview or prior to an individual exiting the building. The term *orphan accounts* refers to resource access accounts that still exist yet do not belong to anybody. Orphan accounts should be discovered during a rights and privileges audit and immediately closed.

Participating in Security Awareness Education

In many companies, it is the responsibility of the security practitioner to participate in and act as a facilitator of security awareness education programs. Not only must the security practitioner deliver the program in front of an audience, in many cases they must author the content of the course.

Types of Security Awareness Education Programs

Many companies, depending on their size, use different types of user awareness training programs:

New Hire Orientation   An indoctrination program is usually delivered within the first few days of employment. During this program, the individual is typically made aware of the dos and don'ts of the company's security policies. They also might sign an authorized use policy (AUP) acknowledging their understanding of the rules and regulations of accessing network resources and company data. Of primary concern in a new hire orientation is the use of personal devices in the work environment. Also, instruction is given on how to access the network from a remote location such as a home office.

Mandatory Security Training   Mandatory security training is required under various regulations such as HIPAA in the medical field as well as various privacy regulations with respect to financial, banking, and credit card industry information. Mandatory training is usually cyclical and is required on an annual or semiannual basis.

Corporate-Wide Security Training   This program is generally required at least once a year by most corporations. It may be offered as a refresher program and in many instances takes the form of computer-based training (CBT).

Specialty Security Training   Specialty computer training includes training programs made available for vendors, customers, extranet users, senior executives, and department managers or offered in special situations. These courses are typically custom designed specifically for the audience.

Working with Human Resources and Stakeholders

It is important to know that as a security practitioner, you may be obtaining information for a security presentation by interacting with other departments. There are two distinct department and groups:

Human Resources   Human resources as a department is charged with not only sourcing and onboarding new employees but also the management aspect of their career during their employment with the company. It is important to include human resources in any training module. The human resources department may include trainers who are expert at either designing courses or facilitating presentations. Also, they are specifically aware of all of the laws and regulations regarding the material that may be presented to individuals, specifically testing and evaluation. It is their responsibility to make sure all training and evaluation of employees complies with federal, state, and other mandates.

Stakeholders   Stakeholders may have an interest in security training. They may be internal to the company, such as department heads, network administrators, and corporate executives, but they may also be external to the company, such as regulators and auditors. Stakeholders may might be involved in creating the content of security awareness training courseware. It is important to make sure the information obtained from stakeholders coincides with the overall security policies of the company.

Senior Executives

It is important to note that senior executives have a serious interest in the security of the company. In many cases, they have signed off on a variety of policies and statements that set forth the direction of the corporate security policy.

Senior Executive Presentation   During a senior executive security presentation, facts and supporting information are presented to illustrate compliance with various corporate security policies.

Senior Executive Security Training   This is a very important training awareness program specifically designed for senior executives concerning the protection of information to which they have access. In many instances, it is the senior executives who are specifically targeted for information concerning mergers and acquisitions, information about change in financial structure, or specific information about new products, strategies, or corporate direction. In many instances, this training involves the protection of cell phones, pads, tablets, and other devices used by senior executives.

Customers, Vendors, and Extranet Users Security Awareness Programs

On many occasions, it is responsibility of the security practitioner to facilitate discussions, training, or webinars for a variety of external users. Depending upon the company, various customers, vendors, or extranet users require indoctrination into the proper use of company assets and company information. It is important to stress the impact of security on both your company and the partnering company.

Summary

This chapter discussed a number of techniques, processes, methods, hardware devices, and protocols that form the foundation for network security. Enacting security in any workplace environment is a complex endeavor, not only requiring knowledge of software and hardware but also understanding the behavior of individuals who may mistakenly or intentionally cause harm to resources and data.

You have seen that, as in many other industries, there is no single solution to a problem or opportunity. Therefore, many companies and organizations developed their own methods for providing a solution. This is a primary reason the security professional is required to be aware of all of the possible solutions.

Various techniques may be used by an (ISC)² SSCP exam candidate to examine and understand the Common Body of Knowledge (CBK) required to pass the exam. One of the techniques is to visualize the solution from start to finish (the example cited was that of a remote user desiring to log in to a corporate network). You have seen how various hardware and software solutions have evolved over time. New and better techniques often replace older techniques. Another learning technique is to group all similar terms into a category. And it's important to note how the exact same item or process might be known by several different names.

During exam preparation, you will come across terms such as TACACS, X.509, 802.11n, AES, and CAT6. Each of these terms originated either through a private company or through some sort of standards organization. You have seen that the standards organizations use a variety of techniques to arrive at a recommendation for the industry. These recommendations, or standards, are for the security professional sources of information for industry-accepted best practices.

The CIA triad features the three central concepts of security objectives that are the essence of all information security systems. The security professional must be completely familiar with the concepts of confidentiality, integrity, and availability and be able to relate any other security topic to one of these three objectives. In addition, there are three categories of security goals: prevention, detection, and recovery. Controlling access to an organization's resources involves a multistep process, which includes identification, authentication, authorization, and accounting.

Finally, it's important to acknowledge that the largest threat to the organization's resources is people.

Exam Essentials

The CIA triad   Know the CIA triad, and be able to describe the concepts of confidentiality, integrity, and availability.

Security Categories   Know the three security categories and be able to explain the actions required of each. The categories are prevention, detection, and recovery.

Access Control Requirements.   Be able to explain the requirements for access control.

The Access Process   Be able to explain the four steps of the access process. The steps include identification, authentication, authorization, and accounting.

Nonrepudiation   Be able to explain that nonrepudiation means that the sender cannot deny sending a message and that, provided special conditions, the receiver cannot deny receiving a message.

Risk   Explain that risk is a concept that indicates that there is a chance of damage or loss based upon exposure to potential threat.

Vulnerability   A vulnerability is a weakness that can be exploited by an attacker.

Controls   Controls, also called safeguards, countermeasures, policies, and procedures, are techniques that can be used to reduce or mitigate risk.

Three Types of Controls   The three types of controls are physical, logical, and administrative.

Prudent Man, Due Diligence, and Due Care   Prudent man, due diligence, and due care are measures taken by security professionals to protect the assets of an organization.

Assets in an Organization   Assets within an organization fall within two general categories: resources and data.

Three As of Security   The three As of security are authentication, authorization, and accounting.

Principle of Least Privilege   The principle of least privilege is the practice of providing users and applications with the least level of access required to perform a task or job.

Account Life Cycle   Privilege management, aka privilege life cycle, refers to the group of activities between user account initiation and the final termination and deprovisioning of an account.

Written Lab

You can find the answers in Appendix A.

1. Write a paragraph briefly explaining the concept of implicit deny.

2. Briefly describe the availability principle in the CIA triad.

3. List the components of AAA.

4. List the three primary security categories.

Review Questions

You can find the answers in Appendix B.

1. What is the definition of the principle of least privilege?

   A. Allowing all users full control over a network to keep administrative responsibilities to a minimum

   B. Keeping the number of system users with access to a minimum

   C. Granting users only the minimum privileges needed to accomplish assigned work tasks

   D. Designing applications that do not have high levels of privilege

2. What is the process of assigning groups of tasks to different users to prevent collusion and avoid conflicts of interest?

   A. Principle of least privilege

   B. Separation of duties

   C. Mandatory access control

   D. Integrity assurance

3. To prevent any one person from having too much control or power, or performing fraudu-lent acts, which of the following solutions should *not* be implemented?

   A. M of N control

   B. Job rotation

   C. Multiple key pairs

   D. Separation of duties

4. What is the primary goal of risk management?

   A. Reduce risk to an acceptable level

   B. Remove all risks from an environment

   C. Minimize security cost expenditures

   D. Assign responsibilities to job roles

5. Which of the following best describes the use of a PIN number?

   A. Authentication

   B. Authorization

   C. Auditing

   D. Access control

6. Nonrepudiation ensures which of the following?

   A. That strong passwords are always used

   B. The accounting of the user actions

   C. That the sender cannot deny their actions

   D. The confidentiality of the database

7. Which item is not part of the primary security categories?

   A. Prevention

   B. Encryption

   C. Detection

   D. Recovery

8. Which of the following is a nontechnical means of enforcing security?

   A. Development of a disaster response plan

   B. Separation of duties

   C. User training

   D. Safe testing

9. Which option is not part of the prevention primary security category?

   A. Placing a padlock on a fence

   B. Using guard dogs instead of security guards

   C. Using virus protection software on all users' machines

   D. Using an alternate site after a disaster

10. What is the most important step the IT department should take when an employee is fired?

   A. Search their desk for USB drives

   B. Erase all data on their laptop

   C. Review the rights and privileges assigned to the user

   D. Deactivate the user's account to prohibit access

11. What is the foundational premise of risk management?

   A. There is always some level of risk.

   B. Computers can be completely secured.

   C. As security increases, costs decrease.

   D. Security and performance are cooperative measurements.

12. What are weaknesses within a network?

   A. Vulnerabilities

   B. Mitigation

   C. Risks

   D. Controls

13. Which of the following options is a part of the CIA triad?

   A. Admission

   B. Availability

   C. Auditing

   D. Administration

14. Which of the following is *not* a security category?

   A Prevention

   B. Remuneration

   C. Detection

   D. Recovery

15. Which of the following types of controls restricts access based upon time?

   A. Temporal time restriction

   B. Date restriction

   C. Time of day restriction

   D. Authorized access hours

16. Which of the following provides a catchall and prevents an action from being taken after everything else has allowed through on a network?

   A. Explicit deny

   B. Deny any

   C. Implicit deny

   D. Global deny

17. Which of the following is a security program used in many banks to verify the ethics and job performance of a bank manager?

   A. Ethical investigation

   B. Mandatory vacation

   C. Mandatory cruise

   D. M of N

18. When it comes to network security, the acronym AAA stands for which of the following?

   A. Authorization, authentication, and accounting

   B. Admission, authorization, and accounting

   C. Authentication, authorization, and accounting

   D. Administration, authorization, and auditing

19. What is a restriction placed on users that denies them access to resources on the weekends?

    A. Temporal differential

    B. Time of week restriction

    C. Time of day restriction

    D. Time-based accounting

20. During an access system audit a number of active accounts were discovered from employees who had left the company over the past two years. What are these accounts called?

    A. Long-term accounts

    B. Orphaned accounts

    C. Pseudo-active accounts

    D. Ghost accounts

Chapter 3

Domain 1: Access Controls

THE SSCP EXAM OBJECTIVES THAT WILL BE COVERED IN THIS CHAPTER:

✓ **Implementing Authentication Mechanisms**

   ■ Understand multifactor/authentication and single sign-on techniques

   ■ Review device authentication implementation

✓ **Utilizing extranet, third-party, and federated access internetwork trust architecture**

   ■ Understand one-way trust relationships, two-way trust relationships as well as the principles of transitive trust

✓ **Know the security practitioner's role in Identity-Management Lifecycle**

   ■ Understanding authorization, proofing, provisioning, maintenance, as well as account entitlement

✓ **Implementing types of Access Controls**

   ■ Understand types of access controls including mandatory, non-discretionary, discretionary, role-based as well as attribute-based access controls

Access control provides users with a method of accessing system resources. It also places limits on how users access the resources, what user actions can be performed, and what resources users can access. Access controls limit general public access by requiring identification, verifying or authenticating the identified user, and then authorizing the user, thus providing them with predefined rights and privileges on the system.

The access control system must provide system administrators with the ability to limit and monitor users who have access to a system and to control or restrain the actions that they can perform. Access control systems define what level the user has on a system based on predefined conditions such as the user's authority level or membership in a group or by matching a security level with a specific category of the information being accessed. Various information access models are available to the security practitioner, and several may be used simultaneously within a business or IT system.

The SSCP access control domain requires knowledge of the techniques and mechanisms that allow security practitioners the ability to protect the organization's systems or resource assets.

An important first step of the identification and authentication process is the identification of the individual user. An access control system must be able to accept the user identification in a format it recognizes and be able to convey this information to a processing system where the identification is compared against a list of users authorized to access the resource.

In this chapter about the access control domain, you will learn about access control models that you can use to determine both the access to a resource and who determines the access permissions. You will also learn about the information control models that can be employed to limit what the user can do once they are allowed access to the information or resource.

The security practitioner must be completely proficient with the three types of controls (physical, logical, and administrative) and should be accomplished at employing each of them to provide a layered security and defense in depth environment.

What Are Controls?

A system administrator or security manager must have the ability to limit risk. Risk is inherent in every IT environment. A threat such as a hacker or intruder identifies and exploits a weakness, referred to as vulnerability. Vulnerabilities exist throughout applications, databases, and entire networks.

The act of limiting risk is referred to as mitigation. The tools available to mitigate a risk are called controls. The access control techniques and mechanisms are described as follows:

Physical Controls   These include doors, locks, and fences.

Logical Controls   These include an access control list (ACL), an intrusion detection system (IDS), firewalls, routers, virus protection software, and activity logging mechanisms.

Administrative Controls   These include banners, signs, policies or procedures, directives, rules or regulations, and documents or log-on screens.

Exam Point

It is important to know that there are three basic types of controls: physical, logical and administrative. You should be able to recognize various devices and techniques employed in each type of control.

In everyday conversations, the word *control* and the word *countermeasures* refer to the same item or concept. In most cases, all three types of controls are in use all of the time. (The three types of controls are described in detail in the section "Types of Access Controls" later in this chapter.)

Exam Point

A control may be physical, logical, or administrative and limits or mitigates a risk.

What Should Be Protected?

The first step in determining the security for an organization is to determine what resources and assets need to be protected. Resources and assets fall into three general categories: physical assets, digital assets and information assets.

Physical Assets   Tangible things such as the building, property or business equipment (which includes network hardware), and people

Digital Assets   Generally consist of the data contained or stored on the IT systems

Information Assets   The content information represented by the digital data

Information assets can be classified based upon the financial value to the business or what harm would be done if information was lost, destroyed, or released to the public. For instance, the business category in which the organization is involved is general public knowledge, but the release of a trade secret identifying exactly how the business creates its product could do irreparable harm to the business. Information assets might be ranked from unclassified to confidential. Or it could be ranked on a valuation scale, such as zero dollars to many millions of dollars of cost in the event of information release or loss.

A task of a security practitioner is to identify the resources and assets requiring protection and rank them using either an asset valuation system or a sensitivity and potential harm system. In risk analysis, there are a number of methods used in performing this task. In all situations, the most valuable asset to be protected is people. For example, in the event of fire, bomb threats, or other life-threatening emergency situations, the safety and well-being of the people in the environment is always the primary concern. People must be evacuated or protected from the threat. Evacuation programs, exit markings, emergency lighting, and fire protection systems as well as emergency evacuation drills must all be part of the general safety policy for the environment or building,

---

Exam Point

The most important asset to be protected is the people.

Why Control Access?

Controlling access is vital to the health of your systems, networks, and data. With access, a user or attacker can do anything to your system. If they cannot get access, they can do nothing to the system. Access controls also provide a level of accountability and the ability to audit what the authorized user is doing while in the system.

Although the concept of access controls may be easy to comprehend, the application is frequently more complex. A balance must be achieved between resource protection, control mechanism cost, and user-friendliness. Controls must be consistent with the organization's security policy; they must provide adequate protection of the resource at a reasonable cost yet not be so arduous that users attempt to find a workaround to save time or effort.

Exam Point

Procedures that ensure that the access control mechanisms correctly implement the security policy are called *assurance procedures*.

An additional concept of access control is referred to as *layered security* or *defense in depth*. This is a simple concept of establishing a number of roadblocks the adversary must cross in order to access the resource.

The *defense-in-depth* strategy utilizes multiple layers of controls and relies upon a couple of concepts:

Discourage an Attack   The first concept is to frustrate or deter the attacker. If the prize is not worth the hassle, perhaps the attacker will move on. When this concept is employed, the attacker may perceive that there are just too many obstacles to overcome, that the time to penetrate these obstacles is too long, or finally, that the ultimate value of the prize being sought is insufficient for the amount of effort expended.

This technique is evident with the application of simple versus complex passwords. A simple password may take several hours to crack, and a complex password, utilizing numbers, special characters, and capitalization, may take 1,000 years to crack using the same computing equipment.

Slow the Attacker   The second concept is to slow down the attacker. For instance, even if the attacker tripped the house alarm, thus notifying the authorities, scaling a fence and picking the padlock would take enough time for the police to arrive and arrest the attacker.

 **Real World Scenario**

Backyard Security

Defense in depth can be illustrated by a backyard storage shed. Imagine that you possess an 8×8-foot metal shed. You keep a lawn mower, a rake, a shovel, and a garden hose in this shed. Your first layer of defense might be simply to always keep the shed door shut. But, in the interest of security, you also place a padlock on the door. Because of your neighborhood, you also place a padlock on the gate to your backyard. Since someone might jump your fence, you elect to install a motion-detector backyard light. After word of a few other neighborhood thefts, you decide to install a video recording system, buy a large dog, connect the shed to the home burglar alarm system, and place a large sign in the yard announcing that you will prosecute thieves and announce that they are "on camera," As shown in the following illustration, each of these items provides a different layer of defense to your defense-in-depth strategy for the backyard shed.

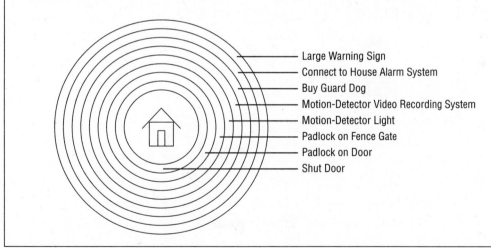

The overall consideration of placing various controls in the path of an attacker is cost. Is it prudent to spend $2,500 on controls such as video equipment, special lighting, and police alarm systems just to protect $300 worth of garden tools and equipment? The security practitioner must be constantly aware of how the cost of controls compare to the value of the systems or data being protected.

Exam Point

The defense-in-depth or layered security concept features placing various controls in the path of a potential attacker.

Subjects and Objects

There are two terms related to access control: subject and object.

Subject   A *subject i*s the user or entity taking the action or accessing a resource such as a database.

Object   An *object* is the item or resource being acted upon. For instance, a user accessing a software application is the subject, and the software application would be the object.

In some cases, items may change relationships (Figure 3.1). In such an event, an object becomes a subject and then reverses roles again. For instance, the user (subject) accesses an application requesting information. The application (object), in an effort to respond to the user (subject), requires information from a database. The application now becomes a (subject) to the database (object). Once the data is retrieved, the application once again reverts to an (object) role and responds to the user (subject).

FIGURE 3.1   The relationships between subjects and objects

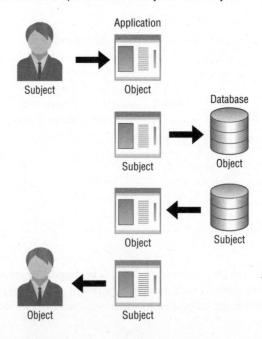

Types of Access Controls

As mentioned earlier, there are three general categories of controls: physical, logical, and administrative. Virtually all controls can be placed in one of these categories. There is a security principle you will hear many times. It is the principle of implicit deny. In simple terms, it refers to excluding everyone except those you have specifically (explicitly) allowed to enter. It is much easier to work with a small group of users or items than it is to work with a large group of items that includes everything. As a simple example, four people work in the server room and require access. It makes sense to give these four people access keys to the room while excluding all other persons.

The same principle might be applied to children viewing television, persons accessing websites at work, or the general public accessing your private business network on the Internet. It is much easier to list what users can do than it is to list everything they cannot do. In the world of security, the list of what the user can access is referred to as *included by exception*, a *white list*, or *explicitly allowed*. The restricted list, or the list of what is not allowed, is referred to as *black list*, or *implicit deny*. Implicit deny is a main feature of most router rule lists. It denies all incoming traffic that has not specifically been allowed by an explicitly written rule.

Physical Access Controls

A *physical access control* is all the items listed in the backyard shed example earlier in this chapter. The purpose is to keep a physical intruder from penetrating a physical property area. The following physical access controls can be used:

- Closed doors
- Locks
- Chains
- Bars across doors
- Cages
- Earthen berms
- Driveway spikes
- Bulletproof glass
- Fences
- Earthen berms

- Lighting
- Security alarms
- Video surveillance
- Guard dogs
- Human guards
- Exterior walls
- Infrared motion detectors
- Glass breakage detectors
- Mantraps
- Intrusion alarms

Physical controls are usually independent of computer hardware, software, and communication systems. Locks, gates, lights, and detectors generally do not report in, with the exception of very high-security installations. Of course, there may be locks that use a logical device such as a card reader or other mechanism to trigger (open) a device. These are still classified as physical access controls.

Physical controls restrict or prohibit access to the physical components of the infrastructure such as wiring closets, wireless access points, server rooms, and communication lines. Physical security is an important concern for the security practitioner in maintaining the layered security and defense-in-depth security concepts and works hand in hand with other access controls. A physical access control is usually the first line of defense.

Logical Access Controls

Logical access controls are those controls used to keep a digital intruder out of a network, host, or system. Logical controls are usually established to protect the data, applications, hardware, and network devices from hackers, malware, intruders, and simply mistakes users can make. These types of controls are usually grouped into two categories with much overlap. The categories are hardware and software. Firewalls, intrusion prevention systems (IPSs) and data loss prevention systems are typical logical hardware devices, whereas some firewalls, virus protection software, and Group Policy enforcement by an operating system are software controls. The following items are logical controls:

- Firewalls
- Routers
- IDSs/IPSs
- Data loss prevention systems
- Unified Communications security devices
- Proxy servers
- Virtual networks
- Virtual private networks (VPNs)
- Application firewalls
- Virus protection software
- Authentication mechanisms
- Encryption

Access Control Lists

A type of logical control used when granting access to major applications, databases, and physical devices and when granting the ability to pass through network controls such as firewalls is the use of *access control lists* (*ACLs*). ACLs are used by some major applications to provide access controls to the data that the application manages. Typically, access control lists contain the identity and access authority for every user (subject). A type of access control list referred to as a *capability table* maintains the permissions assigned to the user, such as read, write, and execute.

An access control list generally appears as a type of database table listing users or subjects in one column and the permissions they are assigned in another. Because ACLs are used to grant and administer file permissions and access, users' permissions may be easily escalated. Care must be taken in the selection of and the number of administrators capable of changing ACLs.

Exam Point:

Logical controls are any network device or software that protects the network hardware and digital information assets of the company.

Administrative Access Controls

Administrative access controls consist of policies, directives, regulations, and rules set up by a company to govern activities taken by individuals or to establish operating procedures. Every company or firm requires various policies. In some cases, these policies are imposed by an outside organization or regulation, such as the *Sarbanes-Oxley Act (SOX)*, the *Health Insurance Portability and Accountability Act (HIPAA)*, the *Security and Exchange Commission (SEC)*, and the *Payment Card Industry Data Security Standard (PCI DSS)*.

Administrative controls begin with policies that address a specific subject, all the way down to the person ultimately responsible for carrying out the action. Many new hires are introduced to IT security administrative controls immediately upon joining a company. They must often read, agree to, and sign an *authorized use policy* (AUP) that specifies how the user must behave when using the networks, information, and IT products of the company (Figure 3.2).

FIGURE 3.2   A typical authorized use policy screen

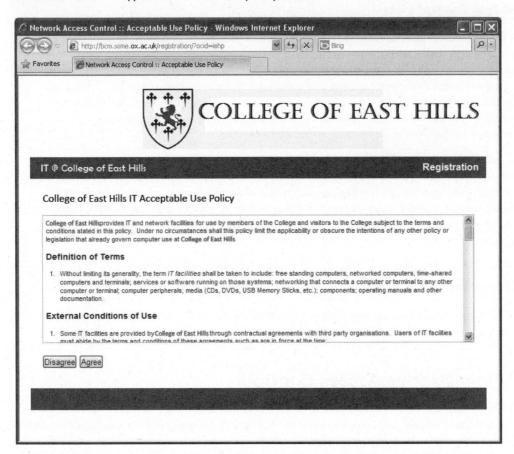

Identification

The first step of access control is *identification*. Many might think that entering a username into a field is the first step in identification. This is not always the case. There may be a preceding step. For instance, in the case of logging into a bank account, the user might be

prompted to click a "log in" link on the bank's home page. This click initiates the identification sequence. In such cases, the bank system responds with a login screen featuring a
field for the username and a field for a user password (Figure 3.3). The blank for the user
name is the request for identification information. In other situations, the swiping of a card
in a gas pump or at a grocery store initiates the login sequence. Access control identification
may also allow access to specific places by swiping an access card at a doorway reader thus
identifying the user and unlocking the door.

FIGURE 3.3   A typical login screen

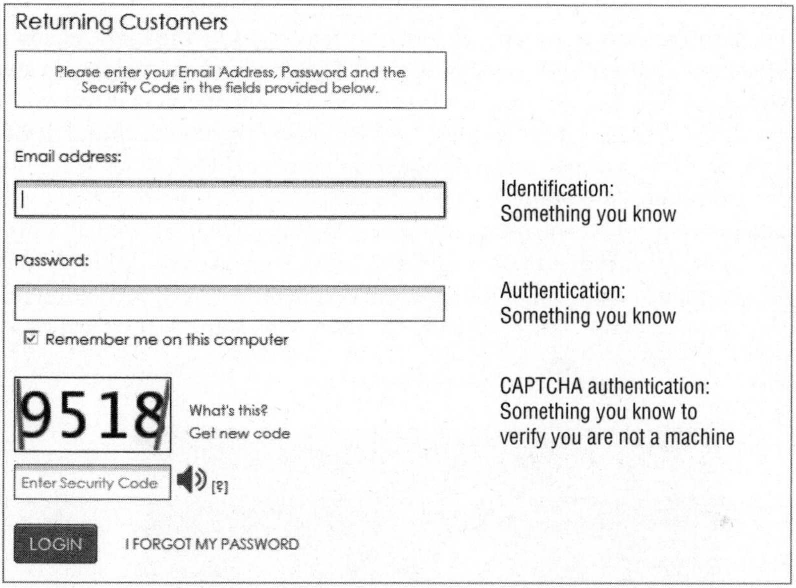

Returning Customers

Please enter your Email Address, Password and the
Security Code in the fields provided below.

Email address:

|

Identification:
Something you know

Password:

Authentication:
Something you know

☑ Remember me on this computer

9518   What's this?
Get new code

CAPTCHA authentication:
Something you know to
verify you are not a machine

Enter Security Code   🔊 [?]

LOGIN   I FORGOT MY PASSWORD

The goal of these systems is to differentiate one user from another. A unique username,
personal email address, or account number will initiate the identification sequence. During
this sequence, the system will compare the received identification information with some
sort of internal database; in the case of a Microsoft system, this might be *Active Directory
(AD)*. In the event the user is not identified, the system may present an error screen or in
some cases a screen offering the user the ability to create a new account. If the user identification is recognized, the system will proceed to the next step. This step usually involves the
request for additional authorization information.

The challenge to security practitioners with regard to identification is that the person
entering the data or swiping the card may not be the person you want to have access.
Anyone knowing that the web page username field requires an email address could easily
type someone else's email address. The person swiping the card might have just stolen it.
This is why more verification information is required before allowing access into the system
or location.

Authentication

Authentication is the process of proving the identity professed by the user. As you have seen, anyone can enter a username or swipe a card. The next step is to authenticate the user to the system (Figure 3.4). The most common method of authentication is to have the user enter a password. On ATMs and gas pumps, or with various credit cards and debit cards, this might be in the form of a personal identification number (PIN). When a credit card is used at some gas pumps, the billing address zip code may be requested. Because most credit cards require only a PIN to withdraw money, the zip code is utilized as a piece of authentication information that a thief would not know. This password, PIN, or zip code, along with the username or identification, is again compared to the information in a system database to determine that the user is actually the user. This is the authentication step.

FIGURE 3.4   User entering PIN into a reader device

The challenge for security practitioners is that besides the attacker using a stolen identification, there are many ways of breaking a password, PIN, or other methods of authentication. If an attacker is both identified and authenticated correctly and allowed into the system, this is referred to in security as a *false positive* and is a serious situation. It means that an unknown person has been granted permission into the system. To combat this possibility, there are many authentication methods that exist.

Exam Point

A false positive refers to a condition where an unknown user has been identified and authenticated and allowed access to a system. This is known as a false positive error. A false negative refers to a condition where a known good user is denied access to the system. This is known as a false negative error.

Many might think that identification and authentication occur only when the user is logging on to the system or network. There are a great many places on a network where identification and authentication can take place. False positive and false negative errors may occur in a number of different situations. The frequency of these errors is referred to as an *error rate*. Generally, all access control and authentication is performed by comparing user information with some type of list. Identification and authentication might take place when the following items are used:

Firewalls and Routers   *Firewalls* and *routers* compare incoming access requests to a set of rules. The rules are established by an administrator and maybe be either broad in nature or very restrictive. For instance, many firewalls might allow HTTP traffic yet restrict traffic from specific URLs. A router may allow or disallow a specific IP address through the use of an access rule programmed into the router.

Intrusion Prevention System   An *intrusion prevention system (IPS)* inspects packets on a network. Packet construction and contents are compared to a type of list called a signatures list. Packets represent the data that a user is sending over a network. An IPS is inspecting packets as if each packet is requesting access. Packets identified by the IPS as being threats to the system are not allowed to pass and are dropped.

Switches   A *switch* is a device that routes network communications based upon the Media Access Control (MAC) address of a device. Switches are programmed with an access list of MAC addresses that may pass through or be denied by the switch.

Virus Protection Software   Similarly to the IPS, *virus protection software* inspects data coming into a network, on a host computer, or currently in storage against a type of list called a signatures list. The signature data file contains profiles of known malicious software. The virus protection software then takes steps to deny access or trigger an alert.

Access control not only identifies and authenticates users to allow access to a network or application, it can be made granular enough to inspect packets on a network or specific host machines and grant or deny access based upon a list or other identification/ authentication technique.

Factors of Authentication

There are several types of authentication methods. They are referred to as factors. A *factor* is an item or attribute that can be specifically linked to the user. Most authentication attributes fall into five main categories:

Something You Know   This includes any information committed to memory or in written form, such as passwords, PINs, the street you grew up on, your favorite teacher, or personal information such as your zip code or account number.

Something You Have   This includes credit cards, digital proximity cards, radio-frequency identification (RFID) devices, hardware tokens, photo ID badges, and smartphones for SMS/text messages.

Something You Are   This includes the use of a biometric system to verify the user's physical characteristics such as fingerprints, palm scans, iris or retina scans, facial feature scans, key stroke dynamics, weight, or speech recognition.

Somewhere You are   This uses a geolocation or geotagging system to physically locate the user by recognizing the user access point or terminal, IP address, satellite triangulation, or cell towers in use.

Something You Do   This makes use of various traits exhibited by the individual. These traits include voice patterns, heart rhythms, handwriting analysis, and keyboard typing characteristics.

The attributes are explained in detail in the following sections.

Exam Point

It is very important to be able to identify the different factors used to authenticate a user.

Something You Know

Something you know is the most common form of authentication. In most instances, the user enters a password. Passwords can prove to be the weakest type of authentication. The security practitioner may employ a number of techniques that increases the security of user passwords:

Never use default passwords.   Users, as well as network administrators, should not use the password that came from the factory. Passwords must be changed on all network hardware items. Users must never be allowed to use *pass* or *password* as a password.

Change passwords often.   Many organizations establish a password change period within a password policy document. This may be as often as every 30 days but should be no longer than every 90 days. Group Policy Manager is usually used to enforce password change policy.

Make passwords sufficiently strong.   Passwords should never be common dictionary words of any language, names, personal identification numbers, pet names, or anything that can easily be guessed. Passwords should be a minimum of seven characters in length and consist of upper- and lowercase letters, numbers, and special characters.

Never write passwords down.   Frequently passwords are found around the user's work area on sticky notes, note pads, diaries, or even books or papers. As a security practitioner, never make a password so complex that it forces the user to write it down and refer to the note.

Never tell your password to anyone.   One of the most popular social engineering attacks is a call from a tech department requesting the user's password. Frequently, someone is away from the office and calls to ask a friend to access their system using their password. Or, a temporary employee is given the password of the permanent employee they are replacing.

Use audit tools to verify password strength.   There are many third-party applications as well as operating system tools that allow the security practitioner to scan passwords and verify the strength by checking for special characters, password length, numbers, and duration on the system.

In Exercise 3.1, you will see how to check the strength of passwords. You will also read helpful text concerning the construction of strong passwords.

EXERCISE 3.1

Microsoft Password Checker

A responsibility of the security practitioner is to educate users on the correct guidelines for creating strong passwords. The use of the Microsoft Password Checker allows users to test their own passwords for strength and security.

1. Open a browser window.

2. Go to www.microsoft.com/security/pc-security/password-checker.aspx.

3. Experiment with the Microsoft Password Checker by inserting typical passwords and noting the output display.

Something you know can also be a secondary authentication question (Figure 3.5). Many financial accounts require a username for identification, a password for initial authentication, and then some personal information not likely known by many others. This additional personal information is usually in the form of several questions the user is asked upon account setup. Such questions might include mother's maiden name, the street where you lived when you were 10 years old, your favorite teacher, the best man, and the city where you were married. The problem with this is that some of this information is readily available knowledge. Users should select questions and answers that are not easily publicly found, such as favorite teacher or best man.

FIGURE 3.5   Typical login verification question

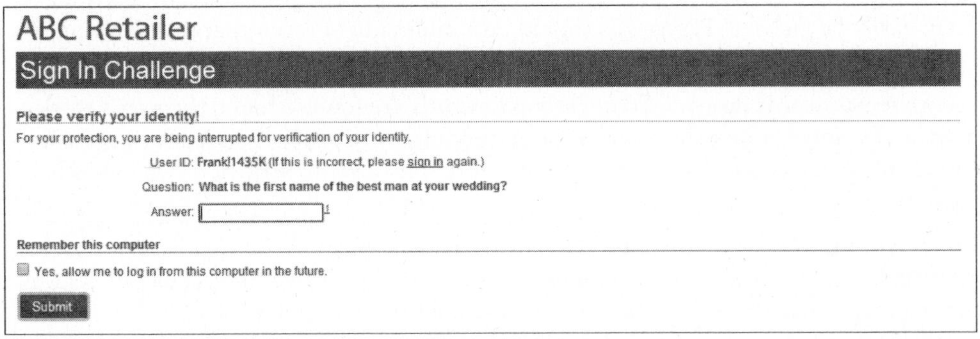

ABC Retailer

Sign In Challenge

Please verify your identity!

For your protection, you are being interrupted for verification of your identity.

User ID: Frank!1435K (If this is incorrect, please <u>sign in</u> again.)

Question: **What is the first name of the best man at your wedding?**

Answer: [   ]¹

Remember this computer

☐ Yes, allow me to log in from this computer in the future.

[Submit]

Another form of something you know authentication is the use of CAPTCHA characters (Figure 3.6). CAPTCHA is the acronym for Completely Automated Public Turing test to tell Computers and Humans Apart. This is a challenge-and-response system featuring a set of numbers and letters in various shapes with varying backgrounds. The challenge is for the user to visually recognize the characters and knowingly retype them into a form. This technique is used to determine if the user is a human or a machine. A machine may be able to break a user's password, but it still would not be able to pass this test. The machine would not be able to visually read or recognize the shapes of the CAPTCHA characters.

FIGURE 3.6   This figure illustrates CAPTCHA characters

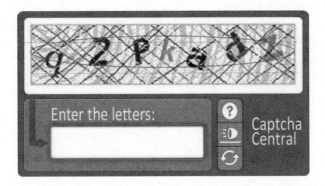

🌐 **Real World Scenario**

Password Policy and Password Management

Many companies have created a password policy that specifies password duration, length, the use of capital letters, numbers and special characters to increase password complexity, how passwords are audited, and other requirements. Typically, the enforcement of such password policies is through the use of Group Policy Manager in Windows. This allows the system administrator to establish password policies that can be applied to all of the users in the domain. The following illustration shows the Windows Server 2012 Group Policy Management Editor with the domain Password Policy selected.

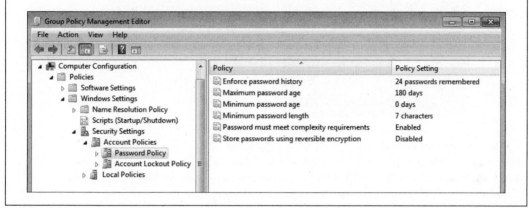

Exam Point

The password policy specifies how often passwords must be changed, password complexity, how passwords are audited, and other password characteristics.

Something You Have

Many people carry an ATM card, driver's license, student ID, smartphone, credit card, or proximity card. Each of these can be used to establish authentication. For instance, if you are stopped by the police, you may verbally state your name, but a driver's license or other identification issued by an authority such as a state department of motor vehicles or a university, in the case of a student ID, is used by the officer to establish if you are stating the correct name. This is an example of something you have.

Many corporate and federal employees are issued proximity keys or cards to access facilities. Specific data is embedded within the card. Although they are not internally powered, they feature a type of antenna that receives a signal from a nearby receiver (Figure 3.7). This stimulates the card and provides sufficient energy for the card electronics to respond to the card reader and transmit information. This technique is also utilized on many toll roads across the country. A small device typically placed on the windshield responds to a signal transmitted toward the auto and the device responds with identification and authentication information allowing the toll authority to debit the person's account.

FIGURE 3.7   Toll authority RFID device

Many businesses provide employees with a personal badge that has a name, ID number, and photo of the employee (Figure 3.8). Many of these badges also contain micro-electronics that allow the individual to access various doors within the facility. Most facilities log the entry and exit of individuals throughout the premises.

FIGURE 3.8   Standard ID badge with proximity chip

Another type of card is a smart card; in government organizations this might be referred to as a common access card (CAC). This type of card features circuitry that stores the user's certificate. The certificate contains the user's public key for authentication as well as encryption, although in this case it is primarily used for authentication. The card is usually placed into a card reader to be read. Since the card might be lost or stolen, a second authentication factor is usually required such as a biometric input, PIN, or password.

Something You Are

Something you are is a physical characteristic that is unique to you and your body. *Biometrics* is the science and technology of recognizing a user based upon their body. For instance, law enforcement can identify individuals by fingerprints, footprints, palm prints, blood samples, and DNA.

All biometric systems require an individual to register or enroll by recording the specific biometric sample into the system. Different biometric system manufacturers referred to this measurement as a *reference profile*, *reference template*, or *biometric signature*.

In business today, various biometric techniques are used to identify and authenticate individuals:

Fingerprints   *Fingerprints* have been used for identification by law enforcement for many decades. A fingerprint is obtained by scanning one or more fingers several times. This *digital finger print image* is used to generate a *finger image identifier record* that can be used to compare with future scans. Fingerprint recognition in biometrics is one of the most widely used techniques now being used on laptops, tablets, and personal cell phones. In *finger-scan technology*, only the features extracted from the fingerprint are stored. This allows one to many rapid fingerprint data searches. In *fingerprint technology*, entire fingerprints are stored on a system, requiring large amounts of storage.

Iris and Retina Scans   *Iris scans* map the colored part of the eye, recording the unique color, patterns, and textures (Figure 3.9). A *retina scan* has proven to be extremely reliable, more reliable than using fingerprints and other biometric techniques. Retina scans are utilized by the government for access into sensitive locations and systems.

FIGURE 3.9   Retina scanning technique

4. When the user requests access, their retinal scan is compared to their stored compressed data points.

1. Most retinal scanners read from the outer iris in toward the pupil edge.

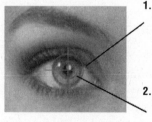

3. The scan data is then sent to a database server where data points are compressed.

2. The retinal scanner then plots the unique patterns of blood vessels using infrared light.

Facial Recognition   Similar to mapping points on a fingerprint, a *facial scan* records and traces various key points on the human face. Using measurements and placement of various features, a video or photograph of a face may be matched to facial signatures in a database.

Weight   Although not as popular as other biometrics, *weight recognition* has been utilized in mantraps to both authenticate an individual and alert authorities in the event of two persons in the mantrap, called "piggybacking." Weight has also been used as alarm systems to warn if an intruder has placed weight on a room floor or object.

Weight Sensors

You may have seen the weight-scanning biometrics technique in the movies. First, the would-be diamond thief repels down from the ceiling so that she won't put weight on the alarmed floor, only to be caught when a small object falls and hits the floor setting of the alarm. Second, in a fictional movie scene, the hero archeologist replaces the golden object with a bag of sand, also setting off an alarm. Both of these are illustrations of weight sensors in use, but in these scenarios they are used as controls against thieves. They can also be viewed as biometric authentication sensors. The first scenario authenticates the room with no weight present. The second authenticates the object with the exact weight. If the weight changes, the object is no longer authenticated.

Palm Prints and Palm Geometry   This biometric method uses the physical *palm geometry* of the palm and fingers to uniquely verify an individual. In systems known as *palm scans*, a bright light is used to scan and map blood vessels within the hand to create a unique palm signature.

Retinography is a process for identifying people by the pattern of blood vessels on the innermost tissue coat of the back part of the eye, called the retina. This identification process makes use of a retina-scanning device that maps the unique pattern of blood vessels on the retina.

Retina Scanning

A typical *retina scanner* uses infrared light for mapping while a user requesting access looks into a scanner device. A low-energy beam of infrared light traces a circular path on the retina at the back of the eye. The device measures the variation in intensity of the reflection of the infrared light from blood-filled blood vessels called capillaries. These capillaries absorb more of the light than the surrounding tissue, allowing the tissue to reflect light, thus outlining the capillaries. Many scanners measure this reflection at between 300 and 400 points along the beam path and then rapidly assign an intensity grade between 0 and 4,500. The sample results are then compressed into a computer file, which is sometimes called a signature, and stored in a biometric server database. The stored data is then compared each time the user is scanned for access.

Retina-scanning devices tend to be very popular in corporations and high-security access points; not only are they fast, they tend to be very accurate with a very low error rate because the eyeballs do not change over time. Retina scan user enrollment is very quick and easy, and eyeball scans are extremely difficult to forge.

There are several challenging aspects to the use of biometrics. Any or all of these might be considered when implementing a biometric system:

Enrollment Time   Every biometric system must initially be set up with every user's unique information. For instance, for a retina scan device, every user must submit to an initial scan.

Error Rate   Every biometric device is comparing a current reading or capture with a saved signature. In some cases, an error can occur that prohibits passage or allows passage when it should not occur.

Acquire Time   Each user wanting access must submit to an acquisition of biometric information. This could be as simple as a fingerprint scan or palm scan or as complex as a retina scan or voice scan. Each scan requires an increment of time to acquire the sample information, and in each case the user must be present and wait during the scanning process.

Throughput Time   Once the biometric sample has been acquired from the user, it must be compared to the stored sample signature in the system database. This requires a period of processing time during which the user remains waiting for access. Should the system malfunction or service be denied, access to the facility or resource might be denied.

One-to-One Search   In this type of database search, the acquired information scan is compared against stored signatures or data samples for a potential match. Only specific data points of the acquired sample information are compared against similar data points stored in the system to speed the sort. Errors may occur when not enough points match.

Exam Point

A security practitioner should know and understand the biometric error types.

Every biometric system faces its own challenges processing information and making decisions to allow or deny access to the user. When specifying a biometric authentication system, various terms and considerations are used.

False Rejection Rate (FRR)   FRR is referred to as a Type I error. This is the percentage of time a biometric system rejects a known good user, thus not allowing access.

False Acceptance Rate (FAR)   FAR is referred to as a Type II error. This is the percentage of time a biometric system falsely identifies as good an unknown user, thus allowing access.

Crossover Error Rate (CER)   The CER is where the false rejection rate (FRR) and false acceptance rate (FAR) cross over (Figure 3.10). A lower CER indicates a better biometric authentication system.

FIGURE 3.10   The crossover error rate (CER) is where the FAR and FRR intersect. The lower the CER, the better the biometric system.

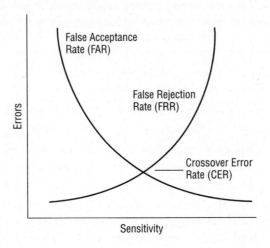

Exam Point

The lower the CER, the better performing the biometric system.

Something You Do

Something you do is a trait that you have developed over the years. This trait is unique to you and has developed either through training, your upbringing, environment, or perhaps something unique to your body construction. Unique biometric scanning devices have been constructed to measure a variety of personal traits to be able to authenticate an individual. These traits are as follows:

Signature Dynamics   This recognizes how the subject creates letters and words. The subject is requested to sign their name or to write out a specific group of words. Items tested may include pen pressure, direction of strokes, and points where the pen was lifted from the page. The scanning system then examines the result and matches specific test points with those saved in memory. *Signature dynamics* is the biometric factor of handwriting analysis.

Voice Pattern Recognition   This acquisition system requires the individual to speak a phrase into a recording device. This is the same phrase that was originally recorded and stored in memory. The system examines features such as inflection points, volume, speaking speed, and pauses. The stored voice phrase in the biometric system is referred to as a *voiceprint*.

Voice pattern recognition is not the same as speech recognition. Voice pattern recognition identifies and records a number of data points based upon unique vocal patterns of the individual. These data points are compared to a saved signature used to authenticate the individual. *Speech recognition* identifies word sounds and matches the sounds to a prerecorded profile of the user. Speech recognition also makes use of *artificial intelligence* as a method of determining the word actually spoken.

Keystroke Dynamics   *Keystroke dynamics*, also known as keyboard pattern recognition, recognizes how an individual types on the keyboard. Various biometric systems measure flight time and dwell time to generate a typing signature. The signature generally captures *flight time*, or the time a user takes between key depressions, and *dwell time*, which is the length of time a key is depressed. The results of using keystroke dynamics as a biometric recognition system are inconsistent because users' typing methods change depending upon mood or environment.

Heart/Pulse Pattern   Researchers have identified that each person's heart beats in the unique pattern. This pattern may be detected with recognition software and used as a biometric authentication system. Typically this is achieved by the user wearing a wristband that monitors their heartbeat and its unique pattern and uses it to unlock phones, computers, and other nearby devices that belong to the user. This technique is somewhat similar to health and fitness trackers, with the current measurement of the user being compared to a stored signature for authentication purposes. *Heart/pulse pattern recognition* is a biometric authentication technique.

Somewhere You Are

Geolocation and *geotagging* are now used by many systems to identify where the user actually is located. Many software applications, retail stores, social media sites, and other systems ask for the user to allow themselves to be geolocated. Users may be identified and authenticated by their location. For instance, several major department stores are pushing ads out to cell phones as you walk through the store. You may receive a coupon on your phone as you drive past a coffee shop or another location. Major credit cards such as American Express will act on location anomalies when a charge is made in a foreign country if the user has no history of traveling to that country.

 Real World Scenario

The Callback

A recent application of a tried-and-true computer system access method is the *callback*. Years ago, when a remote user called in by telephone to connect their modem to a network or mainframe, the computer system would terminate the initial call and call the user

Continues

Continued

back at their location on a known user phone number. Today many banks and financial institutions and other such organizations use the same technique by texting or emailing the user an access code during the login process. Upon receipt, the access code is entered by the user into a field on the logon authorization screen. Once it's matched by the system, the system authenticates the user using the "something you have" method of authentication.

In this instance, the user owns and has access to a cellular telephone with a cell phone number and a texting application, or the user owns an email account. Both the cell phone number and the email account have previously been authenticated as items owned by the user. As with the rapid expiration time of some token access codes, the access code provided by text or email usually have an expiration time of two hours.

Single-Factor Authentication

With *single-factor authentication*, only one factor is used. An example of single-factor authentication is using the password required by a screensaver. The only factor required is something you know, which in this case is the password. Requiring the entry of two or more of the same type of factor is also regarded as single-factor authentication. When a user logs on to a network first thing in the morning, they may be required to enter an identification item such as a username or click a specific icon. The second item requested is usually a password. In this instance, both factors are the same type, something you know. Using two of the same types of factors during authentication is no stronger than using a single factor.

Multifactor Authentication

Multifactor authentication refers to using at least two different types of factors for authentication purposes. In many businesses today, employees are issued a pass card or smart card. This card generally allows access to various authorized doors within the building. In other cases, employees are required to authenticate into secure databases, applications, or other sensitive areas.

The two different types of authentication factors might be a typed-in password and a thumb print. A secure room might require a smart card scan and an iris scan. In any event, for it to be multifactor authentication, the factors must be different. The user cannot use a token and a smart card because they are the same type of factor, as are a thumb print and an iris scan. *Multifactor* means, for example, something I have and something I am, or it could mean something I know and something I have.

Exam Point

Multifactor authentication requires two different types of factors, such as something I know and something I am. Remember that a password and a PIN are still one factor, something you know. Read the exam questions and options on multifactor authentication very carefully.

Token-Based Access Controls

Token-based access control is based upon a *one-time password*. Because the password is used only once, it is very difficult for a hacker to obtain it. The password is also only available for a very limited period of time, usually 60 seconds, after which it changes to a different password. Because the password is displayed only once and for a short period of time, it is almost impossible for an attacker to intercept it.

A *token,* or *token device,* is usually a small hardware device that displays a number (Figure 3.11). The token is synchronized with the authentication server so that the server always knows the number that is displayed. When the user wishes to log in or access an application, they enter the number that is visible at that moment. This indicates to the authentication server that this person has the token in their possession. This is an example of a something you have authentication factor.

FIGURE 3.11   An example of a token

Some hardware tokens are attached to key chains for user convenience. This type of token is referred to as a key fob. The device used to unlock a car door is a type of key fob. It sends a coded message to the car.

A token is synchronized with the authentication server, thus providing a synchronized one-time password. The displayed password usually changes every 60 seconds.

Another type of one-time password is *OPIE*, which is short for *One-Time Passwords in Everything*. This type of one-time password is based on *S/KEY*, a one-time password system used to generate passwords on some Unix systems. It is typically the user's actual password combined with other data and passed through a hashing algorithm. This technique generates a one-time password and makes use of the MD4 or MD5 *hashing algorithm*.

System-Level Access Controls

System-level access controls address two very specific requirements.

The Value of the Information   The first requirement is the value of the information. Information value is strictly in the eye of the beholder. If you are in business, financial and customer data is of utmost concern and value to you, but if you are in the government or military, data concerning troop movements, targets to attack, and logistics may be of utmost concern.

The Method of Accessing the Information   The second requirement is how the information is made available. For instance, can a database owner decide who has access to the data or work object and is there another means of relating the data specifically to the user or subject allowed to access it?

Discretionary Access Control (DAC)

With *discretionary access control (DAC)*, access is granted to objects (data and applications) based upon the identity of the subject. Each subject is granted specific rights to the data. For example, when you share a folder on your desktop with three of your co-workers, you are exercising discretionary access control. As the data owner, you are granting access to your folder. At any time, you may restrict or revoke access to your folder, but the decision is completely yours. In the slightly more sophisticated environment of a Microsoft SharePoint administrator, the administrator may decide which users can read only, edit, or write to a data file. Again, this is completely discretionary based upon the value of the data in the eyes of the administrator, department head, or company.

In the Microsoft SharePoint example, the identity of the user is established by the user credentials at login to the Microsoft SharePoint system. Again, the Microsoft SharePoint administrator may easily, at their discretion, set the rights and privileges of that individual. Once the individual accesses the data folder or file, the software system checks the user credentials and allows the user to perform actions as established by the administrator or data owner. It is important to note that at any time the data owner or administrator may override the existing selections and make changes to the rights and privileges. Typically, the following actions may be granted to the user for a file:

- Full Control
- Modify
- Read & Execute
- List Folder Contents
- Read
- Write
- Special

With discretionary access control, each data file or folder makes use of an access control list (ACL). The ACL lists the user and their permissions on a file or folder. While the ACL is associated with or is attached to an application or resource to control access, the subject may also have a list. This list is referred to as a *capabilities list* and is, in essence, a list of the rights and privileges granted to the user.

Exam Point

In the DAC model, users and data owners have complete discretionary control over their data and who has access to it.

Nondiscretionary Access Control

Nondiscretionary access control (non-DAC) is used when a system administrator, management, or an information tagging/labeling system controls access to objects by subjects. In this case, the access might be granted by policy to a specific group of users. The system administrator is carrying out policy administration.

Mandatory Access Control

Mandatory access control (MAC) uses labels or tags to identify both subjects and objects and is a nondiscretionary access control model. It is the most secure model and is used by the U.S. military and federal government to protect classified data. With the MAC model, every piece of information (object) and every user (subject) have been given a label.

Currently the U.S. government maintains the following levels of information labels:

Top Secret Release of this information is listed as causing "exceptionally grave damage" to national security.

Secret   Release of this information would do "serious damage" to national security.

Confidential   Release of this information would cause "damage" to national security.

Unclassified   This is not a security label but a general catchall for any information not labeled.

In the U.S. government and military, information is "classified" if it is in one of three levels, confidential, secret, or top secret. Individuals with the corresponding labels or clearances may access data. It is not uncommon for data to be compartmentalized. In this case, an individual with a Secret clearance is allowed access only on a "need to know" basis.

Many data labels exist for business data. Most businesses have proprietary information, trade secrets, and internal data that if made public might do substantial harm to the company. Business data may also be classified into compliance categories. Categories such as personal identification information (PII), HIPAA information, and various categories of financial information may be restricted by regulations. The following information security labels are typically used in business:

Confidential   Disclosure of this information may cause irreparable harm to the company.

Internal Use   Disclosure of this information may cause harm to the company.

Public   This classification of information is generally known to the public.

Exam Point

Under the MAC model, subjects and objects are assigned labels or tags. Labels assigned to subjects are called *security clearances* or a *capabilities list*, while labels assigned to objects are called security classifications or *information classifications*.

U.S. Government Classifications

The United States government classifies information according to the degree to which unauthorized disclosure would harm or damage national security. Like many other countries, the United States has three classification levels. From the highest to the lowest, these levels are as follows:

- Top secret (TS, color code orange)
- Secret (S, color code red)
- Confidential (C, color code blue)

Government documents that do not have a classification level can be marked as unclassified (U, color code green).

The color codes refer to the color of the borders on the cover sheets placed on top of secure information, printouts, and documents. Each page of a secure information print-out is also printed or stamped at the top and the bottom with the security classification for that document.

It has recently been made public that an estimated 4 million people have top secret clearance and an estimated 10.8 million government, private contractor, and military personnel have some sort of U.S. government security clearance. It is reported that an additional half-million security clearance requests are processed annually. Because so many people have access to it, top-secret information is put in separate compartments, accessible only to those people who have a *need to know*. The system is referred to as sensitive compartmented information (SCI) for intelligence information, while other highly secret and sensitive information specific to the military and other organizations is protected by compartmentalized special access programs (SAPs).

Sensitive Compartmented Information (SCI)   SCI is divided into 200 to 300 SCI compartments and subcompartments, and each compartment is named with a single code word. These compartments contain information specific to the intelligence community, such as the NSA, CIA, FBI, and other "alphabet" agencies. A famous top-secret SCI compartment is named UMBRA. This code word has been in constant use since 1968 and is used to protect the most sensitive intercepts of communications intelligence. Although officially terminated in 1999, recent NSA leaks indicate that the code word is still in use.

Special Access Programs (SAPs)   SAPs have been created to control access, distribution, and protection of particularly sensitive information, which includes top-secret military information. Each SAP is identified by code words that consist of two unassociated, unclassified words. There are over 100 SAPs, with many having numerous compartments and subcompartments. An example of a top-secret special access program is Yankee White. Persons who have been cleared for this SAP have complete access to presidential workspaces that might contain classified information at any level up to "Presidential Eyes Only" and may also carry a loaded weapon in the presence of the president. This clearance requires the most extensive and thorough background investigation possible.

Administering Mandatory Access Control

You have seen that discretionary access control is administered through the use of an access control list (ACL) attached to each file or folder with changes that can be made on the fly by the data owner. Mandatory access control must be enforced by a completely different mechanism. Typically, in a mandatory access control system, the sensitivity of the objects being accessed is far greater than the objects in a discretionary access control system. Therefore, greater harm or expense may be incurred should subjects be given improper access to highly sensitive data. In a mandatory access control system, something is required to mediate between the levels of access granted to the subject and the security classification of an object. This mediation or decision-making process must be accomplished in an environment of trust, where the hardware and software providing this mediation is above reproach. The theory and application of this hardware and software mediation platform is referred to as a trusted computing base (TCB).

Trusted Systems

Mandatory access control (MAC) is traditionally enforced by the system through the use of a *trusted computer base (TCB)*. This is a protected part of the operating system that includes a *security kernel* and *a reference monitor*. As you have seen with MAC, users or applications are referred to as subjects and are labeled with a security clearance and are included on a capabilities list. The security clearance represents the highest level of information the subject may access. In addition, all data and information is referred to as an object and is classified as, for example, confidential, secret, or top secret. This security classification system is primarily used by the federal government and military agencies.

The primary information framework utilized in MAC requires that a subject that is granted a secret clearance may not access top secret information "read up" from the clearance they currently possess and, once accessing secret information, cannot "write down" that information to a level such as confidential or unclassified, thereby reducing the secret information to a lower security classification. In practice, the trusted computing base is engaged in the comparison between the security clearance labels of subjects and the security sensitivity labels placed on objects.

There are several components to a trusted computing base:

Secure Hardware and Software Environment This may take the form of an isolated server stripped of all services and capabilities not required of the mediation process. The isolation means that it should not be possible for an attacker to be able to change the logic of the reference monitor or access and change the contents of the security kernel.

Reference Monitor The *abstract machine concept* that mediates all access by subjects to objects (Figure 3.12). As part of the TCB, it must always be invoked and available, be verifiable as correct, be protected from modification, and mediate all access requests. Once a subject requests access to an object, the reference monitor accesses a file, known as the security kernel database, that lists the access privileges or security clearance of each subject and the security classification attributes of each object.

FIGURE 3.12   The reference monitor mediates all transactions between subjects and objects.

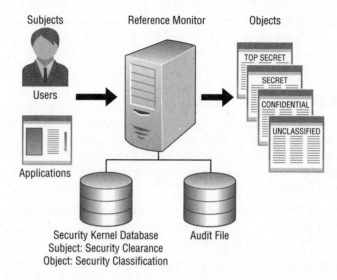

Security Kernel   The component of the trusted computing base consisting of hardware, software and firmware elements that implements an authorized control list (ACL) database, usually referred to as a security kernel database. This database is utilized when mediating (comparing) subject and object labels in a Mandatory Access Control (MAC) authentication system.

Audit   The final requirement is to provide a complete audit file recording attempted security violations, authorized data accesses, data file changes, and authorized changes to the security kernel database.

Exam Point

The *reference monitor* mediates (compares) subject and object security labels prior to allowing access.

Mandatory Access Control Architecture Models

The MAC architecture model provides a framework that can be applied to various types of information systems. In general, these models provide rules that can be applied to subjects before they are allowed to read or write sensitive information. Each of the four models provides a primary goal of either confidentiality or integrity. Each of the models is named after the individuals who created it.

Exam Point

When using the mandatory access control architectural model, the federal government and military are primarily concerned with information confidentiality, while business interests and corporations are primarily concerned with information integrity.

Bell-LaPadula Model

The *Bell-LaPadula model* enforces information confidentiality. It does this by enforcing security through two rules called no read up and no write down.

With the Bell-LaPadula model, an individual with a secret security clearance cannot read top secret information and cannot write secret information down to a security level below secret, such as unclassified.

Simple Security Property Rule (No Read Up)   Subjects cannot read information classified at a higher level than theirs. For example, a person with a unclassified security clearance cannot read a document classified as secret.

The Star Property Rule (No Write Down)   Subjects with access to information at a certain security level cannot write that information to a lower security level. For example, a person accessing documents classified as secret cannot reduce the classification level by writing the information to a lower level. Usually an asterisk (*) is used as a star, as in the * property rule.

The Strong Star Rule   This rule states that if you have read and write capabilities, you are restricted to read and write your data at your level of secrecy, but you cannot read and write to levels of higher or lower secrecy. This is sometimes referred to as the constrained or tranquility property.

As expected, the Bell-LaPadula model is used extensively in the federal government and U.S. military where confidentiality of information is the primary concern.

Exam Point

The Bell-LaPadula model deals with assigning to subjects security labels called security clearances and to objects labels called sensitivity classifications.

Biba Model

The *Biba information model* is primarily concerned with information integrity. The rules are reversed from the Bell-LaPadula model. In the Bell-LaPadula model, we do not want to reduce the security classification of sensitive information. The Biba model seeks to not increase the integrity of information at a lower level.

The goal is that an individual at a certain security level may not read information at a lower level and the individual may not create (write) information at a higher level than their security level.

Simple Integrity Axiom (No Read Down)   Subjects granted access to any security level may not read objects at a lower security level. For example, a business manager may not read or accept actionable orders from an assembly line worker, but the president of the company may issue actionable orders to the manager.

The Star Integrity Axiom (No Write Up)   Subjects at a certain security level may not write to a higher level. Continuing our example, the assembly line worker cannot write actionable orders for the manager and the manager cannot write actionable orders for the president. (Usually an asterisk [*] is used as a star, as in the * integrity axiom.)

The Invocation Property   The invocation property prevents a user at one level from using or invoking the powers or privileges of the user at a higher level.

The Biba model is used primarily in the business environment where data and object integrity is of primary concern. In this model, individuals at a lower level may not create or modify data at a higher level.

Exam Point

The Biba model is concerned with the integrity of objects.

Clark-Wilson Model

The goal of the *Clark-Wilson model* is to enforce separation of duties through integrity rules. This model places a mechanism such as a software program between the subject and object. The software program separates the subject and object. This model enforces data integrity by checking, screening, or formatting data prior to it being placed in the object, such as a database. The Clark-Wilson model enforces what is called "well-formed transactions." This model also enforces such integrity policies as authorized users may not take unauthorized actions and unauthorized users will not be allowed access.

Exam Point

The Clark-Wilson Model is concerned with object integrity and separation of duties and enforces well-formed transactions.

Brewer-Nash Model (Chinese Wall)

The *Brewer-Nash model* is used in many business organizations to prevent conflict of interest situations within the same business. Objects are classified in a manner that indicates conflicts of interest. For example, if a business is providing different services for the same client, each branch or department is isolated from the other with no knowledge of the other departments' activities. This eliminates the possibility of a conflict of interest. This is also referred to as providing a Chinese wall between the two groups. Each group's information (objects) is classified so that it may not be accessed by the other.

Exam Point

The Chinese wall concept prohibits conflict of interest within an organization.

Account-Level Access Control

In any business, there are a number of individuals requiring different access privileges based upon their responsibilities and roles within the organization. Account-level access control allows for a more detailed or granular control ability down to the group or individual level. This is the basis for role-based access control.

Dual Control

Dual control refers to an access mechanism whereby two individuals must work together to gain access. In some cases it is referred to as *split knowledge* as well as *separation of duties*. Dual control may be specifically utilized for access to encryption keys when two or more individuals maintain partial knowledge. When their knowledge is combined access is granted to the item, such as access to an encryption key or encrypted message authentication codebook or physical access. Dual-control access mechanisms are highly relied upon in the U.S. military where total responsibility for access by one individual must be avoided.

 **Real World Scenario**

Access to Military Top Secret Information

The 1995 action movie *Crimson Tide* illustrated a number of military access control techniques in use. The movie plot makes use of a nuclear submarine receiving top secret information by the way of undersea low-frequency flash communications called an emergency action message (EAM). The dual-control technique was illustrated during the retrieval of the message from communications, where two individuals were involved.

The printed communication message had to be kept in plain sight at all times as it was walked to the bridge.

The authenticity of the message was accomplished by yet a third person snapping open a plastic container holding the top secret code word after it was retrieved from a safe. When the message was read out loud to the captain of the submarine, the code word on the message was compared to the code word retrieved from the safe and had to be confirmed as authentic by the first officer. Only then could the captain of the submarine accept the message as authentic. This is an example of the multiple steps used throughout the U.S. military to ensure that critical top secret messages are authenticated and validated through numerous steps.

Device Authentication, Certificate-Based Authentication

In many security situations it is desirable to authenticate not only the individual but also the machine or device they are using. *Certificate-based authentication* requires that a valid digital certificate be maintained on a machine or device from which the user authenticates. Authentication relies upon the certificate information and encrypted user password. This combination authenticates not only the user but the device that they are using. In device-to-device authentication, a similar scenario is used during the authentication process; valid certificate information is used to authenticate devices to each other. Certificate-based authentication may be accomplished through a commercial certificate issued by *certificate authorities (CAs)* such as *VeriSign* or through internal corporate CAs managed by the organization.

A very lightweight version of device authentication may be accomplished through the use of cookies. *Cookies* can be installed on various devices to identify them. Although not significantly utilized for communication encryption, devices may be initially authenticated by banks, financial institutions, and e-commerce sites as having been previously used by the user requesting initial authentication into their system.

Exam Point

Device authentication relies upon digital certificates installed on the device.

Reverse Authentication

With reverse authentication and mutual authentication, not only does the user authenticate to the system when requesting access, they also have knowledge that the system they are contacting is in fact a genuine site. Various techniques have been used, from complex mutual handshake technology to visual cues.

Banks and financial institutions have utilized visual identification cues that only the logging-in user would recognize. It consists of a simple picture they selected upon account initialization. The user is then presented with the picture during login.

The unfortunate downside of this technique is that the end user may not realize that this is an authentication technique or cannot remember that this was a picture that they selected, and other than terminating the session, they have no method of communication or validation other than contacting the institution's customer service department. A more successful method of reverse authentication is actually through the use of *personal security questions*. Personal security questions have been primarily intended as an initial factor of authentication of the user by the institution. But, a spoofing website will not have access to the correct answers to the user's questions. Thereby, even if the spoofing website is capable of obtaining login and password information, access to the real website will still be denied.

Privileged Accounts

Privileged users are typically super-users or administrators who have an elevated level of rights, privileges, and access capability to applications and data. Throughout the IT security organization, privileged account users present special access control concerns. Possessing the ability to bypass many access control methodologies, they may be capable of modifying many normal system controls. Privileged users should always be required to log on to two accounts: their privileged user account and their normal user account which allows access to email and regular daily applications. All privileged accounts should be closely monitored and audited regularly for privilege escalation or de-escalation as the situation requires.

Exam Point

Privileged users, or superusers, should make use of two separate accounts. The privileged account should be used only for privileged account administration purposes. A second account should be used for everyday network access, email, and general applications.

The following are guidelines for privileged accounts:

Account Creation   Assign privileged accounts only as required. Screen, background check, and document users assigned to privileged accounts.

Policies and Procedures   Privileged account holders transcend everyday users and even corporate executives with their access capability. Consider requiring more stringent authorized use policies, nondisclosure agreements, noncompete agreements, and confidentiality agreements for these individuals.

Account Provisioning   Using the "least privilege" concept gives a privileged account only the minimum rights and capabilities required for the role. For example, do not give a database administrator the same rights as a server administrator or system administrator.

Account Monitoring   Always monitor and log all privileged account accesses and actions. Store these logs on a remote server to which the privileged account holder does not have access (separation of duties). Assign an individual to monitor and report on the logs regularly.

Dual Accounts   Always provide the privileged account holder with a regular personal account for email and daily routine access. Never log into a privileged account to perform personal business.

Separate Machines   Ideally, establish a virtual machine to log into the privileged account. This eliminates the possibility of any malware migration onto the privileged machine or the servers and applications being administered.

Escrow Passwords   Passwords, encryption keys, and other account login information may be placed in blind escrow in the event of incapacity or termination.

Account Deprovisioning   Establish a deprovisioning plan to use in the event of incapacity or termination for privileged accounts. The plan should restrict access and change passwords but securely retain information for future access if required.

Privileged accounts, due to the elevated accesses they provide, should be the most heavily logged and monitored accounts within the IT system. You should not only monitor the actions of the privileged superuser but also monitor for potential attacker access violations and privileged escalation attacks.

User Accounts

All corporate employees fall under the user accounts umbrella. *Identity management* refers to the management of all of the accounts within the corporate domain. Each account has an *account life cycle* that must be managed by the IT department. This management of user accounts during the account life cycle is called *identity management*. A general account policy should be established with standards and procedures to be followed during the account life cycle. Finally, a person or department should be specified to carry out the account life cycle tasks. The following events or activities are included as account maintenance during the account life cycle:

Provisioning   During the provisioning phase, accounts are created, and the appropriate application licenses, system rights, and privileges are assigned to the account. *User entitlement* refers to the rights and privileges provided to a user. An important consideration when establishing a new user account is naming and identifying standards established by the policies. This maintains a consistency of account names, email addresses, and private folder names. To speed this provisioning process, many IT departments have established a number of user groups of like roles or privileges and assigned the individual to the appropriate group. These groups might be the accounting department, sales department, senior executives, marketing department, and so on.

This grouping of roles also involves assigning various security privileges, which in this case is role-based access control (RBAC). Some organizations use an automated provisioning application where the HR department enters various new-hire information, including an assigned group or role, and the software application provisions the account using this department-supplied information.

Password Maintenance   This is generally a corporate policy that is usually enforced by a Windows Server Group Policy manager. Passwords should conform to the length and complexity, expiration date, minimum password age, password history, and other provisions within the corporate password policy.

Account Audit   Accounts should be audited on a schedule as specified in a corporate account policy to determine if the current account access rights and privileges match the current role and requirements of the existing position. This prevents privilege escalation with job rotation or reassignment.

Account Proofing   The term *account proofing* has various meanings in different circles. Microsoft has used it to mean requiring an authentication validation, such as a phone number, address, or zip code. In other scenarios, the term refers to verifying that the account belongs to the stated individual through the use of various authentication tests and audit techniques.

Account Privilege Change   A change management process should be established to service the requirements of assigning additional rights and privileges to an individual account.

Account Entitlement   Account entitlement refers to the access enabled or available for any user account. Various government and financial institution regulations require regular annual audits be performed on user accounts that access sensitive applications and data.

Account Deactivation   This is a procedure undertaken immediately upon resignation or termination of an account owner. A corporate policy or service-level agreement (SLA) should be established that triggers account deactivation immediately upon a separation event. All managers and HR individuals must be aware of the policy and how to take immediate action to protect the company assets. Account deactivation removes only the password and user access. All underlying folders and information remain intact.

Account Deprovisioning   This is an organized disassembling of rights and privileges of the user account as well as archiving any folders, data, applications, user history, logs, or other user-specific information as required by policy. Ultimately, hardware is recycled, disposed of, or destroyed as required by policy.

 Real World Scenario

Account Deactivation Plan

With the current proliferation of cell phones, and tablets in recent years, the ability to log onto a corporate network by an individual is immediate. This is the primary reason that an account deactivation plan should be in place for any resignation or termination event.

During a termination event sequence, the terminating manager or HR representative should contact IT and put in place the account deactivation plan, thereby eliminating access to the corporate network and resources by the terminated individual. Ideally, network account access should be terminated during the exit interview or prior to the individual leaving the building. Should this plan not exist or not be enacted, the corporate network and resources could be easily accessed from the lobby or parking lot of the facility by the terminated employee, thus increasing risk to the business.

Exam Point

Account provisioning is the process of assigning rights and privileges to an account. Account maintenance includes the actions taken during the account life cycle.

Account Lockout Policy

The account lockout policy may generally fall under the account password policy. It features an ability to prohibit resource access after a preset number of attempts to log in. This policy directly addresses brute-force password hacking attempts. There are several provisions of this type of policy:

Request to Reset   This is a procedure the user must follow in an effort to reset a password. The help desk or other IT contact verifies the user information and, upon authentication, issues either a replacement or temporary password to the user. In many cases, an automated system may be accessed by the user to access a forgotten password or reset a password.

Threshold of Entry Attempts   This is the number of times an incorrect password may be attempted before the user account is locked out. The lockout may be resolved through a help desk contact procedure or through a wait period.

Wait Period   This is the time duration after the threshold of entry attempts has been reached. In many cases, this period is 30 minutes, after which the user may attempt to enter their password.

Reset Interval   This is the time required that must elapse between password resets. It is typically set at two days. This prohibits the user from resetting their password several times in the same day.

Last Login Notification

The last login notification is a security check. Upon login, the returning user is greeted with a message such as "Your last login was Sunday, May 21, 2014." This may alert the user that there has been a violation on that machine if they did not log in on that day. This technique is popular in high-security environments and the banking industry.

Violation Warning Screen

Some companies enforce user policies by flashing a warning screen on the user machine (Figure 3.13). This may be in response to an attempt to access secure information or a blacklisted website or even inserting a USB drive into the machine.

FIGURE 3.13   Warning screen

Account Callback

This process originally began as a telephone callback when a remote user called in for modem access to a computer system. The system would terminate the call and call the user back to verify their location. Today, many banks and financial and other important institutions will email or text the user with a passcode that must be entered into the account logon screen to further the authentication process.

Guest Account

Many companies establish a guest login on a separate VLAN for guest-level Wi-Fi services within the premises. The guest account may be general in nature and only allow the user to connect with the Internet via a temporary account

This type of account may be assigned to a temporary worker or someone who might be replacing an employee on medical or maternity leave. Based upon the principle of least privileges, this account is usually short term and is allowed access to only the tasks of the person they are replacing but not to items such as the user's email, personal information file, storage locations, or nontask applications.

Contractor Account

A contractor account is a temporary account established for a contractor of a business. A contractor might be a temporary team of individuals, a programmer, or another person who is not a full-time employee of the business. A contractor account may be hosted on a VLAN.

These accounts are based upon the principle of least privilege and are usually tracked with logs. Some contractor accounts may have a duration of several years.

Authorized Use Policy (AUP)

The *authorized use policy* (AUP) is a screen that is displayed to an account at login notifying the user of various requirements or policies they must agree to prior to and during the use of the company resources.

Exam Point

The exam candidate should be aware of both the name and the associated acronym, such as authorized use policy (AUP), will be presented in either questions or answers on the exam.

 Real World Scenario

Account Deactivation Problems

The legal department for a major medical distribution company decided that it wanted to install a Microsoft SharePoint site that would ultimately contain thousands of legal documents, contracts, and other specific company information. After a period, contract administration, marketing and sales, and other departments were added to the Microsoft SharePoint site. The legal department, using its own budget, engaged a small IT contractor firm to create the site for the company. Because the small internal IT department of the company lacked status and budget, it elected not to be involved in this project.

A year later when a new chief information officer joined the company and authorized a penetration test, surprising information was discovered. The new Microsoft Share-Point site created by the outside contractor was hosted externally on cloud servers and accessed by a URL. Access had been granted to the information informally by Microsoft SharePoint administrators within the legal department. The problem that was discovered was that when an employee was terminated or resigned, individual network access accounts assigned by the IT department had been appropriately deleted, but everybody, current or separated from the company, who had ever been added to the Microsoft SharePoint site could still access the site through an external web-based URL.

Role-Based Access Control

Role-based access control (RBAC) is similar to and can be enforced by Group Policy manager (Figure 3.14). Typically, users with very similar or identical roles are identified and placed in a group. Access control is granted to all individuals in the group based upon their membership in the group. This type of administration is ideal for large groups such as call center employees, bank tellers, store clerks, and stock traders or with groups in which numerous adds and drops occur frequently. Once a user is assigned to the group, they receive all the rights and privileges anyone in the group has received.

FIGURE 3.14   Various groups under role-based access control

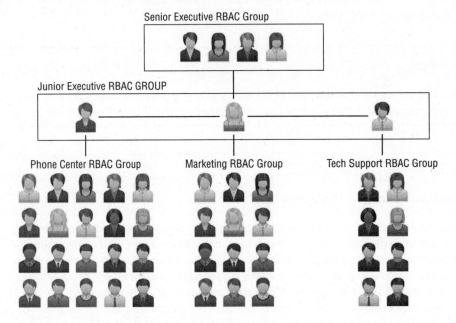

Rule-Based Access Control

Rule-based access control (RBAC or RAC) is based upon explicit rules that have been established to control the activities of subjects. Various rules may be created to allow or restrict access to objects. One such rule is the *time of day restriction*. This rule establishes when a resource or object may be accessed. For example, if the user is never required to access a database on a Saturday or Sunday from either within the building or a remote location, a rule may be established restricting access. It is important to note that role-based access control and rule-based access control may both be referred to as RBAC.

 A typical example of a time of day restriction is by controlling the access of phone center personnel to the network to a certain work schedule. As shown in the following illustration, phone center personnel have access during normal business hours but are restricted during evenings and weekend hours from accessing the network.

Phone Center Time of Day Authorized Network Access							
	Mon	Tue	Wed	Thu	Fri	Sat	Sun
12:00AM							
5:30AM							
6:00AM							
6:30AM							
7:00AM							
12:00PM							
4:30PM							
5:00PM							
5:30PM							
6:00PM							
6:30PM							
7:00PM							
7:30PM							
8:00PM							
8:30PM							
12:00AM							

Exam Point

If you see RBAC in either a question or an answer, read the question carefully for context. Determine if the question is referring to role-based access control and rule-based access control.

 Real World Scenario

Dangerous Workarounds

System administrators must be aware that any restrictions they place on information access and storage retrieval may be met with workarounds from the end users. One major hospital issued a policy that was enforced by the Windows Group Policy, which enforced not allowing anyone to write to a USB storage device. The users could read from a USB device but could not write to it.

During a penetration test, it was discovered that one hospital work group was required to share information among themselves. They did not have access to a shared drive or Microsoft SharePoint, and because they could not write to a USB drive, they just elected to establish a Dropbox cloud account and share the password among themselves. This was all innocent enough in an effort to just complete the task at hand. They thought no harm had been done; they were just trying to expedite their project. Upon investigation, it was discovered that restricted patient account information and specifically HIPAA documents were being stored on the commercial cloud drive using a shared password.

Session-Level Access Control

Session-level access controls restrict or allow actions during a specific communication session. These controls terminate when the session is terminated. A session is a one-time or individual login or access to a resource that involves a beginning and an end and is of a specific duration of time. For example, when you wish to check your bank account balance, you log in to your bank, view the account page, and log off. This defines one session. The following is a list of commonly implemented session-level access controls:

Login Notification   The system provides the user with the last login date and time for user verification.

User Inactivity   The account automatically logs the user off after a period of inactivity.

Multiple Logon Control   Some systems allow the user to establish multiple logins simultaneously. The system should be set to allow only one login from a specific user at one time.

Origination Location   The origination of a connection can easily be established and disallowed per policy. For example, many companies disallow any connection requests from URLs originating outside the United States.

Session Connection Time Limit   Users may be allowed to access a system for a set period of time, after which the session is terminated. This is popular with libraries, coffee shops, hotels, gaming sites, and other paid sites.

Continuous Authentication   *Continuous authentication* is a technique whereby the user is authenticated through every packet sent to the receiver. IPsec, a series of communication and encryption protocols, may be utilized to authenticate each packet as having been sent by the user. IPsec may also be configured to provide message integrity verification, thereby immediately alerting of changes you made to a message en route.

View-Based Access Control

View-based access control, sometimes referred to as a *constrained view control*, is a feature of many software applications as well as databases. Typically a "view" is the screen or page displayed to the user resulting from an application access or database query. This screen or view may have form blanks for the user to enter information or display specific data retrieved from a database. A view is a specific security control mechanism that restricts the user's actions or displays only the data available to them based upon their rights and privileges.

An example of a typical application might be that of a bank teller. Upon entering the customer account number, the bank teller may view a page originating in the database server that specifically outlines the customer's name, address, and current bank account balance. What is restricted from the bank teller but contained in the same database is the customer's credit information, loan payment history, loan balances, other related accounts, and some personal information. The bank teller, based upon their access capability, cannot make any adjustments or changes to the customer's bank loans. Similarly, in the same bank, upon entering customer-specific information, a loan officer will be sent a view from the same database that may include loan history, payments, collateral information, and customer credit scores. All of this information is contained in the same database, yet each user, based upon their role, was served a different view screen and had different capabilities for altering information.

View-based access control may also restrict access to certain data or certain functions provided on application programs. A typical example of this is the sheet or workbook protection mechanism that can be employed in Microsoft Excel. You can lock the entire sheet or just selected cells by using a password so that other users viewing the same sheet do not have the ability to either enter or change data. This could be handy, for instance, if the Microsoft Excel sheet is to be distributed between departments within the company to gather information. The departments will have access to the spreadsheet cells that are unlocked yet be restricted from changing any other information on the sheet. The other restricted information on the sheet may be generated by the originator or designer of the spreadsheet.

Data-Level Access Control

Data-level access control specifically deals with protecting data in any of its three states: in process, in transit, and at rest.

Data In Process   This is data that is currently in use or being acted upon by an application. Many applications feature "rollback" provisions in the event of a transaction error, application malfunction, or hardware failure. This returns the data to the last known good state. Other controls are at the application level and feature error flags and warnings depending upon various conditions established within the application. Input data at the beginning of a transaction is very vulnerable. Controls should be established to validate the input and verify the data prior to beginning a transaction. Some data in process controls feature integrity checking, using a number of techniques such as CRC, parity, or hashing to compare and validate that the data is correct and has complete integrity.

Data In Transit   Of course, data in transit is transmitted from one location to another. The transmitting location must verify the identity and authenticate the receiving user or system. In some cases, the transmitting entity and the receiving entity authenticate each other. Data in transit should be encrypted to prohibit access by any entity other than the authorized receiver, and the transmission process should guarantee integrity that none of the data has changed during transmission.

Data At Rest   Data at rest is in storage. Access to this data should be allowed only by proper identification and authentication. While data is at rest, it should be encrypted and backed up for safety. To prohibit access, such as when a cell phone is lost, a provision should be available to "wipe" or destroy the data at rest. Data at rest on USB drives, laptops, and tablets should always be encrypted.

Exam Point

Data has three states: in process, in transit, and at rest.

Contextual- or Content-Based Access Control

Data-level access control may also be based upon the form or content of the actual data. This type of access control, referred to as *contextual-based access* control or *content-based access control*, is constructed using data content rules. Content-based access control may be illustrated by using lab reports in a major hospital. A specific blood test report might be accessible by the entire nursing staff assigned to a particular unit or floor. But if the same blood test report contained information concerning a specific infectious disease, it might be restricted to only the attending physician. These types of contextual access control rules are difficult to write and maintain, but depending upon the information to be accessed, they can be highly useful.

Physical Data and Printed Media Access Control

Access controls for data stored on removable items such as magnetic tape, magnetic disk, electronic memory devices, optical media, and printed media are normally categorized as handling and storage access procedures. Corporate information that has been identified as requiring any type of security should be physically marked and then treated according to the procedures associated with the category under which it falls. Removable items containing data should require the same identification and authentication access controls and protection as any information accessible on a network.

A variety of corporate policies such as a corporate data retention policy, storage policy, and destruction policy should be created. Sensitive information should be placed in a separate collection bin for sensitive documents, papers, and magnetic media. The following external data and media access controls are typically used:

Offsite Commercial Storage   Specific storage companies offer services to warehouse secure information.

Formal Access Policy   A formal sign-out or access control policy should be followed.

Data Retention Period   Data should be destroyed at the end of a retention period. In many cases, the retention period is specified by a regulatory agency. In some corporations, retention and destruction dates are strictly adhered to by the legal department to counter e-discovery searches.

Media Destruction Policy   A policy should outline the proper destruction or recycling techniques for all paper, hard drives, optical media, PCs, cell phones, and magnetic tapes.

Strict attention should be given to the procedures and methodology of device destruction. In many cases today, data storage devices are completely shredded and destroyed rather than erased and reused.

 Real World Scenario

Knowing the Policy

A national corporation was in the process of upgrading all of its employee cell phones. The instruction to the employees was to send in the old phone when they received a new phone. Upon seeing hundreds if not thousands of cell phones coming into the warehouse, a junior manager for the company, not in the IT department, decided the company might make some money by selling these on the used electronics market.

As you might imagine, after the company sold hundreds of used phones on online bidding websites, some of the new owners of the cell phones began calling into the company. It seems they were finding phone numbers, personal information, and company and customer information on the used phones. Although the national corporation had a data disposal policy for electronic devices set in place by the IT department, the junior manager, not familiar with every IT policy, simply displayed some initiative and a desire for an additional revenue stream. The lesson here is to make sure everybody in your company understands your electronic hardware and information disposal policy.

Assurance of Accountability

Accountability is the end result of the identification and authentication system. The *assurance of accountability* is the guarantee that the user or subject has been proven to be who they say they are. When you use a strong identification and authentication system, users of the system may not deny their actions. With the concept of nonrepudiation, strong identification and authentication plus the implementation of log files are used so that the receiver cannot deny receiving a message.

Exam Point

Accountability is the result of a strong identification and authentication system.

The term assurance is widely used in information technology, project management, financial institutions, and the medical industry, among many other areas. Basically it is a measurement of how a procedure or operation was conducted as compared to established organizational or industry standards and methodology. Assurance is a measure if these procedures and operations are being followed and are successful. For instance, many corporate individuals are evaluated by their managers once or twice a year. In the last few years, many large companies' human resources departments have begun using job assurance measurements in personnel evaluation scales. This technique utilizes two different evaluation scales. One is a scale measuring the degree to which the individual met their goals; the second is, in meeting the goals, how well did the individual use techniques, policies, methods, or "values" prescribed by the company. In essence, the term *assurance* provides a measurement that goals were not only achieved but were achieved using company-approved procedures and methods.

Manage Internetwork Trust Architectures

A trust architecture is a relationship that is established between domains that allows users in one domain access to shared resources that are contained in another domain based upon authentication and authorization. Many organizations establish number of domains on their internal network. The combination of all of these domains is referred to as an internetwork. For example, domains may be established for the marketing department, sales department, and accounting department. It may be obvious that individuals within the sales department may not require access to resources within the accounting department domain. However, users within the accounting department may require access to servers in the sales department domain in order to create daily sales reports. In this case, a type of internetwork trust relationship is established between the accounting department domain and sales department domain.

Trust is a logical relationship between domains that utilizes an authentication process that verifies the identity of the user and an authorization process that determines the rights and privileges the user is granted on the resource domain. Here are some of the terms used in this process.

Trusted Domain The *trusted domain* contains the user requesting access to a resource in another domain. The domain containing the resource "trusts" the domain containing the user. Therefore, the user's domain is referred to as a trusted domain.

Trusting Domain The *trusting domain*, otherwise referred to as the resource domain, contains the resource to which access is desired. For example, a user would be blocked from the trusting domain if they were requesting access to resources and were not a member of a trusted domain.

Simple Trust Relationship In a simple trust relationship, the user in a trusted domain requests access to a resource in the trusting domain. A process is undertaken by the trusting domain to authenticate the user and determine the permissions assigned or authorized to the user by the resource. The resource maintains an access control list (ACL) that identifies authorized users with access levels and permissions for the resource.

One-Way Trust   The simple trust relationship illustrates a *one-way trust* in practice. This means that users in one domain may access resources in a second domain. But since this is a one-way relationship, users in the second domain may not access resources in the first domain. This type of trust relationship is established only for specific purposes.

Two-Way Trust   A *two-way trust* relationship is one in which both domains trust each other and each user in either domain may access the resources of the other. In *Microsoft Active Directory*, all domain trusts are automatically established as two-way trusts.

Transitive Trust   A *transitive trust* relationship is defined by a simple logical equation that if domain A trusts domain B and domain B trusts domain C, then domain A trusts domain C. The transitive trust relationship is specifically used when new domains are created in Active Directory. Domains within Active Directory may be represented as a domain tree or a top-down hierarchical structure. As new domains are created, they inherit a bidirectional trust relationship with the domains above them.

Exam Point

It is important to understand internetwork trust concepts. You should be able to explain one-way, two-way, and transitive trust definitions.

The security practitioner must be familiar with a variety of methods available to identify and authenticate users requesting access to data and resources. In the event the user is in a remote location from the company network, the authentication procedure is referred to as *remote authentication.*

Centralized Authentication

Centralized authentication is a method by which users can log onto a network one time using identification and authentication techniques. *Centralized* refers to the technique of having one central authentication server providing user lookup services and allowing or disallowing access to the data and resources. One centralized system may be used by thousands or tens of thousands of users to access organizational resources.

Decentralized Authentication

With decentralized authentication, every server or application is required to verify the identification and authentication of the user requesting access. As you may imagine, this may be a huge task to maintain adequate access control lists on each and every application and resource within an organization. *Decentralized authentication* may be applied in very specific and vertical instances where a limited number of users have been given rights and privileges to the resource. As the number of users grows, the more arduous the task of administering user rights becomes.

Single Sign-On

Single sign-on (SSO) is an identification authentication technique whereby the user signs on one time and has access to multiple applications. The user authenticates one time, and the system passes this authentication to applications and other entities. This is known as single sign-on authentication. It increases password security by reducing the number of passwords a user must remember. The risk in this process is that an attacker has access to multiple applications if the user password is discovered. Several single sign-on authentication mechanisms exist. One of the most popular is Kerberos.

Kerberos

Kerberos a computer network authentication protocol is named after a three-headed Greek god named Cerberus, known as the hound of Hades. It was originally programmed for Unix by a group from the Massachusetts Institute of Technology (MIT) in the late 1980s. All Microsoft Windows implementations after Windows 2000 use Kerberos as the default authentication protocol.

The current gross model is based on a transitive trust system. In such a system, if A trusts B and C trusts B, then A trusts C. In this example, B is represented by a Kerberos server and A, desiring to access C, would be authenticated by the Kerberos server. All of this is performed through the use of tickets.

The use of this system would be to achieve the following scenario:

Scenario   The user requests authentication by the *Kerberos* system and requires access to any or all of four applications they have permissions to access.

Process

1. Authentication request.

   The user sends an authentication request to the Kerberos authentication server.

2. Authentication reply.

   The Kerberos server responds with a secret symmetric key and a *ticket-granting ticket (TGT)*, which is time stamped.

3. Application access request.

   When the user desires access to a specific application, the user sends the request to a Kerberos ticket-granting server.

4. Session ticket reply.

   Upon receiving the ticket granting ticket, the ticket-granting server responds with a ticket for use with the target application. This ticket contains the symmetric key of the ticket granting server.

5. Presentation of ticket.

The user presents the time-stamped session ticket to the application.

6. Ticket verification.

The application server verifies the session ticket by comparing the symmetric key contained in the ticket with the pre-shared key it has stored. If they match the application server, it has authenticated the user and authentication of the ticket.

In the preceding scenario, the user is authenticated by a server one time. The server issues a ticket granting ticket to the user that can be used to request session tickets or access to servers. When the user wishes to access another server resource, the user issues the ticket-granting ticket and specifies the resource. A resource-specific session ticket is issued to the user. The user presents this ticket to the requested application server. Through the use of pre-shared symmetric encryption keys, the application server verifies the authentication of the user and ticket.

Federated Access

Federated access allows users to be identified and authenticated to multiple networks or systems. Where single sign-on allows users to access servers and applications within a single network system, federated access is an agreement between different companies or networks to allow the identified and authenticated user on one network to access another network.

An example of federated access is evident during the use of popular flight and hotel room booking websites. Once you log on and make your flight or room reservation, you might be asked if you would like to rent a car. When you select a car rental company, your identification and authentication information is passed by means of the federated database to the federated partner. That auto rental company will then allow you to book a rental car using your original sign-on information.

Exam Point

Federated access is the sharing of user information among a select federation of companies, usually within the same industry, such as travel or entertainment.

Cloud-Based Security

The *cloud* is defined as hardware and software provided to a user on a requested basis. The cloud may be both internal to the organization and external, as provided by a cloud service provider. The advantage to using the cloud is that the user generally does not have to own the equipment that provides the cloud services. Also, the user pays only for the services they utilize. In other words, the cloud may expand and contract depending upon what the user is willing to pay.

There are two primary types of cloud services:

Public Cloud   Public clouds are hosted by cloud service providers and made available either as a free service or as a pay-per-use service. Users purchase various storage sizes and other services from the cloud service provider.

Private Cloud   Private clouds are essentially the same as public clouds, the difference being that private clouds are hosted within an organization and the general public is restricted from access.

The concept of the cloud is predicated on the concept of virtualization. *Virtualization* is primarily running an application, database, or operating system that is completely separate from the hardware on which it is running. For instance, a number of virtualized application servers may be running on one physical server. This is the basis for cloud computing.

The following list includes some of the concepts of cloud computing:

Platform as a Service   *Platform as a Service (PaaS)* provides the user with a virtual computer. The user can install software and databases and operate the system as if it were a purchased hardware device sitting on their desk.

Software as a Service   *Software as a Service (SaaS)* makes available a software application that is hosted on a remote server and made available on demand by the user. One advantage to the system is that, as the application programming team makes upgrades and updates to the application, the updates are immediately available to the end user. This reduces the requirements for service packs and updates to be installed by the end users. An example of SaaS is Microsoft Office 365. Another advantage of Software as a Service is that the application is not required to be resident on the end-user device, whether a pad, tablet, or cell phone, in order for the user access the application. This reduces the requirement for memory or processing power on a small device.

Infrastructure as a Service   With *Infrastructure as a Service (IaaS)*, the cloud provider supplies the capability of creating cloud based networks utilizing standard or virtualized networking components. Infrastructure as a Service allows a company to expand very rapidly without having to purchase vast amounts of expensive hardware.

Cloud security is concerned with the following vulnerabilities:

Cloud Vendor Reliability   Cloud vendor reliability encompasses not only the financial viability of a cloud provider but also their ability to provide adequate safeguards and security controls on the cloud equipment.

Data Clearing and Cleansing   Data clearing and cleansing refers to company data that may remain on cloud storage devices after a cloud size is reduced. For instance, a benefit of the cloud is the ability to expand as required. If the space is no longer required and the company elects to contract the cloud size, the question is what happens to the data that remains on the cloud.

Cloud Client Encroachment   Cloud client encroachment refers to a couple of concepts unique to the cloud. Because the cloud is virtualized, a number of clients may all be running on the same hardware. If one client runs afoul of the law, there's a chance that could impact other clients running on the exact same hardware. The second aspect is if one client is attacked, the attacker might access other clients on the same virtualized system.

Regulations and Jurisdiction   Regulations and jurisdiction must be taken into account as cloud providers offer their services worldwide. Data stored on a cloud server system based in Spain may come under the jurisdiction of the Spanish legal system. This may be a primary consideration during a forensic investigation or a security incident response.

Summary

Controls are put in place to limit risk. Access controls are used to establish the methods by which users, called subjects, may access resources, called objects. There are three types of controls. Physical controls in the form of locks, doors, and fences physically provide barriers to entry by locking or securing an entrance. Logical controls in the form of firewalls, routers, and other computer hardware control access to digital resources such as networks and data. Administrative controls in the form of policies and enforced by rules, AUPs, and signs convey information concerning access to either physical or digital assets and resources.

In this chapter we discussed what should be protected within a business or agency. Assets and resources fall into three general categories: digital assets, physical assets, and information assets. Protection of these assets is based upon their value. This value may be expressed purely in monetary terms or may also include subjective expense based upon the harm to the business if an asset was damaged or released to the public. During a risk assessment process, a threat is identified and a control is placed to reduce a vulnerability of the asset. During active access control, we are not only controlling the access by authorized users but also limiting access by unauthorized users, bad actors, and the malware they may send in the direction of our resources and assets.

The security practitioner has a variety of tools and methods available to control access. Foremost is the ability to identify and authenticate the user or system requesting access. The identification and authentication process makes use of one or more factors of information. The use of multiple factors ensures that the user or system requesting access is actually who they claim to be. Users may be authorized to access resources based upon various security access models. These models include discretionary access control, during which the data owner assigns access; mandatory access control, which labels both the user and the data and uses a matching system to allow access; and finally, role-based access control, where users are granted access as members of a group. Various rules may be established, such as time of day access, and this is referred to as ruled-based access control.

The security practitioner should completely understand the requirements for access control and the methods, products, policies, and actions that may be implemented to provide access control and therefore security and protection for assets and resources.

Exam Essentials

Three States of Data   Understand that the three states of data include data in transit, data at rest, and data in process.

Categories of Resources and Assets   Know that the categories of resources and assets to be protected include physical assets, data assets, and information assets.

Controls   Be able to explain that controls are items used to control risk by reducing vulnerability. Controls may be physical, logical, or administrative.

Defense in Depth   Know that defense in depth and layered security refers to the use of a number of controls placed in sequence through which a threat must penetrate.

Subjects and Objects   Understand that the subject is the user or system (actively) requesting access. An object is the (passive) resource or asset of which the subject is requesting access. These roles may change or flip.

Authentication Factors   Be able to explain that a factor represents the source of information presented for either identification or authentication. Factors may be something you know, something you have, something you are, or somewhere you are. Multifactor authentication is the use of information from different factor sources.

Biometrics   Know that biometrics is the type of factor that provides information on something you are. During data acquisition at the time of access, the data may be flawed and two types of errors may occur. A *Type I error* is a false rejection. A false rejection rate (FRR) is the frequency with which the system rejects a known good person. This restricts entry of a person who should be allowed to enter. The *Type II error* is a false acceptance. A false acceptance rate (FAR) is the frequency with which an unknown person is allowed to enter. On a graph, the point where Type I errors and Type II errors cross indicates the crossover error rate (CER). The lower the CER, the more reliable the biometric system.

Internetwork Trust Architectures   Understand that a one-way and a two-way trust relationships deal with the sharing and access of resources between domains within an organization. A transitive trust relationship is established logically; if A trusts B and B trusts C, then A trusts C. This relationship is established when domains are created within Microsoft Active Directory.

Access Control Models   Understand that various access control models exist. Discretionary access control (DAC) is based upon the resource owner deciding who may have access. Nondiscretionary access control is based upon a system administrator or management deciding who may assign access. Mandatory access control (MAC) is performed by applying labels or tags to both the information and the users or subjects requesting access. Role-based access control (RBAC) is based upon the user or subject being a member of a specific group. Rule-based access control (RBAC or RAC) is based upon rules such as those that restrict access at a certain time of day.

Architectural Models   Be able to answer questions concerning the access control architectural models. The Bell-LaPadula model enforces information security. The Biba model enforces information integrity. The Clark-Wilson model enforces information integrity and separation of duties. The brewer-Nash model provides the concept of a Chinese wall to restrict conflict of interest.

Written Lab

You can find the answers in Appendix A.

1. Write a paragraph explaining federated access.
2. What is a primary vulnerability of the single sign-on process?
3. Briefly explain the difference between MAC and DAC.
4. List the three primary categories of access controls.

Review Questions

You can find the answers in Appendix B.

1. When a user is asked for a password by a system, what process is the system performing?

   A. Evaluation

   B. Identification

   C. Authentication

   D. Authorization

2. Authorization for multiple applications using one set of credentials is best described by which of the following?

   A. Authorization

   B. Single Sign-on

   C. Multi-factor

   D. Enrollment

3. If information being protected is critical, which is the best course of action?

   A. The encryption password should be changed more frequently

   B. The data should be used less frequently

   C. The data should be hidden from other processes

   D. Users should be provided public encryption keys

4. What are the three categories of controls?

   A. Physical, detective, and logical (technical)

   B. Administrative, physical, and preventative

   C. Administrative, logical (technical), and physical

   D. Physical, logical (technical), and administrative

5. Which of the following best describes the use of the password generated by a synchronous token device?

   A. The password must be used within a variable time interval

   B. The password must be used within a fixed time interval

   C. The password is not dependent upon time

   D. The password is of variable length

6. Access control is best described as which of the following?

   A. Reduction a social networking

   B. The elimination of risk when allowing users on a network

   C. The use of identification and authorization techniques

   D. The use of federated identities

7. What is the type of access control in the default access control method found in Microsoft Windows which allows users to share files?

    A. Mandatory access control

    B. Rule-based access control

    C. Sensitivity-based access control

    D. Discretionary access control

8. Which of the following types of access control is preferred for its ease of administration when there are a large number of personnel with the same job in an organization?

    A. Mandatory Access Control

    B. Role-based Access Control

    C. Rule-Based Access Control

    D. Label-based Access Control

9. Which of the following best describes the time that it takes to register with a biometric system, by providing samples of a personal characteristic?

    A. Setup time

    B. Login time

    C. Enrollment time

    D. Throughput time

10. Which technique best describes a one-to-one search to verify an individual's claim of identity?

    A. Authentication

    B. Accounting review

    C. Authorization

    D. availability

11. Which of the following is a goal of integrity?

    A. All systems and data should be available

    B. Any changes to applications for equipment must be approved

    C. All data should be encrypted in transit

    D. Data should not change between sender and receiver

12. View-based access control is best described as which of the following?

    A. The concept of hiding data from view while in storage

    B. Limiting the data the user may observe on a computer screen produced from a database

    C. Allowing a user to only view unencrypted data

    D. A rule-based control of a database

13. Which of the following best describes privileged users?

    A. They are anonymous users

    B. They are super-users or administrators

    C. They all must work in the IT department

    D. By default have access to everything on the network

14. Which of the following is true about biometric scan technology?

    A. The full palm print is stored in memory.

    B. A number of points extracted from the item scanned are stored.

    C. Scan data is always stored in the cloud for rapid retrieval.

    D. It is always used with a second method of authentication.

15. Mandatory access control uses which of the following to authorize access to information?

    A. Identity and voice prints

    B. Roles and rules

    C. Subject and object labels

    D. Identity and several factor authentication

16. Which of the following is an example of two-factor authentication?

    A. A password and user name

    B. An user ID and an account number

    C. A PIN and an RFID card

    D. A fingerprint and signature

17. Crossover error rate (CER) refers to which of the following graphical intersections?

    A. Database usage rate

    B. Employee opt-out rate

    C. Symmetric and asymmetric rate

    D. False rejection rate and false acceptance rate

18. The sensitivity adjustment on a biometric authentication device affects which of the following?

    A. Cost of the device

    B. False acceptance rate and false rejection rate

    C. Limitation of the enrollment database

    D. Requirement for continuous adjustment

19. Which of the following best describes session level controls?

    A. Role-based logon controls

    B. Identification and integrity control

    C. Mandatory access controls

    D. Log-off due to the user inactivity

20. Which of the following best describes a password that changes on each logon?

    A. Session level password

    B. Self assigned password

    C. Dynamic password

    D. Variable password

Chapter

4

Domain 2: Security Operations and Administration

SSCP EXAM OBJECTIVES COVERED IN THIS CHAPTER:

✓ Understanding the (ISC)[2] code of ethics

✓ Security policies, baselines, standards and procedures

✓ Data classification

✓ The validation of security controls

✓ Asset management

✓ Testing and applying patches, fixes and updates

✓ Understanding change management

✓ Certification and accreditation of systems and software

✓ Participate in security awareness training

✓ Understand concepts of endpoint device security

✓ Comply with data management policies

✓ Generally understand security concepts

The Systems Security Certified Practitioner (SSCP) must be familiar with an organization's policies, standards, procedures, and guidelines to ensure adequate information availability, integrity, and confidentiality (AIC). The SSCP works closely with the organization's management personnel, system owners, information managers, data custodians, and end users in the application of security policies, data classification schemes, security controls verification, and the monitoring and application of patches and updates. It is important that the SSCP candidate understand the concepts of endpoint device security and change management. As a member of the organization's IT security team, a practitioner may be involved in security awareness training and other milestones in the employee life cycle, such as onboarding, account provisioning and user support, changing rights, and account termination processing.

Security operations and administration is a broad canvas encompassing everything from corporate policies to everyday security activities. The practitioner should be knowledgeable in all of the facets of IT security administration for an organization.

Security Administration Concepts and Principles

Security administration includes the policies, principles, standards, procedures, and guidelines required for availability, integrity, and confidentiality (AIC) of an organization's data and hardware assets. Security administration also defines the roles and responsibilities of individuals within the organization who must carry out various tasks according to established directives. Administrative activities such as change control, configuration management, security awareness training, monitoring of systems and devices, and the application of generally accepted industry practices are the responsibility of IT administrators and security practitioners.

Security administration is performing various functions and activities related to the security of the system or enterprise. It is typically the responsibility of a security administrator, security officer, or security manager. While some of the specific activities are actually performed by frontline personnel such as security practitioners, the responsibility for them resides with the security administrator. But security administration sometimes requires more than assuming duties that somebody else has been performing. Many security administration functions in organizations are handled by various personnel. A typical assignment of the security practitioner is to perform duties that ensure that system security is maintained, security flaws are controlled, and risk to the organization is minimized.

Security administration involves the selection and placement of controls to enforce the AIC objectives within the system to ensure availability, integrity, and confidentiality for all members of the organization. These key administration duties may include configuration, logging, monitoring, upgrading, and updating products and end-user support.

The first thing that comes to mind when someone says IT security are electronic boxes with assorted flashing lights. Although various network hardware devices may be used to detect and mitigate threats on a network, IT security and the security of the enterprise must first be built on a firm foundation of policies and concepts. Without policies and the resulting procedures and guidelines, there would be a complete lack of corporate governance with respect IT security. Security policies are the foundation upon which the organization can rely for guidance.

Network personnel, from network administrators to security practitioners, are required to have a least a working knowledge of networking, security, and risk management concepts and how they impact the enterprise.

Security Equation

IT security and the security of the organization are necessary because of risk. Every enterprise faces uncertainty based on a vast array of threats. The process of measuring, identifying, and controlling the risk environment within an organization is referred to as risk management. Risks are managed by utilizing various controls to reduce them. You have already seen that these controls may be technical or administrative in nature. The following is the description we use in the system security field to identify risk:

> Risk is a function of the likelihood of a threat agent exploiting a vulnerability, and the resulting impact of that action creates an adverse effect on the organization.

In other words, risk can be expressed as the possibility of loss. Risk and risk management will be covered in Chapter 5. The activities of security administration include the creation of policies as a risk mitigation function. Administrative policies recognize that threats exist and put in place controls and conditions whereby the exposure of various organization vulnerabilities may be mitigated.

Exam Point

Risk is the probability that a threat will exploit a vulnerability.

Security Policies and Practices

Policies and practices are put in place by an organization to guide business and personnel actions. In a small entrepreneurial business, policies may be dictated and enforced by the business owner. Not always are these policies committed to writing. In many cases, a policy statement might be explained as, "We've always done it this way." In most cases, when a very small business begins to grow and gains employees, it's actually the human resources department that spearheads the requirement for policy statements. Many of these employee-based policy statements are enacted due to various local, state, and federal regulations. In many cases, the beginnings of a small business security policy take the form of "lock the door and turn off the lights when you leave."

As we move from small and medium-sized businesses (SMBs) into large enterprises, the requirements for formal, well-constructed written documents that are aligned with the mission and values of the enterprise are required. These documents form the foundation to protect the organization's information and assets by specifying the requirements and techniques utilized to control risk. It is through these documents that controls are put in place to reduce risk by mitigating a threat's ability to exploit a vulnerability.

Business, IT, and Security Alignment

The security of any organization or enterprise rests totally on the strategic planning and tactical implementation of security policies and risk mitigation controls. The security plan of the organization should completely coincide with the mission, objectives, culture, and nature of the business. Various security frameworks exist to guide the organization as well as the security professionals responsible for implementing programs through the planning, organization, and documentation that respond to the requirements of the organization. The most popular frameworks include the *National Institute of Standards and Technology (NIST) 800 series of Special Publications*. These NIST publications offer a broad coverage of IT security best practices. Another of the most popular frameworks is the *ISO/IEC 27000 series* of information security standards.

An information security management system (ISMS) consists of the set of policies designed to reduce or mitigate risks to the organization. It promotes the principle that an organization should create, implement, and maintain a complete set of security policies, processes, and systems to manage risks to both hardware and information assets.

The framework initially was published in the United Kingdom as BS 7799 in the mid '90s. By 2000 it was adopted by the International Organization for Standardization (ISO) and retitled *ISO/IEC 17799*. In 2005, the standard was incorporated into the ISO 27000 standards series as ISO/IEC 27002. It is common to place the date of revision after the standard number. The most recent revision is ISO/IEC 27002:2013. The standard is explicitly concerned with information security, meaning the security of all forms of information. There are several information security standards published in the ISO/IEC 27000 series. The two most popular are as follows:

ISO 27001:2013   *ISO 27001:2013* is a specification for the evaluation of the performance of an information security management system (ISMS). Organizations that meet the standard may gain an official certification issued by an independent and accredited certification body on successful completion of a formal audit process.

ISO 27002:2013   Provides organizational information security standards and information security management practices which takes into consideration the organization's information risk appetite. These guidelines include the selection, implementation, and management of risk mitigation controls. ISO/IEC 27002:2013 is a popular, internationally recognized standard of good practice for information security.

Both ISO 27001:2013 and ISO 27002:2013 have been completely rewritten since the 2005 edition. While ISO 27001:2005 specified Deming's *Plan-Do-Check-Act cycle*, in ISO 27001:2013 other continuous improvement processes such as Six Sigma's *DMAIC* (Define, Measure, Analyze, Improve, and Control) may be implemented.

Best Practices

A best practice is an accepted methodology of performing an action that leads to a beneficial result. In many situations, the best practice has developed, over a period of time, through trial and error. Businesses utilize best practices in the form of frameworks, templates, or guidelines. Various methodology frameworks such as Information Technology Infrastructure Library *ITIL*, *Six Sigma*, agile project management, and the *Scrum* agile software development framework are readily adopted by businesses. Practice distribution has been made possible generally through the commercialization of the topic and the proliferation of books, courses, and certifications.

Organizations such as the *National Institute of Standards and Technology (NIST)*, the *International Organization for Standardization (ISO)*, and the *International Electrotechnical Commission (IEC)* work with industry groups as well as governments to develop and publish frameworks of best practices. Once a framework becomes generally well accepted, it will be adopted as an industry standard. A typical best practice recommendation for information security management is the ISO/IEC 27002:2013. Quite often best practices and industry-recognized frameworks become the foundation for corporate policies.

Corporate Policies

A corporate policy is a written document that states high-level goals and directives as established by corporate top management. Corporate policies take the form of a brief statement by corporate top management and provide authorization, intent, and direction. They generally include all of the major areas of the enterprise, such as accounting, legal, human resources, ethics, and regulatory compliance to name a few.

Corporate policies are generally created as a response to various requirements.

Legislative and Regulatory Compliance   Most corporations are required to comply with a variety of legislative or regulatory mandates. Legislative restrictions are in the form of laws passed by a government body. A regulation is generally issued by government department or a recognized regulatory body such as a trade association. Failure to comply with legislative or regulatory mandates may result in fines, sanctions, or even criminal prosecution.

Contractual Requirement   Every enterprise enters into a wide variety of contracts with suppliers, customers, service providers, and partnering organizations. These policies state the intent and direction of top management in relation to the management of a contract or relationship.

Security Policies

The corporate security policy is a statement authorized by top management that defines the overall security for the organization and protection of corporate assets. Chief among corporate assets is information. Therefore, many security policies are referred to as IT security policies because information is contained on computers, servers, and storage devices.

The IT security policy may be viewed as an umbrella policy that encompasses a number of subpolicies or supporting policies that address various activities or risk categories. These subpolicies generally cover areas such as information access, use and disclosure, destruction, and classification as well as physical security, ethics, and various activities associated with the IT infrastructure. Figure 4.1 illustrates the relationship between general corporate policies, the IT security policy, and various subpolicies.

FIGURE 4.1   The relationship between corporate policies, security policies, and supporting policies

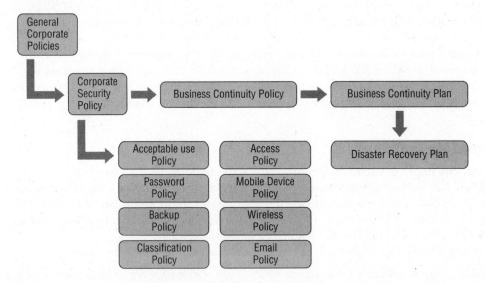

For instance, the enterprise security policy may broadly state that all information system users are required to use a password as an authentication mechanism. The password policy would then specify such details as the structure of a password, password expiration and renewal, re-issuance of a forgotten password, and any other details specific to passwords.

Types of Security Policies

There are different categories of security policies depending upon the structure and requirements of the organization. There are three general types of security policies that together meet the requirements of the overall enterprise security program:

Organizational Policies   An *organizational policy* is established by a person or group with a high level of authority, such as a senior manager or corporate office, and it's usually very broad in nature, impacting the entire organization, corporate division, geographic area, or a country-specific working group. For example, an organizational policy may be created for the XYZ Corporation, the XYZ Corporation Omaha Engine Manufacturing Division, or the XYZ Corporation Asia – Pacific Region.

The same organizational policy may exist for all three entities, with the difference being the scope of the policy in relation to the requirements of the entity. For instance, an organizational policy reflecting the requirement for personal privacy for European operations will have different standards, regulations, and legislation to comply with than one for the Omaha division within the United States. Organizational policy should be clear regarding the specific entity or geography of the intended audience. It should include specific statements about the geography, facilities, hardware, software, data storage, and personnel within the scope of the policy. This is very important in the case of a cloud data storage policy, for example.

The organizational policy may generally state that customer data may be placed in cloud storage. Unfortunately, the organization may find that the cloud storage facilities are based in a country that does not allow search and seizure of the data during a forensics investigation. Therefore, the organization must carefully consider and clearly define the requirements when creating a general organizational policy.

Functional Policies   Functional policies address specific issues or concerns of the organization. They may be used to define requirements related to particular areas of security, such as access control, acceptable use, change management requirements, hardware and software updates, and other operational concerns. An example of a functional policy is a Bring Your Own Device (BYOD) policy. It may state that corporate employees may use their own wireless device to access the organization's network and data based upon certain criteria. The *functional policy* will list the criteria that must be met prior to an individual being allowed access. The criteria may include the requirement of current updates on the system, the use of anti-malware and virus protection, the restriction of different types of data that may be uploaded or downloaded, the requirement for device security, the ability to remote wipe the device in case of theft or loss, and many other requirements that are relevant to the use of personal wireless devices.

Similar to organizational policies, functional policies may include the entire organization, corporate division, geographic area, or country-specific working group within the scope of the policy. An example of the corporate division functional policy might be that personal access to all manufacturing facility workspaces at the XYZ Corporation Omaha Engine Manufacturing Division will require two-factor authentication.

Operational Policies   *Operational policies*, sometimes referred to as system-specific policies, are used to clarify and provide a clear direction on operational topics such as access to specific database information, application software, or networking facilities. An operational policy may state the requirement that a specific action, such as access to an accounts payable application function, requires separation of duties. Another operational policy may state that all accounting personnel workstations will be assigned to a specific virtual network.

Exam Point

It is important to understand the difference between organizational, functional, and operational policies.

The more detailed or granular a policy, the more frequently the policy may be required to be updated or changed. Organizational policies are usually very broad in scope, while an operational policy defines a specific operational requirement or action. For instance, an organizational policy may require that all individuals utilize two-factor authentication for facility access. This is a general statement that applies to all the individuals in the organization. The specific supporting operational policy may state that the XYZ2314 retinal scanner be used as the second factor for authentication at the New Mexico Laboratory Annex. While the organizational policy is long term, spanning many years, the XYZ2314 retinal scanner may be replaced within a year or two, requiring an operational policy and procedural policy change.

Security Policy Endorsement

Although corporate policies may be authored by knowledgeable individuals within the organization or may be adopted from a variety of best practices, policy templates, or frameworks, it is of paramount importance that the top management of the organization support, approve, and endorse the security policy. The security policy should reflect and support the mission and goals of the enterprise. The endorsement by top management provides an authoritative document that authorizes the adoption and implementation of various controls by which to mitigate risk to the organization's assets. The security policy clearly states the direction and goals of top management and reflects the culture, goals, and mission of the organization.

Exam Point

If a policy lacks the endorsement of top management or a corporate executive sponsor, it will be doomed to failure.

Enterprise-Wide Security Policies

Today we operate in a multicultural global economy. As security professionals, we must recognize that our organization may span dozens of countries. Under the umbrella of IT security policies, it is not unusual to have policies specific to a country or a region. The right to privacy is a highly developed area of law in Europe. All of the member states of the European Union are also members of the European Convention on Human Rights. In 1980, the comprehensive data protection system was adopted throughout Europe. The Convention developed the guidelines governing the protection of privacy. It adopted seven principles governing the protection of personal data:

Notice   Persons should be given notice when their data is being collected.

Purpose   Data should only be used for the purpose stated and not for any other purposes.

Consent   Data should not be disclosed without the owner's consent.

Security   Collected data should be kept secure from any potential abuses.

Disclosure   Persons should be informed as to who is collecting their data.

Access   Persons should be allowed to access their data and make corrections to any inaccurate data.

Accountability   Persons should have a method available to them to hold data collectors accountable for not following the above principles.

It is important to understand that from a global perspective, numerous security policies may be required depending upon local laws, customs, and regulations.

Supporting Security Policies

A large number of policies may fall under the umbrella of IT security or corporate security policies. Each of these policies provides guidance on a specific requirement. Here are some of the most common supporting security policies:

Acceptable Use Policy   This policy defines the acceptable use of organizational hardware and information assets. This is one of the first organizational policies most new employees are exposed to, and they usually must sign an acknowledgment of having received it. The *AUP* may also define warning banners that pop up on system login, which may also require acknowledgment by clicking a continue button.

Password Policy   A password policy usually states that a password must be used as authentication for hardware and information access. This policy will address use, creation, structure, system lockout, and the password replacement and renewal period.

Backup Policy   This policy specifies backup procedures for information on individual workstations, servers, databases, applications, or other environments.

Network Access Policy   The network access policy may contain the rights and privileges of specific subjects when they are gaining access to the network. This policy may describe authentication techniques and specific access control mechanisms.

Incident Response Policy   This policy describes how incidents are identified and the specific steps to be taken once they are. As a functional or operational policy, it may list the persons to be notified and actions required to remedy the situation.

Guest Access Policy   This policy describes specific network guests that may be allowed access and the methods they are allowed to use for access.

Remote Access Policy   This policy describes authentication techniques and logging requirements for accessing the corporate network from external sources.

Virtual Private Network (VPN) Policy   The virtual private network policy describes hardware, software, and encryption to be utilized when establishing VPNs for remote access by both users and external systems.

Third-Party Connection Policy   The third-party connection policy describes any methodology used by customers, partners, suppliers, or other entities when connecting with the corporate network.

Wireless Policy   This policy describes the setup and use of the corporate wireless network. It may describe network access, protocols and methodology for encryption, and other details concerning wireless network access.

Encryption Policy   Data should be encrypted both in transit and at rest. The encryption policy describes the methodology and algorithms used to encrypt data in various states. This policy may also describe the requirements for encryption on external devices such as cell phones, pads, laptops, and tablets.

Mobile Device Policy   The mobile device policy is sometimes referred to as a BYOD policy and describes the use of various personally own portable devices both on the premises of the organization and when connected to the organization's network.

Network Security Policy   A network security policy broadly states the requirements for network security and, as a functional or operational policy, describes security requirements and specific controls to be utilized to protect corporate assets.

Data Classification Policy   The data classification policy describes the method and hierarchy of data classification within the organization. It also will describe the criteria for data access, including the assignment of subjects rights to access classified data, and a data declassification scheme.

Retention Policy   This policy describes long-term storage of data, encryption of data while it's in storage, access to stored data, and data destruction criteria.

Physical Security Policy   The physical security policy outlines the controls used to mitigate threats to physical assets. The policy may describe access controls, authentication methodology, and access logging requirements throughout the organization.

Outsourcing Policy   An outsourcing policy may set forth the requirements placed upon external vendors who supply labor, consultation, or physical assets to the organization. Generally these policies describe access controls for the privacy and security of corporate assets.

Email Policy   Email policies generally describe the use of corporate email accounts, data retention, acceptable use, restrictions on personal use, and appropriate email content. Functional and operational email policies may detail email storage, deletion, and forwarding to personal devices.

Employment Policy   Every employer should enforce an acceptable use policy (AUP) as well as other policies that outline acceptable behavior for all employees. The employment policy should describe the qualifications for employment, background check requirement, and required onboarding, training, and indoctrination, including the signed receipt indicating an acknowledgment of receiving a corporate policy manual or employee handbook.

Contractor, Consultant, and Vendor Security Policy   A variety of policies may be required if a business engages contractors, consultants, and vendors on the premises. These policies should specify physical access, acknowledgment of entry, access to specific information or networks, encryption methodology, and other subjects specific to the relationship.

Exam Point

The acceptable use policy (AUP) defines the acceptable use of organizational hardware and information assets.

Security Policy Format and Design

Security policies do not need to be large and bulky to be effective. In fact, most corporate policies are three to five pages and usually no longer than nine pages in length. It is very helpful if all policies follow the same general format.

All policies may be designed to include various statements specific to the policy topic; security policies usually contain many of the following sections:

Purpose Statement   The purpose statement identifies a particular policy and reason for its existence. It is usually a vision or mission statement.

Audience Statement   This statement identifies the intended audience for the policy. For instance, a high-level organizational policy may affect every employee in the enterprise, while another high-level policy of a similar nature may affect only those employees working in the Asia-Pacific region. An operational policy, on the other hand, may be directed at system administrators at the Omaha branch.

Authorization Statement   This statement lists the individual responsible for issuing the policy. In all cases this should be a C-level individual. The authorization statement establishes the ultimate responsibility for this particular policy.

Accountability Statement   This section specifies individuals, by job title, who are responsible for ensuring compliance with the policy.

Standards or Mandate Statement   This section may be optional and, when used, specifies the regulation, legislation, contractual agreement, or business standard the policy enforces.

For instance, the policy may support a particular requirement of the Sarbanes-Oxley Act or a Payment Card Industry Data Security Standard (PCI DSS) v2 requirement.

Policy Detail Statement This section briefly specifies the items or actions that are directed by the policy. For instance, "The IT department at XYZ Corporation will establish a password policy to authenticate all individuals or systems desiring access to the network or data of XYZ Corporation." On the password policy document, this section would detail specific password requirements, such as length, duration, issuance, and identity verification.

Enforcement Statement This section specifies what actions or sanctions may be taken in the event the policy is violated. On occasion, a range of actions or sanctions may be listed, depending upon the severity of the policy violation. It is important to define, by job title, who enforces the policy.

Support and Execution of Security Policies

As you have seen, the corporate security policy is generally broad in nature and makes a single statement. It does not go into detail concerning the "how" and, specifically, the "who" of any aspect of the policy. In the example of the corporate password security policy, the mandate statement was very general. On the specific password policy, more detail was added as to the length of time, identity verification, and other password requirements. This password policy detail is supported by a policy statement, standards, baselines, procedures, and guidelines.

The components of a policy and supporting documents are as follows:

Policy Statement A policy statement is a high-level directive setting forth a mandate in support of the mission goals and objectives of the organization. For example, XYZ Corporation will comply with the Payment Card Industry Data Security Standard (PCI DSS).

Standards *Standards* represent the criteria that must be met by the policy. Standards may be imposed by legislation, regulation, or industry requirements, or they may be imposed by the organization. For instance, the *Payment Card Industry Data Security Standard (PCI DSS)* is a proprietary information security standard for organizations that handle branded credit cards. The PCI DSS standard is mandated by the card brands and specifies various compliance requirements. The corporate *PCI DSS* security policy would list the six requirements as established by the Payment Card Industry Security Standards Council.

Baselines A baseline may be established as the normal or minimal criteria that must be met by the policy. Baselines may list a specific configuration setting for a piece of hardware, such as a firewall, an IDS, or a router. Such a baseline configuration may require that various rules be included in every router. Baselines are used to ensure that the standard minimal or optimal foundation configuration exists for the consistent implementation of the availability, integrity, and confidentiality of information throughout the organization.

Each piece of hardware or software has optimal settings that allow for the most secure implementation. A baseline states a specific configuration criteria required for the hardware or software to meet the functional or organizational policy statement. For example, an organizational policy may state that every user workstation be protected by antivirus software. The functional policy may state that ABC antivirus software be implemented on all user workstations. And a baseline may state that the ABC antivirus software be configured to automatically update on a daily basis using the ABC Professional Signature database. It is also important that configurations be regularly evaluated or audited to ensure that they meet the baseline minimum requirement.

Procedures Procedures are detailed steps that provide a set of instructions for performing a specific task. Some companies, and specifically government/military organizations, might have what is called a standard operating procedure (SOP). Procedures define not only the steps to take but other specific information.

> **Instructions** The chronological steps that the individual must do to complete or finish a task.
>
> **What** The device or tools that should be used and a source of materials specific to the task. This may also describe what reports or logs must be completed when a procedure is finished.
>
> **When** How often or what time of day should the procedure be undertaken.
>
> **Where** Where to find the device, the tools, or the information required by the procedure.
>
> **Who** The person responsible for carrying out the procedure. This may also specify who is responsible to inspect or double-check the quality of the work.

Guidelines Guidelines differ from procedures in that they are generally considered optional and may take the form of a suggested practice. *Guidelines* generally allow the individual to make a discretionary judgment on how to proceed when executing procedural steps. Many guidelines originate from recommendations and best practices and are usually created through trial and error. For instance, a guideline may state, "To avoid skin contact, wear rubber gloves when applying solvent."

It is not uncommon that over time guidelines become accepted practice throughout an organization or industry and are integrated into a procedure as a requirement. Many of today's policies and procedures originated as guidelines.

Figure 4.2 illustrates the hierarchy from general corporate policies to guidelines, including standards, baselines, and procedures.

FIGURE 4.2   Illustration of the hierarchy from general corporate policies to guidelines

```
┌─────────────────────────────────────────┐
│                 Policies                  │
│     Broad-Based Management Statements     │
└─────────────────────────────────────────┘
                     ↓
┌─────────────────────────────────────────┐
│                 Standards                 │
│     Leglislative & Regulatory Constraints │
└─────────────────────────────────────────┘
                     ↓
┌─────────────────────────────────────────┐
│                 Baselines                 │
│      Performance Standards & Criteria     │
└─────────────────────────────────────────┘
                     ↓
┌─────────────────────────────────────────┐
│                Procedures                 │
│          Step-by-Step Instructions        │
└─────────────────────────────────────────┘
                     ↓
┌─────────────────────────────────────────┐
│                Guidelines                 │
│       Suggestions and Recommendations     │
└─────────────────────────────────────────┘
```

Exam Point

It is important to be able to differentiate between and understand the definitions of standards, baselines, procedures, and guidelines.

Policy Documentation

For effective communication, all corporate policies should use a similar template. The template will ensure that each policy document contains the required information and is easy to read and understand. Policy content must be brief and to the point.

Policies may be documented through a number of methods. Of course, one technique would be to print out the pages and place them in a binder. Policies do need to be in writing, but consideration should be given to storage, accessibility, updates, and communication.

Enforcing Security Policies

A method of enforcement must be included in the security policy. The policy should list the definition of a violation (and optionally, its severity) and the punishment, sanction, or action taken. When considering enforcement actions, it is always highly recommended to include the human resources department. Policies must be enforced fairly and without bias. Individuals could claim that they did not know about the policy, the policy changed without them knowing, or that somebody else was not accused when they violated the policy. Numerous legal issues may arise when enforcing a security policy.

The violation of some policies could lead to severe punishment, sanctions, or termination for the employee. In such case, as with onboarding documentation, the employee must sign an acknowledgment that they have received, read, and understand the policy. When feasible, some organizations require a face-to-face meeting with each employee, while other policy notification situations may use emails to employees and require an e-signature document to be returned.

Policy Change and Updating

Over time, some policies must change. Policy change and review should constantly be undertaken by the organization. Because top-level corporate policies are authorized by C-level corporate officers, a formal change review and signoff process should be undertaken. Once a policy is updated, copies should be distributed as specified by the communication plan.

Policy Communication and Awareness

Policies and changes to policies must be communicated to the appropriate audience throughout an organization. Depending upon the policy, not all information is distributed to everybody. A policy that affects only the marketing department is obviously not required to be distributed to warehouse personnel.

When communicating policies and changes, it is important to consider the actions required by the individual. Some of these actions may be more significant than others. For instance, a policy change stating that a specific server will not be available from 10 p.m. to midnight on Saturdays due to scheduled maintenance may have less impact and significance on individuals than a policy that implements a new workgroup data-sharing software application requiring individuals to organize and upload all of their work files within the next week. The communication should be clear on what actions and activities individuals must perform in relation to the policy or policy change.

Many companies utilize their intranet to disseminate policy information. Other policy documentation communication plans might include one or more of the following:

- Pop-up banner upon login
- Newsletters
- Emails from the CEO
- Posters or displays in public areas
- Senior management town hall meetings
- Departmental meetings
- Manager meetings, one-on-one meetings, or workgroup meetings
- Global meetings, management webinars, or conference calls
- Open days or "cafe chats"

Two of the most popular and frequently used methods of policy distribution and awareness are manager meetings and pop-up logon banners. Everyone in the organization logs into their computer workstation on a regular basis. It is fairly easy to include a pop-up or warning banner announcing a policy or a change in a policy. For more detailed explanation or policy distributions that may require a question-and-answer session, manager meetings may be held with departmental staff. Depending upon the details of the policy, "train-the-trainer" sessions may be held with managers to explain the details of a policy and how to answer specific questions. This is especially important if a policy may have an adverse or confusing effect on personnel.

Understanding the *(ISC)² Code of Ethics*

Every security professional certified by (ISC)² or a candidate for (ISC)² certification must commit to the (ISC)² Code of Ethics. The complete code is available on the (ISC)² website and features a preamble that basically states that (ISC)² certified individuals will ensure the safety of society, act honorably, provide competent and diligent service, protect and advance the profession, and adhere to the highest ethical standards of behavior.

In our daily lives and professional relationships, there are three levels of ethics, the (ISC)² Code of Ethics, an ethics statement put forth by one's employer, and each individual's personal code of ethics or character. If an individual senses a conflict between the (ISC)² Code of Ethics, their personal code of ethics, and the ethics of their employer through either word or deed, it is incumbent upon the individual to first attempt to reconcile the conflict internally within the employer organization. If the individual is unsuccessful or is ignored while trying to reconcile ethical differences within the organization, the individual may have the ability to explore remedies external to the organization, such as *whistleblower programs* and legal recourse. Keep in mind that once employed, employees owe their allegiance to the employer. This may be evidenced by various onboarding agreements, ethical statements, and value system programs. But, as witnessed by various Wall Street and financial sector scandals, keeping quiet while witnessing ethical violations could have legal implications, possibly leading to prosecution.

Exam Point

The SSCP exam candidate should read and understand the (ISC)² Code of Ethics prior to sitting for the exam. You will have to agree to it at the beginning of the exam.

Security Development Life Cycle

A security practitioner may be involved in the development of software or applications. It is important that security personnel be involved at the beginning and as a stakeholder in every development project.

The *Security Development Lifecycle (SDL)* is a software development process proposed by Microsoft to reduce software maintenance costs and increase the reliability and security of software. The Security Development Lifecycle incorporates all of the activities to ensure compliance with both operational and security requirements as specified by organizational policy. Security requirements and the inclusion of security controls should be present at the beginning of the development project.

Automated Configuration Management

The security practitioner may be required to manage the configuration files on a variety of network equipment. Configuration management is critical to the success of the IT organization. Various IT devices, including servers, switches, routers, and IDSs as well as other networking items, require configuration and system updates on a regular basis. The larger the organization, the more difficult this task becomes.

While it is always possible to update and configure items manually, many organizations have adopted *automated configuration management*. Automated configuration management provides a centralized method to make changes to a system in an organized manner.

Configuration management is the application of tools that allow for the centralized management of settings, firewall rules, and configuration files that allow networking items to perform their assigned tasks.

The task of configuration management may be broken down into a number of activities. The security practitioner may be responsible for any or all of these configuration management tasks.

Identification   *Configuration identification* is the process of setting and maintaining *operational baselines* that define the system status at any point in time. Identification is similar to *snapshots*, in which the specific parameters of the system are available. An example includes restore points on Microsoft Windows operating systems. A *restore point* represents a specific configuration at a point in time.

Control   Control represents any action concerning change requests and change proposals and their subsequent approval or disapproval. Control may be thought of as a function of the change control process. Various devices may be automatically patched or updated on a regular basis without submitting a change request, while other devices must proceed through a *change proposal*.

Accounting   Accounting is the process of logging and reporting any change to configuration.

Auditing   *Auditing* is verification that a process has been completed according to policy or plan. It may also verify that the product is in compliance with established performance requirements.

Patch Management

Applying relevant patches, *updates*, and fixes may be the responsibility of the security practitioner. Patching devices may be automated or manual in nature and are always procedural based. This means that a procedure exists such as taking an item offline, placing it in administrator mode, connecting a console, and completing many other required steps to update the software contained on the device. Although the word *patch* is frequently used to describe an update or change in a software device, there are many other terms associated with this activity.

Patch A *patch* is a piece of software intended to update an application, operating system, or control program to improve its usability and performance. A patch may be broad in nature and fix or repair various problems identified within the software. *Patch Tuesday* is an industry term referring to when Microsoft regularly releases patches for its software products. Usually on the second and fourth Tuesday of each month at a specific time of the day, patches are made available for manual or automatic download. Other major manufacturers, such as SAP and Adobe Systems, have announced their *Security Patch Day* to coincide and occur on Patch Tuesday.

Security Patch A *security patch* is a specific update to an application, operating system, or control program in response to the identification of a vulnerability. Many manufacturers attempt to distribute security patches as soon as they are tested and available. In some cases, a manufacturer is unaware of a vulnerability and therefore does not have a patch available. An exploit of a vulnerability for which the manufacturer is unaware is referred to as a *zero-day attack*. The term *zero day* indicates that this is the first time the vulnerability has been identified. Microsoft generally releases security patches once a month, and other manufacturers release security patches as soon after a vulnerability identification as possible.

Unofficial Patch *Unofficial patches* are patches provided by third-party individuals or organizations for commercial software. These patches are usually sold by subscription and either fix problems earlier than the manufacturer can release a patch or patch products that are no longer supported by a manufacturer.

 Real World Scenario

What to Do About Windows XP

Tens of thousands of corporate workstations around the world are still running the Windows XP operating system. Microsoft has ended the period of extended support for the Windows XP operating system. This effectively ended the security patch support that was provided by Microsoft. Microsoft has advised that organizations and individuals should immediately move off of the Windows XP operating system platform or face continuous penetration attacks without security updates.

Thousands of corporations (medical institutions, banks, retailers, and manufacturers) around the world, including the European aerospace-defense industry, have XP machines in daily operation and have little intention or ability to make massive upgrades. Various third-party companies have stepped up to offer continued protection for these XP machines on a subscription basis. Some techniques include updating templates or software agents placed on XP machines. A current point of contention is that only Microsoft can update the *Windows XP kernel*. In any event, the market is out there for third-party product support not only for Microsoft products but also for discontinued products of a number of manufacturers.

Hot Patch   A *hot patch* is a patch that can be applied to piece of hardware or software without the requirement to power down or reboot the product, thus making it unavailable to users. This type of patch addresses the availability component of the CIA triad.

Service Pack   A *service pack* is made up of a number of updates, enhancements, fixes, or patches that are delivered by the manufacturer in the form of a single executable file. The executable file will cause the service pack to be installed on the target machine. Service packs are usually numbered and are released on a random basis when a sufficient number of patches and updates have accumulated. Most service packs are cumulative in nature, meaning patches and updates from a previous service pack are incorporated in the current service pack to ensure that all changes are made adequately. Service packs for application software generally replace the existing files with updated software. During this process, the application software may receive a new version number.

Update, Upgrade   *Update* and *upgrade* are industry slang used to describe the installation of any software that either fixes a vulnerability or increases the usability or functionality of the product.

Fix, Quick Fix   A *fix* has become known in the software industry as a rapid repair to an identified problem. In many cases, the fix is related to a very specific problem or possibly a specific user of the software. A hastily released fix that has not been properly tested may raise the risk of possible regressions. A regression is when a fix for a current problem creates problems in prior versions of the product. Testing a fix to address this problem is called *regression testing*.

Hotfix   Similar to a hot patch, a *hotfix* may be applied to a piece of hardware or software that is currently online and in use. Hotfixes have become known in the software industry as providing the ability to fix a bug very rapidly and possibly without going through formal development channels.

Version Numbering

Software version numbering is a method of assigning alphanumeric or numbers to designate the generation or "build" of a software or firmware product. The numbers or alphanumeric designations are generally assigned in increasing order to correspond to changes and developments and new releases of the software product.

Most versioning schemes feature three- to four-digit identifiers and are used to convey the importance or significance between changes. Different manufacturers and producers of software make use of the designations differently. For instance, the designation 2.1.3.4 may indicate that this is the fourth revision (4) of the documentation and the third revision (3) of minor changes. It may also indicate this is the first revision (1) indicating a major change since the last general release. Some manufacturers jump sequence numbers to indicate the importance of an upgrade or software revision change. For instance, Internet Explorer 6 went from 6.1 to 6.5.

The primary version number (2) indicates a new software release with a major functionality change. When manufacturers change the primary version number, it may indicate a substantial change in functionality, usability, or feature set. It may also denote an incompatibility with prior versions. When changing the primary version number, many manufacturers use this opportunity to resell the subscription to the software.

Exam Point

A security practitioner, quite often, is responsible for applying patches, upgrades, fixes, and service packs. It is important to understand the difference between these terms.

Sandbox Testing

It is an industry best practice to thoroughly test any patch, fix, update, or service pack in a nonproduction environment. *Sandbox* refers to a machine or virtual network that is totally isolated from the production environment. Problems experienced during testing within a sandbox cannot escape to the production network. It is never a good idea to distribute patches, fixes, or even service packs without first testing them in an offline environment.

 **Real World Scenario**

Even the Best Have Problems

You might expect that organizations as large as *Apple* or Microsoft have the resources and personnel to thoroughly test patches and updates prior to their release. IT professionals have known for years that this is not always the case. This is why every professional IT shop tests updates, fixes, and service packs offline and on isolated machines or virtual networks prior to distributing them throughout the organization. Professionals know that more times than not, problems have surfaced after the installation of the patch. But what happens if you are a consumer? You have only one product and no capability to test the results of installing the update. What happens in this situation?

In September 2014, Apple immediately pulled an update to *iOS 8*. The new iOS 8 operating system had been released only a week earlier and was plagued by problems. An update was rushed out that was supposed to fix the problems. It seems that upon installation of the iOS 8.0.1 update, iPhones could no longer connect to their cellular network and displayed a message of no service. *iPhone* owners also reported issues with *Touch ID*, which is a feature that allows people to unlock their phones using their fingerprints.

Fortunately, Apple was very quick with a response and removed the patch from availability within an hour. It acknowledged that there was a problem and instructed the affected users to reinstall iOS 8 through *iTunes*. This is not a one-time occurrence; a year earlier, Apple introduced *iOS 7*. Days later it released IOS 7.0.2 to fix identified problems with the initial release.

Industry professionals recommend not being the first person on the block to download and install a patch or upgrade, especially if you cannot test it prior to installation. And, on consumer-grade devices, back up all information prior to any installation or upgrade.

Implementation and Release Management

Release management is part of the software development process, which can be a constantly evolving process or an ongoing cycle of development, testing, and release. Software applications are created, modified, or updated on a regular basis. As part of the process, they are tested and evaluated by both IT quality testing teams and end-user testing teams. Each team is challenged with testing the software to specific design parameters, usually as outlined in the *business requirements document (BRD)*. The IT quality team is charged with testing the automation of the software and how it interacts with databases, storage devices, and other pieces of software, sometimes referred to as *quality acceptance testing (QAT)*, while the user team is testing the software against specific scenarios or business cases, usually referred to as *user acceptance testing (UAT)*.

Once the software is completed and passes the testing environment, it is made ready for deployment. *Software deployment* is a series of steps in which the new software is loaded on a server and distributed to the appropriate user workstations. In some deployment situations, the software remains on the server and is available for end-user logon.

Software Release Activities   The security practitioner may be responsible for one or more activities during the software release process.

Facilitate Communication   Serves as a liaison between the business units and the IT department to ensure proper communication during the release process.

Release Coordinator   Communicates issues, problems, and concerns and coordinates the services of the help desk group to facilitate software deployment.

Software Release Challenges   A software release is not without its own unique challenges. The security practitioner may be involved in communicating or assisting in solving some of the challenges and problems facing the release, including these:

- End-user issues
- Reporting of software defects
- Change requests
- End-user orientation and training
- Defect reporting
- Incident handling
- Identification of risks

Software release can be an ongoing, multifaceted project involving dozens of individuals. In the past, new software releases and updates were made available only upon the completion of particular project. This project methodology is referred to as the *waterfall development process*, where one step leads to the next until the project is eventually completed and distributed to the end users. Software development organizations today utilize an agile development process in which items are developed very quickly, tested, and made available. The *agile development process* has greatly increased the number of possible software releases due to the rapid ability to create or modify software, correct mistakes, and reissue the software.

Change Management

Change management is specifically an IT process in which the objective is to ensure that the methods and procedures for change are standardized and are used for efficient and prompt response to all change requests. Change management is a system that records a request, processes requests, elicits a denial or authorization, and records the outcome of the change to a configuration item.

Changes requiring specific approval may be forwarded to a *change control board (CCB)* or *change advisory board (CAB)* consisting of various authoritative and qualified individuals within the organization who review and approve or deny changes.

Change management is responsible for managing change processes involving the following:

- Network infrastructure
- Specific networking components
- Application software
- Database structure
- Communications processes
- Change and release processes
- Network component modification or upgrades

Exam Point

A security practitioner is quite often responsible for changes to both hardware and software items. It is important to know and understand the principles of change management.

Asset Management

Asset management broadly defines the identification, maintenance, and risk protection of hardware or information assets. The very first step of risk management is identifying the assets that require protection. The security practitioner may be involved in cataloging, maintaining, or decommissioning various organizational assets.

Assets are generally grouped into two specific classes: physical assets, which are also called *tangible assets*, and nonphysical assets, which are also called *intangible assets*. It may be obvious that tangible assets are IT infrastructure hardware components, while intangible assets are data, information, and intellectual property.

Asset Life Cycle

As a security practitioner, you may be involved in providing some service at any point along the asset life cycle. The asset life cycle includes the following steps:

- Design
- Construction
- Commissioning
- Operating
- Maintaining
- Repairing, modifying, replacing
- Decommissioning
- Disposal

Validate Security Controls

The IT environment is constantly changing along with the threats to the organization. IT departments should regularly test security and compliance controls to ensure that they remain both effective and within the scope of the required operational guidelines. The reason security controls require validation is to maintain compliance established by various regulations, such as, for example, FISMA/NIST, PCI DSS, and HIPAA.

It may be the responsibility of the security practitioner to assess, verify, and document the correct operational state of a security control based upon established baselines. During this process, the practitioner accomplishes a number of procedures that may include validation of current updates and patches, validation of correct configuration, and review of logs and documentation.

Data Management Policies

Every organization maintains data related to its business or operation. This information may consist simply of phone numbers and contacts, or it may be regulated information such as patient medical records. The security practitioner can be involved at any level of the maintenance and protection of organizational information.

Data States

Data is classified as being in one of three states: *data at rest*, *data in transit*, and *data in process*. Data at rest is in memory, and data in transit is moving. Data in process is a little more complex because it is data that is being used by a process. Programmers and database administrators are involved with handling data in process. For instance, if two numbers are being added together and the power goes out, what happens to the two numbers, and what happens to the answer? The programmers and database administrators use processes referred to as *rollback* and *roll forward* to reverse the effects of the calculation and restore the data to the state it was in prior to the power going out. Although the security practitioner may not be involved in such programming, it is important to recognize the terminology.

Exam Point

Data may be in in one of three states: data in transit, data at rest, data in process.

Information Life Cycle Management

Information life cycle management (ILM) is the practice of applying certain policies during the creation and maintenance of information. The organization may have several policies concerning the creation, classification, access, handling, and disposal of information. The security practitioner may be involved at any point during information life cycle management, including the classification and disposal of information as per existing policies.

Information Classification Policy

Organizations, whether business, military, or the federal government, possess data requiring various levels of privacy. The strictest data privacy classification in a military organization is top secret. This designation would indicate that the data or information would require the greatest amount of protection afforded any data in the system.

Various organizations are required to classify information based on privacy regulations imposed upon the industry. Information such as trade secrets, Department of Defense or governmental information, patient privacy information, and customer information such as credit cards, addresses, and Social Security numbers are all pieces of information that require protection through privacy. Some organizations separate classifications based on the type of data, such as financial, personal, or institutional secrets. An information classification structure is a set of labels or tags placed on documents and data that specifies the required protection that should be afforded to the information.

Many organizations, including the U.S military and government, use hierarchical based information classification systems. Business and commercial information classification systems are much more abbreviated than those of the military or government usually featuring three layers at most. Typically, this hierarchy includes unclassified, sensitive but unclassified, confidential, secret, and top secret. In the corporate world, a hierarchy may include public, sensitive, and confidential as classification categories.

Most organizations provide security controls based on the value of what is being protected. Many organizations rely on a risk assessment to determine the value of data. There are several ways to determine the value of an asset. The organization could assess the impact of the loss or disclosure of the data, the cost of replacement, and the amount of embarrassment that disclosure or loss of the data could produce. Then, place a higher value on the more serious impacts. The higher the value, the more protection is required. The lower the value, the less protection is needed.

To keep yourself on track, keep the following points in mind when assessing the level of security necessary for data within your organization.

- You cannot protect everything from everyone.

- There are not enough resources and money in the world to totally mitigate all risks.

- Focus on protecting the most important information first, the information that exhibits the highest risks if exposed.

There are two parts to a data classification system:

Object Classification   An object is the data being accessed by a subject. During the process of *object classification*, an object such as a document is labeled (classified) in some manner to illustrate the status of the information. For instance, it may be labeled company confidential, sensitive, or unclassified.

Subject Labeling   A subject is the person or system requiring access to the classified object or data. Generally, the technique of labeling a subject is referred to as issuing a *clearance level*. A clearance establishes the topmost boundary of the information that may be accessed by the subject. For instance, a subject may have a *secret clearance*, thereby establishing that the topmost boundary of access is classified information that is labeled secret. By default, the subject would also be able to access any information classified below the secret level. However, they would not be able to transfer information classified as secret to any other level. For instance, information classified as secret must remain classified as secret.

Data Classification Process

Data classification strategies differ greatly from one organization to the next because each generates different types and volumes of data. The balance may vary greatly from one user to the next between office documents, email correspondence, images, video files, customer and product information, and financial or intellectual property data. Many companies begin to classify data in line with their confidentiality requirements, adding more security for increasingly confidential data. The classification system itself must include an element of centralized control so that data is classified in the context of overall strategic business objectives, such as compliance.

Various tools, software, and methodology exist to assist an organization in the *data classification process*. Generally, organizations opt to classify the most sensitive information first and work down to publicly available information.

Marking, Labeling, and Storage

An organization establishing a data classification policy must also include information concerning the marking, labeling, and storage of classified information. Sensitive information must be adequately identified both physically (by the marking on containers and storage devices) and digitally so that it can be recognized by trusted computer systems. The data classification policy should also include the access control provisions for both current information and information in long-term storage. Some information must be maintained in storage off-site for many years. Some regulations require that sensitive information be retained 7 years and some as much as 10 years. In the case of criminal evidence data, the information must be kept indefinitely. Consideration should also be given to the encryption methodology for long-term storage of data at rest. Currently, the AES encryption algorithm is used for long-term data storage.

Data Declassification

Records management is an expensive undertaking for any organization. The continued maintenance of classified information, including storage and access, should be considered in any data retention or data classification program. Many government agencies and other organizations have responded by developing an open data program. An *open data program* is an attempt to review information and declassify it according to various criteria. Some information that has been gathered may not be declassified. For instance, the Privacy Act of 1974, 5 U.S.C. § 552a, Public Law No. 93-579, established a Code of Fair Information Practice that governs the collection, maintenance, use, and dissemination of personally identifiable information about individuals that is maintained in systems of records by federal agencies. Other regulations, including HIPAA, restrict declassification or dissemination of private client or patient information.

It is suggested that a declassification scheme and methodology be included in any classification policy.

 Real World Scenario

Whose Job Is It Anyway?

With limited budgets all around, it's not unusual to hear department managers argue over whose budget a project or program might impact, and with the lack of a clear security policy, things can fall through the cracks. Two years ago a consulting team was engaged to provide penetration testing for a software development company in the Midwestern

United States. The 7-year-old company had about 800 employees, all based in the same location. The penetration test featured two test components:

- A test of a proprietary account logging application that had been designed and programmed by the organization
- A lightweight social engineering test of the department that was to be assigned to the application

Because it was a software company, the IT department and specifically the software development staff was quite large, totaling over 180 individuals, including analysts, programmers, and project managers. The penetration test of the application went off without a hitch. It was successfully completed within a day or so, and the client received an after action report on the test.

The second test featured three simple social engineering scenarios, one of which tested the employees' knowledge of a specific corporate policy. During the test of a 45-person department, 12 individuals completely failed the corporate policy scenario. Upon investigation it was discovered that these 12 individuals were temporary contractors hired by the department to fill vacancies. Upon further investigation it was determined that the human resources department, acting within the scope of the HR hiring policy, was dutifully recruiting, hiring, onboarding, and training the full-time employees for the company but had no control over temporary employees or contractors. Various departments, including accounting, customer service, and the IT department, were allowed to engage contractors and temporary employees as needed and pay for these individuals out of their operating budgets. During the investigation, it was determined that over one-third of the IT department consisted of contractors or temporary employees who had never been processed through the HR department or received background checks or corporate policy training, and most had access to sensitive corporate information. These individuals were just scheduled as required by staff assistants in the IT department simply by calling the local contracting firm. Many of these individuals were simply issued a visitor badge to access the premises.

Of course, the penetration test consulting company included in its after action report that as many as 140 individuals out of a workforce of approximately 800 worked on the premises every day, and because their status was temporary or they were contractors, they were not included in the HR hiring policy or several of the IT security policies. None were properly screened or received any policy orientation. The HR department even restricted these personnel from corporate training and access to the learning management system (LMS) because they were not "full-time" employees. It became evident that a vague HR employment policy had created a monumental potential security problem for the company that violated a number of customer and client contracts as well as government regulations.

Endpoint Device Security

Any computer hardware device that can be connected to the Internet or a local area network can be referred to as an endpoint device. Endpoint devices include desktop computers, user workstations, laptop computers, tablets, thin clients, smartphones, printers, removable memory such as USB drives, IP cameras, and other business-related computer items. Specialized computer hardware, such as *point-of-sale terminals*, dedicated tablets such as those used in the shipping industry, *barcode readers*, *smart meters* used in the electrical distribution industry, and supervisory control and data acquisition SCADA networking items within the manufacturing industries are classified as endpoint devices.

With the creation of IPv6, the *Internet of Things (IoT)* will force the quantity of endpoint devices into the billions, including household appliances, Internet-enabled medical devices, and other Internet-connected items such as automobiles, communication devices, tools, and process control items.

Endpoint device security is specified in the endpoint device policy and generally consists of endpoint compliance and endpoint defense, as explained in the following sections.

Endpoint Health Compliance

Network access control (NAC) is a technology that uses a set of protocols to enforce a policy for endpoint access to a network. In essence, network access control checks the health of the device requesting network access. An endpoint device security policy might state that the device is required to meet a certain criteria prior to being allowed access to the network. This criteria could include the requirement that current software, current updates, and specific applications be loaded on the device. Upon request to join a network, the network access control technology would check the requesting device to determine that it has the current antivirus protection, the current system updates, and the current system configuration; it also may verify installed software or applications (apps) and confirm the current update level or configuration of the applications.

The second aspect of network access control technology is that through various means, which may include a preinstalled software agent loaded on the device, the network access control software may be able to automatically bring the device into compliance by automatically upgrading the device or correcting configuration problems.

Network access control represents a new and emerging category of security products that investigate a device and check its health prior to allowing access to a network. With the millions and possibly billions of devices within the Internet of Things, Internet-enabled devices such as health monitoring wristbands, refrigerators, washing machines, wearable devices, medical devices such as insulin pumps, and thousands of additional devices all could be compromised by malware or other attacks. It would be highly beneficial to be able to remotely monitor the health of the connecting device.

Although the nature of this technology is currently somewhat controversial concerning privacy issues and the ability to make changes externally on a personally owned device, it's clear that there will be a need for a way to check the health of devices wishing to connect to a network.

Endpoint Defense

Endpoint defense consists of an endpoint-mounted firewall, host intrusion detection systems (HIDSs), and antivirus software. The point at which defense mechanisms should be installed is when the endpoint or host system is initially set up or installed. The problem with endpoint defense is that it is required to be installed and maintained by the end user. It is safe to say that the majority of tablets, pads, and cell phones are currently incorrectly set up. In fact, it is a proven fact that most devices still maintain the *default password* that was on the product out of the box. Another aspect of end-user responsibility is maintaining patches, updates, and new versions of software applications as well as antivirus software.

Various firms offer endpoint security management software. *Security management software* is usually a form of server product that centrally manages the security settings and security components of network-based endpoint computers. Using security management software, applying patches and updates and monitoring the health and well-being of the endpoint device may be accomplished in a central location.

Endpoint defense for systems connected to a network can be carried out through the use of group management policies. A network administrator may assign various rights and capabilities to the user group that are enforced when they log onto the network. These rights and capabilities could include the inability to make changes, use USB devices, download specific software, or take other actions that might compromise the system. Although imposing restrictions on users is never popular, it does restrict the possibility of intrusions and problems with endpoint devices.

Exam Point

Any computer hardware device that can be connected to the Internet or a local area network can be referred to as an endpoint device. Endpoint devices include desktop computers, user workstations, laptop computers, tablets, thin clients, smartphones, printers, removable memory such as USB drives, IP cameras, or other business-related computer items.

Endpoint Device Policy

Endpoint device policies describe the various aspects and requirements of endpoint devices that are connected to the organization's network. By definition, endpoint devices may consist of assets owned by the organization or personally owned devices. It is obvious that endpoint devices owned directly by the organization are much easier to keep in compliance with upgraded software, patches, and other defensive mechanisms.

Personally owned devices may be described by a *mobile device policy*, in some cases known as a Bring Your Own Device (BYOD) policy. It is important today to have and enforce a clear *BYOD policy* within an organization. Employees, contractors, and visitors as well as strangers are attempting to enter your network on a daily basis. Clearly the policy must address authentication mechanisms that allow or restrict access to network hardware and information assets. One of the most important parts of a BYOB policy is what information may be stored on a personally own device and what happens if the device is lost or stolen. Most BYOD policies specify that each device that has the capability of downloading information from the network must have the capability of being wiped or erased remotely if stolen or lost.

Personally owned devices offer many challenges to IT security managers and practitioners. Employees must be trained in the protection of corporate information assets that may be in their possession. For example, many personally owned devices have *VPN client software* installed. Many users automatically store their logon passwords on the device, and if the device is lost or stolen, the thief can immediately log on to the organization's network. In addition, users might log on using public Wi-Fi networks. In some public environments, Wi-Fi networks can actually be spoofed by a rogue operator who is intercepting passwords and text messages being sent over the network. The security practitioner should be involved in educating users in the correct methods of using their own devices.

Security Education and Awareness Training

End users pose the greatest threat to hardware and information assets of an organization. Through inadvertent or willful actions, users have the ability to cause great harm to the organization. Most organizations have already invested heavily in the latest firewalls, intrusion detection systems, and other advanced security technologies. Yet losses caused by security breaches continue to grow each year. The problem is not so much with the security technology as it is with the lack of security awareness among users. All too often the breaches that information security professionals have to deal with are caused by users forgetting to back up critical files, using weak passwords, or opening an email attachment with malicious code.

Social networking attacks prove to be one of the easiest attack vectors available. The uneducated user can be easily exploited. It is important to stress initial and continued security awareness education and training at all levels within an organization.

Organizations need to address the following potential vulnerabilities caused by uneducated end users:

Malware Introduction   Implantation of malware or malicious code within ads with third-party apps owned by an organization can pose real risks ranging from exposing proprietary information, culminating in the devalue of the corporate brand. End users continuously receive emails or solicitations with a "click here" invitation. They need to be informed opening unsolicited attachments and "click here" invitations can trigger the introduction of malware onto their system.

Social Media Platforms   Employees in most organizations are increasingly using social media platforms like Twitter, LinkedIn, and Facebook to communicate with friends, family, and business customers. Individuals are sharing more personal information online which poses a significant threat as new "friends" and "followers," most of whom are unknown, pose social engineering threats. Through *Twitter feeds* and *online posts*, end users could expose corporate information, including nonpublic information of a financial nature that could potentially lead to insider trading. In the event of a corporate crisis where press inquiries were normally made through the public affairs department, end users now simply tweet or post information online, providing a direct link to the press.

Password Exposure   With the introduction of personal end-user devices, the ability for IT administrators to enforce password best practices has disappeared. After years of password breaches and warnings about weak passwords, a large percentage of people are still choosing words like *welcome* or words derived from personal information such as a birthday for passwords. This ultimately places company data and networks at risk. IT administrators have the ability to mandate password construction, expiration, and other attributes through such tools as *Group Policy Manager*. But this is only effective with systems where hosts directly connect to the network.

Network managers and administrators have attempted to create various password policies that invariably include passwords such as &KH67rty&D@, which are virtually impossible for individuals to memorize, thus leading them to have written notes containing passwords in the vicinity of their computer.

Other end users do not take password security seriously. It is been discovered through various industry audits that whole departments shared a single password into a database. It has also been discovered that temporary personnel have been allowed to log in as the person they are replacing for the day.

I Forgot My Password

According to many Internet sources, the use of very simple passwords is still in popular use. Regardless of corporate password policy statements, new-hire orientations, and security awareness sessions, users still opt for simple when it comes to passwords. Here is a list of some of the most frequently used passwords:

123456	00000000
password	qwerty

Continues

Continued

aaaaaaaa	iloveyou
12345678	adobe123
Admin	11111111
abc123	

It has also been noted that when numbers are used, they represent either a four-digit year or a two-digit age. The most popular special character is the explanation point (!). When there is a requirement for an uppercase letter, it is almost always the first character in the password. If there is a requirement for two of something, such as two special characters or two uppercase letters, almost always the same two selections are used: AA or @@ or 22. Pet, children, and spouse names are very common passwords. If a password is assigned to the individual rather than created by the individual, it is almost always written down and stored near the computer.

Mistaken Access   Social engineering against end users is an act of psychological manipulation. It is the art of manipulating people into performing actions or divulging confidential information. Through sympathy, tricks, mistaken identity, and deception, end users may be lured into allowing an unauthorized individual into a location or providing access to an organization's information.

Data Exposure   Technology has also led to the popularity of cloud storage. The ability to access information from anywhere and store and share data is an incredible business tool, but it also presents some challenges. There are a number of cloud services, many aimed at consumers, like *Dropbox*, *Google Drive*, and *Apple iCloud*. However, not every service or vendor has the same security controls, and so many are inappropriate for enterprise use. If employees are untrained, they're more likely to share sensitive documents over unprotected channels and store them on insecure devices, putting company information at risk.

Lost Devices   Sometimes the biggest risks that companies face does not come from the outside but results from end-user negligence. When employees are careless with their devices, it can lead to loss or theft. This can become a serious security issue for companies when a lost device contains sensitive company data. As mobile devices proliferate in the workforce, the ramifications of a lost or stolen device are huge. Personally owned mobile devices are more difficult to remotely wipe when lost or misplaced since they are not under IT department direct control. This can expose corporate data to loss and may result in the breach of sensitive data, potentially triggering state or national data breach notification requirements.

Employee Security Training Policy

The security policy of the organization must include a top-level security training policy. It should clearly state the importance of training at all levels of the organization to mitigate the threat to the organization through end-user conduct, whether it's willful or negligent.

The policy should clearly dictate which department is responsible for end-user security training. It should allocate the appropriate budget and state the expected goals and outcomes of end-user training.

 Real World Scenario

"Just Read It" Training

All too often the debate rages within the company over who is actually capable of or responsible for conducting security training for the employees. Often the corporate training department lacks the skills, budget, or desire to conduct security training and the IT department lacks professional trainers and the budget or personnel to do the training. Therefore, a situation like the one cited here may occur.

Joe's first day on the job was not unlike tens of thousands of other job applicants that have been offered a position by an employer. After some cursory paperwork in the human resources department, he was escorted along with 15 other new hires into a large conference room. The new hires were greeted by Sarah, who introduced herself as an admin in the HR department. She was obviously proud of her position and announced that she had joined the company just six months prior. She quickly passed out folders and announced that she would be conducting the new hire orientation and that there were numerous topics that were required to be covered in a short period of time. Subject after subject was quickly covered, accompanied by PowerPoint slides with bullet lists. It was quite obvious that her skills were centered on human resource programs. She went into great detail about pay programs, direct deposit, health insurance, matching contribution programs, vacation days, and several other subjects of which she had expertise.

Continues

Continued

To Joe this did not seem to be a training class but more of a quick read-through referencing the information folder. It was evident that Sarah was not a trainer as she mentioned but that it was just her turn to conduct the new hire session this week. With 15 minutes remaining in the session, it was apparent Sarah was feeling the time pressure. She announced that the final subject that she was required to cover was security awareness training. As time grew tight, Sarah mentioned that there was not enough time remaining in the session to complete the security awareness training program.

As Joe thumbed through the four photocopied pages marked "Security Training" in the folder in front of him, he raised his hand to ask a question. Sarah mentioned that there was only time for one or two more questions before they had to wrap up and called on Joe. Joe asked Sarah if there was actually a security awareness training program available. Sarah confessed that she was not aware of any formal classes and that it was not one of her favorite subjects and that she knew very little about it. Sensing that Joe wanted more information and that time was drawing to a close, Sarah addressed the group with her closing comment, "If you need more information about security, the pages are in your folder and you can just read about it."

Employee Security Training program

Security awareness training should focus on the threats to the organization as posed by the end users. These individuals should be made aware that such threats exist and be able to recognize the pattern or techniques an attacker may use. They should also be instructed on how to be vigilant so they can identify the potential risks and vulnerabilities that exist.

Several groups within an organization are involved with and have access to various levels of information. Training programs should be focused on users, management, and executives due to their exposure to potentially sensitive information. Special security awareness training programs should be devised for each group to pinpoint the threats and the risks at each of their levels within the organization.

Training Users

Training corporate employees on the subject of security is extremely important. It may be required under the corporate security policy, and in some cases it may be a compliance item under a governmental or industry regulation. It is important for the SSCP to understand various aspects of training because you may very well be involved in either the development or the delivery of security training topics.

Focus   End users can potentially cause a greater loss of information and system assets than all other types of threats. It is imperative that users of the organizations systems be well educated about security threats such as social engineering. Users should be given information to help them make good decisions regarding their use of the systems in their daily activities. User training must also include proper use of personal devices such as cell phones, tablets, and laptops.

Level of Information   User training should consist of basics facts about information systems security as it applies to the environment in which they work. It should include all of the best practices, including how they should exercise the use of proper passwords, how to avoid giving information over the phone, and how to report suspicious activity. User training programs should also concentrate on how to protect corporate data and workstations. They should be aware of threats and vulnerabilities and the risks to their information in their systems.

Specialized training should be provided to any end users handling sensitive or confidential information. This may include individuals with access to customer databases, accounting records, or client information. Individuals should also receive specialized security training in compliance-based areas such as *HIPAA* medical information regulations and patient information privacy.

Delivery Method   Instructor-based training is usually preferred by many organizations. Classroom training promotes direct contact and the ability to perform various interactions such as role-playing or scenario-based activities between individuals. Care must be taken in the selection and training of the instructor so that adequate emphasis is placed upon the correct content. *Computer-based training (CBT)* may be used to complement instructor-based training because it may be available as training on demand, with incremental modules.

Training Frequency   User training should be delivered at a minimum upon new hire and at least on an annual basis thereafter. It is important to support the training on a daily or weekly basis with pop-up banners, email reminders, webinars, and posters.

Training Management

Corporate security training may be tailored to other employees at different ranks within the organization. It's important to recognize the information requirements and perspectives of these individuals in order to make the best use of time and provide for the greatest impact and absorption of the information.

Focus   The focus of management training is protecting the assets of the company while creating efficiencies and productivity throughout the organization. Those in management individuals are interested in cost and time. Management training should concentrate on the consequences involved in not maintaining an adequate security posture. Promoting end-user security should be a job-related task placed on every manager.

Level of Information   Managers, by nature, tend to be concise and bottom-line oriented. They want to know the security requirements of the organization, the funding required, and the results expected. In essence, they require a business case to be made for organizational security. Managers need to understand their responsibilities and how to make security work within their organization including the impact if security fails.

Delivery Method   Manager training is quite different than end-user training. Management training programs should communicate corporate policies with regard to the security of the organization. This type of training session may also provide managers with a train-the-trainer program as well as handouts and materials for their departmental meetings. The managers of the company are primarily concerned with the functions of their business unit. In most organizations, they are conduits of information from higher management down to their staff. Therefore, you may use the following briefing method of communicating security programs to managers.

> **Briefing Paper**   A short summary of the security programs is outlined. A briefing paper specifically states the purpose and actions required in implementing security programs for their unit of responsibility.

> **Formal Briefing**   The formal briefing is where the overall program is discussed, including the current status of the system security manager's responsibilities, actions, and activities.

> **Reminder Memo**   This is a follow-up, a written memo or email that highlights the first and second steps and reminds them of their responsibility.

Training Frequency   Once a year is often enough for manager training, but managers are also users, and it is recommended that they attend user training as well.

Training Executives

Making a presentation on security topics to the senior executives within an organization is a skill that requires understanding both the time available and the amount of information to present. This level of corporate employee requires a high-level presentation that is quite different from end-user corporate security training.

Focus   The success of the company and the protection of business assets is the role of the senior executives of the organization. They are responsible to shareholders and investors for the success of the company. The training focus for executives should be to provide them with enough information to allow them to make quality decisions based upon factual data that will benefit the organization.

Level of Information   At a general level, corporate executives should be made aware of security policies. They should also be informed of general risks to the organization and how they are being mitigated through various programs. Executives realize their responsibilities under legislation, rules, and regulations and the impact that compliance has on the organization. It is also important to include a briefing on the protection of high-level confidential information because many high-level corporate executives are the focus of whaling attacks, spoofing, social networking, and other attacks due to their position and inside knowledge of the organization.

Delivery Method   Short written briefs of one or two pages are the optimal communication method with high-level executives. If the presentation is longer, it will generally not be read.

Training Frequency   Deliver training as requested or required. Top executives have skill levels that allow them to assimilate information very quickly. It is important to summarize information and be prepared to follow the summary with in-depth supporting information.

Executive Level Training—Follow the Money

It is unfortunate that in many organizations senior executives may be ignored by normal corporate training programs. This may be due to the perception that they are too busy or have achieved such a level of knowledge that they do not require awareness training. It is a proven fact throughout the IT security industry that senior executives in an organization can be the most heavily targeted individuals. Whaling and spearfishing techniques as well as targeted device theft and common dumpster diving may be used to gain specific information about the organization.

Various investigations have determined that an increase in executive-level penetration attacks occurs during corporate merger and acquisition periods. Inside information concerning a merger or acquisition can be quite valuable on the street. While the common misperception is that most attackers are only after customer credit card and database information or out to disrupt a network through a denial-of-service attack, in actuality they may be specifically engaged to acquire a certain type of information. The senior executives in any organization should be made aware of these threats and various vulnerability mitigation strategies.

Business Continuity Planning

Every business or organization can potentially face threats or situations that disrupt business processes and activities. For instance, a hurricane might interrupt electrical power to a business location. A tornado or fire might destroy parts of the building in which a business is located. A flood might easily disrupt the operations of a primary supplier of parts to manufacture the company's products. Each one of these interruptions or disruptions can potentially harm the organization.

Business community planning includes all of the steps and activities required to maintain business operations in the event of a disaster or disruption. It must include consideration for those activities required to completely restore business operations. All of the activities and information required to maintain business activities during a disaster incident and the restoration activities necessary to restore the business to a fully operational status are included in a business continuity plan (BCP).

A business continuity plan will take into consideration a variety of threats that might potentially disrupt or interrupt business operations. These threats will fall into the following categories:

Weather/Natural Event/Fire   Weather or natural events may cause a potential business interruption or disruption. Business locations may be exposed to ice and snow, hurricanes, tornadoes, droughts, tsunamis, earthquakes, floods, mudslides, or forest fires, among other events. Fire is one of the most frequent causes for business interruption or disruption. A fire does not need to be major to cause significant problems. A localized fire in a networking or communications cabinet can create significant downtime for an organization.

Human Caused   Human-caused events may be intentional or unintentional and cause business interruption or disruption. This category would include sabotage, neglect, willful misconduct, unintentional errors or mistakes, and other events that could be caused by a person from within or external to an organization an organization. Included within this category are medical emergencies such as the common cold, flu, epidemics, and other biological situations that may directly cause business interruption.

Supply Chain   Any activity that supplies raw materials, finished parts, or services required by the organization to maintain business activities is part of a supply chain. For example, a supplier of automobile tires is in the supply chain for the auto manufacturer. If the tire manufacturer experiences a disaster and could no longer supply tires to the auto manufacturer, the auto manufacturer will experience a disruption or interruption of business.

The failure of internal operations that are required to create or manufacture products such as the machine tool or conveyor system could pose significant interruption or disruption to a business. Services and other activities such as banking and Internet and telecommunication services may be included as part of the supply chain because they contribute to the organization's ongoing business activities.

Utilities   Utilities service is the lifeblood of any organization. An extended lack of utility service could create a significant disruption or interruption of business activities. Basic utilities may include electric power, water, sewage, and telephone service. Other utilities to consider would be telecommunications (including fiber-optic service), microwave communication, satellite communication, and general mail service. Within the utilities category may be grouped basic transportation services, such as UPS, FedEx, and other commercial carriers.

Crime/Terrorism/War   Crime, terrorism, and war pose a significant threat to an organization, with the potential of severe interruption or disruption of the business. Crime could involve a holdup or robbery but could extend to the theft of a valuable business asset such as a customer database. Extortion and embezzlement can also have a significant disruptive influence on a business.

The September 11, 2001, terrorist attacks; the terrorist attack on a cartoon publisher in Paris, France; the attack on the Oklahoma City federal building; and other significant terrorist attacks have illustrated on how terrorism can cause significant business interruption or disruption or even immediate termination of activities, as with the *Sony Pictures* release of a supposedly offensive movie.

Crime also includes the theft of intellectual property. *Edward Snowden* perpetrated a crime against the United States government by exposing *Central Intelligence Agency* classified information. Creating a politically embarrassing situation for the government of the United States, this action illustrates that organizations can be significantly disrupted by the release of sensitive information or the exposure of intellectual property such as trade secrets to competitors.

Attack   An attack is a willful action against a business that causes significant interruption or disruption. Most of the time we think of an attack as a cyber-based intrusion, but an attack can include any activity with the goal of creating harm to the organization. Business interruption may be a result of an attack. For instance, workplace violence such as the Fort Hood shooting or a deranged individual crashing a light airplane into the IRS office building in Austin, Texas, are attacks that have caused business interruption.

Digital   Threats to the digital environment of an organization abound. Business services may be interrupted by hacker intrusion, distributed denial of service, boot sector destruction, and many other techniques. A clear illustration of the damage that can be done digitally to an organization is the attack on Sony Pictures in California. Not only did the terrorist organization, sponsored by a nation-state, manage to expose sensitive corporate information in emails, they also caused major damage to the organization through physical destruction of hardware by destroying boot sectors.

Miscellaneous Causes   Under miscellaneous causes, random equipment failure might top the list. What happens to the data center if the air-conditioning breaks down? How long might be equipment continue working without air-conditioning? What happens if a pipe bursts and floods the server room? Unanticipated random events can cause devastating damage.

These threats and the resulting business disruptions illustrate many of the calamities that face organizations. While risk analysis endeavors to identify various threats and mitigate their effects, it is obvious that a business or organization can never address every threat. There would be no way the promoters of the Boston marathon could have significantly predicted that two brothers from Boston would place a bomb in a spectator area. Through risk analysis, they may have identified that anything could go wrong at any point along the marathon route and thus obtain an insurance policy covering both the marathon participants and spectators in case a spectator brings a legal action against the promoter. The continuity plan, on the other hand, would detail the actions that would be taken in the eventuality that there was a significant disruption or interruption of the marathon.

Exam Point

Business continuity planning (BCP) and disaster recovery planning (DRP) are important for any organization and specifically the IT department. Security practitioners should understand the principles of these programs.

Developing a Business Continuity Plan

The *business continuity plan* is a set of procedures, programs, and supporting plans that have been established to maintain the operations of the organization in the event of disruption or interruption caused by different levels of disaster. In the event of a disaster, responding individuals simply follow a plan consisting of instructions, checklists, or prearranged activities. Each individual can proceed to take the actions necessary to recover from a disastrous situation.

Development of a business continuity plan is a major undertaking for any organization. It requires time and diligence and the participation of many individuals. Successful plan creation is the result of the resolve and commitment of the organization and the commitment of financial resources to the project. Unfortunately, many small to medium-size businesses neglect the creation of a business continuity plan purely because of lack of resources. Although there is some business continuity plan templates available, each business organization must determine which functions are vital to the success of its specific operation.

As with all projects of any substance, the activity begins with a policy or charter that initiates the project. The business continuity plan policy must include the mandate of top management or the sponsorship of a senior executive or executive committee to provide the required directives and financial support the plan creation will require. Without top management or executive support, the creation of the plan will fail.

A business continuity plan consists of several supporting plans or documents (Figure 4.3). These plans are used to identify and prioritize various activities of the organization that must be maintained for the continued viability of the organization. Other documents will detail information concerning backup plans, alternate sites, restoration and recovery plans, and other plans critical to the continuation of the organization.

FIGURE 4.3   The business continuity plan and support plans and documents

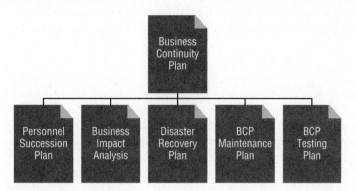

Business Impact Analysis

A *business impact analysis (BIA)* is the first step in creating a business continuity plan. Similar to risk analysis, where all assets are identified and possible threats categorized, the business impact analysis seeks to determine and rank activities and functions that are absolutely required by the operation and without which the operation would cease to exist. The business impact analysis evaluates the financial impact on the organization from a quantitative and qualitative viewpoint.

For example, a warehouse and shipping facility suffered $500,000 in damage during a hurricane. Prior to the damage, the facility was shipping $70,000 worth of products per day. It is estimated that the facility will be down for five days. The quantitative financial impact might be calculated at $350,000 in lost shipping revenue plus $500,000 to restore the warehouse to full operation. The qualitative financial impact is a less precise figure based upon business that had been turned away, customers that will leave and never come back, and bad publicity or reputation in the marketplace and other considerations.

During a business analysis, all of the major activities of the organization are listed and categorized as to their importance or how critical they are to the continued existence of the organization. Every business organization has basic revenue-driving operations and support functions. The BIA seeks to differentiate critical operations from support operations and specify a time frame during which the business can survive without the critical operations. Differing from a risk analysis where potential threats are examined, a business impact analysis considers the impact to the business if the business function ceased operation for whatever reason.

Reason for Outage

When creating a business continuity plan or business impact analysis, it is easy for stake-holders, executives, department managers, and other individuals to become immersed in a conversation concerning what might cause an outage and the probabilities of a hurricane, forest fire, or other threat actually occurring. At the point of creating a continuity plan or business impact analysis, it is not important what the actual threat is. A burst water pipe, a dam breaking, or a river overrunning its bank all have the potential to cause an outage due to excessive water in the facility.

The conversation should be concerned with the assumption that a catastrophic outage (of some type is) has occurred (for whatever reason), causing a 100 percent loss of a process or operation to the organization and then determining which actions and activities are required to sustain any remaining operations or begin a disaster recovery process.

Various steps must be undertaken during the creation of a business impact analysis:

Locate and determine all business processes   It may seem easy to identify simple business processes. A list of departments such as sales, marketing, manufacturing, accounting, IT, customer service, and a few other major groups may be enough. But this process becomes much more complex than a larger organization. Although major departments and work-groups have been identified, what would happen if a localized fire took out the valuable customer database of a small four-person work group?

The list of all the business processes is usually created by contacting senior personnel, department heads, managers, and knowledgeable individuals within the organization. This listing of processes will form the basis of creating an entire picture of the organization.

Determine how critical a process is to the business   The next task is to determine how critical a process is to the business. This may be accomplished through interviews, polls, questionnaires, and other devices used to solicit opinions and information from across the organization. Reconciling of this information is never an easy chore. It may be found that according to the perspective of the individuals polled, their department or business process may be indispensable. Therefore, a ranking system should be devised along with the deci-sion process to determine the critical nature of each business process.

Determine how long the business can survive without a particular process   Once business processes are ranked in order of importance, now comes the task of determining how the business can survive without a particular process. This computation may be undertaken with the assistance of knowledgeable individuals within the organization, such as stake-holders, department heads, and managers.

Where's the Revenue?

Sometimes it is not easy to determine what facets of a business are absolutely required to maintain the business. There are the absolute must haves and everybody else is secondary. When asking the leaders of business units, you might expect each leader to say that their unit is by far the most important to the corporate operation. How do you decide?

Just as a thought exercise, let's consider the automobile industry. Looking at a manufacturer as a whole, consider what you think are the most important activities of the economic process of the company. Sure, it is very easy to say that an automobile assembly plant must be brought back online as soon as possible to continue supplying product or that without parts and supplies the entire operation will grind to a halt. Therefore, suppliers and warehousing are important. Of course it's always easy to consider that without the labor force nothing would be done. While all of these are important components of the auto business, how do we prioritize one over another?

A simple method when evaluating priorities within a business is to consider where the revenue is generated. For companies to remain viable, maintaining their revenue stream is a priority. If there is no money, they are out of business. So in this thought example, we might consider that automobile dealerships currently have plenty of stock on their lots. Currently, manufacturers annually shut down for weeks on end for tooling changes. So evidently both the supply chain and the ability to manufacture and assemble automobiles may not be that high a priority in an emergency. Since automobiles are sold throughout the country in automobile dealerships, the marketing, sales operations, and customer service activity is separated from the main geographic location. So if we consider where the revenue is actually being generated, we might determine that the credit-granting organization within the business is the most important to bring back online. Automobile dealerships rely upon the manufacturer's ability to grant credit to the buying customer for the majority of the automobiles sold. If the credit organization is down for an extended period of time, the primary revenue stream for the manufacturer could be severely impacted, thus jeopardizing the entire business.

Downtime impact timelines   Various terminology may be employed to describe the timeline when a critical operation is down or offline (Figure 4.4). The times can be measured in minutes, days, or weeks and can be determined by both qualitative (numerically based) and quantitative (subjectively based) methods. Usually the correct answer is a combination of both techniques.

FIGURE 4.4 An illustration of the relationship between maximum tolerable downtime and the recovery time objective

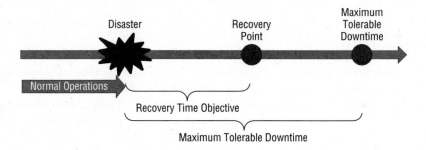

Maximum Tolerable Downtime (MTD) The *maximum tolerable downtime* is an estimate of the maximum time the business process may be down or offline before the organization becomes unable to recover. For instance, if a business warehouse sustains a catastrophic fire and cannot adequately function for a period of 90 days, it may be assumed or a fact that all of the current customers have migrated to other suppliers and that the business can no longer operate.

Recovery Time Objective (RTO) The *recovery time objective* may be stated as the estimated time by which the affected process will be restored. For instance, a fire in a warehouse has destroyed the communications closet containing five servers. All data processing functions to that warehouse are no longer available. The recovery time objective is stated as 14 days to replace equipment, rewire the building, and bring the servers to full operation. The important point to remember is that the RTO must always be less than the MTD. If it is ever longer, the business will fail.

Recovery Point Objective (RPO) The *recovery point objective* acknowledges that during any disaster, records and data may be lost. It is necessary to determine at what point known good records could be restored, after which reliable data and information will not be available. A recovery point objective is directly related to data retention, data storage, and backup methodology employed by the organization. For instance, if daily data is backed up at midnight each night, the recovery point objective will be the prior midnight. Many businesses utilize immediate offsite storage such as cloud storage or another related facility. When this is the case, data can be recovered almost up to the point of disruption, so the recovery point objective is virtually at the point of service interruption.

Figure 4.5 illustrates the relationship between the recovery point objective and the recovery time objective. The recovery point objective indicates the last known good data safely backed up and not affected by the disaster. The recovery time objective is the amount of time required to restore the data from the backup archives.

FIGURE 4.5   The relationship between recovery point objective and recovery
time objective

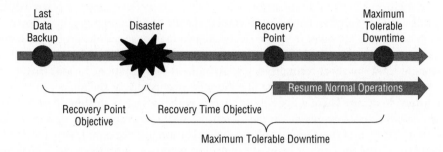

The concepts of maximum tolerable downtime, recovery point objective, and recovery
time objective may be applied to every critical activity identified as a priority to the organization. Although the recovery point objective in the previous example refers to the restoration
of data using backup files, it may also apply to physical or operational assets. For instance, a
recovery point in a customer service office may be established as the point at which customer
service agents are able to resume operations by answering telephones and resolving client
issues. When planning a physical or operational recovery point objective, it is important
to consider alternate or temporary recovery programs. For instance, the customer service
department may be brought back to minimal operational status in an alternate location with
telephone service using temporary tables, paper records, and written forms while the normal
facility, communications equipment, and computer service is being restored.

Disaster Recovery Plans

As a security practitioner, you will be involved in restoration activities after a disaster. You,
along with other team members, perform an integral service in returning IT operations and
other business functions back to normal. A business continuity plan is concerned with maintaining the operations of a system or department after a disaster. As previously discussed,
operations may be continued in a temporary location using a paper-based methodology, but
at least they will be continuing.

Disaster recovery plans encompass a framework of processes and programs focused on
the restoration of computer services, telecommunications, facilities, and operations back to
a predisaster operational state. Since most organizations rely heavily on IT infrastructure,
it is important that IT systems and services be returned to an operational state as soon as
possible. As previously stated, continuity planning and disaster recovery planning sometimes require monumental efforts. These activities require a large degree of coordination,
stakeholder input, and financial resources. Due to the importance of IT infrastructure, the

IT department should create a comprehensive continuity plan and a disaster recovery plan independently of the rest of the organization if necessary. In other words, the IT infrastructure for an organization should take priority and have complete restoration plans available.

Not all disasters are created equal. For instance, the air-conditioning breaking down the server room or the loss of power from the electrical grid may pose serious problems, but they are not as catastrophic as a tornado or hurricane. Some disasters are not disasters at all and only pose significant but short-term problems. To address this situation, various threats may be identified and assessed as to either the likelihood of occurrence or the impact to the organization if they do occur. There will be those threats with a very low likelihood of occurrence and possibly with a very low impact on the operations of the organization if they do occur.

Since all disasters and their impact on the organization are not equal, a method should be available to trigger the correct response plan. For instance, suppose a fire occurs and the information needs to be conveyed to the emergency recovery staff, corporate executives, and other stakeholders. You could easily imagine that the very next question somebody will have is, "How serious is it?" Therefore, many organizations have adopted a three-tier category system to describe an event by listing a disaster level. In this example, we'll list them as level I, level II, and level III disasters, although the title may be different based upon the organization. The descriptions and responses for each disaster level are completely arbitrary and may be assigned or determined by the individual organization. Each disaster level triggers a measured and preplanned response by the organization. Note that the level classification indicates the response to the disaster event, not a description of the cause, which is of secondary concern.

Level I Disaster   This level describes a disaster that is local in nature and affects only a small part of the operation. Although serious, it may be handled in-house and may have a short-term effect on ongoing operations. The short-term effect may be defined as a 6- or 12-hour downtime with total recovery within 48 to 72 hours. Disasters of this nature might include a localized event such as an equipment failure, application or database failure, communication system failure, or other local infrastructure problem.

Level II Disaster   A level II disaster specifies a situation that affects a significant amount of the organization. In this instance, ongoing operations may be affected for up to a week or more. The physical location of some departments may be damaged and unusable. Organization IT infrastructure may be seriously damaged, requiring significant replacement or rebuilding of equipment or wiring. Data storage facilities may have been seriously damaged, requiring replacement or the use of an alternate site.

Level III Disaster   A level III disaster specifies a very serious situation requiring the relocation of IT operations to an off-premises alternate site. This type of disaster may include significant damage to the facility, requiring personnel to evacuate the premises. The facility may be deemed unusable and require extensive repair. The estimated time to restore the facilities to full operational status may be measured in weeks or months.

Disaster Recovery Strategy

Various items and components of the IT infrastructure require different strategies. For instance, should a disaster event occur, there is a significant difference between restoring a server with previously backed-up information and totally replacing server racks and damaged cables and restoring communication equipment. The recovery strategy should include plans and procedures for the restoration or replacement of various components of the IT infrastructure. These plans should include the following sections:

- Assessing the damage and determining what needs to be replaced
- Placing orders for replacement goods or services
- Receiving, installing, and configuring replacement goods
- Loading and testing applications and data
- Certification and accreditation of IT systems and infrastructure

Each section should indicate the job title of the individuals responsible for the management and completion of the activity. It may also detail suppliers, service providers, contractors, partners, and other individuals and entities that may be utilized or contracted to perform a role in the recovery efforts.

A recovery plan may be organized by operational section. For example, different individuals may have responsibilities, and each section may feature different priorities, time-lines, suppliers, and requirements. The following operational sections might be included in a recovery plan for an IT department:

- Physical Facility
- Facility Wiring
- Network Hardware
- Data, Applications, and Operating System Restoration
- Communications Hardware

 Real World Scenario

Where's My stuff?

It was the Friday after Thanksgiving and the entire company had the day off due to the holiday weekend. As many senior staff are apt to do, the chief financial officer elected to go into the office, looking forward to getting some work done without being disturbed. Upon arriving at the office and seeing an incredible commotion, he placed a call to the vice president of operations.

Continues

Continued

"We've had a small fire," he stated, alarming his co-worker.

"How small is a small fire?" was the response.

"I can't see into the building, but you better come quickly," he stated.

All during the half-hour drive to the office, the vice president of operations ran through his head the potential definition of a small fire. Upon rounding the corner and pulling into the parking lot, he quickly received his answer. The entire front of the building was gone, devastated by a fire that had evidently raged for some time. Soot-covered firefighters were working with hoses that were strewn everywhere, littering the parking lot and street in front of the building. Some firefighters were traversing ladders that reached into the upper stories of the building, while others were raking through piles of paper that were still on fire.

Knowing that the small company did not have a formal continuity plan or anything hinting at a disaster recovery plan, the VP of operations realized that he did not even possess the phone numbers of key personnel within the company. He asked the fire chief if his office had been involved in the fire and if there was any way that he could get back to where his records were on his desk, including his phone book. The fire chief informed him that the structural integrity of the building was such that they could not let any civilians in at this point.

A wave of incredible helplessness spread over the two senior company officials as they watched the mayhem unfold in front of their eyes, knowing that not only did they not have any plan in place, they did not even have access to vital information to even begin the formation of a plan. As the last embers of the fire were extinguished and the firefighters started gathering up their hoses, both individuals looked at each other hopelessly with an expression of "what do we do next?"

Figure 4.6 illustrates a graphical technique of prioritizing disaster response by analyzing the impact to the business if a catastrophic event should occur. Obviously, plans to restore high-impact, high-probability processes take precedence over low-impact, low-probability processes. This type of planning chart will easily illustrate restoration priorities. Business processes that are very important to the business would be placed in the upper-right quadrant, indicating that the continuity of these processes has high significance to the continued operation of the business.

FIGURE 4.6   An illustration of restoration priorities based upon the importance of the asset or department to the organization and the impact to the organization if it is unavailable or lost during a disaster

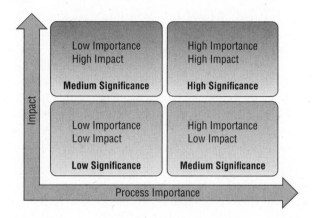

Plan Testing

Continuity plans and disaster plans required testing. Testing is the method of identifying weaknesses, reviewing assignments and updating plan information. It also verifies that the plan meets the organization's needs and requirements and that all individuals responsible for action items are knowledgeable and competent regarding their responsibilities. The primary goal of testing includes the following activities:

- Fulfill testing, exercise, and maintenance requirements
- Conduct training for the business continuity team supervisory individuals
- Conduct orientation for all staff positions
- Conduct actual changeover or simulated scenarios
- Update plans to incorporate "lessons learned from" exercises

Various methods may be used to test the plans with varying degrees of risk to the organization and commitment of time and resources:

Checklist Test   The checklist test enables individuals to review the continuity plan or disaster recovery plan to ensure that all procedures and critical areas within their responsibility are addressed. During this test, they meet update information including contact and duty assignment information. This type of test is conducted at the individuals work space, office or cube and requires the least amount of effort and resources. Some organizations may also referred to as a desktop test.

Tabletop Test   In a tabletop test, individuals assigned to the test being conducted will assemble in a conference room. Here they will review the continuity plan or disaster recovery plan and proceed through the plan step-by-step, outlining their personal responsibilities. Sometimes referred to as a structured walk-through test, this test enables the group to discuss the plans and update them where required. During the tabletop test or structured walk-through test, a specific scenario may be discussed and individuals may role-play their assigned activities. In one such test it was discovered that a key person from the finance staff was required to be part of the continuity team because they were the only staff members who had purchasing authority.

Simulation Test   A typical emergency situation may be practiced during a simulation test. In this type of test, individuals role-play their assignments to bring the simulation to a successful conclusion. They are instructed to go through all the exact steps they would in the event of a real emergency situation, the steps being coordinated by the continuity plan leader. The leader might designate a specific time for the start of the test.

At that time, the continuity plan leader announces the type of emergency, such as a fire and evacuation of part of the building with an outage of all network operations and communication within that area. The leader may then declare the potential impact of the event. For instance, nationwide customer service is completely interrupted for the next 20 hours. Since the current work location is no longer available, the team leader designates the location that will be used as an alternate site for the coordination of all activities. All responsible participants will relocate all of their available resources to the newly assigned location. If they are responsible for other individuals, they have to locate these people and deliver them to a predefined location.

The simulation tests is a very accurate training tool because, invariably, people will forget things, not have transportation, not have backups available, or find that communication is inadequate. The simulation test is typically conducted once a year in many organizations due to the fact that it may interrupt or disrupt business activities during the testing period.

Parallel Test   A parallel test is similar to those tests where software applications are run in parallel with the actual business environment to test how well they will perform. In a parallel test, duplicate systems or alternate processing sites may be brought online and run in parallel with the existing data processing system. This type of test can tend to be complex and expensive. The benefit is that in the event anything goes wrong with the parallel test, the primary processing environment is not affected.

Full Interruption Test   A full interruption test entails a complete power up of an alternate site, switch over and power down of the primary site. This test is very risky and expensive. Typically, only the business activities requiring the highest level of continuity are switched to the alternate site. The challenge on many full interruption tests is to bring the primary site back online.

How to Communicate

Most continuity plans require individuals to contact each other by some means. Key plan personnel, supervisors, and team leaders must communicate with each other as well as communicate with all affected participants and staff members. During the disaster of 9/11, cellular telephone systems were completely jammed with calls and no one could get through. It has also been seen that during two major hurricanes, cellular telephone towers were knocked out for a period of time.

Most professional disaster emergency response teams, as well as hospitals and other critical operations such as police, fire, and emergency rescue, switch to battery-operated, noncellular radio communication equipment with handheld walkie-talkie systems issued to all key personnel. For an accurate test of your organization's continuity plan, a scenario might be devised where the participants do not have access to cellular telephones.

Succession Planning

With proper *succession planning*, backup personnel are available in the event that key personnel are lost or unavailable. Backup personnel may be required to fill key business leadership positions in the company or IT department. Succession planning increases the availability of experienced and capable employees who are prepared to assume these roles if they are required.

Succession planning is key within an IT department. It begins with the process of hiring competent well-rounded personnel. They should then be cross-trained in many different disciplines. Specifically for disaster planning, the disaster plan should clearly list, by job title, the succession to the top decision-making role during a disaster. This is simply accomplished in some organizations by a "call list" that includes the individuals who should be notified of an event or situation. The point is, in a disaster scenario, a clear leader and decision-maker must be denoted. In the event a primary person is not available, the authority should immediately be instilled with a backup person.

In planning for succession, individuals should be cross-trained in disaster preparedness and information should be shared among both the primary and backup persons who are responsible to take action. Plans including procedures, documentation, policies, and other documents should be identified and shared.

Disaster Planning Alternate Sites

Business continuity plans require the listing of alternate plans for the continuation of IT operations should a disaster occur. Of course, in some level I disasters, as previously described, IT operations may continue in the same location. A level III disaster may mean that a location is no longer suitable or available for continued IT operations and therefore a decision must be made to relocate, on a temporary basis, to an alternate site or facility. It is important during the creation of business continuity plans to carefully consider and preplan alternate sites. These alternate sites should be arranged for and contracted in anticipation of any need arising.

A variety of site selections and alternative methods are available for the continuity of business operations:

Hot Site   A *hot site* is a physical location available for immediate switchover of processing operations. A hot site typically contains power, heating, ventilation and air-conditioning, security, connectivity, servers, workstations, and networking devices that may be substituted for the existing production environment. Data may also be mirrored to the hot site, requiring little or no installation or update. A hot site is set aside exclusively for the use of the organization. The hot site installation and contract is very expensive.

Warm Site   A *warm site* is a computer facility that is contractually available and has some power, heating, ventilation and air-conditioning, connectivity, and basic networking equipment. Organizations may be required to install servers, workstations, and other networking devices in order to make a warm site fully operational. Obviously, a warm site will take longer to bring online than a hot site. Some suppliers of warm sites offer mobile capability. The mobile site features IT equipment mounted in semitrailer vans that may be brought to an organization's location. A major consideration is that in the event of a major catastrophic event affecting a number of organizations, a warm site may not be available due to the number of organizations under contract to use it.

Cold Site   A *cold site* is a facility that has power, heating, ventilation and air-conditioning, and little else. It does not have communications or computer equipment. If an organization has to set up an alternate site for processing, they would have to bring in and set up every device. Although it's the least expensive of the site alternatives, bringing a cold site online would involve a substantial undertaking and expense.

Virtual Site   With the proliferation of cloud services, various cloud providers are providing Infrastructure as a Service (IaaS) disaster recovery sites. Under these programs, the organization's existing IT infrastructure may be established under virtual conditions in the cloud. Data and applications may be made available almost immediately under the circumstances.

Partnership/Cooperative Site   A partnership/cooperative site also known as a reciprocal site involves an agreement between two companies to share resources in the event of a disaster. In such a situation, excess capacity by the way of servers, storage, computer workstations, and other resources may be made available should one or either company experience a disaster situation.

Several scenarios should be envisioned when planning for alternate sites or the relocation of operations. The assumption might be that if a disaster affects a geographic region, various scenarios may occur.

Alternate Site Proximity   A general rule of thumb is that an alternate site should be no closer to the original site than 20 miles. This takes into consideration general geographic disasters such as earthquakes, floods, hurricanes, tornadoes, forest fires, or other events that might affect not only the organization but every business within a radius of several miles. This was evident during 9/11 when a company's backup location was the second World Trade Center tower. Consideration should also be given to the transportation of individuals, data, and hardware to the alternate site as well as room and board of individuals while at the alternate site.

Competition for Resources   When disaster affects a geographic region, it affects all the companies and businesses as well as potential suppliers and providers within the area. The business continuity plan and disaster recovery plan should take into account that the resources required for recovery may not be available because they are being utilized by other organizations within the same vicinity. This includes contracts for alternate sites. Another organization may have contracted for a priority position in using an alternate site. As part of a contingency plan, many companies maintain a quantity of small-denomination currency and even have gold on hand to use to barter for services, equipment, and supplies in an emergency.

Exam Point

It is important to understand the difference between the different types of alternate sites.

Summary

The systems security certified practitioner must be familiar with the organization's policies, standards, procedures, and guidelines to ensure adequate information availability, integrity, and confidentiality.

In this chapter you learned that security administration defines the roles and responsibilities of practitioners within the organization who must carry out various tasks according to established policy and directives. Practitioners may be involved with change control, configuration management, security awareness training, and the monitoring of systems and devices. The application of generally accepted industry best practices is the responsibility of the IT administrators and security practitioners. Key administration duties may include configuration, logging, monitoring, and upgrading and updating products as well as providing end-user support.

We discussed the importance of policies within an organization. Without policies and the resulting procedures and guidelines, there would be a complete lack of corporate governance with respect to IT security. Security policies are the foundation upon which the organization can rely for guidance. Included with these policies is the concept of continuity of operations. Continuity of operations includes all actions required to continue operations after a disaster. A policy of disaster preparedness and a disaster recovery policy provide the steps and required information to restore operations.

The configuration and management of various systems and network products may be the responsibility of the security practitioner. This chapter covered patching and upgrading systems. We also looked at the version numbering methodology used to identify various versions of software, firmware, and hardware and discussed release management and the responsibilities involved in the distribution of software changes throughout the organization.

Data classification policies and the responsibilities of the security practitioner were discussed. The practitioner may be involved in both the classification process and the declassification process with regard to data management policies.

The security practitioner may be involved in conducting or facilitating security awareness training courses or sessions. During the sessions, malware, social media, passwords, and the implications of lost devices can be discussed. Different groups of individuals that require training were identified.

Business continuity and disaster recovery plans are important programs to initiate within an organization. The security practitioner may be involved in originating or maintaining such plans and will definitely be involved if the plan needs to be exercised. A business impact analysis is key to the origination of a business continuity plan. Plans should be tested by a variety of methods to ensure that individuals are aware of their responsibilities and that all of the details of the plans have been considered.

Exam Essentials

Importance of risk   Understand that risk is a function of the likelihood of a given threat agent exploiting a particular vulnerability, and the resulting impact of that creates an adverse event in the organization.

Corporate Policies   Understand that corporate policies must be aligned with the mission and values of an organization.

Support of Top Management   Be aware that the success of any policy requires the support and authorization of top management or a sponsoring high-level executive, without which it is doomed to fail.

General Types of Policies   Know that organizational policies, functional policies, and operational policies are types of policies.

Policy Construction   Understand that policies consist of standards, baselines procedures, and guidelines.

The (ISC)² Code of Ethics   All SSCP candidates should read and understand the (ISC)² Code of Ethics.

Configuration of Hardware and Software   Know that the security practitioner is required to patch, upgrade, and make changes to both hardware and software.

Change Management   Understand all of the techniques and methodology required in change management, and be able to support the change management policies of the organization.

Data Management Policies   Be able carry out the tasks required of data management policies, including data maintenance, classification, and declassification.

Endpoint Device Security   Understand the requirements of endpoint device security concerning firewalls, host intrusion detection systems, and antivirus software, and be able to support endpoint device policies.

End-User Training   Be aware of the types of end-user and security awareness program training required by the different job levels of individuals within the organization.

Business Continuity Planning   Know and understand that as a practitioner, you will be involved in business continuity planning and participating in both tests and actual implementation of plans as required.

Written Lab

You can find the answers in Appendix A.

1. Write a paragraph explaining the importance of executive-level endorsement of a policy.
2. What is a primary difference between standards, baselines, and procedures?
3. Briefly explain the difference between a hot site, a warm site, and a cold site.
4. Describe the difference between recovery time objective and recovery point objective.

Review Questions

You can find the answers in Appendix B.

1. Proper security administration policies, controls, and procedures enforce which of the following?

   A. The elimination of risk

   B. The total reduction of malware

   C. The AIC objectives

   D. Separation of duties

2. Which of the following best describes a threat exploiting a vulnerability?

   A. DDOS

   B. Risk

   C. A hurricane

   D. Power supply brownout

3. Which of the following best describes a security policy?

   A. It describes the requirement for shareholder satisfaction

   B. Lists potential risk targets within the organization

   C. Makes extensive use of baselines and guidelines

   D. Completely aligns with the mission, objectives, culture, and nature of the business

4. Which of the following best describes a federated relationship?

   A. Numerous franchises in a geographical area

   B. The airline industry

   C. HIPAA patient privacy requirements for healthcare providers

   D. Third-party companies and their networks share customer data based upon a single sign-on to a primary organization

5. Which of the following is an example of compensating control?

   A. A padlock on a gate

   B. A chain on the hotel room door

   C. A red bucket of sand with the word, "Fire"

   D. An insurance policy

6. What must every policy possess in order to be successfully implemented?

   A. An enforcement provision

   B. Scope and statements from stakeholders

   C. Senior executive endorsement

   D. Controls and procedures statement

7. What does an acceptable use policy AUP state?

   A. That the organization assets may not be used on weekends

   B. That USB drives may not be used

   C. The acceptable and unacceptable uses for organizational resources

   D. That users may not visit shopping sites during work

8. An Acceptable Use Policy (AUP) is what type of control?

   A. Administrative

   B. Corrective

   C. Detective

   D. Compensating

9. Which of the following should be included in every policy that states possible penalties or restrictions for individuals?

   A. A copyright notice

   B. An enforcement statement

   C. A statement from the author

   D. A preamble of rights

10. Organization policies are generally created in response to the requirement to meet certain criteria. Which of the following best details these requirements?

    A. Baselines

    B. Standards

    C. Procedures

    D. Policy Requirements Document (PRD)

11. Which of the following is a typical method of communicating a policy or policy change?

    A. Intranet announcement

    B. Handouts

    C. Instagram announcement

    D. Phone e-mailed blast

12. Which of the following is the third canon of the (ISC)^2 Code of Ethics?

    A. Act honorably

    B. Ensure the safety of society

    C. Meet all CEU requirements for this certification

    D. Provide competent and diligent service

13. What is a service pack?

  A. A piece of software intended to update an application

  B. A piece of software written by user group intended to fix a problem

  C. A piece of software intended to inform users of a software vulnerability

  D. An executable program that loads a number of fixes and system upgrades

14. Which of the following best describes an environment to test a patch or a service pack?

  A. As they are received from the manufacturer

  B. In a sandbox

  C. In a production environment

  D. In a simulator

15. What is a typical commercial or business information classification scheme?

  A. Unclassified, sensitive but unclassified, secret, and top secret

  B. Unclassified, business casual, confidential

  C. Public, company confidential, company secret

  D. Public, sensitive but unclassified, confidential, secret, and top secret

16. If subjects receive a clearance, what do objects receive?

  A. Data Tag

  B. Mandatory Access Control label

  C. Access point

  D. Classification

17. Which of the following best describes endpoint device?

  A. Router

  B. Computer printer

  C. Switch

  D. HIDS

18. Which of the following is part of the business continuity plan?

  A. The recovery downtime objective

  B. The restoration of accounting data into databases

  C. Recovery point objective

  D. The maximum tolerable off-line time

19. Which of the following best describes a disaster recovery plan?

    A. Makes use of probability analysis

    B. Uses the Business Information Plan to determine procedures

    C. Documents procedures to restore equipment and facilities to the condition they were in prior to the disaster

    D. Specifies time required to restore data with different backup schemes

20. Which of the following best describes maximum tolerable downtime?

    A. The amount of time a business process may be off-line before the viability of the organization is in severe jeopardy

    B. The point at which data recovery should begin

    C. The amount of time between RPO and RTO

    D. The time required to restore data from a backup

Chapter

5

Domain 3: Risk Identification, Monitoring, and Analysis

SSCP EXAM OBJECTIVES COVERED IN THIS CHAPTER:

✓ **Understand the risk management process**

- Risk visibility and reporting
- Risk management concepts
- Risk assessment
- Risk treatment
- Audit findings

✓ **Understand security assessment activities**

- Participation in security testing and evaluation
- Interpretation and reporting assessment results

✓ **Operate, maintain, and monitor systems**

- Events of interest
- Reviewing log files

✓ **Analyze monitoring results**

- Security analytics, metrics, and trends
- Visualization
- Event data analysis
- Communicate findings

IT risk management is the primary focus of the concept of IT security in an organization's IT operations. All organizations depend on IT operations and the information systems that are developed from that technology to successfully carry out the mission and business function of the enterprise. Frequently, portable devices such as digital assistants, tablets, laptops and cell phones are being integrated within the IT systems of the organization.

Possible threats challenge the organization from many different directions, many of which require continuous and ongoing threat identification and monitoring processes that determine the application of controls. Organizational IT systems are subject to serious threats or attacks that could have an adverse impact on the availability and integrity of the organization's hardware systems, information storage, and information telecommunications.

Managing security risks to information systems is a complex, multifaceted undertaking. There are levels of responsibilities throughout the organization that are necessary to meet the goals and objectives of risk management. Senior leaders and management provide corporate policies and governance, organizational managers provide planning and implementation to meet the requirements of these policies, and individuals such as security practitioners are charged with ensuring that the controls designed to reduce risk meet operational baselines efficiently and effectively. The System Security Certified Practitioner will always be familiar with the enterprise's policies, as well as the standards, procedures, and guidelines that will ensure due-care protection of its information as well as its hardware assets. Through the use of risk analysis, assets and their vulnerabilities are identified as well as potential threats that may exploit these vulnerabilities. A variety of tools and reporting techniques are used to reduce the impact of threats to the organization.

The systems security certified practitioner will be involved at many levels of risk identification, threat assessment, intrusion discovery, and eventual remediation and restoration activities. It is important to have a thorough understanding of risk, vulnerabilities, and threats that face organizations IT infrastructure. These will be processes and projects in which Systems Security Certified Practitioners will contribute both knowledge and skills.

Understanding the Risk Management Process

Risks may take many forms in an organization, including IT risk, financial risk, operational risk, commercial market risk, operational security risk, and personal exposure to risk. A senior management team of any organization is continuously burdened with the identification and mitigation of risks in any category that may result in damage or harm to assets of the organization. The most common risk management approach used by organizations is to identify, assess, manage, and control potential events or situations. Various processes are used to effectively perform risk management. *Information risk* management is the process of acknowledging and identifying risks, mitigating risks by the reduction of threats or vulnerabilities through the use of controls, and implementing strategies to maintain an acceptable risk level.

Risks are categorized depending upon the type of risk or the aspect of the business they affect. The top executives must consider every risk to an organization.

Defining Risk

The definition of risk is stated as the probability or likelihood that a certain event or incident may occur that will have an adverse impact on an organization and the achievement of its mission or objectives. Since risk has been defined as a probability of something occurring, it may be represented by a mathematical function.

$$\text{risk} = \text{threat} * \text{vulnerability}$$

When information technology risk is defined, we are basically speaking of the unauthorized use, disruption, modification, exfiltration, copying, inspection, or destruction of information or information processing hardware or software assets. Company managers will use various tools such as risk analysis and risk assessments to analyze the potential risks that may impact organizational assets. There is no such thing as a risk-free environment, and there is no way to totally reduce risk to zero. The tools, devices, and techniques IT managers and security practitioner use are referred to as controls to reduce the level of risk. Residual risk is any risk remaining after the implementation of safeguards and controls. For instance, an asset valued at $100,000 may have a $100,000 insurance policy placed upon it. But that $100,000 insurance policy may have a $5,000 deductible, which is the amount an organization pays in the event of loss. Obviously, with a total loss, the insurance company would reimburse the organization $95,000. The residual risk would be the $5,000 deductible.

Risk Management Process

The *risk management process* is simply a business function that involves identifying, evaluating, and controlling risks (Figure 5.1). As you have seen, risks are prevalent throughout the organization. For example, a commercial market risk may occur when a competitor may lower its prices below what it costs another company to manufacture the same product. A major supplier may have a fire, thus eliminating a supply of raw material to the organization. A hurricane might cause the manufacturing facility to be closed down for an extended period of time. Each of these represents risks to the organization and must be addressed through the risk management process. For instance, in the example of the major supplier experiencing a fire, management would have recognized that nondelivery of production materials would pose a threat to the organization. During a risk analysis process, threats that might affect a major supplier would be identified. In the event such threats came to fruition, causing the supplier to not be able to supply raw materials, plans would be in place to purchase the raw materials through other suppliers. Although this scenario is simplistic in nature, it illustrates the process behind risk management.

FIGURE 5.1   The process of risk management

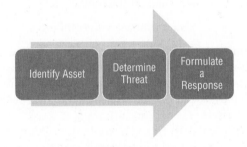

The loss of information processing hardware, software, and information is a serious risk to any organization. *Information risk management (IRM)* is the process whereby risks to IT hardware, software, and information assets are identified and threats and vulnerabilities are reduced to an acceptable level and controls are implemented to maintain that level. At the heart of information risk management are decisions concerning priorities and monetary resources. The question for senior management is what assets to protect and how much to budget to protect it.

Several categories of risks to IT hardware, software, and information assets must be considered. The following are some of the categories that represent threat sources to an IT organization:

Weather   Hurricanes, tornadoes, snowstorms, avalanches, floods, tsunamis, dry spells, and freezing temperatures

Utility and Services   Disruptions of utilities and services such as water, electrical power, natural gas, telephone system, microwave communication, cellular communication

Human Activities   Mistakes, neglect, sabotage, theft, vandalism, hacking, mischief

Business Process   Equipment malfunction, supply-chain interruption, quality control problem, market pricing

Information Technology   Equipment misuse, loss of information, damage or outage of IT equipment

Reputation   Theft of customer information, release of trade secrets and proprietary processes, release of sensitive and confidential corporate information

---

Risk Reduction

The goal of the senior management of any organization is to determine a level of acceptable risk. The process of reducing risk is referred to as *mitigation* (another term for *reduction*). The process of reducing risk might be achieved by reducing the threat level. This can be achieved by reducing the possibility of threat events over a period of time or by reducing the impact that a particular threat may cause. Risk can be reduced by reducing assets vulnerability. By using a stronger lock or type of door the vulnerability of the door is reduced if it is attacked by a threat. The lock or door would be referred to as a control. Other techniques may be used to mitigate (reduce) risk, such as avoidance, transference, and acceptance.

The determination of risk requires the knowledge of various attributes that exist in every scenario where there is risk, as detailed in the following sections.

Assets

Assets are resources that an organization uses to fulfill its mission or business objectives. *Resource* in this context may be very broad and refer to any asset including time, people, money and physical items. When defining risk, we are considering the possibility of loss of a resource. Assets and resources always represent value to the organization. Resources may be grouped into two major categories: tangible assets and intangible assets.

Tangible Assets   A *tangible asset* represents a physical item that may be touched. The following assets are considered tangible assets:

- Buildings and structures
- Tools and equipment
- Raw goods and finished goods

- Furniture and business equipment
- IT hardware and software
- Environmental systems
- Documentation

Intangible Assets   An *intangible asset* represents an item is not physical in nature. The following assets are intangible assets:

- Trade secrets, methodology, and intellectual property
- Proprietary or sensitive information
- Customer or supplier databases
- Contracts and agreements
- Policies, plans, and records
- Information stored by any means
- People

Exam Point

It is important to understand that there are tangible assets and intangible assets and that they may be ranked by the impact on the organization if they were damaged or lost.

Ranking Assets

Assets may be ranked or prioritized within an organization. During asset analysis, a variety of scores will be utilized to rank assets. Of course, the people within an organization are ranked as the highest value asset and must be protected at all costs. The second highest asset ranking will be critical assets. If critical assets are lost or compromised, the viability of the organization is jeopardized. Where hardware items, facilities, and products available from third-party vendors are ranked lower, critical assets in any organization generally include information assets such as customer/vendor data, trade secrets, proprietary information, intellectual property, and information generated by or critical to the ongoing operation of the organization.

Exam Point

The most important assets in any organization are the people.

Threats

Threats are defined as any incident or event that represents the probability to harm an organization. Harm to an organization's IT infrastructure may be in the form of authorized access, data manipulation or change, denial of access, destruction of assets and an authorized information access and release. Threats to an organization are caused by a number of different threat actions. Common sources of threats are natural, human, or environmental. While it is easy to assume that a hurricane is a threat, it is in fact just a threat source. What this means, in essence, is that the hurricane is the actor that causes the threats. The actual threat caused by the hurricane is referred to as the *threat action* or a *threat agent*. A *threat vector* is the path which a threat takes to cause an action.

While threat sources were identified in the section "Risk Management Process" earlier in this chapter, the actual threat that they pose may be individually identified. For example, a hurricane is a threat action. This means that a variety of threats to the organization may be posed during a hurricane. Each of these threats will follow a specific threat vector to harm the organization:

- The roof collapsing or windows and doors blowing out due to excessive wind.

- The facility flooding because of high water or the penetration of rain, floods, or tide water.

- The disruption of power or communications due to excessive wind.

- The destruction of physical assets such as computer hardware, network cabling, and infrastructure due to fire caused by the hurricane.

- The disruption of people. For example, people may not be available, access may be denied, the environment might be too dangerous, or communication access to information assets may be impossible regardless of where the people are located.

So while we may look at a number of different threat actions as being potential threats, in fact many of the threats are the same; they are just caused by different threat actions. For example, a fire, a flood, a wind storm, or a catastrophic mud slide may all cause the destruction of physical assets, such as computer hardware, networking, and infrastructure. As a security professional, you must plan for the resultant action of a threat regardless of the actual cause. The reality is that if the power goes out, the appropriate response must be determined regardless of why the power went out. An event triage is a process during which damage is assessed and restoration priorities are determined. During an *event triage*, you may predict that the power will be out for two hours, for example, or for four days; your prediction will influence your decisions for the proper recovery response. In any event, the power is out regardless of whether it was caused by a hurricane or forest fire.

The actions of humans pose the greatest risk to any organization. While hurricanes, tornadoes, and forest fires may be spectacular during the event and create great harm to the organization, the frequency and complexity of threats created by people far outweigh any other threat to the organization. Threats posed by the human element may be grouped into two categories:

Insider Threats   Insiders are individuals with internal access to the organization's information assets or networks. They may be employees, contractors, temporary workers, or persons with specific access rights, such as customers, clients, or suppliers. Insiders pose the largest single threat to an organization because insiders are supposedly trusted individuals. Insider *threats* may take the form of sabotage, fraud, theft of assets, disruption, or espionage.

External Threats   *External threats* may be may be posed by people who are external to the organization. Because these individuals external, they must work harder at penetrating the organization's security controls and defenses. This means that they do not have access to passwords or proprietary information as would an employee or contractor who has access to the network. These individuals may be hackers, hacktivists, script kiddies, disgruntled employees, industrial spies, or international terrorists.

Exam Point

The greatest threat to any organization is posed by humans.

Vulnerability

Vulnerability is any flaw or weakness that may be attacked or exploited by a threat. A vulnerability may be characterized by either an intentional flaw or weakness placed by an individual or an unintentional flaw such as a mistake in manufacturing. For example, a programmer might intentionally create a back door in a software application. If not detected during a code review, the back door could provide access to the programmer or other people with malicious intent.

Any information system, application, controls, or information assets could be exploited by a threat or a threat agent. For instance, an unpatched or unsupported application or operating system on a host machine or server could create a security vulnerability. From a corporate risk perspective, the security of the entire IT security environment must take into consideration the physical aspects of the building and structure, HVAC, fire suppression, physical lockdown, and access restrictions as well as vulnerabilities to the electrical power, communications, and network infrastructure.

Vulnerabilities may be grouped into two different categories:

Intentional Vulnerability   An *intentional vulnerability* is a willful action that places an asset in jeopardy. An example of unintentional vulnerability is creating access where none existed before or purposefully instigating a situation where assets are exposed to a threat. Intentionally placing malware on a system that creates a back door, allowing an outside visitor access to sensitive hardware, and escalating a user's rights so they can access sensitive information are all examples of creating an intentional vulnerability.

Unintentional Vulnerability   An *unintentional vulnerability* takes the form of a manufacturing defect, programming error, or design flaw in either hardware or software. An example of unintentional vulnerability is a "zero-day attack" that takes advantage of a previously unknown vulnerability. Unintentional vulnerability may also be caused through negligence, lack of patching and maintenance, lack of effective policies and procedures. Accidents happen. With appropriate planning, training, and other mitigation techniques, the possibility of accidents can be reduced. But still, accidents can happen. Insurance underwrites offer uninsured motorist insurance policies to mitigate the effects when an accident occurs and the other driver lacks insurance; your insurance policy will cover your loss even though the lack of insurance on the other driver's part may be intentional in nature. Your vulnerability to having an unintentional accident and the other driver not having insurance represents the reason for your insurance policy.

Controls

Controls are the mechanisms utilized during the risk management process to reduce the ability of a threat to exploit a vulnerability, which would result in harm to the organization. Controls may also be used to reduce the level of a vulnerability. For example, a control that might be used to keep a thief (threat) from exploiting the door (vulnerability) on a backyard work shed might be a heavy lock (control) on the shed door. This effort would reduce or mitigate the vulnerability of the door of the shed. The methods used to reduce or mitigate a threat, on the other hand, might include a heavy lock on the backyard gate, motion-sensing lighting in the backyard, and a guard dog. Therefore, by reducing a vulnerability and reducing the threat, the result is reduction of the overall risk.

There are three categories of controls:

Administrative Controls   Administrative controls are put in place to enforce a policy.

Technical Controls   Technical controls, also referred to as logical controls, are controls placed on the network, computer system, or communication network. Technical controls take the form of hardware, software, or firmware.

Physical Controls   Physical controls are controls used to protect physical assets, such as fences, doors, locks, signs, lights, and other physical safeguards.

Exam Point

There are three types of controls: administrative, technical, and physical.

Safeguards

The terms safeguards and controls are used interchangeably and describe any device, procedure, or action that provides a degree of protection to an asset. Controls are a general category of procedures, mechanisms, and techniques that make up the layered defense model; safeguards are generally described in terms of preventative activities or devices put in place as a result of a risk analysis. A safeguard is generally the use of a control mechanism of some type, the concept of defense in depth provides for the use of multiple controls in a series. Second- or third-tier controls are sometimes referred to as safeguards because they may mitigate a threat that manages to pass through the primary control mechanism.

Compensating Controls

Every control can have a built-in or inherent weakness. A *compensating control* is a device, procedure, or mechanism that addresses the inherent weakness of the primary control. In most cases, a compensating control addresses conditions or situations that the primary control misses.

Countermeasures

During a risk analysis, various threats as well as vulnerabilities are identified. *Countermeasures* generally describe specific activities, procedures, or devices which are put in place to mitigate an identified risk or vulnerability that has been identified during the risk analysis process. Examples of countermeasures include:

- A specific information systems security policy
- Specific topics covered during security education, awareness, and training
- Logical access controls for privacy requirements
- *Proxy servers*, HIPS, NIPS, *air gap techniques*
- Targeted firewall IP exclusion rules
- *Honeypots*

Exam Point

A compensating control is a device, procedure, or mechanism that addresses the inherent weakness of the primary control.

Exposure

Exposure is defined as the estimated percentage of loss should a specific threat exploit the vulnerability of an asset. For example, if a server is valued at $10,000 and each time it is attacked $5,000 is required to rebuild the system, then the exposure factor is 50 percent. Exposure is always expressed as a percentage that when multiplied by the asset value results in the amount of loss during each attack. For instance, the example scenario above restated as a mathematical equation would appear as: $10,000 × .50 = $5,000

Risk Analysis

The *risk analysis* process is an analytical method of identifying both threats and asset vulnerabilities and determining the likelihood and impact should the threat event occur and exploit the identified vulnerability.

Risk Impact

Understanding *risk impact* is an important factor in risk analysis and risk assessment programs. The amount of impact or damage a threat may cause to an asset may determine the risk level to be dealt with. It may be determined that although a risk exists, the value or importance of the asset is such that it may not be worth protecting or that the cost to protect it outweighs the value.

Exam Point

Compensating controls "compensate" or make up for inherent weaknesses in a primary control.

Risk Management Frameworks and Guidance for Managing Risks

Risk management requires the knowledge of best practices, industry standards, and a structured risk analysis method whereby assets and threats may be classified to determine the efforts required to reduce the risk to the organization. Through the years a structured series of standards and methodology has evolved in the form of frameworks.

Frameworks have originated through interaction with industry groups, consultants, and a variety of working committees managed by a standards organizations. Three frameworks have become widely utilized throughout IT security and are discussed in the following sections.

ISO/IEC 27005

The *ISO/IEC 27000 series* is a group of standards that offers guidance to IT security management organizations. The International Organization for Standardization (ISO) and the International Electrotechnical Commission (IEC) have published an extensive series of best practices, recommendations, and guidelines. The ISO/IEC refers to its family of standards as an *information security management system (ISMS)*. The most popular of the standards in the series is *ISO/IEC 27002*, which is a security code of practice and guidelines for IT security management. *ISO/IEC 27005* offers a framework based upon a broad scope of various factors within the organization. This type of framework allows each organization to address the risks based upon their own ISMS. This framework covers such areas as the following:

- Information security risk assessment
- Information security risk treatment
- Information security risk acceptance
- Information security risk communication
- Information security risk monitoring and review

NIST Special Publication 800-37 Revision 1

While the ISO/IEC 27000 series has its foundations in establishing a structure of practices within an organization and then certifying and accrediting the organization for meeting established benchmarks, *NIST Special Publication 800-37 Revision 1*, "Guide for Applying the Risk Management Framework to Federal Information Systems," was created to guide IT organizations within the U.S. federal government with a more practical approach to risk management. The *National Institute of Standards and Technology (NIST)* had its origination as the *National Bureau of Standards* and is a nonregulatory agency of the U.S. Department of Commerce. NIST is responsible for developing information security standards and guidelines, including minimum requirements for federal information systems. Although the news bulletins and publications originated as guidelines for federal agencies, they are widely applied throughout private and public businesses and organizations.

There are a variety of terms associated with NIST publications:

FISMA   The National Institute of Standards and Technology was given statutory responsibilities under the *Federal Information Security Management Act (FISMA)*. Under the law, NIST is responsible for developing information security standards and guidelines. The determination as to which standards to mandate upon federal information systems under the law has been given to the secretary of commerce.

FIPS   *Federal Information Processing Standards (FIPS)* are standards approved by the secretary of commerce as compulsory and binding standards for federal agencies.

Special Publications   *Special Publications (SP)* are documents issued by NIST with recommendations and guidance for federal agencies. Only select Special Publications are mandated for compliance by federal agencies.

The *risk management framework (RMF)* that is detailed in *NIST SP 800-37 Revision 1* offers a six-step process for implementing information security and risk management activities into a cohesive system development life cycle. The risk management methodology described by NIST and this Special Publication is composed of the following steps:

Step 1: Categorize   The information system is examined to determine a category for the system. During this process, the information that the system processes, stores, and transmits is evaluated. This evaluation is used to determine the asset value and potential risks to the system.

Step 2: Select   Baseline security controls are selected based on the category of the system. For example, a system that processes classified data must include a selection of controls that mitigate risks for federal information systems in that category. The baseline selection may then be augmented with additional controls, or existing controls may be modified or customized based on the needs of the organization.

Step 3: Implement   In this step the selected security controls are installed and properly initiated throughout the system. The controls must be documented to show the implementation within the system and what category of risks they mitigate.

Step 4: Assess   An assessment process is utilized to determine if the controls are installed and set up correctly, operating effectively, and meeting the risk mitigation requirements as established by the risk management plan for the system.

Step 5: Authorize   Authorization occurs when an acceptable level of risk is achieved based upon the implementation of controls.

Step 6: Monitor   This step involves the ongoing assessment of the baseline operation of a control and its risk mitigation effectiveness. This process also includes a change management process that documents not only changes to the control and the resulting impact analysis but also environmental changes throughout the system. Management reports also produces result of information system monitoring.

Simply put, a risk management framework is a continuous methodology of categorizing the system based upon a number of criteria and then implementing and monitoring various risk mitigation controls (Figure 5.2). This is referred to as a system security life cycle approach.

FIGURE 5.2   *NIST SP 800-37 Revision 1 risk management framework*

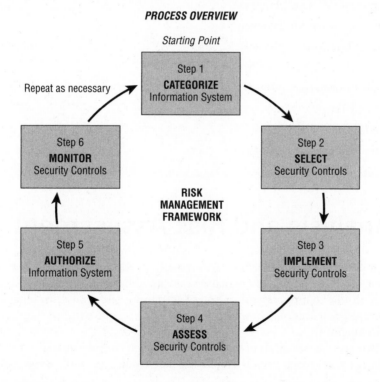

The categorization of the system can be quite extensive, requiring the determination of the system architecture.

System Architecture This may include the business processes, mission, architectural type or model, and boundaries between the system and other related systems.

Input Constraints This includes all of the items that must be considered, such as laws, policy, goals and objectives, availability, costs, and other input.

NIST Special Publication 800-39

NIST Special Publication 800-39, "Managing Information Security Risk: Organization, Mission, and Information System View" is a NIST document that concerns security risk in an IT environment. It was authored by the Information Technology Laboratory (ITL) at the National Institute of Standards and Technology, which provides technical leadership to the nation's measurement and standards infrastructure. ITL should not be confused with ITIL, which is the Information Technology Infrastructure Library, a six-book series of best practices for the IT services industry. ITL provides research, guidelines, and outreach efforts in information systems security for industry, government, and academic organizations.

NIST Special Publication 800-39 contains these major topics:

- Components of Risk Management
- Multi-tiered Risk Management
- Tier 1 – Organizational View
- Tier 2 – Mission/Business Process View
- Tier 3 – Information Systems
- Trust and Trustworthiness
- Organizational Culture
- Relationship among Key Risk Concepts

This publication offers a very good starting point to understanding risk and IT security.

Risk Analysis and Risk Assessment

Risk analysis and risk assessment define various methods for understanding risk within an organization. To be effective, risk management should be a culture and process that is fully integrated throughout the organization. Determining asset value, deciding upon risk mitigation controls, and eventually monitoring and assessing the value of the controls in an everyday environment.

There are two processes that an organization uses when considering risk. A risk assessment is an analytical approach usually employing facts and costs, while a risk assessment may provide a more detailed approach utilizing a much broader scope of the information such as impact analysis and information provided by subject matter experts.

Risk Analysis

Risk analysis is the method by which we identify and analyze risk. Risk analysis is performed by identifying potential threats and vulnerabilities to arrive at a risk determination. The application of numerical analytical techniques is employed to determine asset value and thereby arrive at the cost of controls required to reduce or mitigate the overall risk associated with the asset. There are two general methodologies used to analyze risk: quantitative and qualitative.

Quantitative Risk Analysis

The quantitative risk analysis process involves accumulating various facts and figures about an asset. These facts and figures may include information such as original cost, total cost of ownership, replacement cost, or other monetary amounts. The organization then utilizes this information to determine the total cost that should be budgeted for controls that are used to reduce risk to an acceptable level. The term that describes quantitative risk analysis is *Formal Risk Modeling*. Here are some examples of establishing asset value:

Example 1   An e-commerce server produces $10,000 in revenue per hour. It requires four hours to rebuild after a 100 percent loss.

Example 2   A customer database is valued at $200,000. In the event of an attack, it will require six hours to restore the database from a backup location.

Example 3   A communications closet contains two servers, three routers, and two switches with a combined value of $16,000. In the event of a localized fire, all items may be lost.

The example figures cited here may have been determined based upon the cost to replace the items, the salaries of technical individuals, and possibly an estimated cost of lost revenue due to downtime, among other estimated costs.

The following costs or activities should be considered when values are assigned to assets:

- Cost to replace the asset if lost
- Acquisition cost, including freight and purchasing costs
- The effect or cost on other assets
- Labor costs to replace the asset
- Indirect labor costs, such as salaries, contractors
- Cost of development
- Liability costs such as the potential damage to other devices
- Liability costs such as damage to reputation
- Total value of the asset to the organization that would be lost if the asset was attacked

Quantitative Risk Analysis Formulas and Impact Analysis

Asset valuation determined by various analytical methodologies, can be used to determine the impact of the loss of an asset to the organization. There are several variables that can be used to determine the impact of a loss as a cost to the organization. It might be imagined, not every attack results in a 100 percent loss and that not every attack is successful. Therefore, when using a quantitative risk analysis amount to consider might include, for example, losing 60 percent of an asset or that a successful attack may happen only two times a year.

Exam Point

Quantitative risk analysis considers monetary facts and figures as well as other measurable quantities that may be expressed as costs to arrive at asset valuation. On the other hand, qualitative risk analysis is a subjective process usually based on a number of related aspects of the asset. In the qualitative risk analysis, the value of the asset may be simply listed as high, medium, and low.

The ultimate question we are seeking an answer to is how much we should spend on a countermeasure. The following are the calculations that will assist us in answering this question:

Single Loss Expectancy (SLE)   SLE is the cost (in dollars) that can be lost if a risk event happens. A single loss is of course a one-time loss. But, as mentioned, not every event results in a total loss. So a factor must be used in the equation to represent the amount of loss we expect. So, if

$$AV = \text{asset value in dollars}$$
$$EF = \text{exposure factor expressed as a percentage}$$

the equation would appear as follows:

$$SLE = \text{asset value (\$)} * \text{exposure factor}$$

or

$$SLE = AV * EF$$

In this equation, if an asset was worth $10,000 and we expect it to lose only half of its value with any given risk event, the equation would be as follows:

$$\$5,000 = \$10,000 * .5 \ (50\%)$$

Annualized Lost Expectancy (ALE)   The ALE is the total cost (in dollars) for all of the SLEs occurring during the year. The number of times we anticipate the risk event will happen during the year will be represented by annualized rate of occurrence (ARO). For instance, if an event happened once a year, ARO = 1; if an event happened twice a year, ARO = 2. So, the equation would appear as follows:

$$ALE = \text{single loss expectancy (\$)} * \text{annualized rate of occurrence (\%)}$$

In this equation, if the SLE is $5,000 and we expect two risk events to happen in a year, the equation would be as follows:

$$ALE = SLE * ARO$$

or

$$\$10,000 = \$5,000 * 2 \ (200\%)$$

Annualized Rate of Occurrence   The annualized rate of occurrence, or ARO, is always written as a probability from 0.0 to 1.0, where 1.0 or 100 percent represents one annual occurrence. If we expect two annual occurrences, ARO would equal 2.0, and if we expected an event to happen every two years, the ARO would equal .5.

Normally, the ARO is derived based upon historical or empirical knowledge. For instance, the frequency of hurricanes or floods in a geographic area is recorded in almanacs and government weather services. On occasion, the ARO may the derived based only on past personal experience. For instance, the hacker was able to bypass the firewall four times during the last year. This will result in ARO of 4.0.

Exposure Factor (EF)   An *exposure factor (EF)* refers to the harm or amount of loss that might be experienced by an asset during a risk event. The EF is always written as a percentage or probability and may be expressed in either of the following manners:

$$EF = 100\%$$
$$EF = 1.0$$

This would represent catastrophic or complete 100 percent loss of the asset.

$$EF = 50\%$$
$$EF = .5$$

This EF would represent a 50 percent loss of the asset.

Exam Point

It is important to know the basic asset valuation formulas.

Qualitative Risk Analysis

Qualitative risk analysis is based upon the intuition and individual knowledge of the organization's subject matter experts as opposed to the facts and figures of quantitative risk analysis. Qualitative is a subjective valuation system in which asset value is determined based on other factors rather than accounting costs. During the qualitative analysis, variables such as customer flight, cost to rebuild goodwill, estimated loss of potential revenue, bad publicity or press, and the loss of the ability of staff members to maintain productivity.

In qualitative risk analysis, dollar figures may be difficult to assign due to the subjective result. For instance, it is difficult to place an exact dollar figure on damage to goodwill. In many cases, the results of qualitative analysis are addressed in terms of high, medium, and low or on a scale from 0 to 5.

Analysis vs. Assessment

Although *analysis* and *assessment* are often used interchangeably, they do not have the same definition. You perform an analysis, and the results of the analysis enable you to make an assessment.

Analysis Information-Gathering Techniques

On many occasions, it will be the responsibility of the security practitioner to participate in the risk analysis process. Information may be gathered under different subject information categories that will be used during the analysis process.

Determine a list of assets.   Sometimes it is a major undertaking to locate hardware in racks, closets, and ceiling spaces or to identify software assets such as purchased applications, licenses, databases, proprietary information, and intellectual property stored away on servers and user workstations.

Determine potential threats to an asset.   This activity may involve both historical data and expert opinions.

Determine annual rate of occurrence.   This activity may involve log data and historical information.

Determine how much of an asset was lost based upon prior attacks.   This is attempting to determine the exposure factor based upon historical information.

This information is required for accurate calculations during risk analysis. Much of it comes from accounting data sources and historical data, while other information might be available from *subject matter experts (SMEs)* Subject matter experts such as database administrators, network managers, and administrators as well as technical staff may supply knowledge concerning the performance of an asset. Another source of data used in risk calculations may be supplied by department managers, executives, or general users based upon recollections or memory of loss occurrences.

The following techniques can be used in gathering information relevant to an asset within its operational boundary or knowledge area.

Questionnaire   Risk assessment personnel can develop questionnaires. Different types of questionnaires can return relevant information. For instance, a questionnaire may ask for identification of all hardware and software items within a department. A separate questionnaire may ask the number of times an asset was unavailable for service. To avoid confusion, a clear nomenclature should be established describing the asset by name or inventory asset number. It is suggested that questionnaires be used during both onsite and in-person visits.

Onsite Interviews   Onsite interviews might be deemed much more effective than attempting to retrieve questionnaires that were previously sent to individuals. It may, in fact, be easier and faster to discuss information in person to be included on a questionnaire.

Onsite interviews often allow the interviewer to observe the asset and determine operation and asset security.

Document Review   During a document review, all things pertinent to an asset are examined, including system documentation, directives, policies, user guides, and an acquisition document. Security-related documentation such as spot reports, risk assessment reports, system test results, system security plans, and system security policies might be examined. Important documents also include prior impact analyses or asset criticality assessments.

Scanning Tools   A wide variety of scanning tools are available that scanned for potential vulnerabilities on both networks and host devices. Scans may be both active and passive. Active scans are scams that are initiated for a particular purpose such as identifying weak passwords, open ports, or vulnerabilities in applications. Passive scans may be performed continuously as actions occur on a regular basis. For example, passive scans may review individual passwords as they are created by users on a daily basis.

Risk Assessments

Risk assessments are the primary method used during effective risk management to implement risk reduction strategies. Because risk management is a continuous process throughout the *System Development Lifecycle (SDLC)*, it is a process that can be used to identify, assess, and classify threats against the asset and determine the optimal mitigation technique or control to reduce risk. During this process, many operating parameters may be monitored and adjusted with the appropriate reports generated to facilitate management decision making.

Risk assessments build on risk analysis and incorporate the identification of specific risks, the likelihood of occurrence, the impact, and recommendations for controls. Even in small organizations, risk analysis and risk assessments require a substantial commitment of funds, personnel, and time. As might be expected, large organizations require teams to continuously perform risk assessments. In any organization, cost, time, and ease of use are primary concerns. Therefore, a proven framework may be adopted to provide efficient risk assessments.

NIST Special Publication 800-30 Revision 1, "Guide for Conducting Risk Assessments," offers guidance for conducting risk assessments of federal information systems and organizations. The *NIST Special Publication 800-30 Revision 1* publication has been adopted by a large number of organizations worldwide and forms the foundation of their risk management strategy.

The Special Publication outlines the risk assessment component of risk management and provides a step-by-step process on how to prepare for risk assessments, how to conduct risk assessments, how to communicate risk assessments to key organizational personnel, and how to maintain the risk assessments over time.

In the original version of *NIST Special Publication 800-30*, which is now retired, a nine-step risk assessment process was outlined in detail. It was designed to be similar to a project plan, using typical project management concepts, and each of the nine steps included an input, a process method, and an output. Although effective and comprehensive, it proved to be very bulky and detailed when applied to hundreds of assets. There was a requirement for simplification featuring both speed and adaptability.

In the most recent version, *NIST Special Publication 800-30 Revision 1*, the risk assessment process has been distilled down to four primary steps. All of the original nine steps are still included in the process. Figure 5.3 illustrates the four basic steps in the risk assessment process and the specific tasks for conducting the assessment.

FIGURE 5.3   The four risk assessment process steps from the *NIST SP 800-37 Revision 1* risk management framework

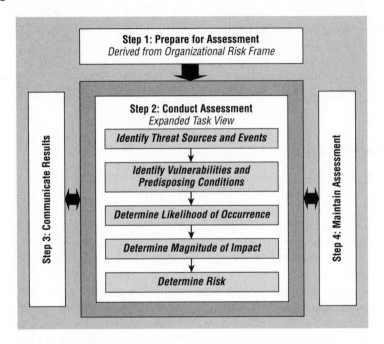

Step 1: Preparing for the Risk Assessment   The first step in the risk assessment process is to prepare for an assessment. The objective of this step is to provide a base framework of information concerning the risk goals of the organization, assessment methodologies to be used, and procedures for selecting risk factors and outlining various requirements, such as policies and regulations that impact the risk assessment. In preparation, there are five general categories of information that should be determined:

- Identify the purpose of the assessment.
- Identify the scope of the assessment.
- Identify the assumptions and constraints associated with the assessment.
- Identify the event information to be used as an input to the assessment.
- Identify the risk model and analytical approaches.

Step 2: Conducting the Risk Assessment   The second step in the risk assessment process is to conduct the assessment. The objective of this step is to come up with a list of risk information that includes resources and events and identifies vulnerabilities and the possible likelihood that a threat may exploit them. Organizations may apply their own criteria to prioritize the threats and vulnerabilities they wish to mitigate. In practice, keeping within available resources, many organizations generalize threat sources, events, and vulnerabilities only as necessary to accomplish the risk assessment objectives. Conducting risk assessments includes the following specific tasks:

- Identify threat sources that are relevant to the organization.
- Identify threat events that could be produced by those sources.
- Identify vulnerabilities within the organization that could be exploited by a threat sources.
- Determine the likelihood that an identified threat source would initiate specific threat events and the likelihood that a threat event would be successful.
- Determine the adverse impact to the organizational operations and assets as a result of the exploitation of a vulnerability by a threat.
- Determine the risk information based upon the combination of the likelihood of a threat exploitation of a vulnerability, the impact of such an exploitation of the organization, and any uncertainties associated with the risk determination.

Step 3: Communicating and Sharing Risk Assessment Information   Decision-makers across the organization require the appropriate risk-related information to guide risk decisions. The third step in the risk assessment process is to communicate the results of risk assessments with managers and other individuals. Sharing information consists of the following specific steps:

- Communicating the risk assessment results.
- Sharing detailed information developed during the execution of the risk assessment to enable to make accurate management decisions concerning risk mitigation.

Step 4: Maintaining the Assessment   In all organizations and enterprises, risk assessment, asset valuation, and threat and vulnerability identification is an ongoing process. The acquisition of new networking products, the requirements of new controls to mitigate risk, and changes to the system over time revealed by risk monitoring techniques, all contribute to changes to the overall risk landscape. The objective of this step is to keep the risk assessment current by noting and logging changes in risk knowledge as it occurs. This monitoring provides an organization with the ability to determine the effectiveness of risk controls, identify risk impacting changes, and verify that the systems and controls operate within established guidelines and baselines. In essence, the maintenance of the risk assessment verifies the compliance with the organization's risk strategy. Maintaining risk assessments includes the following specific tasks:

- Monitor risk factors identified in risk assessments on an ongoing basis.
- Update the assessment when new products or services are acquired, substantial organizational changes such as mergers and acquisitions occur, and the regulatory environment changes.

Managing Risks

As part of the overall risk management plan, organizations analyze and assess risks. During this process, assets are identified, potential threats are determined, and vulnerabilities are evaluated to determine the probability that a threat will exploit a vulnerability and therefore cause harm to the organization.

The next step in the process of managing risks is to formulate a risk treatment plan. A treatment, by definition, is a strategy by which risks are reduced by mitigating threats and reducing the likelihood that a vulnerability may be exploited. The treatment plan is a list of procedures, devices, controls, or steps that may be taken in an effort to reduce risk or minimize the impact once a threat event has taken place.

Treatment Plan

The treatment plan details how the organization plans to respond to potential risks. It outlines how risks are managed regardless of whether they are low, high, or acceptable risks and outlines preferred strategies for dealing with identified risks. Sometimes treatment plans are referred to as risk assessment plans, but in actuality, the treatment plan is the result of an assessment plan. The primary purpose of the *risk treatment plan* is to determine precisely who is responsible for the implementation of controls in what time frame and with what budget. It may also detail the response to an event or incident.

Risk Treatment

Once an organization identifies risks, it must choose from among several different strategies to deal with the risk. Risk treatment involves identifying a range of options for mitigating techniques that may be used to reduce risk. Risk treatment also refers to the overall process of prioritizing risks, evaluating various mitigation options by weighing their benefits and costs, preparing and implementing a risk reduction plan, and then monitoring the mitigation process.

The following risk response options are available for the treatment of risks:

Acceptance   When an organization acknowledges a risk and makes a conscious decision to just live with it, the organization is demonstrating *risk acceptance*. In the event of a total loss, the organization is willing to accept the cost of replacement. The decision to accept a risk may be the result of various situations or considerations:

   Cost   The cost of a control can outweigh the damage if a threat situation is realized.

   Limited Damage   Very little damage might occur if a threat situation is realized.

Residual Risk   *Residual risk* is risk remaining after a control has been put in place. For instance, an insurance policy may cover 100 percent loss of a $100,000 house and have a $2,000 deductible clause. In the event of a total loss, the residual risk would be $2,000.

Transference   When the responsibility for the payment of loss is placed on a third party, it is called *risk transference*. In most instances, it would involve an insurance company. Transferring a risk may also involve an outside source that handles the risk and is responsible for various activities such as investigation, litigation, asset recovery, and claim processing. It's important to note that transferring risk does not mean the risk is going away. It just means that somebody other than the organization is responsible for payment. It is important to note that the ultimate responsibility still remains with the asset owner.

Reduction   *Risk reduction* or mediation is the process whereby a control is put in place to reduce risk. Risks are always present, and no risk can be reduced to zero. Therefore, only the application of various controls will effectively reduce a risk to an acceptable level. As you have seen, controls can take many forms.

The effect of risk may be addressed by reducing the possibility that a threat will exploit a vulnerability prior to the event being triggered, or it may be reduced through incident response activities that limit continuing damage after an event is triggered. Prior to an event, appropriate controls may be used to reduce the likelihood of an event being triggered. After an event, the appropriate testing taken by a damage control team or an incident response process can limit damage caused by the event.

Avoiding Risk   *Risk avoidance* is to eliminate a risk situation. For instance, if you never climbed a ladder, you would never fall off. To avoid risks, you may identify them from prior experience and analyze what steps can be taken to eliminate a risk situation. There's a fine line between risk reduction and avoiding risk. For example, if you never wanted to have an auto accident on Elm Street, you could avoid the risk by always driving down Main Street. This helps to avoid the risk of having an accident on Elm Street, but in fact the risk of an accident still exists.

Risk Treatment Schedule

The *risk treatment schedule* documents the plan for implementing preferred risk mitigation strategies for dealing with identified risks. A risk treatment schedule is an output of the risk assessment phase. Risks have been identified, and various controls have been selected to reduce risk. The risk treatment schedule is a listing of risks in order of priorities. Figure 5.4 illustrates a typical risk treatment schedule.

FIGURE 5.4 Typical risk treatment schedule

Although each risk treatment plan can be customized specifically for an organization, at a minimum the plan should include the following sections:

Risk Identification Number   For example, identified risks can be sequentially numbered in a hierarchy format such as 1.0, 2.0, and 3.0 as the main risks, with 1.1 as a sub-risk and 1.1.1 as an underlying risk under this risk.

Name of Risk   Risks are listed in order of priority.

Risk Treatment Technique   List techniques such as acceptance, avoidance, reduction, and transference.

Selected Control   Include a list of controls selected to reduce the risk.

Risk Rating after Treatment   Use high, medium, and low or a 1-to-10 risk rating scale.

Cost Benefit Analysis   This is an optional analysis of the cost benefit of the control that mitigates risk.

Person Responsible for Implementation of the Control   Usually listed by department and role.

Timetable for Implementation   This is a date when the control will be fully operational.

Control Monitoring Method   This is a description of how to monitor the control after it is in place. Baselines and standards to be used should be specified.

Incident Response   A brief description of the intended response to an incident. This field may also refer to an incident response plan document.

Although the risk treatment schedule takes the form of a spreadsheet template, many of the fields are brief descriptions. The risk treatment plan should include full documentation supporting the identification of a risk during a risk assessment activity, an impact analysis, a control selection criteria, control baselines and standards, and an incident response document.

Risk Register

A *risk register* is a primary document used to maintain a record of risks. It is a direct output of the risk assessment process. A risk register includes a detailed description of each risk that is listed. Although the risk register may appear to overlap the risk treatment schedule, the two documents serve different purposes. The risk treatment plan should include complete documentation concerning the identification of threats and asset vulnerabilities. It also prioritizes risks so they can be addressed with available resources. The risk register might include the following fields or columns:

- Risk Identification Number
- Name of Risk
- Name or Title of Team Member Responsible for the Risk
- Initial Date Reported
- Last Updated
- Impact Rating
- Impact Description
- Probability of Occurrence
- Timeline for Mitigation
- Completed Actions
- Future Actions
- Risk Status

 Real World Scenario

Ignoring Risk

Many of us have seen or heard of companies that are managed by 110 percent positive, bottom-line, results-driven, can-do attitude, get-it-done type individuals with sometimes more drive and ambition than common sense. In some industries, and specifically high-dollar-sales organizations, this attitude may be quite normal, but it can lead executives and managers into risk-prone behaviors. They try to emphasize positive thinking by

Continues

Continued

ignoring the possible unfortunate consequences of the possibility of risks. They will be quick to tell you that anything can be overcome if you think positive and work hard. This attitude can lead to a belief that acknowledging a risk or a flaw exhibits weakness.

Unfortunately, the outcome of this activity is that when the threat occurs, they have no controls in place to reduce their exposure to risk. You cannot cure a devastating disease simply by willing it away or ignoring it. Statements such as "We never expected that," "Wow, didn't see that coming," "Now that's a surprise," and "It was just a matter of time" indicate attitudes of individuals or companies that did not conduct a risk assessment, took no preventative actions, and had no mitigation controls or responses prepared when the event occurred.

Procrastination, another method of ignoring risk, may manifest itself with a statement such as "We're too busy right now to be concerned with the risks" or a hasty reply such as "That's not a problem." In some instances, procrastination is evident when time and attention is given to everything but an important risk matter.

Another method of ignoring risk is simply to rename it or place it into a different category. For instance, in recent years, the news media has reported on conflicts that have happened around the globe. The perspective of combatants may be altered by renaming them. One person's "freedom fighters" may be another person's "terrorists." By renaming a risk, we are allowing it to be viewed in a completely different light. Ignoring risk is not a proper risk treatment method. Individuals, companies, and nations that ignore risks do so at their own peril.

Exam Point

Understand the four risk response options: accept, transfer, reduce, and avoid.

Other types of risk treatments exist that do not fall into the preceding categories. It is nearly impossible to predict all possible risks. In this case, the organization may acknowledge that other risks exist. If an unknown risk event is triggered and identified, it may be placed into an existing general response category. This type of response is called *control and investigation*. The damage is controlled by a general preplanned process, and then an investigation is launched as to the source of the threat, the scope of the attack, and the amount of damage caused.

For example, a *network intrusion prevention system (IPS)* could be attacked through an exploit of a previously unknown flaw in its operating system. This type of attack is called the zero-day attack because it is previously unknown to the manufacturer, and therefore no patches or mitigation techniques are known. The zero-day attack can exploit a vulnerability, allowing an attacker to place a Trojan on the network. The Trojan can enable its malware component to open a back door to a database application. Although the organization may not have listed this device as a possible risk in its risk register, it still may have taken action. The attack might immediately have been classified as an Internet intrusion, and an incident response team might immediately be called in to control any damage. After an event, an investigation should be undertaken to identify the specific attack.

Risk Visibility and Reporting

Most organizations today have an insufficient understanding of risk and an inability to identify and prevent risks. Many managers have insufficient knowledge of the potential of threats and vulnerabilities within the organization, let alone have the resources or a plan to address the risk event once it happens.

Organizations with limited risk visibility are continuously in a reactive state. Most organizations have insufficient understanding of how risk affects daily operations. The culture of many organizational groups is engaged almost exclusively with accomplishing daily tasks, and most managers are rarely able to comprehend the big picture or gain visibility into a risk landscape. Executives and managers at all levels are not risk aware even within their own workspace. Should a risk event occur, the focus is placed on fixing problems and putting out fires rather than on risk prevention.

Enterprise Risk Management

Enterprise risk management (ERM) is a program designed to change the risk culture from reactive to proactive and accurately forecast and mitigate the risk on any key programs. For ERM to be successful, it must be undertaken at an organizational level. This means that it must become part of the overall culture of the organization in order to identify and reduce risks on a proactive basis. To accomplish this task, senior management must decide to make the risk management program more visible throughout the organization.

Without access to comprehensive risk data, an organization may find it difficult to identify its outstanding risks and their probability of occurrence, causing forecasts to be less accurate. There may also be a disconnect between the information used by employees in the field and the information used by executive decision-makers.

An introduction of an enterprise risk management program may involve any of the following:

- Employee risk awareness workshops
- Risk identification across the organization
- Use of risk dashboards
- Incident reporting and incident response reports
- Implementation of an executive risk board or advisory committee
- Continuous monitoring of operational systems

An organization-wide ERM monitors the entire risk surface of an organization, which may include the monitoring of regulatory compliance, financial activities, and the physical attributes of the facilities as well as IT network risks. The ERM program is intended to raise the awareness of risks to the organization and enhance the reaction time to either mitigate the risk, thereby reducing the exposure, or react to the risk minimizing damage.

Continuous Monitoring

Managing the risk landscape involves many more actions than just identifying risks, establishing controls, and responding to problems. It involves a *continuous monitoring* requirement for the effective communication of the status of system internal controls, where threat events may be discovered immediately or as soon as possible after the incursion. Rapid identification of problems or weaknesses and quick response actions help to reduce the cost of possible risk events.

An ideal situation would be to continuously manage risk through real-time metrics. To perform this type of monitoring program, performance baselines must be established for all controls being monitored. These controls should trigger an alert in the event of state changes or even activities outside of normal operating parameters. The baselines must be monitored due to inevitable changes over time.

Passive Monitoring   *Passive monitoring* is characterized by capturing traffic crossing a network or device, usually from a span port or mirror port on a switch or router directly or off the network using a network tap. Typically, the information is in the form of network traffic or packets and is recorded in log files for future review. Although the data is collected in real-time directly off the network, it is reviewed offline at a later time.

The amount of data captured during passive monitoring can be substantial. Various software tools may be used on the data to search for anomalies. During the log review, various anomalies or activities are noted, requiring some procedure to be followed.

During passive monitoring, logs are accumulated through various machines manually or routed to a monitoring console. The serious deficiency with passive monitoring in many organizations is that logs may not be examined on a timely basis. The passive monitoring activity is extremely helpful in device troubleshooting.

Active Monitoring   *Active monitoring* is an approach in which special packets are introduced to the network in an effort to measure server and other device performance. It is ideal for the emulation of various scenarios and testing *Quality of Service (QoS)*. System administrators utilize active monitoring to test the speed, accuracy, and statistical qualities of the overall network and various devices. On many occasions, these tests are required to meet various contractual compliance standards. Active monitoring is a test mechanism usually triggered by a system administrator or other individual in an effort to test a device for the entire network.

Real-Time Monitoring   *Real-time monitoring* may also be referred to as automated monitoring. Various items such as network intrusion prevention systems (NIPSs) and other devices continuously monitor intrusions based upon a variety of signatures, behavioral characteristics, or heuristics. When intrusion is detected, the device immediately alerts the operator of an event. If the event is determined to be an intrusion, it then becomes labeled as an incident.

Depending upon established procedures and protocol for a designated type of intrusion, the Computer Emergency Response Team (CERT) may be required to perform necessary activities. The difference between real-time monitoring and active monitoring is that real-time monitoring is continuously listening to the traffic on the network and automatically sending alerts based upon some criteria.

Even with real-time monitoring, human response may not be sufficient. Various devices such as a network intrusion prevention systems may discover an intrusion and immediately trigger an action, such as modifying a firewall rule that closes a port or blocks an IP address. This automatic response would be much more timely and efficient than a human response.

Security Information and Event Management (SIEM)   *Security Information and Event Management (SIEM)* software products are combined with hardware monitoring devices to provide real-time analysis of security alerts. In many cases, SIEM devices are sold as hardware units that monitor the network and devices on the network while aggregating data from all the various logs. Once the data is accumulated, the device correlates it. Through automated analysis, the data is turned into useful information.

If an anomaly is located, operators are alerted based upon the severity of the intrusion. For instance, operators may be notified to mediate issues by special screens that appear on their consoles. These devices may also be configured to alert administrators by telephone or pager. Less severe intrusions for anomalies can be displayed on dashboards or in various reports.

Exam Point

Security Information and Event Management (SIEM) software products are combined with hardware monitoring devices to provide real-time analysis of security alerts.

Security Operations Center

Many organizations employ an in-house or a third-party *security operations center (SOC)* to monitor the physical perimeter, *CCTV* cameras, and facility access (Figure 5.5). An *information security operations center (ISOC)* primarily monitors the organization's applications, databases, websites, servers, and networks. The ISOC provides real-time situational awareness and is a primary center for network defense.

Many security practitioners are initially employed in an ISOC that provides an excellent opportunity to learn about the network and the business of the organization. The ISOC staff includes security engineers, system administrators, and other IT personnel and network professionals that have certifications such as the (ISC)[2] Certified Information System Security Professional (CISSP).

Real-time security operations are sometimes outsourced by service providers that provide managed services to monitor the client's network on a 24/7 basis. This is ideal for both the small to medium-sized organizations as well as organizations that have numerous branch offices or facilities.

FIGURE 5.5   A typical security operations center

Threat Intelligence

Time is of the essence in the world of cybersecurity. On the other end of the spectrum, organizational resources such as personnel, money, hardware infrastructure, and necessary skill sets are scarce. Threat intelligence is a method by which the organization has up-to-the-minute information concerning zero-day attacks, threat profiles, malware signatures, and other vital pieces of information required to protect the organization's resources.

The sharing of cyber threat information and threat intelligence has been strained at best. It does make sense, however, that if one company is attacked, other companies might want to know so that they can protect their own assets. The problem has been with current laws. The sharing of information between companies in the same industry may appear to be in violation of *Security and Exchange Commission* regulations. Many are concerned that sharing specific threat intelligence with the government may violate privacy laws and regulations.

Various laws proposed in the U.S. Congress have failed on a number of counts. Unfortunately, although logic dictates the wisdom of sharing information, the business sector's fear of sharing information with the government is based on distrust due to the possible opening of a door that would allow the government to use data that is acquired in a surveillance program. While generally private-sector organizations agree that attack information should be readily shared, the disagreement is with proprietary data such as customer lists and personally identifiable information.

A way around the current legal hurdles and legislation or lack thereof is by using a shared central proprietary attack database. Appliances are currently on the market that identify zero-day attacks or other anomalies and immediately upload the data to a proprietary database. Other appliances from the same company can access the database and immediately protect their user networks from the identified attack. Using this technique, only the intrusion data is shared while the end users remain anonymous. This may become an extremely viable method for participating organizations to share attack information as soon as it's available.

Analyzing Monitoring Results

The performance and availability of networks are constantly under threat from both internal and external sources. The security practitioner requires an understanding of monitoring techniques as well as how to interpret the results gathered during the monitoring process. Network devices are sometimes widely dispersed throughout an organization. This may also include offsite networks and remote offices.

Network monitoring involves two general categories of information:

Network Device Status   Network administrators require increased visibility into the network infrastructure to help identify potential failures in critical services and applications that may be caused by number of reasons. When troubleshooting network equipment, it is important to seek the root cause of the problem. For instance, a server may be offline and unavailable, but a network monitoring tool indicates that the cause is actually a faulty router. This type of analysis will indicate that the server was not the problem, the router was.

Device Management Protocols   Network devices communicate their status using *Simple Network Management Protocol (SNMP)* v1, v2c, or v3 or *Internet Control Message Protocol (ICMP)*. The two protocols access network devices utilizing special packets. For instance, using ICMP, the security practitioner can send a ping message to a device to determine if it is working. If the device is working, it will return the ping. ICMP is a simple method to determine the status of a network device.

SMNP Protocol   For a more detailed view of the network device, SNMP is usually employed. Many networks have hundreds or thousands of network devices, including hosts, servers, switches, and routers. This protocol poses a query to the SNMP-enabled device asking for the status of the function queried. Using the Simple Network Management Protocol, a network administrator may monitor network usage and performance, user access, and detect potential or existing network faults. SNMP is currently built into a large number of network products by manufactures and thereby can be used on a very large number of devices throughout the network environment.

SNMP makes use of information contained in a management information base (MIB). The MIB is a collection of information stored in a database of network devices such as routers, switches, and servers and can be accessed using SNMP. The managed object can represent a characteristic of the device being managed. SNMP includes the following components:

SNMP   Simple Network Management Protocol (SNMP) is an application-layer protocol. It is one of the widely accepted protocols for managing and monitoring network elements. Most of the professional-grade network elements come with a bundled SNMP agent.

Managed Device   A managed device is a part of the network that requires some form of monitoring and management, such as, for example, routers, switches, servers, workstations, printers, UPSs, and other devices.

SNMP Manager   A manager or management system is a separate entity that is responsible for communicating with the *SNMP agent* implemented network devices. This is typically a computer that is used to run one or more network management systems.

SNMP Agent   The agent is a program that is packaged within the network device. Enabling the agent allows it to collect the management information database from the device locally and makes it available to the *SNMP manager* when it is queried.

Management Information Database (MIB)   The SNMP agent on each device may be specifically configured to obtain and store various device parameters. This information is stored in a database called a *management information base (MIB)*. When queried by the SNMP manager, the SNMP agent on the device responds with the information contained in the management information base. The SNMP manager adds this information to the *network management system (NMS)*.

Security Analytics, Metrics, and Trends

As a security practitioner, you will undoubtedly be involved with monitoring the security aspects of networks and network-connected devices. This is different than the device monitoring discussed earlier. Device monitoring is a method of gauging the health of a device and the health of the network. During security device monitoring, various alerts will be generated based upon established templates or parameters of a network device.

There's a wide range of log files that track various events on the network. Servers and devices record a wide range of items in logs sometimes called *syslogs*. In practice, syslogs are used to gather information, usually in a database that may contain data aggregated from many different types of systems. The messages maintained in a syslog can be customized through templates to indicate facility level, location, type of activity, and the severity of the alert (such as emergency, critical, or error warning). The type of message the program is logging is indicated by the facility level. Various applications across the organization may have different facility level codes. Of importance to the security practitioner will be the levels of message severity. There are eight severity levels:

Code 0 Emergency   This is the highest alert, possibly affecting major sections of the network or applications.

Code 1 Alert   This indicates a major problem, such as the loss of a central application or communication method.

Code 2 Critical   This represents the loss of a backup or secondary device.

Code 3 Error   When detected, this means that the failure of an application or system was not critical in nature.

Code 4 Warning   Warnings are usually set to indicate that a threshold is near. For instance, server utilization is at 90 percent.

Code 5 Notice   These messages indicate potential problems that should be investigated.

Code 6 Information   These are status messages and no action is usually required.

Code 7 Debug   Debug messages are utilized by developers and programmers.

Event Data Analysis

Event data analysis is the process of taking raw data from numerous sources, assimilating and processing it, and presenting the result in a way that can be easily interpreted and acted upon. While the science of mathematical data analysis is quite extensive, the security practitioner should understand the sources of the data and what the data represents.

For many years, dashboards have been used to represent the correlation of data from numerous sources. At a glance, practitioners, analysts, administrators, and executives have been able to absorb large amounts of data when represented as a digital numerical display, dial with a pointer needle, bar chart, pie chart, or some other visual display technique. Microsoft products, such as Microsoft Excel, offer excellent capability to display graphs and dashboards of complex data. Excel tools such as those for formatting content, conditional formatting, pivot tables, and advanced data filtering have been used in IT data analysis.

Many vendors offer specialized tools that can be used to filter log files, memory dumps, packet captures, and other sources of raw IT event data. In many cases, data templates are used or modified to select the specific event data of interest. For example, log data or packet captures can be analyzed to identify the IP source of specific traffic. Large amounts of data over a period of time can be quickly analyzed to determine various factors such as frequency, length of visit, actions taken or data accessed, and other valuable information that can be used during investigation.

Visualization

Visualization is a technique of representing complex data in a visual form rather than a tabular form such as a list. Even simple network diagrams can be extremely complex and hard to understand. Visualization takes advantage of the human brain's capability of learning and processing complex information based upon visual input. It has been proven that the brain will notice intricacies and details all at once. This allows us to analyze and absorb vast quantities of abstract information at the same time. Prior to graphic visualization, flow charts, graphs, diagrams, and other techniques were used to depict the relationship between items on a network. As networks became much more advanced and complex, paper-based graphing techniques became inefficient.

Information visualization and IT network design is an emerging field of information communication. Data analysis is indispensable when diagnosing problems facing large data communication networks. By viewing the entire network as a spatial diagram of connected nodes and network devices, the analyst can easily visualize large amounts of information and apply reason and insight rather than analytical skills in deciphering information. Many vendors supply visualization software that will map entire networks and allow the user to zoom out or zoom in to comprehend the amount of information they desire. Future iterations of visualization software will be able to display problems and recommend solutions graphically.

In the past, IT network information has been represented by various methods, including nodes illustrated as hanging off of a central bus, host workstations and servers as circles network designs, tree diagrams for Ethernet networks, and clouds representing the Internet or other mass communication technology. Figure 5.6 represents a data visualization of a large network. Major work centers are represented by the larger circles. Work groups of satellite offices are represented by smaller circles in groups, and finally individual nodes are represented by single circles.

FIGURE 5.6   Data visualization

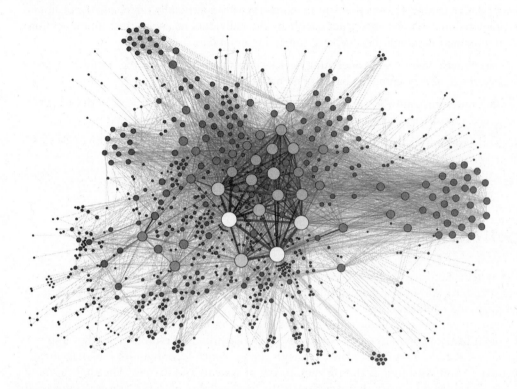

Communicating Findings

The results of data analysis van be communicated using a number of methods. The decision as to the medium or media to be used to convey the information is directly related to the speed of the communication. For example, displaying data on a computer screen is much faster than printing out a pile of paper. Also, utilizing a dashboard to quickly visualize data is much faster than analyzing a spreadsheet with columns of information.

Various roles within the organization require data to make informed decisions. Each of these roles generally requires the data in which they are specifically interested. Data should be presented in a manner that is actionable by the individual receiving the communication. The following roles might be receiving and acting upon data:

Security Practitioner   Data concerning device error situations, misconfigurations, tasks to be performed, and assignments based upon network conditions

Database Administrator/Server Administrator   Data concerning software or device performance, intrusions, penetrations, error conditions, and malfunctions

Network Administrators   Performance reports, reliability, traffic flow, quality of service, security situations

Executives   Operational summaries, executive reports, compliance reports

Summary

The Systems Security Certified Practitioner must be familiar with the organization's policies, standards, procedures, and guidelines to ensure adequate information availability, integrity, and confidentiality.

Security administration includes the roles and responsibilities of many persons within the organization who must carry out various tasks according to established policy and directives. Practitioners may be involved with change control, configuration management, security awareness training, and the monitoring of systems and devices. The application of generally accepted industry best practices is the responsibility of the IT administrators and security practitioners. Key administration duties may include configuration, logging, monitoring, upgrading, and updating products as well as providing end-user support.

In this chapter, the importance of policies within an organization was stressed. Without policies and the resulting procedures and guidelines, there would be a complete lack of corporate governance with respect to IT security. Security policies are the foundation upon which the organization can rely for guidance. These policies also include the concept of continuity of operations. Continuity of operations includes all actions required to continue operations after a disaster event occurrence. An associated policy of disaster preparedness and a disaster recovery policy provide the steps that are required to restore operations to a point prior to the disaster.

The configuration and management of various systems and network products may be the responsibility of the security practitioner. Various concepts of patching and upgrading systems were discussed in this chapter. Version numbering is the methodology used to identify various versions of software, firmware, and hardware, while release management includes the responsibilities involved in the distribution of software changes, upgrades, or patches throughout the organization.

This chapter covered data classification policies with regard to the responsibilities of the security practitioner. The practitioner can be involved in both the classification process and the declassification process for data management policies.

Security education and awareness training was also discussed in this chapter. The security practitioner may be involved in conducting or facilitating security awareness training courses or sessions. During the sessions, topics such as malware introduction, social media, passwords, and the implications of loss devices can be covered. Different groups of individuals will require training.

Business continuity and disaster recovery plans are important programs to initiate within an organization. The security practitioner will be involved in originating or maintaining such plans and will definitely be involved if the plan is exercised. A business impact analysis is central to the creation of a business continuity plan. The plan should be tested using a variety of methods to ensure that individuals are aware of their responsibilities and that all of the details of the plan have been considered.

Exam Essentials

The Importance of Risk   Understand that risk is a function of the likelihood of a given threat agent exploiting a particular vulnerability, and the resulting impact of that creates an adverse event on the organization.

Information Risk Management (IRM)   IRM is the process whereby risks to IT hardware, software, and information assets are identified and reduced to an acceptable level and controls are implemented to maintain that level.

Risk Reduction   The goal of any organization is to reduce risk to an acceptable level. The process of reducing risk is referred to as mitigation (another term for reduce). Risks can never be reduced to zero.

Two Types of Assets   There are tangible assets and intangible assets.

Compensating Controls   Compensating controls address any weakness in a primary control.

Quantitative Risk Analysis and Qualitative Risk Analysis   Quantitative risk analysis is numerical or value based, usually expressed as costs in dollars. Qualitative risk analysis considers items upon which a value may not be placed.

Four Primary Methods of Treating Risks   The four methods of treating risk are acceptance, transference, reduction, and avoidance.

Risk Visibility   Risk visibility is a method organizations use to understand risks and their potential impact.

Continuous Monitoring   Continuous monitoring is the passive, active, or real-time method of acquiring data about applications, devices, or the network.

Obtaining Data from Network Devices   Two primary protocols, ICMP and SNMP, are used to communicate with network devices.

Data Visualization   Visualization is a technique where very complex data is presented in graphical form for rapid visual analysis.

Written Lab

You can find the answers in Appendix A.

1. Write a paragraph explaining the difference between quantitative analysis and qualitative analysis.

2. What is a primary difference between a threat and a vulnerability?

3. Briefly explain SLE, ALE, ARO, and EF.

4. Describe the four methods of treating risk.

Review Questions

You can find the answers in Appendix B.

1. What is a primary goal of security in an organization?
    A. Eliminate risk
    B. Mitigate the possibility of the use of malware
    C. Enforce and maintain the AIC objectives
    D. Maintain the organizations network operations

2. Which of the following provides the *best* description of risk reduction?
    A. Altering elements of the enterprise in response to a risk analysis
    B. Mitigating risk to the enterprise at any cost.
    C. Allowing a third party to assume all risk for the enterprise
    D. Paying all costs associated with risks with internal budgets

3. Which group represents the most likely source of an asset being lost through inappropriate computer use?
    A. Crackers
    B. Employees
    C. Hackers
    D. Flood

4. Which of the following statements is *not* accurate?
    A. Risk is identified and measured by performing a risk analysis.
    B. Risk is controlled through the application of safeguards and countermeasures.
    C. Risk is managed by periodically reviewing the risk and taking responsible actions based on the risk.
    D. All risks can be totally eliminated through risk management.

5. Which option *most* accurately defines a threat?
    A. Any vulnerability in an information technology system
    B. Protective controls
    C. Multilayered controls
    D. Possibility for a source to exploit a specific vulnerability

6. Which *most* accurately describes a safeguard?
    A. Potential for a source to exploit a categorized vulnerability
    B. Controls put in place to provide some amount of protection for an asset
    C. Weakness in internal controls that could be exploited by a threat or a threat agent
    D. A control designed to warn of an attack

7. Which of the following choices is the *most* accurate description of a countermeasure?

   A. Any event with the potential to harm an information system through unauthorized access

   B. Controls put in place as a result of a risk analysis

   C. The annualized rate of occurrence multiplied by the single lost exposure

   D. The company resource that could be lost due to an accident

8. Which most closely depicts the difference between qualitative and quantitative risk analysis?

   A. A quantitative risk analysis does not use the hard cost of losses; a qualitative risk analysis does.

   B. A quantitative risk analysis makes use of real numbers.

   C. A quantitative risk analysis results in subjective high, medium, or low results.

   D. A quantitative risk analysis cannot be automated.

9. Which choice is *not* a description of a control?

   A. Detective controls uncover attacks and prompt the action of preventative or corrective controls.

   B. Controls perform as the countermeasures for threats.

   C. Controls reduce the effect of an attack.

   D. Corrective controls always reduce the likelihood of a premeditated attack.

10. What is the main advantage of using a quantitative impact analysis over a qualitative impact analysis?

   A. A qualitative impact analysis identifies areas that require immediate improvement

   B. A qualitative impact analysis provides a rationale for determining the effect of security controls

   C. A quantitative impact analysis makes a cost benefit analysis simple

   D. A quantitative impact analysis provides specific measurements of attack impacts

11. Which choice is *not* a common means of gathering information when performing a risk analysis?

   A. Distributing a multi-page form

   B. Utilizing automated risk poling tools

   C. Interviewing fired employees

   D. Reviewing existing policy documents

12. Which choice is usually the most-used criteria to determine the classification of an information object?

   A. Useful life

   B. Value

    C. Age

    D. Most frequently used

13. What is the prime objective of risk management?

    A. Reduce risk to a level tolerable by the organization

    B. Reduce all risks without respect to cost to the organization

    C. Transfer all risks to external third parties

    D. Prosecute any employees that are violating published security policies

14. A business asset is *best* described by which of the following?

    A. An asset loss that could cause a financial or operational impact to the organization

    B. Controls put in place that reduce the effects of threats

    C. Competitive advantage, capability, credibility, or goodwill

    D. Personnel, compensation, and retirement programs

15. Which is *not* accurate regarding the process of a risk assessment?

    A. The possibility that a threat exists must be determined as an element of the risk assessment.

    B. The level of impact of a threat must be determined as an element of risk assessment.

    C. Arisk assessment is the last result of the risk management process.

    D. Risk assessment is the first step in the risk management process.

16. Which statement is *not* correct about safeguard selection in the risk analysis process?

    A. Total cost of ownership (TCO) needs to be included in determining the total cost of the safeguard.

    B. It is most common to consider the cost effectiveness of the safeguard.

    C. The most effective safeguard should always be implemented regardless of cost.

    D. Several criteria should be considered when determining the total cost of the safeguard.

17. Which option most accurately reflects the goals of risk mitigation?

    A. Determining the effects of a denial of service and preparing the company's response

    B. The removal of all exposure and threats to the organization

    C. Defining the acceptable level of risk and assigning the responsibility of loss or disruption to a third-party, such as an insurance carrier

    D. Defining the acceptable level of risk the organization can tolerate and reducing risk to that level

18. Of the following choices which is *not* a typical monitoring technique?

    A. Passive monitoring

    B. Active monitoring

    C. Subjective monitoring

    D. Real-time monitoring

19. Which option is *not* a risk treatment technique?

    A. Risk acceptance

    B. Ignoring risk

    C. Risk transference

    D. Risk reduction

20. Which of the following is *not* a control category?

    A. Administrative

    B. Physical

    C. Preventative

    D. Technical

Chapter

6

Domain 4: Incident Response and Recovery

SSCP EXAM OBJECTIVES COVERED IN THIS CHAPTER:

✓ Incident Handling

✓ Preparation prior to incidents

✓ Incident Discovery, and Escalation

✓ Incident Reporting and Feedback

✓ Incident Response

✓ Implementation of Countermeasures

✓ Forensic Investigations

✓ Forensics Teams

✓ Preservation of an Incident Scene

✓ Evidence Acquisition and Handling

✓ Chain of Custody of Evidence

✓ Evidence, Inspection and Analysis

✓ Interpretation and Reporting Assessment Results

✓ Develop and Support a Business Continuity Plan (BCP) and a Disaster Recovery Plan (DRP)

✓ Emergency Response Plans and Procedures

✓ Alternate Site Processing Strategies

✓ Restoration Planning

✓ Implementing Data Backup and Redundancy

✓ Business Continuity Plan (BCP) and a Disaster Recovery Plan (DRP) Testing and Drills

As a Systems Security Certified Practitioner (SSCP) you may be called upon to be a member of an incident response team and take an active part in security investigations. As an integral member of the security team you will be required to determine the difference between an event and an incident using many tools, logs, and monitoring techniques. Once an incident is identified, you may be required to take specific corrective or recovery actions, follow procedures, and record events according to incident response plans. You will need an understanding of how to handle incidents using proven methods that result in the preservation of a scene as well as careful acquisition, recording, and tracking of evidence. You will be expected to use plans and procedures that produce consistent results during an incident investigation.

As an IT team member, you may be required to perform duties in support of business continuity. A thorough understanding of the business continuity plan will enable you to take the required actions assigned to you during an incident or crisis that may cause potential harm to a portion or all of the business. It will be important for you to understand the terminology and techniques that may be applied during such an event.

In the event that parts of the enterprise are physically damaged, you may be involved in recovery operations. The disaster recovery plan will illustrate concepts and how they can be used in order to mitigate damages and recover business operations during an emergency event. You'll also be required to understand the recovery process so the business operations can be restored as quickly as possible.

Event and Incident Handling Policy

The *incident response policy* is part of the overall IT security policy for the organization. It is a high-level document that generally includes all aspects of the organization and all geographic locations. With very large organizations that span globally diverse countries or that include independent operating units or divisions, a number of incident response policies might be written to address individual locations or corporate requirements. The incident response policy establishes the foundation, authorities, and concepts upon which all incident response plans can be built.

The incident response policy includes the following components:

Policy Charter A brief statement from the chief executive officer or highest executive sponsoring the policy on behalf of the organization.

Objectives of the Policy   A brief statement stating the desires of management to formulate plans, establish procedures, identify responsibilities, and take the required actions to discover and respond to incidents in a timely manner according to plan in an effort to mitigate damage to organizational assets.

Standards   A statement that the policy must adhere to laws, regulations, or standards to which the organization is subject.

Scope and Limitations   A statement concerning the breadth and depth of the policy. This may refer to the limitations of this response policy if there are separate policies for international divisions and other business units such as acquired or merged corporations, which may have their own policies.

Roles and Responsibilities   A statement defining the high-level responsibilities of executives and managers to formulate incident response plans, ensure the provisioning and assignment of individuals, and ensure that when activated the plan will be effective.

Terms and Definitions   A list of terms and definitions that enable all individuals to communicate effectively and consistently.

Adherence   A statement that details mandatory adherence to all plans, processes, and procedures created under the policy.

Penalties   A statement detailing a range of penalties that may be applied when lack of adherence to the policy occurs.

Standards

Standards are the criteria that the organization must meet or be in compliance with in order to avoid fines or other actions levied against the organization. Standards may be required to meet a contractual agreement between partner organizations. In some industries, industry standards such as the Payment Card Industry Data Security Standard (PCI DSS) are enforced to set various performance criteria and reporting standards. Federal regulatory bodies may also apply standards that must be adhered to during normal business and during times of crisis.

Standards imposed by industry organizations and regulatory agencies should be applied to an incident response policy. That may include requirements with respect to reporting the occurrence of an incident, recording aspects of handling the incident, and reporting the final outcome and incident closure.

Procedures

Procedures are lists the steps or activities that response teams should follow to perform all required duties as listed in an incident response plan. An organization may have several different incident response plans, depending on the nature of the incident.

Guidelines

Guidelines are informal lists of best practices or good practices either internal to the organization or as listed in various best practice frameworks such as an Information Technology Infrastructure Library (ITIL). A guideline may be a recommended course of action that is not included as an established procedure.

Exam Point

An incident response plan is the direct result of an incident response policy.

Creating and Maintaining an Incident Response Plan

When creating an *incident response plan*, individuals responsible should take into consideration various terms and definitions to be used throughout the organization. These terms and definitions should be integrated into the plan so that all of those involved may refer to the same terminology. Here is a list of some of these terms:

Event   An event is any occurrence of state change on a network, a system, a device, or software. The state change refers to an on/off condition, just as with a light switch. An event could be as simple as a user logging on, an application opening a specific port, the detection of certain type of packet on the network, or CPU usage reaching a set marked level. In other words, anything that happens could be listed as an event. All events as well as all activity might be logged. In some instances, events might be logged only after they reach a certain threshold.

On any network, there could be a great number of events happening all the time. Only a small fraction of these events might be classified as incidents.

Incident   An incident is an event that could cause harm to the organization. All incidents are events. In most organizations, an incident is defined as an activity that is a serious threat to or violation of the security policies, security practices, or acceptable use policies of the organization.

Clipping Level   A clipping level is a threshold of activity that, after crossed, sets off an operator alarm or alert. For instance, an intrusion detection system (IDS) may be set for a specific level of monitoring. In a denial-of-service flood, a large number of a certain type of packet will flood the network. Normally, intrusion detection system may be set to ignore this type of packet, but once the flood of these packets eclipses the threshold of the clipping level, the operator is alerted or other action is taken.

Alert, Warning, Alarm   An alert, warning, or alarm is a method of gaining the operator's attention. In many contexts, an alert is an email message to the operator stating that some noticeable activity has occurred. Warnings and alarms may appear on the operator's console in the form of banners, sounds, or other techniques to gain the operator's immediate attention.

Baseline   A baseline is an established criteria for measuring normal events as well as normal activity and traffic on the network. Baselines may be established for various network locations, network devices, as well as server performance on the network. They can be utilized for detecting events that are outside normally, established criteria.

Tuning   *Tuning* is the act of adjusting a device such as an intrusion detection system or intrusion prevention system to detect events, intrusions, and other anomalies that have exceeded the clipping level set for the device.

Exam Point

An event is any occurrence on a network, device, or system. An incident is any event that has the potential of doing harm to the organization. All incidents are events. Not all events are incidents.

The incident response plan will detail the activities that should take place once an incident is detected. Some organizations may refer to the activities as an incident response cycle. The following phases are involved in a normal incident response plan:

Prevent and Protect   Of course, all organizations, as good practice, should perform risk assessments and, based upon the identified threats and vulnerabilities, take the necessary steps to mitigate any threats to the network. As a matter of ongoing operations, the network should be regularly monitored and all events should be logged appropriately. The prevent and protect cycle should be ongoing for all networks.

Detect   When prevention and protection efforts are unsuccessful, an operator should be alerted to take immediate action and implement an incident response plan. This plan should include the ability to identify and contain malicious and unauthorized activity on critical networks. The detection could be automated through the use of a monitoring device, software, or hardware appliance. This automatically creates an operator alert when a set threshold has been reached or exceeded.

Detection can also be manual, such as through log analysis, operator investigation, or observation. Operators using investigation or intuitive processes determine that there is a problem on the network.

Analyze   Analysis of a suspicious event is conducted to discover whether the event is in fact an incident and whether it is malicious or unintentional and to assess its impact, scope, and severity. Events must be classified as to their cause and impact because of the vast number the events that occur on a daily basis.

A great many sources can be used when analyzing data and information. In some cases, analysis involves tracking the event through various devices on the network. *Triage* is a medical term used in the analysis of events or situations and setting priorities. By setting priorities, incident response team can address various events and incidents in an orderly fashion.

Respond   Each organization has its own response and containment procedures based upon its distinct mission and different authorities. Response should be immediate in an effort to mitigate damage and contain the intrusion. Various actions undertaken by the team should be recorded for future reference. Response to intrusion should never be delayed in an attempt to find out where the attack originates. Immediate protection of the local enterprise environment must be the primary consideration.

Activities during the response include activating response teams, notifying management and executive members, and initiating contact with law enforcement agencies. Response activities should also minimize the knowledge that an attack has happened and contain the information on a need-to-know basis. Incident response plans must have a complete media communication section identifying spokespersons and the information that may be disseminated.

Resolve   The resolution of any cyber incident involves mitigating immediate damages and taking the actions required to prohibit additional attacks from the same vector. The resolution may include determining a source of attack, if possible, and taking actions such as adding firewall rules to guard against future activities. Resolution may also involve an after action report outlining a definition of the incident, actions taken, and future mitigation techniques.

Exam Point

The five action steps of an incident response plan are prevent and protect, detect, analyze, respond, resolve.

An incident response plan should be created to address various levels of escalation of an incident. Not all incidents are created equal. Therefore, various response strategies may be implemented, depending on the triage or estimated severity of damage an incident may create. A typical table of alert levels is illustrated in Table 6.1.

TABLE 6.1 Alert levels

Level	Label	Description of Risk
4	Severe	Highly disruptive levels of consequences are occurring or imminent.
3	Substantial	Observed or eminent degradation of critical functions with a significant level of risk.
2	Elevated	Early indications of the potential of risk.
1	Guarded	Baseline of risk acceptance.
0	Normal	Normal operations.

Utilizing various levels or stages to describe an event is beneficial. For instance, different cyber incident stages may involve different personnel on a response team. Also, reporting responsibilities may depend on the stage.

Law Enforcement and Media Communication

A communication plan is a vital part of an incident response plan. During an incident or disaster event, the news media, business partners, and government agencies may require incident reports, event information, and news release or press statements concerning the event. It is very important to clearly describe in an incident response plan who within the organization is responsible to handle a press or law enforcement contact and what the correct message should be. On the other hand, through training, orientation, and policy, all personnel should be aware of how to handle any media inquiries and to whom to forward media inquiries. It is also important to include incident nondisclosure statements and all third-party vendor and contractor contracts.

Consideration should be given to the communications released to both law enforcement and the news media.

Law Enforcement Communication An incident response plan must include the notification criteria of law enforcement agencies such as local police, FBI, and Secret Service. Depending upon law enforcement jurisdictions and international laws or regulations notification requirements will differ. For example, those organizations covered by the Health Information Portability and Accountability Act (HIPAA) and regulatory bodies such as the Department of Health and Human Services must report certain information breaches that affect individuals, to the media and certain other government agencies. On the international stage, many countries have adopted information reporting requirements based on the breach of privacy through the release of personally identifiable information (PII).

A major consideration when law enforcement is involved is determining the amount or type of evidence that can be collected. In some instances, private information, personal identification information, HIPAA-restricted information, and corporate confidential information may be part of the evidence of an incident. Evidence that is collected may become public through various court procedures.

An incident response plan should clearly specify the person or persons from the organization who are authorized to contact law enforcement and under what circumstances triggers the contact. It should also state what information they can provide and what services they can request. The response plan should include all of the law enforcement agency communication contacts, including with the name of the individual and their working hours and after-hours contact information. Meetings should be held with all law enforcement contact personnel prior to any incident to gain a full understanding of the responsibilities of all parties.

Media Communication   News media organizations in the world of 24/7 news coverage can be quite competitive in obtaining information that has the potential of being sensationalized through media outlets. Depending on how high the profile of the organization is or the type of information breach, media outlets may swarm the organization for information. Incident response teams should be trained and tested on how to redirect media questions and inquiries. It is important that all individuals within an organization understand the importance of information dissemination. Clear restrictions should be placed on the release of incident or information breach information through unauthorized channels such as Twitter, Facebook, or other social media sites.

The incident response plan should also include the departments responsible for handling dissemination of specialized information such as the legal department, public-relations department, investor relations department, and marketing department. Each of these departments should be involved in an incident response plan and determine how they will handle distribution of different types of authorized information that should be released to the media, shareholders, customers, and affected individuals.

 Real World Scenario

Media Risk

A small 150-employee organization in the Midwest decided to engage a security contractor to assist them in creating a business continuity and disaster recovery plan, which they were contractually required to provide to a government agency. The company had been founded by a person who knew how to provide the service but did not pay much attention to information security. The company was a processor of Medicare information for a Veterans Administration program servicing veterans.

Upon initial investigation the security contractor observed that data was not encrypted on any storage device, clerical staff members left stacks of papers with personally identifiable information on their desk when they went to lunch, and almost everybody had direct access to the entire veterans database. When brought to the attention of the owner of the business, the initial response was that it was under consideration to secure the databases and that to change internal operating procedures would take time and money. The security contractor calmly responded, "Since your company deals with both Medicare and veterans' personally identifiable information, in the event of a breach, just imagine your parking lot filled with large television vans with huge satellite antennas. Do you have your speech prepared for the evening national network news shows?" A plan was put in place very quickly.

Exam Point

It is important to identify the persons responsible for releasing information to both law enforcement and the public media.

Building in Incident Response Team

An *incident response team* is the core of the incident response plan. The members involved in an incident response team may vary depending upon the structure of the organization or the nature of the incidents encountered The proper structure of an incident response team includes representatives of the IT department, the human resources department, legal services, public relations, executive management, accounting/auditing, and the physical security department. A good incident response team consists of named individuals, and their alternates, who participate in training and exercises to adequately perform their duties during an incident. Ad hoc or "only person available" team membership should be avoided, but if that's the normal response action for a department, each person that might respond should receive incident response training. Secondary or supporting team members should also be identified, such as network administrators, database administrators, and technical experts.

An incident response plan should also identify third-party forensic companies that may be engaged depending upon the severity level of the incident.

Accusations during an Investigation

Due to severe legal implications, all incident response team members must be trained to not make any accusations, whether direct or inferred, against any individual during an incident or investigation. As part of the incident response plan, the human resources department should be immediately involved if an employee, contractor, or third party is suspected in an incident. The human resources department will consult corporate policy when taking action involving an individual and will act accordingly.

Incident response teams may be constructed both on needs and geographic requirements. Here are some of the different types of teams:

Full-Time Response Team   This type of incident response team features full-time members who respond to incidents on a daily basis. Very large corporations, financial institutions, banks, and other organizations require full-time response teams based on the frequency of incidents.

Functional Response Team   Functional response team members report to other managers and departments throughout the organization and become members of incident response teams when they are required. A typical structure for an incident response team involved members from the HR department, legal, information security, IT, and other departments make up an incident response team.

Outsourced Response Team   Many organizations contract out network and system monitoring as well as the response to intrusions. Managed service contracts that involve handling incidents and providing incident response or offered by large organizations such as Hewlett-Packard, Dell and IBM. In many cases, the contract will also involve some local individuals within the company to assist the third-party response team. A hybrid incident response team is the combination of an external team and an internal team.

Search and Seizure during an Incident Investigation

The Supreme Court of Ohio in December 2009 ruled that the U.S. Constitution's Fourth Amendment prohibition against unreasonable searches and seizures requires police to obtain a warrant to search a cell phone. The decision generated considerable comment across the country because it was the first such ruling from a state supreme court. Since that time, lower courts around the country have reached different conclusions in cases involving police searches of cell phones and personal digital devices belonging to suspects. The U.S. Supreme Court has assumed, without deciding, that citizens have a reasonable expectation of privacy in their cell phone text messages.

When designing an incident response plan, it is important to consider the legal implications, within the local legal jurisdiction, of obtaining evidence or information from personally own devices through search and seizure. Plan designers should obtain legal opinions as well as possibly including the topics of search and seizure of personal devices on corporate property in acceptable use policies. All response team members should receive training concerning the seriousness of search and seizure activities during an investigation.

Incident Response Records

Incident response plans should be the requirement that the incident response team should be required to make incident response plans and keep activity records starting at the beginning of the incident and continuing through resolution. Team responders should record all actions and activities, either during the process or immediately thereafter, to completely document all actions taken during the event. The collection and documentation of all evidence, description of the scene, statements from individuals, and evidence processing notes must be filed and maintained in the event of a formal forensics examination or eventual legal action. Team responders should record all actions and activities, either during the process or immediately thereafter, to adequately document all actions taken. In the event of a forensic examination or eventual legal action, the collection and documentation of all evidence, description of the scene, statements from individuals, and evidence processing notes must be filed and maintained.

Many incident response teams regularly review after-action reports to identify areas of improvement.

A wide range of incident report templates are available on the Internet. At a minimum, the following incident response information should be recorded:

- Date and time of incident
- Type of incident or incident level
- Incident summary
- Incident discovery information
- Actions taken by individuals
- Contact information for individuals involved
- After-action report

Security Event Information

All digital records associated with an event that leads to an incident response must be retained. Event discovery or alerts may be triggered automatically through the use of intrusion prevention systems (IPSs) or intrusion detection systems (IDSs) or a number of other software solutions or hardware appliances. Events may also be discovered through manual review of system logs or other blog information.

Security Information and Event Management (SIEM) systems are used to provide a common platform to collect historical log information as well as real-time information from monitored devices. (Note that other texts may refer to this subject as Security Event and Information Management, or SEIM.) Applications are available that provide easy searching through multiple logs for correlating event information. The output logs of both real-time and historical investigations should be stored for an appropriate retention period. Corporate policy may require that event logs be kept for an indefinite period of time. The default on some log acquisition systems is 30 to 60 days.

> **Exam point**
>
> Security Information and Event Management (SIEM) may be used to provide a common platform to collect historical log information as well as real-time information from monitored devices.

Incident Response Containment and Restoration

The incident response plan should provide the details of all actions to be taken during a specific incident. Actions might include isolating the device from the network by, for example, disconnecting the Ethernet plug or pulling the power plug from the wall to shut down the affected network equipment. Plans may differ depending upon forensic investigation requirements. For instance, a forensic investigation might include disconnecting the device from the network but keeping the unit powered up so that volatile RAM memory can be recorded or examined. A Faraday bag may be utilized to shield a device that is connected to a wireless access point. A Faraday bag is designed as a shield to prohibit a device from transmitting or receiving radio signals.

Exam Point

A Faraday bag is designed as a shield to prohibit a device from transmitting or receiving radio signals.

It is never advisable to not take action and "monitor" an attack while it is in progress. In some cases, an IT individual may attempt to trace an attack back to its origin rather than terminating the attack. Such a trace is usually fruitless as attackers have many ways of disguising their actual location. Devices such as log files, monitoring appliances, honeypots, bastion hosts, and other devices may record the IP address or vectors of an attack. If an attack is discovered and not stopped, the organization may face various legal liabilities.

Exam Point

It is important after the discovery of an attack to start incident response activities immediately to stop the spread of an attack throughout the organization. It is never advisable to "monitor" an attack while it's in progress.

Many corporate incident response policies require that a post-incident restoration action be invoked after an attack. These usually require that the attack unit be reimaged or restored from known good backups. Rarely are devices placed back into service after only one anti-malware or antivirus scan.

Exam Point

Best practice restoration of a device after an incident should include reimaging from a standard image or from a known good backup.

Implementation of Countermeasures

Countermeasures are usually put in place as a response to a risk analysis. In many cases they are intended to mitigate specific threats or vulnerabilities. Controls involve a much broader category of risk mitigation tools and may be put in place in response to best practices or due care. In many situations, the terms countermeasure and control are used interchangeably.

As an SSCP, you may be involved in implementing countermeasures throughout the organization. These countermeasures may include hardware devices such as IPSs/IDSs, antivirus software, anti-malware software, and network-based hardware appliances. Countermeasures, such as intrusion detection and prevention devices, must be adjusted or tuned correctly to be effective on a network. A false sense of security may be prompted by an ineffectively adjusted protection device. Every network protection device should have an established baseline and the performance of the device should be measured regularly against the baseline.

The application of countermeasures in a network or on a device such as a host computer does not relieve the operators or administrators from responsibility. User training is important so that controls and countermeasures are installed and operated correctly.

Exam point

An ineffective countermeasure is worse than none at all because it provides a false sense of security.

Understanding and Supporting Forensic Investigations

Thanks to many crime shows, many are familiar with the science of forensics and a forensics investigation. We all know it involves the identification and analysis of materials usually found at an incident scene. Usually at the point of acquisition, the decision as to whether it constitutes evidence has not yet been determined. The goal of forensics and the forensics examiner is to analyze material using professional assessment techniques to answer various questions for investigators.

Digital forensics involves the investigation of computer related incidents and the gathering of computer related information that may have originated during an incident or an attack. All materials collected during a digital forensic investigation are subject to the same procedural guidelines and practices so that the evidence may be presented in a legal court trial.

A number of organizations establish guidelines for use during computer forensic investigations:

Identifying Evidence   Responding individuals must begin documenting everything that they find at an incident scene. They must record the facts as they present themselves, such as the location of devices, witness statements, obvious evidence, and suspected evidence owners as well as the nature of the incident. It also involves identifying the potential harm to the organization.

Collecting or Acquiring Evidence   Adhering to proper evidence collection and documentation techniques while minimizing incident scene contamination is vitally important. A chain of custody must be provided whereby every transition of possession is completely documented. It is important to preserve the accuracy and integrity of evidence through proper collection techniques at an incident scene. The chain of custody must be preserved from the moment the material is collected.

Examining or Analyzing the Evidence   The evidence is investigated and analyzed using sound scientific tests and methods which are acceptable both in the forensic community as well as in the court of law. The use of proven investigation tools to determine character and ownership of the evidence is required and may be required to be replicated by other forensics examiners.

Presentation of Evidence and Findings   Forensics examiners must present their evidence, findings, and professional opinions in documentation such as court presentations and legal briefs. Quite often, forensics examiners are required to testify as expert witnesses.

Incident Scene

In general practice, it's advisable to refer to the physical location of an incident as an incident scene rather than a crime scene. This avoids a rush to judgment as well as possibly unfounded or inaccurate accusations of individuals at the location.

In the case of the cyber incident, the incident scene is located in two environments:

Physical Environment   The physical environment is of course the actual location of the hardware involved. This may include simply the user workstation, a server in a rack, or even an entire network domain. In some cases the physical environment may be quite small, such as a cell phone, pad, or individual laptop.

Digital Environment   The incident scene in a digital environment may be much more complex and require greater expertise to acquire materials and evidence. Some evidence may be retained in volatile RAM or on an attached hard disk drive, other evidence concerning the same incident may be stored on servers, network-attached storage, storage area networks, and even cloud-based storage. With each of these remote locations, increasingly sophisticated techniques may be required to acquire the evidence.

First responders to digital incident must be trained on how to preserve a digital incident scene. If evidence is contaminated, changed, or altered it is no longer any use during the investigation. During an attack or other incident, users should be educated to step away from their host machines workstations or other digital equipment to allow the incident response team and forensics examiners to gather material and data.

It is a well-known fact in forensic science that just observing evidence changes it. For instance, let's say that you want to check a file to see when it was last accessed. By doing this, you put the current date on that file.

Volatility of Evidence

The *volatility of evidence* determines the priority that evidence must be collected. The volatility is determined by the life expectancy of evidence once power is withdrawn. As might be expected, evidence resident in RAM will be deleted or eliminated once power is withdrawn.

The following list includes evidence from the most volatile to the least volatile:

- CPU, cache, and register contents
- Routing tables, ARP cache, process tables, kernel statistics
- Random access memory (RAM)
- Temporary file system/swap space/page files
- Data on hard disk
- Network archive data/storage area networks/network attached storage
- Remote-based cloud storage
- Data contained on archival media, disk-based backup, tape-based backup, USB drives

Forensic investigators usually acquire and process data in the order of volatility. Some incident response plans call for immediate disconnection and shut down of the target host or server. This eliminates the accessibility to any volatile memory that might be stored in RAM or register type devices.

Forensic Principles

Dr. Edmund Locard was a pioneer in forensic science and formulated Locard's exchange principle, which states that the perpetrator of a crime will bring something to a crime scene and leave with something from it. This is the foundation of trace evidence, that the perpetrator may leave dirt, hair, fingerprints, smudges, oils, or other residue at a crime scene. It also holds that the trace evidence from a crime scene will leave with the perpetrator, such as carpet fibers and other minute pieces of evidence that may link the perpetrator to the location.

In digital forensics, Locard's exchange principle holds that any perpetrator of an intrusion leaves behind trace evidence within the system. This trace evidence may be used to identify the attacker.

Exam point

Locard's exchange principle states that the perpetrator of a crime will bring something to a crime scene and leave with something from it.

Chain of Custody

Chain of custody refers to a forensic principle whereby each movement or transfer of data must be recorded and logged appropriately. If the chain of custody is disrupted by any means, evidence may not be presented in court. Evidence should be appropriately identified, including the circumstances under which it was collected it, including a detailed description of the material when it was collected, as well as other important information. In most cases, evidence is packed in poly bags for transport to a forensic laboratory or storage location.

The evidence documentation must include, at a minimum, the following information:

- Date and time of collection
- Description of the evidence
- Who collected the evidence
- Incident identification or summary
- Evidence discovery information
- Actions taken by individuals
- Contact information for individuals involved
- Chain of custody
- Other collection or handling information

Proper Investigation and Analysis of Evidence

Proper steps must be taken to ensure that data could not be altered. While working with a live hard disk, the forensic investigator will use a specialized write-block hard disk controller that will prevent the writing of any information on the hard drive during an investigation. Figure 6.1 illustrates an industry-standard write blocker attached to a hard drive under investigation.

FIGURE 6.1   A hard drive attached to a Tableau portable forensic write blocker

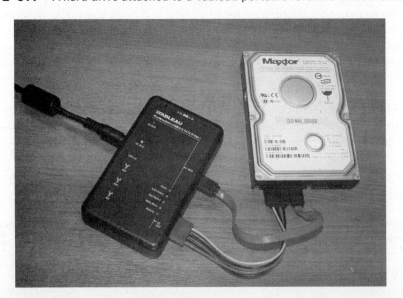

All data on a hard drive under investigation should immediately be copied using industry-standard bit copy software. Products such as EnCase, developed by Guidance Software, and Forensics Toolkit from Access Data offer a suite of tools used by digital forensic examiners to not only create a bit-for-bit copy of hard drive data but also hash the contents to ensure data integrity between the original hard drive source and the copy. The hash value will ensure that no changes have been made to the original disk image. The hash value for an image can be calculated and compared with the original hash value of the data. A data copy should always be used during an examination, while the original is stored as primary evidence.

Interpretation and Reporting Assessment Results

While the forensic examiner is performing the examination of the evidence, they will allow the character of the evidence to lead to various suppositions and potential conclusion possibilities. This is the interpretation process that the forensic expert will use to determine the importance or significance of various pieces of the evidence information. Through experience, training, and proven forensic examination techniques, the forensic examiner will interpret the data and formulate a conclusion. On occasion, the data will be insufficient to draw any conclusions.

Once the forensic examiner has examined the evidence, they will prepare a report. The examiner's report is very important as it provides information concerning the evidence, the analysis techniques, and the resulting findings to the incident investigator, the prosecutor, other attorneys and possibly the court by way of testimony. Forensic examiner reports differ in content but generally contain the following sections:

- Summary of findings
- Identity of the reporting agency
- Incident or case identifier or submission number
- Incident or case investigator
- Identity of the forensic examiner
- Identity of the submitter (if different)
- Date of receipt of evidence
- Date of report
- Descriptive list of items submitted for examination, including serial number, manufacturers, make, and model
- Identity and signature of the examiner
- Brief description of steps taken during examination, such as string searches, graphics, image searches, and recovering erased files
- Detail of findings
- Results/conclusions

It is quite common for either legal side of the court case to request to see the "examiner's notes." The forensic investigator must keep a log of every action taken and test applied during the evidence examination process.

Understanding and Supporting the Business Continuity Plan and the Disaster Recovery Plan

As a security practitioner, it is essential to understand both business continuity and disaster recovery programs for the organization. It is almost certain that you will be involved in either or both programs, either during the planning and creation phase or in the event that one or either plan must be put into action.

These plans are created with the assistance of key personnel such as department heads, executives, and subject matter experts throughout the organization. Each plan is the result of an executive-sponsored policy that directs the creation and implementation of such a plan.

The very survival of the business or enterprise rests upon the accuracy of the procedures directed in each plan. A great many businesses neglect to either formulate a plan or maintain the plan over time.

Emergency Response Plans and Procedures

Emergency response plans differ from incident response plans in that an incident response plan usually refers to a network intrusion. Emergency response is generally much broader in nature. For instance, an incident may be a network intrusion that plants malware on several host machines. An emergency is the network being down for an appreciable amount of time, affecting ongoing business operations.

There are two types of emergency response plans:

Disaster Recovery Plan   A *disaster recovery plan (DRP)* is a documented set of procedures used to recover and restore IT infrastructure, data, applications, and business communications after a disaster event. A disaster may be natural, in the form of a flood, tornado, or wildfire, or it may be man-made, in the form of a terrorist attack or willful destruction of property. Man-made disasters can be intentional or unintentional.

Business Continuity Plan   The *business continuity plan (BCP)* is a documented set of procedures used to continue business operations in some form to enable the organization to maintain its business capacity during some event. This plan may entail substituting equipment or workspaces, temporarily relocating equipment and individuals, and reducing or eliminating noncritical services for a period of time. An event for which a business continuity plan can be used might be a localized fire, power outage, weather-related event, or man-made disaster.

Business Continuity Planning

Business continuity planning is a set of procedures and prearrangements that can be put into action in the event of a disaster. The effort of the continuity plan is to maintain, as best as possible, business as usual in the face of a crisis. The business continuity plan is the result of a business continuity policy approved at the executive level. A substantial commitment of personnel and funds is required to achieve an actionable plan. Without significant corporate executive support, a business continuity plan stands little chance of success.

A number of terms are used when creating a business continuity plan. These terms are described in the following sections.

Business Impact Analysis

A *business impact analysis* is performed to determine the resulting impact to the business of the full or partial loss of an operational functional unit of the business. For instance, a manufacturing unit was shut down because of a hurricane flooding the facility. What effect would it have on the overall performance of the business? In some cases, manufacturing may be shifted to another location. If manufacturing cannot be shifted to another location, the issue becomes how long the business can survive and be a viable entity without the manufacturing unit.

The business impact analysis determines the functions of the business that are critical and functions of the business that are noncritical. Every business is unique and, depending upon the types of goods and services provided, has both essential and nonessential business functions within it. In order for a business impact analysis to be successful, all functions of a business, essential or not, must be identified. Once identified, they are categorized as to essential or nonessential activities. This categorization may be simply ranking the activities on a 1-to-5 scale with, for example, 5 being the most essential.

Maximum Tolerable Downtime

Maximum tolerable downtime (MTD) is the total amount of time the organization can be without the department or business function before irreparable harm is done to the organization. In other words, the maximum tolerable downtime is the point after which the survivability of the business is in question. In some circles, maximum tolerable downtime may also be referred to as *maximum tolerable period of disruption (MTPoD)*.

Recovery Time Objective

Recovery time objective (RTO) is a point in time when a lost or "down" business functionality has been totally restored. Each operational business function may support a different recovery time objective depending upon the function or service. Recovery time objective can be categorized in minutes, hours, days, weeks, or even months. Of course, recovery time is based on a great many factors, including labor, repair parts, new equipment delivery, and event facility repair and build-out. Naturally, the recovery time objective cannot be longer than the maximum tolerable downtime.

Recovery Point Objective

Recovery point objective (RPO) specifies a point in time to which data can be restored. The recovery point could be the last full backup plus any completed incremental or differential backups that might've taken place after the full backup. The more frequent the

backup, the less data will be lost during a business disruption event. For instance, if the organization uses a dual-write technique such as a RAID-1 mirror backup where the second drive is a cloud drive or off-premises drive, the recovery point objective could be at the point of the business disruption event.

Figure 6.2 illustrates a timeline with the business disruption event in the center (the crash event). The maximum tolerable downtime (MTD) indicates the maximum time the organization can be without the business operational unit. The recovery time objective (RTO) is the point at which full operation will be restored, and the recovery point objective (RPO) indicates the point in time at which reliable data for backup purposes is available. Notice that the vertical line represents cost. The bell-shaped graph represents a cost versus timeline. For example, the closer you move the recovery time objective to the business disruption event, the more it will cost the organization. The closer you move the recovery point objective to the business disruption event, meaning that backups are made more frequently (up to complete data mirroring), the more costly it is for the firm to create the backups.

FIGURE 6.2 A cost/timeline graph illustrating the relationship between MTD, RTO, and RPO

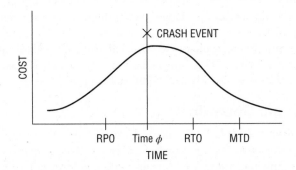

Since business units require IT processing to perform their duties, IT systems and business network capabilities must be fully operational prior to the maximum tolerable downtime (MTD) of the departments served.

Disaster Recovery Planning

After a disaster event, it is extremely important to restore IT services and functions. The restoration process may be detailed for a disaster recovery plan. The high-level disaster recovery policy is an executive-supported policy that sets forth the creation of the disaster recovery plan (DRP).

In the event of a disaster affecting IT operations, all IT personnel, including you as an SSCP, will participate in recovery efforts to restore IT services as soon as possible. As you have seen, in business continuity planning, the majority of business operations are contingent upon active and reliable IT services and functions.

The difference between a disaster recovery plan and an incident response plan is that an incident response plan details the methods and procedures used to detect and stop an imminent threat to the organization's IT assets while the disaster recovery plan is designed to rebuild, recover, and restore damaged assets to full operational capacity. Restoration operations may take a period of time and significant coordination and effort to rebuild or refurbish facilities, restore order, restore and provision hardware products, and restore data and applications from backup sources.

There are some things to consider during the creation of the disaster recovery plan. Some of these considerations are detailed in the following sections.

Identification and Ranking of Disaster Types

As with incident response planning, a disaster recovery plan begins with identifying various disaster types. Disasters may be the result of either natural causes or man-made causes. Natural disasters include hurricanes, tornadoes, mudslides, forest fires, floods, and other disasters caused by weather-related events, and man-made disasters, either intentional or unintentional, may be caused by fires, bombs, terrorist activities, civil unrest, and acts of war, just to name a few.

It is very difficult to have a large number of disaster plans with a response to each particular type of disaster. Imagine communicating to a senior executive on the phone that IT operations has experienced a disaster due to fire. The very next question might be, How big was the fire? Was it localized? Did it take down the entire IT installation and facility? And how serious was it? So as you can see, the overall effects of disasters might differ.

Many organizations find it convenient to establish a disaster classification system to describe to all individuals the severity of the disaster and the type of restoration response to expect. Figure 6.3 illustrates a typical disaster classification chart. In this example, there are only three grades of disasters—one, three, and five—which allows for other numbers or levels of classification to be substituted if required. Other columns may be added to indicate programs of plans to invoke, persons to notify, and other disaster information.

FIGURE 6.3   A typical disaster classification system

Disaster Scale	
5	Extremely severe disruption caused by a major disaster. Extensive loss of business assets.
3	Moderate localized disruption. Facility damage, localized loss of business functionality.
1	Isolated disruption. Minor loss of assets and business functionality.
P	Planning activities for impending disaster.

Disaster Preparation

On occasion, certain disasters come with a warning. For instance, depending upon the geographic location of the organization, an IT operation such as a data center may have knowledge of an impending hurricane, forest fire, or potential flood hours if not days ahead of time. In this instance, a disaster preparation plan may be invoked, where critical data is backed up to an offsite location or to a cloud service provider, which should be of significant geographic distance from the primary IT location so as not to be involved in the same disaster.

Provisions may be made to protect facilities from wind, flood, or fire, and protection must be afforded to all staff members in expectation of a disaster event. Remember, the primary concern in any disaster is the safety and preservation of human life.

Identification of Physical and Virtual Assets

The IT organization should have a complete inventory of all hardware assets and virtual assets at the physical site. This would include all network hardware, network telecommunications equipment, telephone communications equipment, user workstations, wiring diagrams, and a complete description of all configurations of network equipment such as routers, switches, firewalls, and servers. Virtual assets such as applications and data should be inventoried, and the inventory should be recorded. Naturally, in the case of disaster preparedness, all of this information should be stored and backed up to a geographically remote location.

Exam point

The primary concern in any disaster is the safety and preservation of human life.

Availability of Restoration Products, Building Components, and Labor

Various considerations must be made during the creation of a disaster recovery plan. Consideration must be given to the sources and availability of products used to restore the physical facility as well as networking electronic components required to rebuild the data center. Along with the inventory of hardware assets, a list should be created of potential sources of replacement products. The disaster recovery plan should include the methods of purchasing and paying for replacement products in the event that the accounting department and purchasing department have been displaced by the same disaster.

During significant natural disasters such as Hurricane Katrina and Hurricane Sandy, the availability of goods, supplies, building materials, and labor were at a premium. As part of their disaster planning, some large corporations keep small denomination currency and gold to use as larger to pay for goods and services during a severe emergency. In the event of a severe natural disaster, credit cards will be of little use due to a power outage or an Internet outage.

Labor and personnel must be considered in the creation of a disaster recovery plan. During a severe natural disaster, third-party labor such as contractors and a skilled labor force may either not be available or be available to the highest bidder. On the other hand, it might be anticipated that the organization's personnel may not be available either, through lack of transportation, personal disaster, and through lack of basic services.

🌐 **Real World Scenario**

Disaster Preparedness – Communication Plans

Hurricane Sandy will prove to be one of the most destructive storms to ever hit the continental United States. Dozens of states were affected during the storm, including some of the most densely populated areas in the country. It is estimated that over $65 billion in damages were inflicted by the storm over numerous states, knocking businesses, communications, and basic services completely offline for days.

As lessons are learned from recent disasters such as Hurricane Katrina, Hurricane Sandy, and other major disasters such as tornadoes that have leveled entire cities, a primary service requirement surfaces above all others during a disaster. That service is communication. For an organization's personnel, students within a university, parents and children, and the general population as a whole, the ability to communicate is vitally important both in preparation for the disaster and, especially, during the aftermath.

It is been learned that organizations and government should plan for and make use of multiple communication methods to convey messages. These include regular telephone service, cellular telephone service, citizens band and ham radio services, AM and FM broadcast radio services, television, and social media services including SMS, email, and text.

As a lessons learned from Hurricane Sandy, it is recommended that every disaster recovery plan include multiple paths of contacting individuals. Messages should be brief and to the point. All instructions must be complete, unambiguous, and relayed in such a fashion as to be completely understood. It was also determined that organizations and governments should train their individuals in the use of all communication methods and especially how to rely on social media technology that can be monitored, such as Twitter for continuous information updates and communication.

Interim or Alternate Processing Strategies

During a disaster event and recovery operation, the primary IT facility may not physically be available to carry out IT operations. In some disaster scenarios, it may be temporarily disabled, while in other, more severe scenarios, it may be totally destroyed and need to be totally rebuilt.

The disaster recovery plan must include the possibility of relocating IT operations. The different relocation options will respond directly to the recovery time objective. For instance, services may be made available for almost instant switchover, while other services may require the transportation and configuration of hardware in a remote location. Each strategy affects the variables of time to restore services and cost to restore services.

Hot Site   A *hot site* is an alternate IT processing facility that can be brought online within a very short period of time. The hot site will maintain duplicate equipment but no applications or data. The hot site will maintain duplicate equipment and duplicate sets of data. To be effective, the hot site should be significantly geographically separate from the primary site so it's not involved in the same disaster. If the hot site is not an integral function of the organization and is a third-party contractor location, in many cases it is utilized for a short period of time, measured in either hours or days, while a less costly alternate site is made ready.

Warm Site   A *warm site* is an alternate IT processing facility that has equipment installed and usually configured. The warm site does not have duplicate data installed and must be provisioned from backups. It is less costly than the hot site and still requires hours and sometimes days to bring online.

Cold Site   A *cold site* is a location that is provisioned with HVAC, power, and communications lines and can be used for complete IT restoration. A cold site does not have network hardware or communications equipment. Equipment would have to be ordered, shipped in, and installed. After installation, all data would have to be restored from backups. With testing and configuration, a cold site offers the longest recovery time, requiring in many cases weeks of preparation. But on the other hand, it is the least costly.

Contracted or Mutual Sites   A contracted or *mutual site* is made available through an arrangement with the IT department of another organization, where the other organization offers equipment and processing time under a contract or by mutual agreement. This type of an arrangement may also be between different IT departments or divisions within the same organization. In some instances, a mutual site is referred to as a multiprocessing site—one site cannot support the entire IT department, so multiple sites are used as a type of cluster. Normally this scenario is similar to a warm site, where the contracting organization offers access to IT processing capacity and data must be restored from backups to begin operation.

Cloud Sites   Cloud providers now offer a service that consists of the use of either a hot site or a warm site, depending on costs and requirements. Using the Infrastructure as a Service (IaaS) model, the cloud service provider can rapidly duplicate the client's IT service configuration and provision data from backup locations. Some organizations are making use of cloud sites for immediate switchover, while other organizations make use of a less costly service that will require a little more time to bring online.

Mobile Sites   A *mobile site* is a site usually based in 18-wheeler trailers. Under contract, this type of site may be transported to the required location. Mobile sites can be expanded by connecting trailers of equipment together. Mobile sites are usually self-contained and feature a portable generator system to power the equipment. Depending upon the contract, 18-wheeler trailers may be dedicated and outfitted with the exact equipment required to duplicate the IT operation. Transportation, availability, and available communications infrastructure should be prime considerations in using a mobile site and a disaster recovery plan.

When employing any of the types of recovery site options, the planners must consider several important factors:

- Transportation of essential personnel to the backup location
- Room and board for essential personnel at the backup location

- Commitment of essential personnel, which may be hindered by the possibility of the destruction of homes, local infrastructure, and dislocation of immediate family
- Salaries, payment for personnel living expenses, and transportation

It is important to consider cross training of personnel or duplicate personnel with alternate skill sets and the availability of contractors in the remote recovery site location.

Restoration Planning

Disaster preparedness and restoration planning is the formulation of plans that reduce the vulnerability to threats and provide a set of procedures for restoration after a disaster event. In addition to the safety and protection of human life, many other items must be taken in consideration during the creation of a disaster recovery plan:

- Power and essential communications
- Personnel in the labor force
- Essential supplies such as shelter, food, and water
- Transportation
- Building materials and construction components
- Data processing hardware and infrastructure components
- Data communications
- Backup data

Disaster preparedness planners, when creating a disaster recovery plan, should consider alternate sources for any of these requirements.

Backup and Redundancy Implementation

It is important that as a security practitioner you are familiar with all of the different types of backup and data restoration solutions. Data backup and restoration solutions are driven by two primary considerations: time and cost. As you saw with recovery time objectives (RTOs) and recovery point objectives (RPOs), fast recovery times and minimal data loss come with a price. By varying the time frame, not only is the cost affected, but the type of technology used for data backup storage may change.

Not all data needs to be backed up equally. When creating a backup program for the organization, data may be prioritized by importance or frequency of use. For instance, data required for immediate use, such as customer information or accounting data, may be considered vitally important to corporate operations. The decision might be made to prioritize this data and back it up in such a manner as to provide a very fast restoration process. Other data, such as sales transactions, database archives, or archived communications such as emails, may be backed up using a method that is far less expensive and may require a much longer time to restore.

In years past, data was backed up sequentially on magnetic tape. Many may remember the reel-to-reel tapes featured in science-fiction movies. While some of these devices still exist in mainframe computer centers, most tape backup today is performed on tape cartridges and specialized machines. It is not unusual to back up data on DVDs and hard disk arrays and to the cloud.

When removable media is involved, various backup scenarios may be used. The selection of the backup scenario is based upon several factors:

- Required time to back up all of the data
- Required time to restore all of the data
- Cost of labor in time and effort
- Cost of backup media (life of backup media)

When considering these criteria, several backup scenarios can be employed. Of course, at some point in time all of the data must be backed up, which is usually referred to as a full backup. The selection of backup techniques between full backups depend upon the criteria. Various backup techniques are described in the following sections.

Mirrored Backup

A *mirrored backup* features the immediate writing of data to two different locations. "Online data" refers to data that is backed up in the local IT facility. The second copy of the data is transmitted to a separate storage device located in a distant location so as to be separate from any natural disaster. A mirrored backup may also be cloud based.

A mirrored backup requires the use of two identical storage devices. These identical storage devices may be in physically separate locations. A mirrored backup is the most expensive type of backup/restoration system and is usually used for vital data that must be immediately available at all times. Mirrored backups are not used for archive data, applications, operating systems, or other types of data that might be backed up to magnetic or optical media.

Full Backup

A *full backup* is the contiguous copy of the entire system and data. A full backup may include the entire operating system, applications, and data associated with the system. It may also refer to a subset of data. For instance, a full backup may be created of the customer transactions database. This database may have been prioritized as being vitally important to the organization and therefore has its own backup schedule. Normally, full backups to tape or offline storage are made at least weekly.

Differential Backup

A full backup may be created once a week, then daily backups must be made of the transactions for each day. The *differential backup* records all of the transactions since the full backup. For instance, the transactions occurring on Monday will be recorded. On Tuesday, all of the transactions occurring on Tuesday will be added to the backup of all of the transactions occurring on Monday. On Wednesday, all of the Wednesday transactions will be added to the backup of all of the Monday and Tuesday transactions. So on each day, the transactions are just appended to the previous day's backup file.

The advantage is in the event of a restoration, only one file must be added to the full backup file to create a record of all transactions that have occurred. The disadvantage may be in media cost; the backup for each day requires more media because of the amount of data stored each day. Figure 6.4 illustrates the concepts of a differential backup.

FIGURE 6.4   An illustration of a differential backup

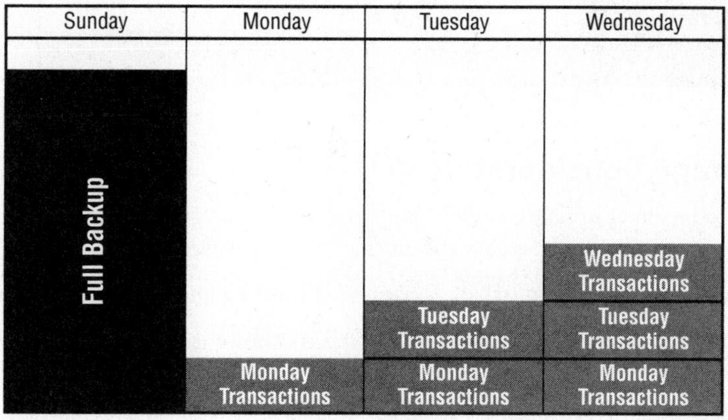

Incremental Backup

Again, assuming a full backup was created once a week, daily backups must be created for the transactions of each day. In the case of *incremental backup*, the transactions occurring on Monday are backed up into a file. Tuesday's transactions are backed up into a second file. Wednesday's transactions are backed up into a third file. Thursday and Friday transactions are similarly backed up into separate files. In the event of a restoration, each of the files must be added to the others and finally to the full backup to form a contiguous data file containing not only all of the existing information from Sunday but also the information from the rest of the week.

The advantage to this program is that each day's backup may be created much faster. Each day's data is in one file. The cost of media for each day is reduced because it is only storing one day's worth of information. The obvious disadvantage is that if a full restoration is required, it takes much longer to combine all of the different daily files together with the full backup prior to being able to restore all the data to the affected device. Figure 6.5 illustrates incremental backup.

FIGURE 6.5   An illustration of an incremental backup

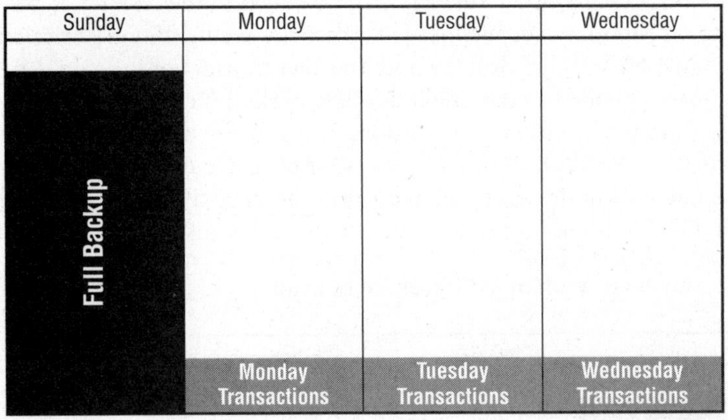

Backup Storage Considerations

Data that is stored as backup is extremely important to the organization. When formulating a backup program, various aspects should be given consideration:

Data Encryption   Data stored in offsite locations should be encrypted for protection.

Reliable Transmission Methods   Data transmitted to offsite locations should be both encrypted and hashed to provide confidentiality and integrity of the data.

Bonded Courier Service   If tapes are created onsite and physically stored in a separate location, the transportation service should be bonded and reliable.

Restricted Off-Site Access   Backup data stored offsite must not be able to be accessed except by authorized personnel performing a restoration.

Proper Identification of All Physical Media   Tapes should be labeled and bar-coded, and the tape label should be encoded on the tape itself for identification purposes. All labeled materials stored offsite should be recorded and the records should be maintained in an inventory.

Exam Point

You should be able to describe the difference between full backup, incremental backup, and differential backup.

Electronic Vaulting, Remote Journaling, and Clustering

Electronic vaulting is another name for transmitting data offsite to either a physical storage location or a cloud storage location. At the physical storage location, the transmitted data is recorded onto tape or media, while on the cloud storage location, virtual storage techniques may be employed. With electronic vaulting, data transmission should be encrypted and validated for integrity, such as employing IPsec as a transmission encryption and integrity coding system.

Journaling is a database term that refers to recording transactions and creating a transaction log. A transaction log may be used in conjunction with the last known good database copy to create an up-to-date database. If an IT transaction is interrupted, a journal can be used along with the original database copy to restore information as of the last transaction.

Clustering refers to using a combination of servers or systems to reduce the risk associated with a single point of failure. A cluster of anything provides a configuration that reduces risk and provides high availability. A term used in clustering is *automatic failover*, which provides system redundancy. In the event of a failover, the secondary system takes over all server operations, and the failover is transparent to the user. This is primarily used in environments that require high availability and continuous use.

Load-balancing clustering is a technique of utilizing various servers and systems in an array to spread the workload. In this technique, various algorithms are used to send work to each one of the cluster servers so that one server does not receive all of the workload. Load-balancing clustering differs from server clustering in that server clustering provides redundancy of servers while load balancing provides availability of servers.

Redundant Array of Independent Disks

Redundant Array of Independent Disks (RAID) is a method of storing data across several different hard disks. Using this system, data is written to a series of hard disks in such a manner as to provide either speed or data redundancy. A RAID array can be viewed as a stack of two or more hard disks that are written to using either software or hardware implementations.

RAID is based on several data recording concepts that may be combined in a number of ways to reach the desired results. These recording concepts include parity, mirroring, and striping.

Parity Parity is performed by adding a separate bit to the data to provide data integrity. Parity is an old data integrity method that provides the reliability of being able to determine if a bit has been dropped during the transmission process.

Mirroring Using this technique, the system writes data to separate hard disk drives. Mirroring is accomplished using either hardware or software; it requires writing data to two disks at the same time. The advantage to data mirroring is data redundancy. The disadvantage is that both drives must write at the same time, thus reducing the writing speed.

Striping Striping is a method of writing information to all disks at the same time. Data is broken down into either bytes or blocks. The advantage of striping is speed because a part of the information is written to each disk at the same time.

Different RAID levels are specified by a number that indicates a particular type of configuration. It is important to know that some RAID levels offer redundancy while other RAID levels offer speed.

RAID-0   This configuration stripes data across multiple hard drives. The benefit is speed and access. There is no data redundancy.

RAID-1   This configuration features writing identical data to two different storage locations such as cloud storage or local hard drives. It offers a simple data redundancy configuration by having identical information written to two different locations.

RAID-2   This configuration stripes data across multiple disk drives at the bit level. It is difficult to implement and generally not used.

RAID-3   This configuration stripes data across multiple drives at the bit level and uses a separate disk drive for the parity bit. This RAID level is rarely used.

RAID-4   This configuration is similar to RAID-3, but it stripes data across multiple drives at the block level. It also uses a separate disk for the parity bit. The RAID-4 level is very rarely used in a production environment.

RAID-5   This configuration is one of the most popular RAID configurations. RAID-5 uses a technique of striping data across multiple drives and incorporating the parity bit on each of the drives. If a drive fails, the data may be reconstructed using the data and parity bit contained on the other drives. A minimum of three drives must be used in a RAID-5 implementation.

Various other types of RAID configurations exist that are based on combinations of the preceding RAID techniques.

Business Continuity Plan and Disaster Recovery Plan Testing and Drills

The business continuity plan (BCP) and disaster recovery plan (DRP) should be verified at least once every year. This procedure is accomplished through the use of a variety of tests and drills with the personnel involved. The various types of tests are based on time, cost, complexity, and risk to the organization. For example, taking the IT department offline to test the capability of a failover to a remote site might pose a substantial risk to the organization. However, many government and military organizations perform this type of test to test readiness in the event of an emergency.

There are various types of tests used to validate either the business continuity plan or the disaster recovery plan:

Checklist Test   The checklist or desk check test is performed by the personnel involved in the plan. Primarily, it involves mentally understanding their responsibilities, reviewing procedures, and updating contact and other required information. Individuals are asked to document any changes or updates made to their areas of responsibility since the last checklist test.

Structured Walk-Through Test   In a structured walk-through test, individuals with responsibility of performing some action or activity in the plan, as well as individuals from key departments involved in the plan, attend a structured walk-through meeting. During the meeting, those involved validate that the plan is correct and that they understand their responsibilities. The structured walk-through test is the most common of the plan tests and may be performed frequently across different business units.

Simulation Test   The simulation test features actual steps that would be taken during an actual emergency or disaster. For instance, files may be restored from backup, generators may be started and switched over, and other physical items may be tested. This is a simulation, and all individuals involved are aware of that. The normal business of the organization is not affected by a simulation test. The output of a simulation test is to specifically test the validity of the plan and the activities, techniques, and responsibilities as specified in the plan.

Parallel Test   A parallel test involves performing IT processing using alternate techniques such as a hot site or warm site. Throughout this test, organizational activities are not interrupted. This type of test must be planned for and budgeted because it incurs substantial cost to the organization. Individuals must be transported to an alternate site, data must be restored from remote backups, and processing must occur as if it were a production site. On many occasions, auditors or observers record the activities.

Full Interrupt Test   In full interrupt testing, business operations are interrupted and the alternate site is brought online into full operation. Processing is performed using the alternate site data and equipment. As can be imagined, this type of test is very intrusive and disruptive to ongoing operations. The organization faces great risk when performing full interrupt testing. A number of things can go wrong, including not being able to bring the original site back to full production mode in a timely manner.

Exam Point

You should be able to describe the different testing methods for a business continuity plan and a disaster recovery plan.

As an SSCP, you will be expected to perform many roles as assigned during both continuity and disaster preparedness testing. You must understand the reasons for the testing and the importance of your role to its success.

Summary

As a security practitioner, you will be closely involved with various aspects of planning, testing and possibly executing incident plans, business continuity, and business recovery plans. As such, it is important to understand the basic concepts of each practice.

In this chapter, you gained an understanding of how to handle incidents using consistent and applied techniques. You learned what the elements of an incident response policy are and that, as in all policies, it must have executive-level support. The incident response plan is the result of a policy directive and requires the interaction and input of many corporate individuals, including heads of departments and subject matter experts. The incident response plan requires a commitment in both time and funding. It also requires training individuals so they understand their responsibilities as possible members of the incident response team. You saw how incident analysis, sometimes referred to as triage during multiple incidents or attacks, is used to prioritize the efforts of the incident response team to mitigate harm to the organization.

During forensic investigations, you may play a role as part of an incident response team while gathering information as well as evidence from the incident scene. In this chapter you learned how to recover and record evidence and provide a continuous tracking method, referred to as chain of custody. We also discussed Locard's exchange principle, which states that a perpetrator will always leave something at the crime scene and will also take something from the crime scene.

You learned the importance of a business continuity plan. The business continuity plan provides the responsibilities, criteria, and procedures to maintain business operations as close to normal as possible during an incident or a disaster. This involves prioritizing business activities that must be maintained before business activities that are support operations. The disaster recovery plan is put into action after a disaster occurs. It provides the responsibilities, criteria, and procedures necessary to restore and recover back to normal operations after a disaster.

We discussed the various techniques of backing up data and providing redundancy for data storage as well as network operations. We also discussed the importance of testing so that every individual is aware of their responsibilities and plans are carried out as intended.

Exam Essentials

Events   Understand that an event is any observable occurrence in a system or network. An event may be as simple as a user logging on, an application opening a port, or data transferring between systems.

Incidents   Know that an incident is an event with the potential to cause harm to the organization. An incident is usually considered an intrusion by an outside force, but it may also be caused by an internal user. An incident may also be intentional or unintentional.

Incident Response Plan   Understand that an incident response plan is a set of established responsibilities, criteria, and procedures to be initiated upon the discovery of an incident.

Nature of an Incident Response Team   Understand that the incident response team is an assortment of multidisciplined individuals from across the organization who aid in the mitigation of harm and the containment of an incident.

User Workstation or Server and Restoration Techniques after an Attack   Know that it is easier to rebuild a workstation or server from an image file or a backup than it is to try to eradicate a virus or root kit from the system.

Chain of Custody for Forensics Evidence   Understand the specific steps and criteria required for the acquisition, handling, recording, and processing of evidence so that it's valid and admissible in a court of law.

Gathering Evidence Based on Volatility   Live evidence, or evidence still in memory, may be collected by the forensic team while the target machine still has power. Know that the evidence is always gathered from the most volatile memory such as CPU cache and primary memory such as RAM, and then the secondary memory locations such as hard disks, USB drives, or even cloud storage.

Hard Disk Forensic Examination Techniques   Understand that data is retrieved from a hard disk using a bit copy software technique to ensure that every bit is recorded correctly. A write blocker prohibits any information from being written onto the drive. Any examination of the data is performed on a hashed copy while the original is maintained in a safe storage.

Business Continuity Planning   Understand that business continuity planning results in the development of a business continuity plan, which is a set of responsibilities, criteria, and procedures to be followed when an incident or disaster event occurs. The purpose of a business continuity plan is to maintain business operations as normally as possible after the occurrence of an incident or disaster event.

The Concepts MTD, RTO, and RPO   Know that the concepts involved in business continuity planning involve maximum tolerable downtime, recovery time objective, and recovery point objective.

Alternate Site Processing Strategies   Understand that, during a disaster, the business continuity plan may call for the use of a cold site, warm site, or hot site or possibly a multiple-processing site or mobile site as an alternate location for the organization's data center.

Written Lab

You can find the answers in Appendix A.

1. Write a paragraph explaining the difference between business continuity planning and disaster recovery planning.
2. Describe what is performed during triage.
3. Briefly explain MTD, RTO, and RPO
4. Describe the activities of an incident response team.

Review Questions

You can find the answers in Appendix B.

1. Which is the *most* volatile memory?
   A. Hard disk
   B. CPU cache
   C. RAM
   D. USB drive

2. Which option provides the *best* description of the first action to take during incident response?
   A. Determine the source and vector of the threat.
   B. Follow the procedures in the incident response plan.
   C. Disconnect the affected computers.
   D. Alert the third-party incident response team.

3. Which option *most* accurately describes continuity of operations after a disaster event?
   A. Controlling risk to the organization
   B. Planned procedures that are performed when a security-related incident occurs
   C. Planned activities that enable the organizations critical business functions to return to operations
   D. Transferring risk to a third-party insurance carrier

4. When considering a disaster which of the following is *not* a commonly accepted definition?

   Which choice
   A. An occurrence that is outside the normal functional baselines
   B. An occurrence or imminent threat to the enterprise of widespread or severe damage, injury, loss of life, or loss of property
   C. An emergency that is beyond the normal response resources of the enterprise
   D. A suddenly occurring event that has a long-term negative impact on major IT infrastructure

5. Which of the following is *not* an accurate statement about an organizations incident response policy?
   A. It should require the ability to respond quickly and effectively to an incident.
   B. It should require the prevention of future damage from an incident.
   C. It should require the retaliation against repeat attackers.
   D. It can require the repair of damage done from an incident.

6. Which option is *not* a responsibility of the person designated to manage the continuity planning process?

   A. Providing information and direction to senior management staff

   B. Providing stress mitigation programs to employees after an asset loss event

   C. Analyzing and identifying all critical business functions

   D. Coordinating and planning integration among business units

7. Which disaster recovery/emergency management plan testing type is considered the *most* cost-effective and efficient way to identify areas of overlap in the plan before conducting a more demanding training exercise?

   A. Full failover test

   B. Structured walk-through test

   C. Tabletop exercise

   D. Bullet point test

8. Which of the following options *best* describes a cold site?

   A. An alternate processing facility with established electrical wiring and HVAC but no data processing hardware

   B. An alternate processing facility with most data processing hardware and software installed, which can be operational within a matter of hours to a few days

   C. An alternate processing facility that has all hardware and software installed and is mirrored with the original site and can be operational within a very short period of him him him him time

   D. A mobile trailer with portable generators and air-conditioning

9. Which of the following statements is an incorrect description of a control?

   A. Detective controls monitor for attacks and instigate preventative or corrective controls.

   B. Controls reduce the possibility that vulnerabilities will be attacked.

   C. The effect of an attack is reduced through the use of controls

   D. Restorative controls reduce the likelihood of a deliberate attack.

10. Which of the five disaster recovery testing types creates the *most* risk for the enterprise?

   A. Simulation

   B. Parallel

   C. Structured walk-through

   D. Full interruption

11. Which of the following options would require the longest setup time?

   A. Mobile or portable alternate IT computing service

   B. Hot site

   C. Cold site

   D. Warm site

12. A backup site is *best* described by which of the following options?

   A. A computer facility with electrical power and HVAC but with no applications or installed data on the workstations or servers prior to the event

   B. A computer facility with available electrical power and HVAC and some print/file servers. No equipment has been installed at the site.

   C. An alternate computing location with little power and air-conditioning is but no telecommunications capability

   D. A computer facility with power and HVAC and all servers and communications. All applications are ready to be installed and configured, and recent data is available to be restored to the site.

13. What is the prime objective of the continuity plan?

   A. To make sure everyone understands their responsibility and the procedures they must follow

   B. To inform everyone that a disaster or incident event has occurred

   C. To maintain business operations, as best as possible, until all operations can be restored

   D. To rebuild the facility after disaster occurrence

14. Which option *best* describes an incremental backup?

   A. Daily backups are appended to previous backups.

   B. Daily backups are maintained in separate files.

   C. Daily backups are appended to the full backup.

   D. Daily backups are mirrored to the cloud.

15. Which option is *most* accurate regarding a recovery point objective?

   A. The time after which the viability of the enterprise is in question

   B. The point at which the most accurate data is available for restoration

   C. The point at which the least accurate data is available for restoration

   D. The target time full operations should be restored after disaster

16. Which team is made up of members from across the enterprise?

   A. Dedicated full-time incident response team

   B. Functional incident response team

   C. Third-party incident response team

   D. Expert incident response team

17. Evidence should be tracked utilizing which of the following methods?

   A. Record of evidence

   B. Chain of custody

   C. Evidence recovery tag

   D. Investigators evidence notebook

18. Prior to analysis, data should be copied from a hard disk utilizing which of the following?

    A.   Write protect tool

    B.   Block data copy software

    C.   Bit data copy software

    D.   Memory dump tool

19. Upon arriving at an incident scene, the incident response team should do which of the following?

    A.   Turn off the affected machine to stop the attack.

    B.   Follow the procedures specified in the incident response plan.

    C.   Quickly unplug the Ethernet plug.

    D.   Take photographs of the crime scene before it can be disturbed.

20. A clipping level does which of the following?

    A.   Reduces noise signals on the IT infrastructure

    B.   Removes unwanted packets

    C.   Defines a threshold of activity that, after crossed, sets off an operator alarm or alert

    D.   Provides real-time monitoring

Chapter
7

Domain 5: Cryptography

SSCP EXAM OBJECTIVES COVERED IN THIS CHAPTER:

- ✓ Concepts & Requirements of Cryptography
- ✓ Cryptographic systems and technology
- ✓ Data Classification and Regulatory Requirements
- ✓ Public Key Infrastructure and Certificate Management
- ✓ Security Protocols

As a Systems Security Certified Practitioner (SSCP), you may be called upon to be a member of a team and take an active part in the security of data in transit and at rest. Security practitioners utilize cryptographic solutions to meet several fundamental roles, including confidentiality, integrity, and authentication, otherwise known as the CIA triad. The practitioner must be aware of and utilize various cryptographic systems that are designed for the purpose in mind.

Confidentiality includes all of the methods that ensure that information remains private. Data at rest, or data in storage, is information that resides in a permanent location. The data might be stored on a local hard disk drive, on a USB drive, on a network (such as a storage area network or network attached storage), or even in the cloud. It may also include long-term archival data stored on tape or other backup media that must be maintained in storage for a number of years based on various regulations.

Data in transit is the data that is moving from one network to another, within a private network, or even between applications. Perhaps the most widely required goal of cryptosystems is the facilitation of secret communications between individuals and groups. While in transit, data must be kept confidential. This type of data is generally encrypted or encapsulated by an encryption algorithm. Data in transit might be traveling on a private corporate network, on a public network such as the Internet, or on a wireless network, such as when a user is connected to a Wi-Fi access point. Data in transit and data at rest require different types of confidentiality protection.

Data integrity ensures that a message has not been altered while in transit. Various mechanisms are used to ensure that the message received is identical to the message that was sent. Message integrity is enforced through the use of message digests created upon transmission of a message. The recipient of the message rehashes the message and compares the message digest to ensure the message did not change in transit. Digital signing of messages is also used to provide, for example, proof of origin. Integrity can be enforced by both public and secret key cryptosystems.

Authentication is a major function of cryptosystems. A shared secret key may be utilized to authenticate the other party because they will be the only ones to have the same key. Another authentication method is using a private key in an asymmetric cryptographic system. The owner of the private key will be the only person who has it and can be the only person to decrypt messages encrypted with their own public key. This technique authenticates that this person is who they claim to be. This technique provides irrefutable proof that the sender is who they say they are. This particular technique is referred to as non-repudiation.

Throughout this chapter we will explore different techniques used throughout modern cryptographic systems.

Concepts and Requirements of Cryptography

The use of cryptography is eons old. Ancient leaders and monarchs required the ability to send messages to distant armies while keeping the content of the messages confidential. Some primitive messages were written on leather straps that were wound around rods of various sizes. The leather strap was then sent to the receiver who then wound it around their own rod of the appropriate size. This enabled the receiver to read the message on the leather strap. Other types of encryption involved encrypting messages using a circular device; an inner circular ring with an alphabet of letters on it could be rotated against an external ring with another alphabet of letters. Depending upon how the rings were rotated, different characters would match up. Identified as a Caesar cipher, this was one of the initial substitution ciphers. The term *ROT-3* indicated that the internal circular mechanism was rotated three characters. The corresponding letter was then read on the outer circular device. Decryption mechanisms like this were in use up through the American Civil War.

Beginning in the Industrial Revolution, various machines were designed to encrypt and decrypt messages, specifically messages sent in wartime. The machine age of cryptography ushered in the use of automatic encryption machines such as the German enigma machine as well as the Japanese red and purple machine. These types of mechanisms created cryptographic messages that were very difficult to decipher.

Today, computers both encrypt and decrypt messages at ever-increasing speeds. Organizations are challenged by ever-increasing speed of computers. Careful consideration must be given to cryptographic systems used for very long-term data storage. According to *Moore's law*, processing power generally doubles every 18 months. This implies that messages encrypted by today's standards may eventually be broken very easily within just a few years.

Terms and Concepts Used in Cryptography

As a practitioner, you must understand the terms and techniques used in the area of cryptography. Cryptographic methods are used to ensure the confidentiality as well as the integrity of messages. Confidentiality ensures the message cannot be read if intercepted, while integrity ensures that the message remains unchanged during transmission.

As with any science, you must be familiar with certain terminology before you study cryptography. Let's take a look at a few of the key terms used to describe codes and ciphers.

Key Space   A *key space* is the number of keys that can be created based upon the key length in bits. For instance, if the key is 128 bits in length, the total number of keys that might be created would be represented by 128 bits. This is roughly $3.40282367 * 10^{38}$.

Algorithm   An algorithm is a mathematical function that produces a binary output based on the input of either plaintext or ciphertext. A cryptographic algorithm produces ciphertext or encrypted text based on the input of a plaintext message in a cryptographic key. A hashing algorithm produces a message digest of a set length with input of any size plaintext message.

One-Way Algorithm   A *one-way algorithm* is a mathematical calculation that takes the input of a plaintext message and outputs a ciphertext message. When a one-way algorithm is used, it is mathematically infeasible to determine the original plaintext message from the ciphertext message. One-way algorithms are primarily used in hashing or for verifying the integrity of a message. Plaintext messages are hashed to create a message digest. The message digest is always the same length, depending upon the hashing algorithm.

Encryption   Encryption is the process whereby ciphertext is created by processing a plaintext message through an encryption algorithm and utilizing an encryption key and possibly an initialization vector that results in encrypted text.

Decryption   Decryption is an opposite process to encryption. Ciphertext is processed through an encryption algorithm using a reverse process, which results in plaintext.

Two-Way Algorithm   A *two-way algorithm* as a mathematical function that may both encrypt and decrypt a message.

Exam Point

Understand the difference between one-way and two-way algorithms. A hashing algorithm is one-way because it is virtually impossible to determine the original plaintext based upon only the hash value. Asymmetric and symmetric algorithms are referred to as two-way algorithms because they perform both encrypt and decrypt functions.

Work Factor   The *work factor* is the time and effort that it would take to break a specific encrypted text. For example, the longer the password, the longer it would take to discover it using brute force. The work factor is a deterrent to a would-be crypto analyst if the effort to break an encryption would require more time and resources and assets than the value of the encrypted information.

Initialization Vector   An initialization vector is an unencrypted random number that is used to create complexity during the encryption process. It works by seeding the encryption algorithm to enhance the effect of the key. The encryption algorithms utilize an initialization vector, and the number of bits in the IV is usually equal to the block size of the encryption algorithm. The IV may be required to be random or just nonrepeating, and in most cases it need not be encrypted. An initialization vector used by an asymmetric algorithm is usually the same size as the block size that the algorithm processes.

> **Exam Point**
>
> Understand that an initialization vector is an unencrypted random number that is used to create complexity during the encryption process. It works by seeding the encryption algorithm to enhance the effect of the key.

Cryptosystem   The *cryptosystem* involves everything in the cryptographic process, including the unencrypted message, the key, the initialization vector, the encryption algorithm, the cipher mode, the key origination, and the distribution and key management system as well as the decryption methodology.

Cryptanalysis   *Cryptanalysis* is the study of the techniques used to determine methods to decrypt encrypted messages, including the study of how to defeat encryption algorithms, discover keys, and break passwords.

Cryptology   *Cryptology* is a science that deals with the encryption and decryption of plaintext messages using various techniques such as hiding, encryption, disguising, diffusion, and confusion.

Encoding   Encoding is the action of changing a message from one format to another using a coding method. It is different than encryption because encoding is the alteration of characters. For instance, an alphabet can be represented by a series of ones and zeros by using an ASCII code. An alphabet can also be transmitted in the form of dots and dashes using Morse code. Entire messages can be encoded by using specific colored flags or the position of flags or by flashing lights between ships at sea.

Decoding   Decoding is the art and science of reading various dots and dashes produced by an electromagnetic Morse code receiver or by visually identifying flag signals or flashing signal lights.

Key Clustering   *Key clustering* is when two different cryptographic keys generate the same ciphertext from the same plaintext. This indicates a flaw in the algorithm.

Collusion   *Collusion* occurs when one or more individuals or companies conspire to create fraud.

Collision   A *collision* is when two different plaintext documents create the same output hash value, which indicates a flaw in the hashing algorithm.

Ciphertext or Cryptogram   The text produced by a cryptographic algorithm through the use of a key or other method. The *ciphertext* cannot be read and must be decrypted prior to use.

Plaintext   *Plaintext*, or clear text, is a message in readable format. Plaintext may also be represented in other code formats, such as binary, Unicode, and ASCII.

Exam Point

Understand the difference between key clustering and collisions. Key clustering is when two different cryptographic keys generate the same ciphertext from the same plaintext. Collisions occur when two different plaintext documents create the same output hash value. This indicates a flaw in the algorithm.

Hash Function   A one-way mathematical algorithm in which a hash value or message digest is a fixed-size output. The output is always the size specified by the hash function regardless of the original size of the data file. It is impossible to determine the original message based upon the possession of the hash value. Changing any character in the original data file would completely change the hash value. A hash function is utilized as a three-step process:

1. The sender creates a hash value of the original message and sends the message and the hash value to the receiver.

2. Upon receipt, the receiver creates another hash value.

3. The receiver then compares the original received hash value with the derived hash value created upon receipt.

If the hash values match, the receiver can be assured that the message did not change in transit.

Key   The *key*, or *cryptovariable*, is the input required by a cryptographic algorithm. Various cryptographic algorithms require keys of different lengths. Generally, the longer the key, the stronger the cryptographic algorithm or resulting crypto text. A symmetric key must be kept secret at all times. An asymmetric key will feature a public key and a private key, and the asymmetric private key must be kept secret at all times. Keys are always represented by the number of bits—for instance, 56 bits, 256 bits, or 512 bits. There are 8 bits in every character, so a 128-bit key is only 16 alphabetic characters long. A 16-character, 128-bit alphabetic key might be represented as "HIHOWAREYOUTODAY."

A Key by Any Other Name

It is important to note that several terms or names may relate to the same thing. For instance, in cryptography, we know that there is a key, and this key should be kept secret. What may be confusing is that this secret key may be referred to by any one of the following terms: secret key, private key, shared key, pre-shared key, hidden key, session key, master key, key encrypting key, and a few other terms. Remember, the only key that is not part of this group is the "public key" that is part of the asymmetric key pair (public key and private key) and is used in public-key cryptography (PKI). If it is not specifically called a public key, then it must be a secret key and must be a part of the secret key group of terms listed here.

Symmetric Key   A *symmetric key* is a key used with a symmetric encryption algorithm that must be kept secret. Each party is required to have the same key, which causes key distribution to be difficult with symmetric keys.

Asymmetric Keys   In *asymmetric key* cryptography, two different but mathematically related keys are used. Each user has both a public key and a private key. The private key can be used to mathematically generate the public key. This is a one-way function. It is mathematically infeasible to determine the private key based only upon the possession of the public key. On many occasions, both keys are referred to as a key pair. It is important for the owner to keep the private key secret.

Exam Point

It is important to understand the use of the term *key pair*. Because each party has a key in symmetric cryptography, some may refer to the keys as a *key pair*, although the keys are identical. In asymmetric cryptography, each party has two keys: a public key and a private key. They may also be referred to as a *key pair*. It is important to understand the context in which the term is used.

Symmetric Algorithm   A symmetric algorithm uses a symmetric key and operates at extreme speeds. When using a symmetric algorithm, both the sender and the recipient require the same secret key. This can create a disadvantage in key distribution and key exchange.

Asymmetric Algorithm   An asymmetric algorithm utilizes two keys: a public key and a private key. Either key can be used to encrypt or decrypt a message. It is important to note the relationship of the keys. A message encrypted with the user's public key can be decrypted only by the user's private key and vice versa. Asymmetric algorithms, by design, are incredibly slow compared to symmetric algorithms.

Exam Point

It is important to know that symmetric algorithms are magnitudes of speed faster than asymmetric algorithms.

Digital Certificate   The ownership of a public key must be verified. In a public key infrastructure, a certificate is issued by a trusted authority. This certificate contains the public key and other identification information of a user. The digital signature is issued by a recognized trusted certificate authority and generates a web trust whereby the key contained in the certificate is identified as being owned by that user. For instance, when you're logging on to purchase something from Amazon.com, the Amazon.com certificate would contain

Amazon's public key. This public key will be used to initiate the logon process. As soon as possible, a secret symmetric key is exchanged, which results in a high-speed secure link between the user and Amazon.com for purchasing purposes.

Who Do You Trust?

Would you agree with me that if a public-key is public, therefore anyone can access it? Also, if there is a piece of information that everybody can access, doesn't it therefore make sense that someone might be able to fake this piece of information? This is the exact problem that we have in public-key cryptography, which uses both public and private keys. What if Amazon wasn't really Amazon, or Sears wasn't really Sears? The question is, how do I know that you are the real owner of the public key? There must be some way of branding your name on a public key so that absolutely, without a doubt, it links you or "binds" you to that key. There should be no doubt that you own that key. This problem is solved by the use of certificates. A certificate is like a notary public of the cryptographic world. A third-party verifies that the public key is yours and that you are in fact you. As long as everyone trusts this third party, the system works.

Certificate Authority   A *certificate authority* is a trusted entity that obtains and maintains information about the owner of a public key. The certificate authority issues, manages, and revokes digital certificates. The topmost certificate authority is referred to as the root certificate authority. Other certificate authorities, such as an intermediate authority, represent the root certificate authority.

Registration Authority   The *registration authority* performs data acquisition and validation services of public key owners on behalf of the certificate authority.

Exam Point

A certificate authority is a trusted entity that obtains and maintains information about the owner of a public key. The certificate authority issues, manages, and revokes digital certificates.

Rounds   This is the number of times an encryption process may be performed inside an algorithm. For instance, the AES symmetric algorithm features 10, 12, and 14 rounds based upon key length.

Exclusive Or (XOR)   The exclusive, or *XOR*, is a digital mathematical function that combines ones and zeros from two different sources in a specific pattern to result in a predictable one or zero. It is a simple binary function in which two binary values are added together. For instance, Table 7.1 is a mathematical truth table that illustrates A XOR B, or that the addition of 0+0 or 1+1 always outputs a 0. If the two values are different, such as 0+1 or 1+0, then the output will always be a 1. The XOR function is a backbone mathematical function used in most cryptographic algorithms. It is depicted in drawings as a circle with crosshairs $\oplus$.

TABLE 7.1   The XOR truth table

Input A	Input B	Output (XOR Result)
0	0	0
0	1	1
1	0	1
1	1	0

Nonrepudiation   Nonrepudiation is a method of asserting that the sender of a message cannot deny that they have sent it. Non-repudiation may be created by encrypting a message with the sender's private key. It may also be created by hashing the message to obtain a hash value. Then the sender signs the message by using the sender's private key to encrypt a message hash value. Non-repudiation may also be referred to as providing "proof or origin" or "validating origin." The origination point is proven by the encryption of the message or hash value with something that exists only at the origination point. For instance, the sender's private key in asymmetric cryptography or a commonly held secret key in symmetric cryptography.

Nonrepudiation may also be imposed upon the receiver of a message. This concept requires that the receiver be authenticated with the receiving system and system logging must be initiated. Thus, the receiver, if audited, cannot deny receiving the message.

Exam Point

Remember that nonrepudiation is a method of asserting that the sender of the message may not deny that they have sent a message. This assertion is created by associating something that only the sender possesses, for example, their private key or a commonly shared secret key.

Transposition   *Transposition* is the method of placing plaintext horizontally into a grid and then reading the grid virtually. This transposes the letters and characters.

Session Keys   *Session keys* are encryption keys used for a single communication session. At termination of the communication session, the key is discarded.

One-Time Pad   A *one-time pad* is the foundation concept of much of modern cryptography. Secure Sockets Layer (SSL), IPsec, and dynamic one-time password tokens are all based on the concept of a one-time pad. The concept is that a real or virtual paper pad contains codes or keys on each page that are random and do not repeat. Each page of the pad can be used once for a single operation, and then it is discarded—never valid or to be reused again. The one-time use of an encryption key is the most secure form of encryption possible.

Exam Point

The one-time use of an encryption key is the most secure form of encryption possible.

Pseudorandom Number   Modern computers cannot create true random numbers. At some point numbers begin to repeat. Users of cryptographic systems must be very careful about the information source on which to base the random number generator. Some *pseudorandom number generators* are based on keystrokes, and others are based on random traffic on a network or cosmic radiation noise. The worst random number generators are based on anything that is predictable, such as the time and date of the system clock.

Key Stretching   *Key stretching* is used to make a weak key or password more secure. The technique used in key stretching is to perform a large number of hashing calculations on the original key or password in an effort to increase the workload required to crack or break the key through brute force.

The common method of key stretching is to increase the number of bits from the original key length. For example, a typical password used in business is between 8 and 12 characters in length. This represents only 64 to 96 total bits. Normally, symmetric algorithms require at least a key length of 128 bits for reasonable security. In an effort to stretch a key or password, it is processed through a number of variable-length hash functions. These functions may add one or two bits to the length of the password during each iteration. Passwords may be processed through dozens or hundreds of hash functions, resulting in a total length of 128, 192, or even 256 bits in length. Any attempt to use brute force to crack the key with this length would require a tremendous work factor. This may result in the hacker giving up long before becoming successful.

In-Band vs. Out-of-Band Key Exchange   Keys must be distributed or exchanged between users. In-band key exchange uses communication channels that normally would be used for regular communication including the transmission of encrypted data. This is usually determined to be less secure due to man-in-the-middle attacks or eavesdropping. Out-of-band key exchange utilizes a secondary channel to exchange keys, such as mail, courier, hand delivery, or a special security exchange technique that is less likely to be monitored.

Substitution   *Substitution* is the process of replacing one letter for another. For instance, when using the Caesar cipher disk, the inner disk is rotated three places, ROT-3, and the corresponding letter can be used as a substitute in the encrypted text.

Confusion   Confusion increases the complexity of an encrypted message by modifying the key during the encryption process, thereby increasing the work factor required in cryptanalysis.

Diffusion   Diffusion increases the complexity of an encrypted message. For instance, very little input or change during the encryption process makes major changes to the encrypted message. Diffusion is also used during a hash algorithm to change the entire hash output for each character modification of the original message.

Salt   A *salt* is the process of adding additional bits of data to a cleartext key or password prior to it being hashed. Salting extends the length of a password and, once the password is hashed, makes the processes of attacking hashes much more complicated and computationally intensive. Rainbow tables are commonly used in attacks against hashed passwords. The salted password prior to hashing the password will usually make using a rainbow table attack infeasible and unsuccessful. A large salt value prevents pre-computation attacks and ensures that each user's password is hashed uniquely.

Exam Point

A salt consists of adding additional bits of data to a cleartext key or password prior to it being hashed. Salting extends the length of a password and, once the password is hashed, makes the processes of attacking hashes much more complicated and computationally intensive.

Transport Encryption   Information must be kept confidential when sent between two endpoints. Transported encryption refers to the encryption of data in transit. IPsec is a very popular set of transport encryption protocols.

Key Pairs   The term *key pair* refers to a set of cryptographic keys. A key pair refers to the public and private key in public key infrastructure (PKI) and in a asymmetric cryptosystem.

Block Cipher (Block Algorithm)   An algorithm that works on a fixed block of characters. Most block algorithms utilize standard block sizes such as 128, 192, 256, or 512 although other block sizes are possible. If the number of characters remaining in the last block are less than the block length of the encryption algorithm, the remaining unused character spaces may be padded with null characters.

Stream Cipher (Stream Algorithm)   This is an algorithm that performs encryption on a continuous bit-by-bit basis. Stream ciphers are used when encryption of voice, music, or video is required. Stream-based ciphers are very fast.

Stream ciphers are utilized anytime information such as voice or video data is flowing from one place to another. Stream cipher performs its encryption on a bit-by-bit basis as opposed to a block at a time as with a block cypher. Through a mathematical process called an exclusive OR (XOR), the original information of ones and zeros is merged with an encryption keystream of information. The encryption keystream is generated with the use of the key, which controls both the encryption and decryption processes.

Stream-based ciphers have a set of criteria that should be met for the cipher to be viable:

- The keystream should be unpredictable. An observer should not be able to determine the next bit if given several bits of the keystream.

- If an observer is given the keystream, they should not be able to determine the original encryption key.

- The keystream should be complex and should be constructed on most or all of the encryption key bits.

- The key string should contain many ones and zeros and should go for long periods without repetition.

The weakest area for any encryption algorithm is repetition. Keystreams should be constructed in such a way as to go for very long periods of time without repetition. Most keystreams will repeat at some point. This point in time should be highly unpredictable.

Exam Point

It is important to remember that there are two types of algorithms: a block cipher (or block algorithm) and a stream cipher (or stream algorithm). A block cipher encrypts one entire block at a time. A stream cipher XORs the bits of a plaintext message one at a time with a keystream to create ciphertext.

Rainbow Tables   *Rainbow tables* are pre-computed hash values intended to provide a reverse lookup method for hash values. Typically, passwords are stored on the computer system in a hash value. Brute-force attacks and dictionary attacks are typically used in password breaking or cracking schemes. The use of this brute-force technique requires significant computing resources and possibly an extended period of time. A rainbow table is a list of hashes that include the plaintext version of passwords. Through the process of comparing the saved password hashes to the rainbow table hashes, the hacker hopes to uncover the original plaintext password.

Cryptographic Systems and Technology

It is important for an SSCP to have a thorough understanding of cryptographic systems and the technology associated with the systems. This includes the various types of ciphers and the appropriate use of ciphers and concepts, including nonrepudiation and integrity. As a security practitioner, you may be involved in various aspects of key management, beginning with key generation, storing keys in key escrow storage, and eventually key wiping or clearing, which is key destruction.

Block Ciphers

Block ciphers operate on blocks, or "chunks," of the data and apply the encryption algorithm to an entire block of data at one time. As a plaintext document is fed into the block-based algorithm, it is divided into blocks of a preset size. There may be 2 blocks or 4,000 or more blocks, depending on the size of the original data. If the data is smaller than one block or if there is not enough data for the final block, then null characters are placed in the block to pad to the end. Different algorithms have different block sizes, usually in multiples of 64 bits, such as 128, 192, 256, 320, 512, and so forth.

Block Cipher Modes

There are many challenges facing the administrator of a cryptographic system. Among them is the fact that messages may be of any length; they can be as short as one sentence or as long as the text of an encyclopedia and then some. The second challenge is selecting an algorithm with an appropriate key length. One problem with block cipher algorithms is that encrypting the same plaintext with the same key always produces the same output ciphertext. As you can see, it would be impractical to change the key between every block to be encrypted. Therefore, systems have been devised to increase the complexity of the cipher output utilizing the exact same key. Most of these techniques use an additional input called an initialization vector (IV). The initialization vector provides a set of random or nonrepeating bits that may be used during the cipher computation.

Over the years, various cipher modes have been devised to encrypt blocks of text using several methods or combinations of a key and an initialization vector and in one case just a counter. These methods may look complex at the beginning. But, as we will see, it is just a means of making the keystream more complex and ensuring that all of the blocks of cipher text are equally encrypted in a secure manner.

There are five basic block cipher modes that the security practitioner must be aware of. Each of these modes offers a different method of utilizing a key and an initialization vector. You'll notice that there is a primary binary mathematical function utilized in all of the modes. This is the binary function XOR, or exclusive OR. In each of the five modes, the XOR function combines the ones and zeros coming from one direction with the ones and zeros coming from another to output a unique set of ones and zeros based upon the combination of the two sources. In some cases, the streams of ones and zeros will be an input into another part of the cipher mode to be used to encrypt the next block.

In each of the diagrams, there is a block cipher encryption algorithm. Originally this encryption algorithm was DES. In 2001, the National Institute of Standards and Technology (NIST) added AES to the list of approved modes of operation.

The five basic block cipher modes are as follows:

Electronic Codebook Mode   The *electronic codebook (ECB mode)* is the most basic block cipher mode. Blocks of 64 bits are input into an algorithm using a single symmetric key. If the message is longer than 64 bits, a second, third, or fourth 64-bit block will be encrypted in the same manner using the same key. If all 64-bit blocks are the same text and we're using the same symmetric key, each output block of cipher text would be identical. Electronic codebook mode is used only on very short, smaller than 64-bit messages. Figure 7.1 illustrates that each plaintext block is processed by an algorithm using a symmetric key. If the key is the same and the block is the same, the process will produce the identical ciphertext. This diagram illustrates three blocks being processed. There may be as many blocks as required, and each block is encrypted separately.

FIGURE 7.1   Electronic codebook (ECB) mode

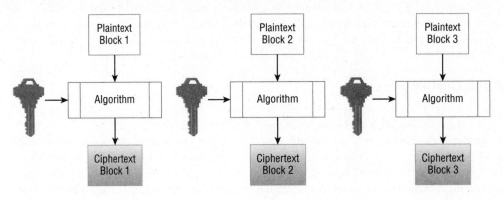

Cipher Block Chaining Mode   Cipher block chaining (CBC) mode is one of the most commonly used of the block cipher modes. Plaintext message is combined or XORed with the initialization vector block by block. Each block is then encrypted into the ciphertext block. Instead of reusing the initialization vector, the system uses the previous ciphertext block in place of the initialization vector. This continues until the entire message is encrypted. In Figure 7.2, you will notice that the first plaintext block is XORed with the initialization vector and then encrypted. The resulting ciphertext block is then XOR (in substitution of the initialization vector) with the second plaintext block, and so forth, until the entire message is encrypted.

FIGURE 7.2   Cipher block chaining (CBC) mode

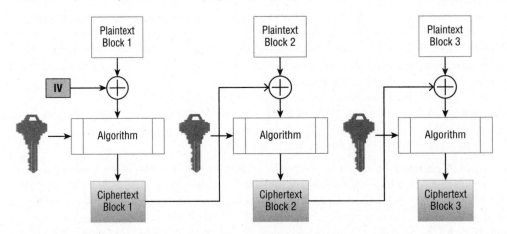

Cipher Feedback Mode   *Cipher feedback (CFB) mode* is the first of three stream cipher modes. Although both DES and AES are block ciphers, both cipher feedback mode and output feedback (OFB) mode are used in a streaming cipher methodology. In cipher feedback mode, there are a number of different block sizes that can be used. Typically, the 8-bit block size is selected because that's the size of a common character. The purpose behind the cipher feedback mode is to encrypt one character at a time, bit by bit. This is accomplished by sending an initialization vector into a shift register, which shifts out 1 bit at a time.

Each bit shifted out is encrypted by the encryption algorithm and then XORed with a bit shifted out of the plaintext shift register. Figure 7.3 illustrates that the XOR output of the encrypted initialization vector in the plaintext is then fed back into the second block cipher encryption and again is XORed with each bit of the second plaintext block. This continues until the entire message is encrypted.

FIGURE 7.3 Cipher feedback (CFB) mode

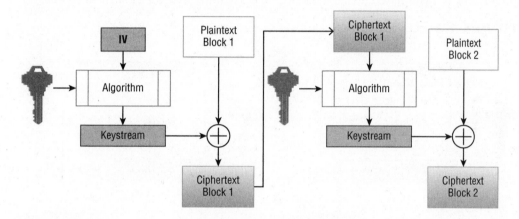

Output Feedback Mode The *Output feedback (OFB) mode* is the second of the stream cipher modes. It is a very similar operation to the cipher feedback mode with the exception that it uses the encrypted initialization vector as the input to the second block cipher encryption. This method allows the keystream to be prepared and stored in advance, prior to the encryption operation. Figure 7.4 illustrates that the initialization vector is encrypted and then fed to the next block cipher, encrypted once again, and fed to the next block cipher.

FIGURE 7.4 Output feedback (OFB) mode

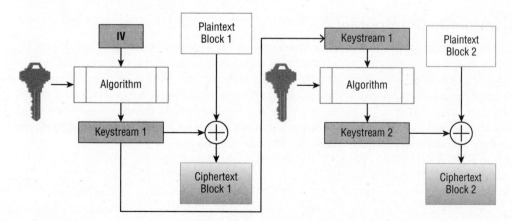

Counter Mode   *Counter (CTR) mode* is the third of the stream cipher modes that turn a block cipher into a stream cipher. It's similar in operation to output feedback mode. A keystream is generated and encrypted through a block cipher algorithm. In this case, rather than use an initialization vector, a 64-bit random data counter is used, which is initiated by a number used only once, or *nonce*. The counter increments by one digit for each block that is encrypted. As in output feedback mode, the counter is encrypted and then XORed to the plaintext on a bit-by-bit basis. This mode does not feature the feedback technique and causes the keystream to be separate from the data. This makes it possible to encrypt several blocks in parallel. Figure 7.5 illustrates how each block is encrypted separately from the others. The only similarity is that each block has a counter that is incremented by one.

FIGURE 7.5   Counter (CTR) mode

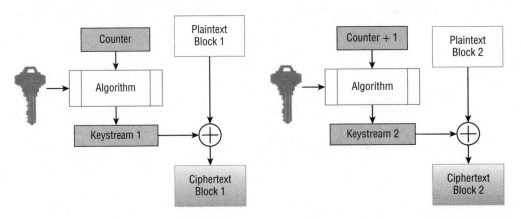

Exam Point

Block cipher modes are used to address the situation in which the same secret key encrypting the same block of plaintext will always produce the same ciphertext.

Symmetric Cryptography

Symmetric cryptography, sometimes called private key or secret key cryptography, uses a single shared encryption key to both encrypt and decrypt data. Symmetric cryptography is referred to as two-way cryptography. A single cryptographic key is used to encrypt and decrypt the information. Symmetric cryptography can be used to encrypt both data at rest and data in transit. When encrypting data at rest on a hard disk, the user possesses a single secret encryption key. Figure 7.6 illustrates that when data in transit is encrypted, both the receiver and the sender require access to the same symmetric key.

FIGURE 7.6 Symmetric cryptography using one shared key

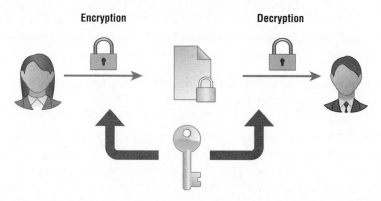

Symmetric cryptography provides very strong encryption protection provided the symmetric key has not been compromised and has been kept a secret. Key exchange and distribution has proven to be a common problem in symmetric cryptography. Each sender and receiver must possess the identical symmetric key. In the event many senders and receivers communicate using the same key, a problem surfaces if any member leaves the group. New keys must be exchanged. In another example, every person in the group shares a unique key with every other person in the group. As you can see, if this is a large group, it will require a very large number of keys. A simple equation may be used to determine the total number of keys required:

$$N * (N - 1) / 2$$

For instance, if there are 10 individuals in a workgroup and each requires a symmetric key to communicate with another within the same workgroup, the equation would appear as follows: 10 * 9 / 2 = 45 keys required. The key management problem increases if, for example, two additional individuals join the workgroup: 12 * 11 / 2 = 66 keys required. By just adding two individuals, 21 additional keys were required.

Symmetric keys may be exchanged both in-band and out-of-band. An in-band exchange makes use of the same communication medium to exchange the symmetric key and the encrypted data. This type of exchange is subject to man-in-the middle or eavesdropping attacks. The out-of-band symmetric key exchange is favored because it uses other methods of symmetric key exchange, such as mail, email, or printed messages, and other methods of exchanging a symmetric key. Public key infrastructure (PKI) is a method of exchanging symmetric keys by first using asymmetric cryptography in establishing a communication link. Once the initial communication link is established, the symmetric key is exchanged, at which time both receiver and sender switch to symmetric cryptography to gain speed.

Symmetric cryptography and the use of a symmetric key is magnitudes of speed faster than asymmetric cryptography due to use of computationally intense mathematical algorithms used in asymmetric algorithms.

> ### Exam Point
>
> Symmetric cryptography is magnitudes of speed faster than asymmetric cryptography.

Various types of symmetric key algorithms exist. Some are less popular than others, and some have risen to the top ranks of standards and are used to encrypt U.S. government top-secret information. The following is a listing of various symmetric key algorithms:

Data Encryption Standard   The *Data Encryption Standard (DES)* was the premier symmetric key algorithm for encryption adopted in the mid-1970s by the national Bureau of Standards (now NIST). DES featured a 56-bit key size, which is very small by today's standards. The cryptographic algorithm was broken in 1999. Also in 1999, Triple DES was prescribed as a potential alternative to DES. By 2002, DES was replaced by the Advanced Encryption Standard (AES). The block cipher modes mentioned previously were designed with DES as the central symmetric algorithm.

Triple Data Encryption Algorithm   *Triple DES*, or *3DES*, is a symmetric algorithm that applies DES three times on each data block. 3DES makes use of three keys, one for each operation. The three keys are combined in ways to create three different keying options:

- All three keys are unique.
- Key 1 and key 2 are unique; key 1 and key 3 are the same.
- All three keys are identical.

3DES features several modes of operation utilizing two keys or three keys. Each mode works on a single block at one time. The four most popular modes of operation are as follows:

Using two keys

- Encrypting using key 1, encrypting using key 2, then reencrypting using key 1.
- Encrypting using key 1, de-encrypting using key 2, then reencrypting using key 1. (In some cases it is referred to as key 3, but it is identical to key 1.)

Using three keys

- Encrypting using key 3, encrypting using key 2, then reencrypting using key 1. This is referred to as EEE3 mode.
- Encrypting using key 3, de-encrypting using key 2, then reencrypting using key 1. This is referred to as EDE3 mode.

Advanced Encryption Standard   The *Rijndael cipher* was selected as the successor to both DES and 3DES during the AES selection process. It was included as a standard by NIST in 2001.

AES makes use of a 128-bit block size in three different wavelengths of 128, 192, and 256 bits. The U.S. government denoted that all three key sizes were adequate to encrypt classified information up to the secret level and that the key sizes of 192 and 256 bits offered adequate encryption strength for top secret classified information.

International Data Encryption Algorithm   The *International Data Encryption Algorithm (IDEA)* was submitted as a possible replacement for DES. It operates using a 120-bit key on 64 bit blocks. During encryption. IDEA performs eight rounds of calculations. It is currently unpatented and free for public use.

CAST   CAST-256, which uses the initials of the creators, Carlisle Adams and Stafford Tavares, was submitted unsuccessfully during the AES competition. Currently in the public domain, *CAST* is available for royalty-free use. Based originally on CAST-128, which uses smaller block sizes, CAST-256 utilizes 128-bit blocks and key length of 128, 192, 160, 224, and 256 bits.

Blowfish   *Blowfish* is a strong symmetric algorithm and is referred to as a fast block cipher due to its speed when implemented in software. Developed in 1993 by Bruce Schneider, Blowfish is still in use today. It provides good encryption rates with no effective cryptanalysis. It is currently packaged in a number of encryption products.

Blowfish works on a 64-bit plaintext block size and utilizes a key of 32 bits to 448 bits. The algorithm is slow at changing keys because the keys are precomputed and stored. This makes Blowfish unsuited for some types of encryption applications.

Twofish   *Twofish* is a symmetric algorithm that was also a contender during the AES competition. A team of cryptographers led by Bruce Schneider developed Twofish as an improved extension of Blowfish. The algorithm makes use of 128-bit blocks in a similar key structure of 128, 192, or 256 bits. It also is in the public domain but is less popular than Blowfish.

RC4   *RC4* is very popular software stream cipher that is used in a number of implementations. The algorithm has known weaknesses, and while it is extensively used in protocols such as Transport Layer Security (TLS), major organizations such as Microsoft and others have recommended disabling RC4 where possible. Originally designed by Ron Rivest in 1987, the algorithm was the backbone of several encryption protocols, including SSL/TLS, Wired Equivalent Privacy (WEP), and Wi-Fi Protected Access (WPA).

RC5   *RC5* is a simple symmetric key block cipher. The algorithm is somewhat unique in that it has a variable block size of 32, 64, or 128 bits and a variable key length from 0 to 2040 bits.

Table 7.2 compares block cipher algorithms and lists the typical block sizes and key sizes.

TABLE 7.2   Block cipher algorithms

Algorithm	Block Size	Key Size
Advanced Encryption Standard	128	128, 192, 256
Data Encryption Standard (DES)	64	56
Triple Data Encryption Standard (3DES)	64	168
International Data Encryption Algorithm (IDEA)	64	128
Blowfish	64	32–448
Twofish	128	128, 192, 256
RC5	32, 64, 128	0–2040
CAST	64	40–128

Asymmetric Cryptography

Asymmetric cryptography is also called *public key cryptography*. Asymmetric cryptography makes use of asymmetric cryptographic algorithm. Between symmetric and asymmetric, asymmetric is by far the more versatile. It makes use of a key pair for each user, which consists of a public key and a private key. The user may easily generate both keys as required.

The public and private keys have a mathematical relationship. The private key is generated first, which then generates the public-key. This is referred to as a one-way function because although the private key generates the public-key through a mathematical computation, it is mathematically infeasible for anyone to determine the private key if they have only the public key.

It is important for the security practitioner to understand the relationships between the public key and the private key in an asymmetric cryptosystem. A key possessed by an individual may decrypt a message encrypted by the other key in the key pair. It is important to visualize this relationship because it is the foundation of asymmetric cryptography. In Figure 7.7, Bob and Alice each possesses a public and private key. Each individual must keep their private key secret. They are the only person who knows the private key. This concept will become the foundation of proof of origin and nonrepudiation. As illustrated, the key relationship is only between the key pair possessed by each individual. In other words, either key may be used to encrypt a plaintext message, and only the opposite key, either public or private, may be used to decrypt the message.

FIGURE 7.7   The relationships of public and private keys in an asymmetric cryptographic system

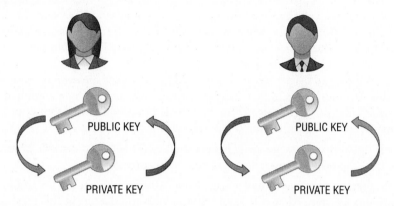

Asymmetric cryptography is much more scalable than symmetric cryptography. In asymmetric cryptography, the public key may be freely and openly distributed. In Figure 7.8, Bob encrypts his message with his private key. This is a secret key and only he knows it. He then transmits the message to Alice. Alice then decrypts the message using Bob's public key.

FIGURE 7.8   Proof of origin encrypted message with a private asymmetric key

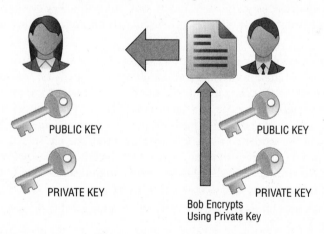

Although in this illustration Bob has encrypted the message using his private key, the message can be decrypted by any person accessing Bob's public key. So this type of message transmission, where the message is encrypted by this method, is not, in fact, secure. Although the message is encrypted, a man-in-the-middle attack can easily decrypt it. The use of this technique is to provide the *proof of origin*. By encrypting a message with his private key, Bob has proven that he is the only person who could have sent the message. Logic follows that if Bob's public key can successfully decrypt the message, only Bob using his private key could have encrypted it. Therefore, only Bob could have sent the message.

In most cases, proof of origin as well as confidentiality of the message is required. To accomplish this, the message is in fact encrypted twice. Bob is sending a confidential message to Alice encrypted with his private key. He is providing both proof of origin and confidentiality. He would perform the following steps:

1. Encrypt his plaintext message using his private key. This would provide proof of origin because he is the only person who has access to his private key.

2. He would then encrypt the same message using Alice's public key. This would provide confidentiality because Alice is the only person who could decrypt this message with the use of her private key.

Upon receiving the message, Alice must perform two steps:

1. Alice would first decrypt the entire message using her private key. Since the message was encrypted with her public key, she is the only person able to do this.

2. She would then decrypt the message once again using Bob's public key. Since Bob encrypted the message using his private key, only his public key could be used to decrypt it. This proves irrefutably that Bob sent this message and provides proof of origin.

Digital signatures are widely used to sign messages. A digital signature provides both proof of origin (and therefore nonrepudiation) and message integrity. Message integrity is the function of proving that the message did not change between the source and the receiver. This is accomplished by passing the original plaintext message through a hashing algorithm to obtain a message digest or hash value. This message digest or hash value is then encrypted using the sender's private key. By encrypting the message using the private key, the sender is providing proof that they are in fact the sender. Figure 7.9 illustrates the use of a private key to encrypt a hash value to create a digital signature. The steps Bob would take to digitally sign the message would be as follows:

1. Bob would hash his plaintext message to arrive at a hash value or message digest.

2. Bob would then encrypt the hash value or message digest with his private key.

It is important to note that a digital signature does not provide confidentiality; it only provides proof of origin, nonrepudiation, and message integrity. Should confidentiality be required, Bob would encrypt the entire message using Alice's public key as illustrated in Figure 7.9.

FIGURE 7.9   The creation of a digital signature by encrypting a hash of a message

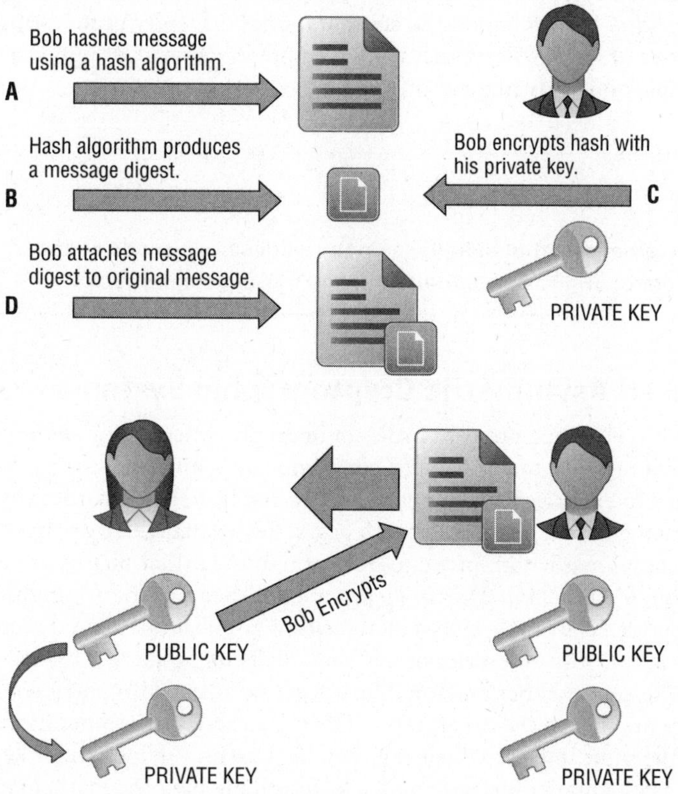

Bob hashes message
using a hash algorithm.

A

Hash algorithm produces
a message digest.

B

Bob encrypts hash with
his private key.

C

Bob attaches message
digest to original message.

D

PRIVATE KEY

PUBLIC KEY

Bob Encrypts

PUBLIC KEY

PRIVATE KEY

PRIVATE KEY

Asymmetric cryptography is much slower than symmetric cryptography due to the very intensive calculations and high processor overhead required. Asymmetric cryptography is generally not suited for encrypting large amounts of data. It is often used to initiate an encrypted session between a sender and receiver so that a symmetric cryptographic key may be immediately exchanged. Once this happens, both the sender and receiver switch to a symmetric cryptosystem, which increases the communication process by magnitudes of speed.

The most widely used asymmetric cryptography solutions are as follows:

- Rivest, Shamir, and Adleman (RSA)
- Diffie-Hellman
- ElGamal
- Elliptic curve cryptography (ECC)

The most famous public key cryptosystem, RSA, is named after its creators Ronald Rivest, Adi Shamir, and Leonard Adleman. In 1977 they proposed the RSA public key algorithm that is still in mainstream use and is the backbone of a large number of well-known security infrastructures produced by companies like Microsoft, Nokia, and Cisco.

The *RSA algorithm* is based upon the computational difficulty of factoring large prime numbers. Each user of the RSA cryptosystem generates a key pair of public and private keys using a very complex one-way algorithm.

Exam Point

It is important to remember that a digital signature does not provide confidentiality. It provides only proof of origin, nonrepudiation, and message integrity.

Non-Key-Based Asymmetric Cryptographic Systems

Key distribution has continued to be a problem in cryptosystems. For example, the receiver and the sender of a message might need to communicate with each other, but they have no physical means to exchange key material and no public key infrastructure in place to facilitate the exchange of secret keys. In such cases, key exchange algorithms like the Diffie-Hellman key exchange algorithm prove to be useful in the initial phases of key exchange.

In 1976, *Whitfield Diffie and Martin Hellman* published a work originally conceptualized by Ralph Merkle. The Diffie-Hellman algorithm establishes a shared secret key between two parties through the use of a series of mathematical computations. In essence, each party has both a secret integer number and a public integer number. Each party respectively sends the public integer number to the other party. Through a series of computational steps, each party arrives at the same integer, which can then be used as a shared secret key.

In 1985, Dr. T. Elgamal published an article describing how the mathematical principles behind the Diffie-Hellman key exchange algorithm could be extended to support an entire public key cryptosystem used for encrypting and decrypting messages. The ElGamal signature algorithm is a digital signature scheme, which is based on the difficulty of computing discrete logarithms rather than like the Diffie-Hellman mathematical process of using the multiplicative group of integers modulo.

The ElGamal signature algorithm is still in use today. When it was released, one of the major advantages of the ElGamal algorithm over the RSA algorithm was that RSA was patented and Dr. Elgamal released his algorithm freely and openly to the public.

The *ElGamal* cryptosystem is usually referred to as a hybrid cryptosystem. In use, the message itself is encrypted using a symmetric algorithm and ElGamal is then used to encrypt the symmetric key used for the symmetric algorithm. This allows unusually large messages to be transmitted to a receiver and decrypted using the symmetric algorithm and key for message encryption, and the asymmetric encryption for symmetric key exchange.

The disadvantage to ElGamal is that the algorithm doubles the length of any message that it encrypts, thereby providing a major hardship when a very large message is sent over narrow bandwidth or when decrypting a very large message with a low-power device.

Exam Point
The Diffie-Hellman key exchange results in each party deriving a shared secret key.

Elliptic Curve and Quantum Cryptography

In 1985, two mathematicians, Neil Koblitz from the University of Washington and Victor Miller from International Business Machines (IBM), independently proposed the application of the *elliptic curve cryptography (ECC)* theory to develop secure cryptographic systems.

RSA, Diffie-Hellman, and other asymmetric algorithms are successful because of the difficulty in factoring large integers composed of two or more prime numbers. The problem with this is the required overhead and processing time to perform the calculation.

The mathematical concepts behind ECC are quite complex. It is important that the construction of parts of cryptographic systems operate as a one-way function. This means that they may easily compute a value in the forward direction, but it should be very near impossible to determine a starting point. For instance, in asymmetric cryptography, the private key and public key are mathematically linked. The private key can be used to generate the public key, but by having possession of the public key, it is impossible to generate or determine the private key.

The security for an elliptic curve protocol is based upon a known base point and a point determined to be on an elliptic curve. The entire process depends upon the ability to compute a point multiplication and the inability to compute the multiple and knowing both sets of points. In summary, it is assumed that finding a discrete logarithm of the elliptic curve element would take an infeasible amount of work factor.

Basically, elliptic curve cryptography is a method of applying discrete logarithm mathematics in order to obtain stronger encryption from shorter keys. For example, an ECC RSA 160-bit key provides the same protection as an RSA 1,024-bit key.

Quantum cryptography is an advanced concept that offers great promise to the world of cryptography. The concept takes advantage of the dual nature of light at the quantum level where it both acts as a wave and is a particle. Quantum cryptography takes advantage of the polarization rotation scheme of light. Successful experiments with quantum cryptography have involved quantum key distribution. With this technology, a shared key may be established between two parties and can be used to generate a shared key that is used by traditional symmetric algorithms. The unique nature of quantum cryptography is that any attempt to eavesdrop on the communication disturbs the nature of the quantum message stream and will be noticed by both parties.

Quantum cryptography technologies are currently in development or in limited use. The prediction for the future is that once it's mature, quantum cryptography will at once replace all existing cryptographic systems and also be able to break existing cryptography.

Hybrid Cryptography

Hybrid cryptography makes use of both asymmetric and symmetric cryptographic communications. This type of cryptography takes advantage of the best attributes of both asymmetric and symmetric cryptography.

The desire is to use symmetric encryption because you can encrypt large amounts of data and it offers great speed. The drawback is in the difficulty of the key exchange. Asymmetric encryption allows for easy key exchange, yet it is very slow and does not encrypt large amounts of data well.

To use hybrid cryptography, you would establish a communication session using asymmetric encryption. Once the session is established, a very large data file would be encrypted with the symmetric key and sent to the receiver. The symmetric key used to encrypt the large data file would then be encrypted with the receiver's public key and sent to the receiver. The receiver decrypts the symmetric key using their private key and then decrypts the large data file using the symmetric key.

This method is used extensively when initiating secure communications using asymmetric cryptography and then switching to a much faster method of encryption using symmetric cryptography.

Exam Point

Hybrid cryptography is based upon initializing an encrypted session utilizing asymmetric encryption to encrypt and send a symmetric key to the other party. Therefore, both asymmetric cryptography as well as symmetric cryptography are used in the same encrypted session. This is the foundation of SSL/TLS-encrypted sessions most often used in e-commerce.

Steganography

Steganography is simply hiding one message inside another. Known as hiding in plain sight, steganography may be used to hide a text message inside a photograph, an audio recording, or a video recording. It's most popularly employed for hiding a text message inside a photograph such as a JPG or GIF. The steganography algorithm encodes the text message by modifying the least significant bit of various pixels within the photograph.

Using this technique, the text message will be embedded within the picture file but will be undetectable to the naked eye. Proof of existence of the message may be determined by hashing the original photograph and comparing it to a hash of the photograph and the message. In this case, the hash values will not be equal. Steganography is fairly simple and fast to achieve using a number of free algorithms. In some cases, the message may be encrypted prior to embedding within a photograph. Figure 7.10 illustrates a JPEG before and after the text has been embedded. Note that the pictures look remarkably the same to the naked eye.

FIGURE 7.10   The process of steganography

Image without data file   Image with data file

Digital Watermark

A *digital watermark* is identification data that is covertly included in either image data or audio/video data. Digital watermarks may be used to verify the authenticity or integrity of an object file or to indicate the identity of the owners. They are utilized to identify the copyright or ownership of an object file. Digital watermarks may very well maintain its integrity even though the underlying media is significantly altered. This is important in such technologies as *Digital Rights Management* (DRM) where ownership of the media and content is important to prove. As with steganography, an application is required to both embed and read the watermark.

Unlike metadata, which may be listed with the file and include the author, date of creation, and other information, a watermark is invisible to the naked eye. Most watermarks cannot be changed by either data compression or manipulation of the original, such as cropping a photograph. A digital watermark is purely passive marketing of information and does not prevent access or media duplication. Digital watermarks have been used extensively in the music industry and motion picture industry to detect the source of illegally copied media.

Hashing

Hashing is a type of cryptography that does not use an encryption algorithm. Instead, a hash function produces a unique identifier that may usually be referred to as a hash, hash value, message digest, or fingerprint. The hash function, or hashing algorithm, is a one-way function, meaning that the hash may be derived from a document using the hashing process but the hash value itself cannot be used in a reverse function to derive the original document.

Hash values or message digests always produce a fixed-length output regardless of the size of the original document. Hash functions also use the technique of the avalanche effect. Changing one character in the original document will change the entire hash value. For instance, hashing an entire document will create a unique hash value. Typing the letter *a* anywhere in the document will completely change the hash value. Typing another *a* in the document will completely change the hash value again. This ensures that an attacker would not be able to determine what character was typed by studying the hash value. And, if two of the same characters were typed consecutively, the hash value would change in such a manner as to not identify the two characters. Figure 7.11 illustrates a number of different hashing algorithms and their output values. Notice the difference between hash values when just one number is changed at the end of the sentence.

FIGURE 7.11   Comparison of hash values

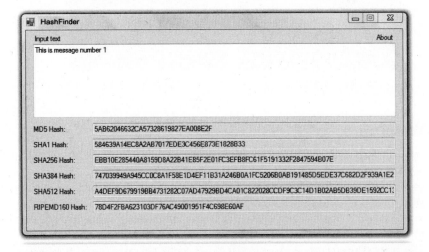

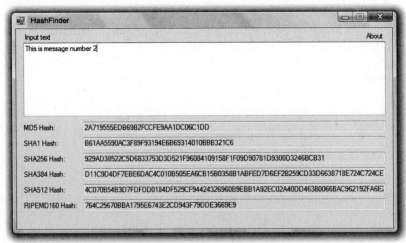

A hash is used to detect whether a document has changed. To verify the integrity of a document, the document is hashed by the sender, and the hash value is included with the message. Upon receipt, the receiver hashes the message once again, and the hash values are compared. If the hash values are the same, the message did not change in transit.

Hashing algorithms make use of a variable-length input file and output a fixed-length string of characters. For example, *Message Digest 5 (MD5)* produces a hash output of 128 bits. This means that regardless of whether a simple sentence or an encyclopedia is put through the hashing algorithm, the output will always be 128 bits. The *Secure Hash Algorithm (SHA-2)* hash function is implemented in some widely used security applications and protocols, including TLS and SSL, PGP, SSH, S/MIME, and IPsec.

The hashing algorithm must be collision free. This means that two different text messages cannot result in the same hash value. In the event that this happens, the hashing algorithm is flawed.

Table 7.3 illustrates the various hashing functions and the resulting length of their hash value.

TABLE 7.3   Hashing functions and their hash value lengths

Algorithm	Hash length
Secure Hash Algorithm (SHA-1)	160
SHA-224	224
SHA-256	256
SHA-384	384
SHA-512	512
SHA-512/224	224
SHA-512/256	256
SHA3-224	224
SHA3-256	256
SHA3-384	384
SHA3-512	512
Message Digest 5 (MD5)	128
RIPEMD	160

Exam Point

Remember that a hashing algorithm provides message integrity. Hash values or message digests are always a fixed length, depending upon the hash algorithm.

Message Authentication Code

A *Message Authentication Code (MAC)* is a message authentication and integrity verification mechanism similar to a hash code or message digest.

When it's in use, a small block of data that is typically 64 bits in length is encrypted with a shared secret key. This block of data is appended onto a message and sent to the receiver. The receiver will decrypt the 64-bit data block and will then determine that the data has not changed in transit.

Authentication is provided to the receiver by the knowledge that the sender is the only other person to possess a secret symmetric key.

A MAC integrity block can take the form of the final encryption block of ciphertext that was generated by the DES encryption algorithm using CBC mode. To arrive at the final encryption block in CBC block mode, a large number of computations in encryptions have taken place. The receiver determines the final block of the algorithm in CBC mode and compares the two blocks. If they match, the receiver can be assured that nothing has changed. The system works because the CBC mode would propagate an error through to the final block if anything changed in the message. The disadvantage of this method of providing both message integrity as well as sender authentication is that it is a very slow process.

HMAC

A *keyed-hash message authentication code*, or *HMAC*, features the use of a shared secret key, which is appended to the message prior to hashing, to prove message authenticity. Message authentication codes are used between two parties that share a secret key in order to authenticate information transmitted between the parties. The hash function performs the normal message integrity.

In use, the sender combines the original message with a shared secret key by appending the key to the original message. This combination message and secret key is then hashed to create an HMAC value. The original message without the secret key appended plus the HMAC value is then sent to the receiver. The receiver will append their secret key to the original message and hash the message, creating their own HMAC. If the HMAC received from the sender and the HMAC determined by the receiver are the same, then the message did not change in transit, proving integrity, and the sender is authenticated by the fact that they have possession of a shared secret key.

Exam Point

Understand the difference between message authentication code (MAC) and keyed-hash message authentication code (HMAC). When using a message authentication code, the sender encrypts a small block of data with a shared secret key. When using a hashed message authentication code, a secret key is appended to the original message and then hashed by the sender. The original message and the HMAC value are then sent separately to the receiver.

Key Length

One of the most important security parameters that can be chosen by the security administrator in any cryptographic system is key length. The length of the key has a direct impact on the amount of processing time required to defeat the cryptosystem. It may also have a direct impact on the processing power required and amount of time required to process each block of data.

According to U.S. government and industry standards, the more critical your data, the stronger the key you should use to protect it. The *National Security Agency (NSA)* has stated that key lengths of the 128 bits, 192 bits, and 256 bits of the AES algorithm are sufficient to protect any government information up to information classified as secret. It has also stated that information classified as top secret must be encrypted by AES using either 192-bit or 256-bit key lengths.

The obvious exception to the rule is elliptic curve cryptography. Due to the calculations used within the algorithm, a shorter key length may be the equivalent to a much larger key length and other algorithms. For instance, it's reported that a 256-bit elliptic curve cryptosystem key is equivalent to a 3,072-bit RSA cryptosystem public key.

It is important to take into consideration the length of time the data must be stored with regard to the length of the cryptosystem key. Moore's law states that processing power (actually, the number of transistors capable of being packed onto a IC chip) doubles about every 18 months. If this is a fact and it currently takes an existing computer one year of processing time to break a cryptosystem key, it will take only 3 months if the attempt is made with contemporary technology 3 years down the road. If records must be retained under a regulatory environment for 3, 7, or 10 years, the appropriate key length must be selected.

Non-repudiation

Non-repudiation prevents the sender of a message from being able to deny that they sent the message. In asymmetric cryptography, non-repudiation is invoked when a sender uses their private key to encrypt a message. Any recipient of the message may then use the sender's public key to decrypt the message. Since the sender was the only person to have access and knowledge of the private key, they cannot deny that they encrypted the message and therefore sent it. The only exception to this rule might be if the sender's private key has been compromised, in which case both the private key and the public key should be discarded.

Non-repudiation is also dependent upon proper authentication. The sender must be properly authenticated to the system and therefore have proper access to the private key. Of course, should an unauthenticated intruder access the individual's private key, non-repudiation would be invalid.

Authentication verifies the authenticity of the sender as well as the recipient of the message. Non-repudiation may also be proved by the receiver provided that the receiver is strongly authenticated into their system and that all of their activities and actions are being actively logged. Therefore, the receipt of the message may be traced to the appropriate receiver.

Non-repudiation is enacted in asymmetric cryptography by the action of the sender encrypting the message with the private key. The only person who could have access to the private key would be the sender. Non-repudiation may be enacted in asymmetric cryptography through the use of a symmetric key. In this case, only the receiver and the sender possess the symmetric key. The symmetric key is a shared secret. Should either party received a message from the other encrypted with the symmetric key, authentication is provided by the fact that the sending person must possess a secret symmetric key. Therefore, they are who they purport to be. A threat to this might be the interception of a private key or secret symmetric key by third-party eavesdropper.

This type of non-repudiation is utilized in the single sign-on methodology of Kerberos. The ticket-granting server maintains a shared secret symmetric key. Each resource in the Kerberos realm also possesses the same shared secret symmetric key or a unique key shared key that is also shared by the ticket granting server. Upon presentation of a ticket containing the key from the ticket-granting server, the resource may conclude that the ticket is valid and authentic by comparing the resource secret key to the ticket granting server security that was included in the ticket. In this case, nonrepudiation may also be used as authentication.

It should be noted that if any more than two individuals possess access to a shared secret symmetric key, such as folks in a workgroup, non-repudiation cannot be achieved. It is impossible to determine, in such an arrangement, who actually used the symmetric key to encrypt the message.

Exam Point

Non-repudiation prevents the sender of a message from being able to deny that they sent the message.

Key Escrow

Key escrow is the process in which keys required to decrypt encrypted data are held in a secure environment in the event that access is required to one or more of the keys. Although users and systems have access to various keys, circumstances may dictate that other individuals within the organization must gain access to those keys.

In a symmetric system all entities in possession of a shared secret key must protect the privacy and secrecy of that key. If it is compromised, lost, or stolen, the entire solution, meaning all entities using that key, is compromised.

In an asymmetric system, each user is able to use their private key to decrypt messages that have been encrypted using their public key. If a user loses access to their private key and the message is encrypted with their public key, the message will be lost.

An escrow system is a storage process in which copies of private keys or secret keys are maintained by a centralized management device or system. The system should securely store the encryption keys as a means of insurance or for recovery if necessary. Keys may be recovered by a key escrow agent and can be used to recover any data encrypted with the damaged or lost key.

Key recovery can be performed only by a key recovery agent or group of agents acting under specific guidance and authority. In some cases, recovery agents may be acting on behalf of a court under the authority of a court order.

A *key recovery agent* or group of agents should be trusted individuals. Many corporate, government, and banking situations require more than one trusted key recovery agent to be involved as in a two-man policy or dual-control. In such case, a mechanism known as *M of N control* can be implemented. M of N is a technique where there are multiple key recovery agents (M), and a determined minimum number of these agents (N) must be present and working in tandem in order to extract keys from the escrow database. The use of M of N control ensures accountability among the key recovery agents and prevents any one individual from having complete control over or access to a cryptographic solution.

Keys can be stored in either hardware solutions or software solutions. Both offer unique benefits and shortcomings. Hardware key storage solutions are not very flexible. However, as a key storage device, hardware is more reliable and more secure than a software solution. Hardware solutions are usually more expensive and are subject to physical theft. Some common examples of *hardware key storage* solutions are smart cards and flash memory drives.

Software key storage solutions generally offer customizable and flexible storage techniques. Anything electronically stored is vulnerable to electronic attacks. Electronic storage techniques rely on the host operating system, and if insufficient controls aren't in place, keys may be stolen, deleted, or destroyed.

Centralized key management is a system where every key generated is usually stored in escrow. Therefore, nothing encrypted by an end user is completely private. In many cases this is unacceptable to a public or open user community because it does not provide any control over privacy, confidentiality, or integrity.

🌐 **Real World Scenario**

Federal Back Doors

In the late 1990s, the federal government, through the National Security Agency (NSA), developed a centralized key management scheme that it wished to implement throughout the business community. A controversial tamperproof hardware chip called a *clipper chip* was proposed to be mounted in all commercial devices. The *skipjack algorithm* was to provide encryption. Key escrow for the skipjack algorithm was provided by a *Law Enforcement Access Field* (LEAF). The concept created much controversy at the time with the suggestion, by some, that the entire mechanism allowed an easy back door for the NSA, thereby providing access to anyone's secrets. Needless to say, it was never implemented. But to this day, government officials such as the U.S. Attorney General and the Director of the FBI, among others, plead the administration's case to Congress that laws should be passed providing the government full access to private encrypted files.

Decentralized key management allows users to generate their own keys and submit keys to a centralized key management authority but to maintain their personal keys in a decentralized key management system as they desire. This limits the number of private keys stored by the centralized key management authority but also increases the risk should something be encrypted with a secret key that is not accessible by a recovery agent.

Exam Point

Understand that key escrow is utilized to securely store encryption keys in the event that a key is no longer accessible and must be retrieved.

Key Management

As an SSCP, you should be aware of the various mechanisms, techniques, and processes used to protect, use, distribute, store, and control cryptographic keys. These various mechanisms and techniques all fall under the category of management solutions.

A key management solution should follow these basic rules:

- The key should be long enough to provide the necessary level of protection.
- The shorter the key length or bit length of the algorithm, the shorter the lifetime of the key.
- Keys should be stored in a secure manner and transmitted encrypted.
- Keys should be truly random and should use the full spectrum of the keyspace.
- Keys sequences should never repeat or use a repeating IV.

- The lifetime of a key should correspond to the sensitivity of the data it's protecting.

- If a key is used frequently, its lifetime should be shorter.

- Keys should be backed up or escrowed in case of emergency.

- Keys should be destroyed through the use of secure processes at the end of their lifetime.

In centralized key management, complete control of cryptographic keys is given to the organization and key control is taken away from the end users. Under a centralized key management policy, copies of all or most cryptographic keys are often stored in escrow. This allows administrators to recover keys in the event that a user loses their key, but it also allows management to access encrypted data whenever it chooses. A centralized key management solution requires a significant investment in infrastructure, processing capabilities, administrative oversight, and policy and procedural communication.

Cipher Suites

A cipher suite is a standardized collection of algorithms that include an authentication method, encryption algorithm, message authentication code, and the key exchange algorithm to be used to define the parameters for security and network communication between two parties. Most often the term *cipher suite* is used in relation to SSL/TLS connections, and each suite is referred to by specific name.

An official TLS Cipher Suite Registry is maintained by IANA (International Assigned Numbers Authority) at the following location:

`www.iana.org/assignments/tls-parameters/tls-parameters.xhtml`

A cipher suite is made up of and named by four elements. For example, CipherSuite "TLS_DHE_DSS_WITH_DES_CBC_SHA" consists of the following elements:

- A key exchange mechanism (TLS_DHE)

- An authentication mechanism (DSS)

- A cipher (DES_CBC)

- A hashing or message authenticating code (MAC) mechanism (SHA)

In practice, a client requesting a TLS session will send a preference-ordered list of the client-side supported cipher suites as part of the initiation handshake process. The server will reply and negotiate with the client based on the highest-preference cipher suite they have in common.

Ephemeral Key

An *ephemeral key* is a one-time key generated at time of need for a specific use or for use in a short or temporary time frame. An example might be a key that is used only once for a communications session and then discarded. Ephemeral keys are by definition in contrast to static or fixed keys, which never change. Ephemeral keys are used uniquely and exclusively by the endpoints of a single transaction or session.

Perfect Forward Secrecy

Perfect forward secrecy is a property that states that a session key won't be compromised if one of the long-term keys used to generate it is compromised in the future. In essence, perfect forward secrecy is a means of ensuring that no session keys will be exposed if a long-term secret key is exposed.

Perfect forward secrecy is implemented by using short-term, one-time-use ephemeral keys for each and every session. These keys are generated for a one-time use and discarded at the end of each session or period of time. Session keys may also be discarded and reissued based on the volume of data being transmitted.

Perfect forward secrecy also requires that if the original session key is compromised, only the part of the conversation encrypted by that key would be exposed. It also ensures that if the original asymmetric keys are obtained or disclosed, they could not be used to unlock any prior sessions captured by an eavesdropper or man-in-the-middle trap.

Cryptanalytic Attacks

Any cryptographic system is subject to attack. In some cases this may benefit the cryptographic community by establishing weaknesses and popular cryptographic algorithms. Cryptographic algorithms are often made public for just such attacks to test their veracity. In the real world, attacks against cryptographic systems happen every day. The following list explains various common attacks against cryptographic systems:

Brute-Force Attack   In a brute-force attack, all possible keys are tried until one is found that decrypts the ciphertext. It stands to reason that the longer the key, the harder it is to conduct a brute-force attack. Depending on key length and the resources used, a brute-force attack can take minutes, hours, or even centuries to conduct.

Rainbow Table Attack   A rainbow table is a series of precomputed hash values along with the associated plaintext prehashed value. This provides the original plaintext and the hashed value for the plaintext. For instance, the password "grandma" would be contained on the rainbow table along with its hash value. The use of rainbow tables are used as a method of deconstructing or reverse-engineering a hash value. Since passwords are stored on systems as hash values, if an attacker obtains access to the list of hashed passwords, they could process them against a rainbow table to obtain the original password. Rainbow tables may be obtained in different hash lengths.

Known Plaintext Attack   In a *known plaintext attack*, the attacker has access to both the plaintext and the ciphertext. The goal of the attacker is to determine the original key used to encrypt the ciphertext. In some cases, they may be analyzing the algorithm used to create the ciphertext.

Chosen Ciphertext Attack   In a *chosen ciphertext attack*, the attacker has access to the encryption mechanism and the public key or the private key and can process ciphertext in an attempt to determine the key or algorithm.

Chosen Plaintext Attack   In a *chosen plaintext attack*, the attacker has access to the algorithm, the key, or even the machine used to encrypt a message. The attacker processes plaintext through the cryptosystem to determine the cryptographic result.

Differential Cryptanalysis   *Differential cryptanalysis* is the study of changes in information as it is processed through a cryptographic system. This method uses the statistical patterns of information changing as it progresses through a system. Several cryptosystems, including DES, have been broken through differential cryptanalysis.

Ciphertext-Only Attack   The *ciphertext-only attack* is the most difficult attack. The attacker has little or no information other than the ciphertext. The attacker attempts to use frequency of characters, statistical data, trends, and any other information to assist in placing the ciphertext.

Frequency Analysis   *Frequency analysis* is the study of how often various characters show up in a language. For instance, oftentimes in the English language, a single character may be an *I* or *A*, while the frequency of two characters together might be *qu, to, be,* and others. This will assist the crypto analyst in breaking the encryption.

Birthday Attack   A *birthday attack* is based on a statistical fact, referred to as the birthday paradox, that there is a probability of two persons having the same birthday depending upon the number of persons in a room. For instance, if there are 23 persons in a room, there is a 50% chance that two of them have the same birthday. This increases to a 99.9% chance if there are 75 persons in the room. This type of statistical attack is used primarily against a hash value in that it is easier and faster to determine collisions based on two plaintext messages equaling the same hash value than it is trying to determine the original plaintext for a given hash value. The birthday attack technique relies on the statistical probability that two events will happen at the same time and that it will be faster to achieve a result using that method rather than having to exploit every possibility such as using brute force.

Dictionary Attack   A *dictionary attack* is commonly used in a brute-force attack against passwords. A dictionary attack may either be used as a brute-force attack whereby no words are known or filtered down into some suspected plaintext words such as a mother's maiden name or names of pets. These plaintext words are then forced into a specific input space, such as a password field.

Other dictionary attacks hash various dictionary values and compare them against the values in a hashed password file. Dictionary attacks may be successful when some information is known about the individual, such as, for instance, pet names, birth dates, mother's maiden name, names of children, and any words associated with a person's working environment (such as the medical or legal field).

Data Classification and Regulatory Requirements

Various military, regulatory, and government agencies require that specific types of information be classified in a manner that restricts access to the information. In the government and military, this may be a standard information classification system based upon need to know. In a regulatory agency, information may be classified based upon privacy concerns, such as restricting access to *personal identification information (PII)*.

Data may be assigned a classification or given a label based upon the sensitivity of the information and who should have access to it. Considerations may be given to how much harm might be inflicted upon the organization if this information was disclosed. The owner of information is the person who classifies the information at a specific level. In many organizations, the custodian is the person responsible to ensure that access is granted only to persons who are privileged to access specific information at a classification level. The custodian is involved in the availability of information.

U.S. Military and Government Security Classifications   The United States military and government are primarily interested in information security and confidentiality. In the U.S. government and military, information is "classified" if it is in one of three levels: confidential, secret, or top secret. This scheme also includes unclassified. Access to secure information is achieved by labeling the information with a classification and the subject or person desiring access to the information with a security clearance label. In such cases, a trusted computing base, utilizing a reference monitor, mediates all access to classified government information by subjects desiring access.

Business and Industrial Security Classifications   Business and industrial entities are interested in information integrity over information confidentiality. A variety of governmental regulatory agencies, as well as contractual relationships, require businesses to maintain the confidentiality of certain personally identifiable information. For instance, hospitals must be concerned with HIPAA information, while companies dealing with credit card transactions must be concerned with the privacy of industry-standard Payment Card Industry (PCI) information. Many organizations have fewer information security levels than the government or military. These levels may include trade secrets, business confidential, sensitive, and public information categories.

Safe Harbor Regulations   All organizations are affected by various regulatory environments within the geographic or jurisdictional boundaries in which they operate. On occasion, new laws, ordinances, and regulations take effect, which affect the organization. The *safe harbor provision* is typically a set of conditions that, if applied in good faith, may temporarily or indefinitely protect the organization from legal action or penalties imposed by a new regulation or law.

Exam Point

The safe harbor provision is typically a set of conditions that, if applied in good faith, may temporarily or indefinitely protect the organization from legal action or penalties imposed by a new regulation or law.

Privacy, Compliance, and Requirements   As the international community grows through the World Wide Web many privacy laws and regulations pose an ever-growing list of challenges on businesses and organizations. *Personally identifiable information* (PII) in the form of Social Security numbers, account numbers, banking information, and health records is very valuable. Credit card theft and resale has been rampant for years. But personally identifiable information through stolen medical records is even more valuable. It is important for the organization to place proper controls and safeguards on this type of information.

Personal data or personal identification information is defined as any information that belongs to or may identify a real person. The *European Data Protection Directive* mandates that personal data must be protected when the information is required in a legal action or to protect the life of the subject, is provided with the consent of the subject, or is provided within the scope of public interest.

Under the European system regulation, the data controller has the responsibility for the protection of data and must implement all appropriate controls to maintain the privacy of personal data. The European Data Protection Directive also includes that individuals have the right to know the identification of the data controller, the recipient of the data, and how the data is stored. The EDPD includes the rights that an individual has if data isn't accurate or if it's exposed to the public. The directive mandates that very sensitive and private data, such as data relating to sexual orientation, health, religious, or philosophical orientation, is among the most sensitive data of an individual.

End-User Privacy Training   All individuals within an organization maintain a certain level of security awareness. This includes the protection and security of corporate information. The release of restricted information may incur fines or penalties to the organization. As a security practitioner, you may be involved in communicating the proper actions that must be taken to safeguard information. Various contractual obligations as well as governmental regulations require that formal security awareness training be conducted throughout an organization on an ongoing basis. All individuals must attend such training and be assessed for their understanding of information protection requirements.

Security awareness training may cover a number of topics. The following topics are related to information security and privacy restrictions:

- The protection of classified or personally identifiable information maintained on computer systems
- The authentication required to access classified or personally identifiable information
- Responsibilities of third parties, including contractors, clients, and customers, with regard to classified or personally identifiable information
- The proper handling of information in printed form and the associated disposal and destruction of classified and personally identifiable information
- The consequences, including fines, sanctions, and penalties, of disclosing classified or personally identifiable information

Public Key Infrastructure and Certificate Management

A *public key infrastructure* consists of software, hardware, organizations, and trust architectures used to validate ownership of a public key by an individual or organization.

In asymmetric cryptography, each entity has both a public and a private key. The private key is permanently bound to one party because it is a secret and the owner is the only person or entity that knows the secret key. The public key, on the other hand, is known to everyone and could easily be spoofed by an attacker claiming to be the owner of the key.

Public-key infrastructure is effective because all of the parties involved trust the issuer of a digital certificate. The ownership of public keys is validated through the trust placed in a certificate authority.

Digital Certificates

Digital certificates are used to prove the authenticity of a key owner and bind a asymmetric cryptography public-key with the identification of the owner. The *X.509 version 3* format specifies a standard for the public key infrastructure (PKI). Certificate revocation lists as well as the structure of a trusted system of certificate authorities are included in the X.509 version 3 format.

Fields within a digital certificate include information on the identification, date of issuance, expiration date, as well as the plaintext public key belonging to the certificate owner. Figure 7.12 illustrates a typical digital certificate and part of the public key in the scroll window.

FIGURE 7.12   A typical digital certificate

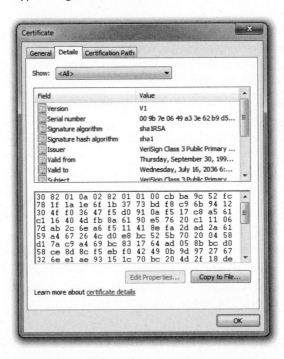

Digital certificates may be preinstalled on Internet browsers through an arrangement between a merchant and the creator of the Internet browser. Certificates that identify the public key of merchants such as Amazon.com are preinstalled on Internet browsers. Certificates, not preinstalled in a browser, may be automatically or manually installed as required. Every certificate includes a path between the Internet browser and a certificate authority for verification purposes.

Exam Point

It is important to remember that a certificate contains the user's public key and that it validates the owner of the public key using a trust system.

The Certificate Authority

A *certificate authority (CA)* is the trusted issuer of a certificate. In most commercial e-commerce transactions the certificate authority is a trusted entity such as Semantic, GoDaddy, GlobalSign, and many others. Large organizations may have internal certificate authorities that issue certificates specifically for the organization.

The certificate authority issues a digital certificate that contains a public key and the identity of the owner. Each digital certificate contains a digital signature of the certificate authority, thus proving that this digital certificate was issued by the certificate authority. Through a trust relationship between the parties and the certificate authority, all parties are assured that the public key contained on the certificate is the public key of the entity listed on the certificate.

Certificates may be issued and maintained on behalf of the certificate authority by *intermediary certificate authorities*. It is due to these intermediary certificate authorities that a certificate will indicate a path to a top-level *or root certificate authority*.

A *registration authority (RA)* is an entity given the responsibility of obtaining or maintaining certificate owner information. On behalf of the certificate authority, the RA may obtain and verify the information provided by the owner and match that with the public key. Under the X.509 standard, the RA may also be involved in certificate expiration and revocation and the maintenance of CRL lists.

The certificate authority administers the certificates by obtaining both the identification of the key owner and the public key and then adding the certificate to a database of certificates to be administered. Certificates are available upon request to any entity requiring verification of a public key. The certificate authority also manages the expiration of keys, either through normal expiration dates or through a compromise activity that invalidates the certificate.

Exam Point

It is important to remember that the information contained in a digital certificate is based upon the X.509 format standard and that a certificate authority digitally signs the certificate.

Certificate Expiration or Revocation

All certificates have an expiration date, although some expiration dates may be 20 years in the future. On occasion, certificates are compromised because either the private key associated with the public key has been made public or some other action has occurred that invalidates the public key. In such a case, all of the users of the certificate should be made aware that the certificate is no longer valid. This is achieved by the certificate authority publishing a *certificate revocation list (CRL)*. Certificate users may check the certificate revocation list either manually or automatically.

The *Online Certificate Status Protocol (OCSP)* is an Internet protocol used to determine the status of a certificate. At any time a party to a transaction may verify the status of a certificate by issuing a request to an OCSP server. The server responds to the request by either validating that the certificate is active and current or indicating that the certificate has expired or been revoked.

A browser such as Microsoft Internet Explorer version 7 and above supports OCSP validation requests. Other Internet browsers, such as Google Chrome, disable automatic OCSP checks due to privacy issues. Figure 7.13 illustrates a typical banner that is presented by a web browser to alert the user that a certificate is invalid, expired, or nonexistent. Users are warned from continuing on with the transaction due to the fact that the other party's public key cannot be verified.

FIGURE 7.13   A certificate warning banner

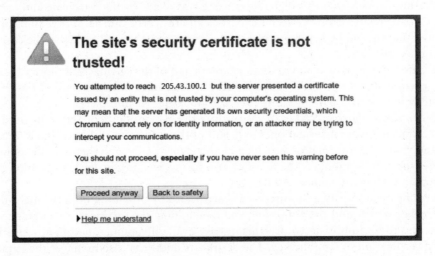

Exam Point

A certificate authority (CA) is the trusted entity that issues a certificate. A registration authority (RA) gathers and verifies information on behalf of the certificate authority. Certificates that have been compromised or have expired are placed on a certificate revocation list (CRL). Validation of certificates may be performed by using the Online Certificate Status Protocol (OCSP).

Key Management

In today's world of e-commerce and business, cryptographic communication is essential. Central to cryptographic communication is the secrecy of keys and validation of the ownership of public keys. Key storage, key distribution, and key generation are all subjects that a security practitioner must be aware of.

Key Generation

Modern cryptography uses integers for keys in both symmetric and asymmetric cryptographic systems. Keys may be randomly generated on any computer by using a *random number generator (RNG)* or a *pseudorandom number generator (PRNG)*. Both a random number generator and a pseudorandom number generator are computer algorithms that produce data of a nonrepeating nature, thereby random. Both of these random number generator algorithms require a seed value to begin their processes. In some cases, the algorithm will use a characteristic known as system entropy to begin the process. The second method of providing a seed is the use of a password or passphrase that is concatenated within the system to provide a suitable seed for the random number generation process.

Keys may be generated automatically by an application or manually by entering a value.

Key Distribution

Key distribution is a major consideration in developing or selecting a cryptosystem. In symmetric cryptography, each party must possess the same key. As you have seen, distribution of this key may be accomplished through a number of means. The terms *in-band* and *out-of-band* refer to transferring key material to the other party. *In-band* refers to transmitting, or sending, a key over the existing communication connection. Eavesdropping and man-in-the-middle are typical attacks on key exchanges. *Out-of-band* is the term used to describe the transmission of key material through any other means. This may include notes, handwritten messages, security transfer pouches, or verbal exchange, to name a few.

Earlier we discussed the Diffie-Hellman key exchange for symmetric key exchange. This method dealt with factoring large prime numbers with the final result that each party obtained the exact same resulting number. This resulting number became the symmetric key.

Asymmetric key exchange features the use of a public/private key pair. As previously described, the private key is a secret key. The public key may be used by any party, but the ownership of the public key should be verified through a trusted certificate system.

A key distribution center (KDC) provides key management for the Kerberos single sign-on application. Each Kerberos user establishes a master key, which is used to communicate between the user and the key distribution center. In the Kerberos system, a symmetric key is embedded in the ticket-granting ticket. Each time the user wishes to access a resource in the Kerberos realm, the user uses the master key embedded in the ticket granting ticket to access the key distribution center, which then provides the user with the session key embedded in the session ticket.

Key Encrypting Keys

Session keys are one-time use keys used during a specific communication session between sender and receiver. At the termination of the session, the keys are disposed of and never used again. During the establishment of a session, both the sender and receiver are required to obtain the same secret session key. The solution is to use a *master key* to generate session keys. Using this technique, both the sender and receiver have a master shared key that they maintain all of the time. When they begin a session, they encrypt the session key with the master key and exchange the session key confidentially. A *derived key* is a session key that has been created based on a long-term key, hash algorithm, or other derivation function. In some cases, the derivation function is based on a seed of the user's password or passphrase.

The distribution of session keys is still difficult and requires transmission of the key through an untrusted network like the Internet. In practice, the master key, also called the *key encrypting key (KEK)*, is used to create a session key. In effect, this places a wrapper or encapsulation around the session key while it is transmitted across the untrusted network.

Although the session/master key distribution method predates PKI-based asymmetric key exchanges, as well as computational symmetric key exchanges, such as Diffie-Hellman, it is still used today in such protocols as SSL and PGP and various banking and point of sale devices.

Exam Point

A key encrypting key (KEK) is a shared master key that is used to encrypt and exchange session keys between two parties. It is easier to have one shared key permanently on hand that is used to encrypt all of the session keys that are exchanged prior to a communication session.

Key Retrieval

Secret keys must be kept secret. Through unfortunate circumstances, encryption keys may be lost or corrupted. A corporate policy may dictate that a key escrow system be used to maintain duplicate copies of keys. In some cases, master keys are stored that create subkeys for use throughout the organization. Master keys are put in a place to access the keys in case, for example, the secret key is lost. This plan must also include safeguards so that access to the secret keying information is controlled in such a way that excessive access is not granted to any one person. Using more than one person to access sensitive information stored in a key escrow location is a control against collusion.

Dual Control   Dual control is a system that requires two individuals to take separate actions to access the key escrow. For example, the process of accessing a safe deposit box at a bank requires the bank's key to be inserted by a bank representative and the user's key to be inserted by the owner of the safe deposit box.

Two Man Rule (Two Person Rule)   The two man/person rule is used when accessing a high-security area where extremely sensitive information is stored. The United States military and government agencies utilize the two-man rule when accessing high-security information. Corporate information confidentiality policy may require that two authorized persons must be involved in any attempt to access cryptographic materials. This may also incorporate the use of dual physical access, such as two keys, two locks, two physical barriers, or other access controls.

Split Knowledge   Split knowledge is a system in which part of a secret is shared among two or more individuals. Each individual has only their part of the information. In order for access to be successful, all of the information from each individual must be provided. In this situation, each individual cannot determine another person's information based upon what they individually possess. For example, a very simple explanation might be to write down a key on a piece of paper and cut the piece of paper in half, dividing the key into two parts. Distribute the two pieces of paper to two different people. The only way to retrieve the entire key is for the two people to share their split knowledge.

M of N Control   M of N control is similar to the two man rule and the split knowledge rule. This type of control is used if access is required and the person or people authorized for access are not present. Under this plan, M represents the number of people required to access the key escrow or secure material. N represents the total number of people that may be substituted in such a situation. For example, three individuals (M) in a nuclear facility must each take an action in a security situation. In the control room, there are nine individuals (N) authorized to act as one of these three persons. Therefore, any three of the nine individuals may take the authorized security action. M of N control also prohibits collusion because all of the individuals must agree to a course of action or it cannot be taken.

Segregation of Duties   Segregation of duties, also referred to as separation of duties, is where one person is required to complete each part of a task. Using the example of key escrow, one person might access the key contained in key escrow while a second person must decrypt the files using the retrieved key. For example, a third person may verify that each of the other two persons performed their actions correctly. In a purchasing department, this may be simply illustrated as the person who places the purchase order is not the same person who checks in the received merchandise.

Key Storage and Destruction

Secret keys and secret keying material must be protected and kept confidential. Proper storage and destruction as well as making changes are very important aspects to key management and may be tasks assigned to a security practitioner.

Keys, as well as secure keying materials, may be subject to long-term attacks such as brute force or other attack methodologies. Corporate key confidentiality policy should require that confidential keys and keying material be stored in air-gaped facilities as well as in heavily encrypted *hardware security module modules* (HSM).

Air gap refers to the technique of maintaining a host, network, or electronic storage mechanism that is physically separated from the outside world (Internet) by not having any inbound or outbound connections.

Keys should be destroyed upon expiration, if compromised, or if they are in frequent use. The more frequently a key is used, the shorter the life span it should have. Prior to destroying a key, data must be re-encrypted with a new key.

Zeroisation, in some cases referred to as *clearing*, is a technique used to completely erase a key from an electronic device or a memory module such as a hard drive, smart card, or USB drive so that magnetic information may not be retrieved by any known method. In most cases, zeroisation is the technique of overwriting a memory location to a U.S. government standard of seven times (or the new standard of three times) with either all zeros or alternating ones and zeros to ensure that no remaining data in the form of magnetic remnants may be present on the media. Zeroisation may also be required for all supporting documentation, encryption materials, and other information relating to the use of or creation of the key.

Exam Point

Zeroisation, in some cases referred to as *clearing*, is a technique used to completely erase a key from an electronic device or a memory module such as a hard drive, smart card, or USB drive so that magnetic information may not be retrieved by any known method known method.

Secure Protocols

The security practitioner should be familiar with secure protocols used in data transmission. Secure protocols are used every day in e-commerce and to connect end users to end users and networks to networks. Many of the security protocols feature a variety of setup options depending upon the required result.

IPsec

Internet Protocol Security (IPsec) provides encryption security for the Internet Protocol (IP) and authentication for each IP packet of a communication session. Encryption and authentication for each packet represent granular methods of confidentiality and authentication. IPsec can provide authentication, data origin authentication, data integrity, data confidentiality (encryption), and replay protection.

IPsec a can provide communications between two hosts (transport mode), between two security gateways or routers (tunnel mode), and between gateway and host (network to host).

The IPsec has a number of different components. As a security practitioner, it is important to recognize these components and their purpose within the IPsec protocol.

Internet Key Exchange (IKE)   The IPsec protocol requires that a symmetric session key be available for encryption purposes. A key may be exchanged out of band or maybe created using the Diffie-Hellman key exchange. The Oakley Key determination protocol is a protocol that is based upon the Diffie-Hellman key exchange technique has also been employed in IKE.

Security Associations (SAs)   The Security Association provides each party with the symmetric session key. Each party will also agree upon the encryption algorithm to be utilized during the session.

Authentication Header (AH)   The *authentication header (AH)* supports access control, packet origination authentication, and connectionless integrity. Encryption is not performed by the authentication header. The authentication header may be used with the encapsulating security payload header.

Encapsulating Security Payload (ESP)   ESP is the encryption mechanism in IPsec. It provides for a header and a trailer that encapsulates the packet. Within the header are various fields that include authentication as well as integrity for the packet. ESP provides protection against replay attacks.

Security Parameter Index (SPI)   The security parameter index is a unique value assigned to a communication between two parties. It is a tag that identifies preselected encryption rules and algorithms when more than one transmission session is being conducted.

IPsec may be used in two different modes: transport mode and tunnel mode. Each of these modes illustrates the versatility of the IPsec family of protocols.

Transport Mode   The transport mode of IPsec is used for host to host, peer-to-peer, and endpoint-to-endpoint communication. In this mode, the packet contents are protected while the original IP header is exposed for internal routing.

Tunnel Mode   The tunnel mode of IPsec is used for network-to-network, gateway-to-gateway, or firewall-to-firewall communication. Normally, it is expected that this type of communication would be conducted across insecure networks such as the Internet. In tunnel mode, the original IP packet, including the payload, is encapsulated into a new packet with a new header.

Either mode may utilize the authentication header with the encapsulating security payload header and trailer. IPsec was originally included as a mandatory security implementation in IPv6. In a later IPv6 revision, it was deemed to be optional in an IPv6 implementation.

🌐 Real World Scenario

Bob's Bicycle Shop

Last year Bob opened a bicycle shop on the south side of the city. Business increased steadily over the first six months and then skyrocketed during the holiday end-of-year rush. He could hardly keep enough inventory in stock during this busy season. As business returned to normal by late January, Bob began thinking of how he could expand his business. After some consideration, he settled on the idea of opening a new store on the north side of the city.

His major concern involved managing the remote store and the logistics of placing orders for inventory, recording customer purchase transactions, and handling general accounting activities. He called Jim, a computer consultant and friend who had set up his small network. After expressing his desire to establish a new store location and his concerns of monitoring day-to-day operations, Bob asked Jim for his advice. Jim suggested that a duplicate network be set up in the second store and that both networks be tied together. He explained to Bob that he would install the second network and connect both store networks together using an IPsec-based virtual private network (VPN).

As the new store was being readied for the grand opening, Jim set up the new network and established a VPN tunnel. After careful consideration, Jim elected to use IPsec in tunnel mode as the VPN. He also selected ESP encryption to encrypt all of the data packets sent between stores. He then created a symmetric key to share between both locations. Finally, both individual local area networks were configured to appear as one large network.

Bob couldn't have been more pleased. He was able to connect the cash registers in the remote store to his accounting system in the first store. And he was also successful in running his inventory and ordering software application, which now encompassed both store locations. As an unexpected bonus, Jim connected several IP video cameras in strategic locations in the new store for safety and surveillance.

Bob was up and running in no time with his new store and network connectivity, all thanks to the implementation of an encrypted IPsec tunnel.

Exam Point

IPsec is a versatile Internet security protocol that is based on an established connection from host to host in transport mode or network to network in tunnel mode.

Secure Sockets Layer and Transport Layer Security

Both SSL and TLS use asymmetric cryptography and digital certificates to initiate communication using public and private key pairs and immediately switch to symmetric cryptography after having exchanged a symmetric "session" key. Both protocols are widely popular and are used in applications such as electronic mail, instant messaging, voice over IP (VoIP), Internet faxing, and web browsing.

Secure Sockets Layer   *SSL*, or *Secure Sockets Layer*, is the Internet protocol that provides authentication and encryption during a session. SSL works at the Transport layer of the TCP/IP protocol stack and utilizes a shared secret key. SSL is now considered insecure because it is vulnerable to the POODLE attack. Padding Oracle On Downgraded Legacy Encryption (POODLE) is a type of attack against SSL 3.0. This type of attack makes use of a fallback provision to the SSL 3.0 protocol. This fallback to a less secure state is also interoperable with legacy systems or software implementations.

Transport Layer Security   *TLS*, or *Transport Layer Security*, is the successor to SSL3.0. Although they perform similar operations, SSL and TLS are incompatible.

The technique to establish a communication session is as follows:

1. The client contacts the server and requests communications. It sends a list of cipher suites that it supports.

2. The server picks one of the suites and notifies the client of the selection. The server then sends the client its digital certificate containing its public key.

3. The client may check the validity of the certificate by checking a certificate revocation list or automatically using the new OCSP protocol.

4. The client then generates a random number and encrypts it using the server's public key. Upon receipt, the server decrypts the message using its private key. The random number now possessed by both the client and the server becomes a master key to generate session keys.

This concludes the setup process of the initial communication between the client and server, and all messages are now encrypted and decrypted using the session key. The session key is disposed of upon termination of the communication session. The SSL/TLS communication is always set up between the server and the Internet browser on the client.

 Real World Scenario

Heartbleed

Heartbleed has recently been in the news. It is a type of security bug that affects OpenSSL cryptography, which is widely implemented in the Transport Layer Security (TLS) protocol.

Continues

Continued

You need to understand a little bit about transport layer security in order to understand the Heartbleed security problem. The transport layer security protocol as well as the datagram transport layer security protocol required a quick and simple method of maintaining a secure open communication session without having to renegotiate after a period of inactivity. In practice, the technique is for one end of the device of the communication to send a text string in the form of a 16-bit integer to the other end of the communication. The receiving device is required to return exactly the 16-bit integer to the origination. This "Hello again, just checking to see if you are still there." handshake technique was termed the *Heartbeat Extension* for the TLS/DTLS protocols.

Sounding simple enough, it was immediately adopted as RFC 6520 and incorporated in several versions of OpenSSL. Unfortunately, there was an error embedded in the return request portion of the code. To exploit the error, a man-in-the-middle attacker would send a malformed packet containing the normal 16-bit integer, but instead of requesting exactly a 16-bit integer to be returned, the attacker could specify up to 64 Kb to be returned. This would possibly expose any data from recent OpenSSL communications. This recent data could easily include encryption keys, session cookies, authentication information, and personal information such as Social Security numbers, credit cards, or personally identifiable information (PII).

This type of attack is possible due to improper data validation and is referred to as a buffer over-read, or missing bounds check, attack, which results in more data being returned to the attacker than needed. The attacker exploiting the Heartbleed security bug has no control over what data is returned. However, this is a secure communication link, the 64 Kb would contain confidential information possibly of value to the attacker.

Since the Heartbleed bug was introduced by OpenSSL, it has been reported that hundreds of thousands, if not over 1 million, servers, websites, and hosts have been affected by the Heartbleed bug problem. Officials across the industry have commented that this is possibly the most damaging bug since the Internet to be used for commercial commerce. Other critics point to the fact that the OpenSSL organization is producing critical software that is used widely across the industry and yet is run by a handful of unpaid volunteers and is terribly underfunded. All in all, many are of the opinion that this points to a much larger over-arching problem within the IT industry involving open systems and open software. This involves the fact that seemingly good software is designed, changed, or implemented on a worldwide basis that is not properly vetted or tested by organizations due to possible lack of funding or implementation of proper controls and safeguards.

Exam Point

SSL/TLS utilizes symmetric cryptography after a handshake session during which secure key material (a random number) is sent from the client to the server using the asymmetric public and private keys of the server. The SSL/TLS communication is always set up between the server and the Internet browser on the client.

Summary

As a security practitioner, you can expect to be closely involved with cryptographic systems, key management, and the use of such cryptographic elements as certificates.

Confidentiality is a major security goal of any organization. You have seen that different types of organizations—whether government, military, or private industry—have a requirement to maintain the confidentiality or secrecy of information. Information as an asset has value. The intentional or unintentional release or dissemination of confidential information can have substantial damaging effects on an organization. U.S. military classifies data as top secret, secret, and unclassified, while business organizations might classify data, trade secrets, business confidential, sensitive, and public information. You have seen throughout this text that it is naïve for an uninformed individual to assume that hackers are after only credit card information. In fact, other information within the organization may have far greater value. Medical records, for instance, contain valuable data such as Social Security numbers, Medicare numbers, insurance company information, and much more exploitable information. Major events such as a merger or acquisition, introduction of a new product, approval by a regulatory agency, and a serious security incident could affect the value of a company's stock prices or its relative position within the marketplace. It is therefore very important to maintain the confidentiality and secrecy of various types of information.

The security practitioner must be aware of the different types of encryption algorithms as well as how they are used in encrypting data in transit and data at rest. You should understand the transmission and use of different types of keys because you may be called upon to manage keys, access key repositories or escrow locations, or eventually destroy keys. It is important to understand the use of digital certificates in relation to keys in that they prove or bind the ownership of the key to a public key through a trust mechanism referred to as a certificate authority.

Finally, security practitioners may be called upon to create or conduct end-user training with regard to the use of encrypted data in files as well as the creation and protection of keys.

Exam Essentials

Trusted Third Parties   Certificates work because they have been issued by a trusted entity referred to as a certificate authority. This third-party entity validates or certifies that the public key is bound to the key owner. Users of the public key can rely upon this trust system when using a public key on a certificate issued by a trusted certificate authority

Digital Certificates   Each party in an asymmetric cryptographic system has a public key. The ownership of a public key must be proven without a doubt to all users of the public key. This is achieved through a digital certificate that contains the public key and the owner's information. This binds the owner to the public key through a trust system. Digital certificates are issued and maintained by certificate authorities.

X.509 Version 3 Certificate Standard   Digital certificates are based on the X.509 version 3 certificate standard. Some of the required components are the subject's public key, the CA's distinguishing name, a unique serial number, and the digital signature of the certificate authority on the digital certificate.

PKI   The public key infrastructure (PKI) focuses on proving the identity of communication partners, providing a means to securely exchange session-based symmetric encryption keys through asymmetric cryptographic solutions, and providing a means to protect message integrity through the use of hashing.

Centralized Key Management   Centralized key management specifies a method the organization uses to maintain complete control of all keys. In centralized key management, all keys are stored in a centralized storage location or key escrow. Access to any confidential information is at the discretion of management.

Decentralized Key Management   In decentralized key management, end users generate their keys and submit keys to centralized authorities only as needed. The end user's private key is always kept private, so they are the only entity in possession of it.

Software Key Storage   Software key storage makes use of electronic mechanisms to securely store encryption keys. Most software solutions offer customizable options but may still be vulnerable to electronic attacks. Software key storage introduces risk into the protection of keys from both internal and external threats.

Hardware Key Storage   Hardware solutions are more reliable and more secure than software solutions. They can, however, be expensive and are subject to physical theft. Some common examples of hardware key storage solutions are smart cards and flash memory drives. Hardware key storage devices that are air-gaped from possible network intrusion or attack may be more secure than any device that might be attacked from either external or internal means.

Private Key Protection   In a symmetric cryptographic system, all entities in possession of the shared secret key must protect the privacy and secrecy of that key. If the key is compromised anywhere or by anyone, all of the encrypted information may be compromised. In an asymmetric cryptographic system, the user's private key must be secret at all times.

Key Revocation and Status Checking   Keys and certificates can be revoked before they reach their lifetime expiration date. Status checking is the process of checking the lifetime dates or prior revocation status against the current system date by checking the certificate revocation list (CRL) or querying an Online Certificate Status Protocol (OCSP) server.

Key Zeroisation   Zeroisation is a technique used to completely erase a key from an electronic device or a memory module such as hard drive, smart card, or USB drive. In most cases, zeroisation is the technique of overwriting a memory location to a U.S. government standard of seven times (or recently referenced three times) with either all zeros or alternating ones and zeros to ensure that no remaining data in magnetic remnants is present on the media.

Hierarchical Trust Models   A hierarchical trust model structure has a single top-level root certificate authority (CA). Below the root CA are one, two, or more subordinate CAs. The root CA is the start of the trust hierarchy. All CAs and participants in a hierarchical trust model ultimately rely on the trustworthiness of the root CA.

Written Lab

You can find the answers in Appendix A.

1.   Write a paragraph explaining the difference between symmetric and asymmetric cryptography systems.

2.   Describe what is performed during the Diffie-Hellman key exchange.

3.   Briefly explain CA, RA, CRL, and OCSP.

4.   Describe the activities necessary to create a digital signature.

Review Questions

You can find the answers in Appendix B.

1. When hashing a message, which of the following security goals is being provided?

    A. Confidentiality

    B. Encryption

    C. Accounting and availability

    D. Integrity

2. Which key is used to provide proof of origin?

    A. The sender's public key

    B. The sender's private key

    C. The receiver's public key

    D. The receiver's private key

3. Which best describes a multiple-person technique for use to recover a corrupted key?

    A. Separation of duties

    B. Multiple-key agent rule

    C. Staged multiple interaction

    D. M of N

4. Which choice is not a commonly accepted definition of *symmetric key*?

    A. A key that may be publicly exchanged

    B. A key that can be used for authentication

    C. A key used in Kerberos SSO

    D. A key that must be kept secret

5. Which of the following is an inaccurate statement about an organization's encryption policy?

    A. Private keys should be protected at all times.

    B. Local data should always be encrypted with the user's public key.

    C. The longer the storage, the longer the key.

    D. Important keys should be kept in a storage location or key escrow.

6. Which choice is not a proper method of managing keys?

    A. Keys frequently in use should be replaced frequently.

    B. Key expiration dates should be carefully monitored.

    C. Memory locations of keys should be overwritten seven times.

    D. Keys may be sent to and reused by a different department.

7. What is key clustering?

   A. The identification of several keys used in symmetric key algorithms

   B. When two different keys encrypt a plaintext message into the same ciphertext

   C. When one key encrypts a plaintext message into two different cipher text messages

   D. When one key in a keyed hash function generates different message digests

8. Which choice is the most accurate description of a collision?

   A. Two plaintext documents are corrupted when using the same symmetric key.

   B. Two plaintext documents result in the same ciphertext.

   C. Two plaintext documents result in the same hash value.

   D. Two ciphertext documents are decrypted using the same asymmetric key.

9. What is the correct description of a certificate?

   A. A certificate contains the owner's private key.

   B. A certificate contains the owner's public key.

   C. A certificate contains the owner's symmetric key.

   D. A certificate always contains a user's key.

10. Which of the following is not part of a certificate's trust architecture?

    A. Certificate authority

    B. Registration authority

    C. Certificate gateway

    D. Certificate revocation list

11. An initialization vector (IV) when used in a cipher block mode serves what purpose?

    A. Adds to the encryption power of a password or key

    B. Enhances the strength of an owner's public key

    C. Ensure that the code is repetitive

    D. Increases the speed of computations

12. Which of the following would best describe a block cipher?

    A. A cipher that encrypts data as it receives it

    B. A cipher that encrypts a set group of data at one time

    C. A cipher frequently used to encrypt VOIP communications

    D. A cipher that requires a public key to operate

13. Which of the following best describes a one-way function?

    A. A asymmetric function

    B. A symmetric function

    C. A hash function

    D. A Message Authentication Code

14. Which option best describes the encryption technique of a Caesar cipher?

   A. Diffusion

   B. Confusion

   C. Replacement

   D. Substitution

15. Which of the following options best describes the concept of hiding information in plain sight?

   A. Confusion

   B. Steganography

   C. Rapid polarization

   D. Elliptic curve

16. Which best describes actions in asymmetric cryptography?

   A. Only the private key can encrypt, and only the public key can decrypt.

   B. Only the public key can encrypt, and only the private key can decrypt.

   C. The public key is used to encrypt and decrypt, but only the private key can decrypt.

   D. If the public key encrypts, only the private key can decrypt.

17. Which of the following is most correct in a digitally signed message transmission using a hash function?

   A. The sender's public key encrypts the message.

   B. The sender's private key encrypts the hash.

   C. The hash and the message are encrypted by the receiver's private key.

   D. The hash and the message are encrypted by the receiver's public key.

18. Which of the following is not a symmetric encryption algorithm?

   A. RSA

   B. DES

   C. Twofish

   D. AES

19. Upon receiving a digital signature, what must the receiver do to verify integrity?

   A. Use a symmetric key to decrypt the message authentication code

   B. Use an asymmetric key to decrypt the hash in the HMAC

   C. Use the sender's public key to decrypt the hash value

   D. Use the receiver's public key to decrypt the hash value

20. Which of the following is not a characteristic of a symmetric key algorithm?

   A. It is slower than asymmetric algorithms.

   B. Most algorithms are available for public scrutiny.

   C. Work factor is directly related to key size.

   D. Key distribution can be a problem.

Chapter

8

Domain 6: Networks and Communications

SSCP EXAM OBJECTIVES COVERED IN THIS CHAPTER:

✓ Network Models

✓ Network Design Topographies

✓ Ports and Protocols

✓ Converged Network Communications

✓ Network Monitoring and Control

✓ Access Control Protocols and Standards

✓ Remote Network Access Control

✓ Data Plane and Control Plane

✓ Network Segmentation

✓ Secure Device Implementation

✓ Firewall and Proxy Implementation

✓ Network Routers and Switches

✓ Intrusion Detection and Prevention Devices

✓ Telecommunications Remote Access

✓ Wireless & Cellular Technologies

✓ Traffic Shaping Techniques and Devices

✓ Wireless Transmission Security

An organization's data and information flow through and between a large number of network devices. These devices may be hardwired within the organization's premises or interconnected through the Internet. Users may connect to the network through a hardwired connection from their host workstation or through the use of wireless connections.

As an SSCP, is important for you to understand all of the communication paths within the network, whether wired or wireless, and the different types of signaling protocols that are used to control devices or inform other users of the type of information that is being transmitted.

In this domain, we will investigate various theories and concepts used in modern networks and look at the devices that interconnect users to each other as well as to data sources. With the advent of voice and multimedia over digital networks, you need to understand the importance of prioritizing the transmission of information, which is known as traffic shaping. Also, intruders can take advantage of your networks, so you must implement detection measures as well as appropriate controls to mitigate the damage they might do.

Network Models

Networks are founded on the principle of device-to-device telecommunications. No longer are computers stand-alone devices that work in total isolation. It is only natural that a user must connect to another user or to a remote data source. Originally, computer systems were only required to communicate with other devices within their local premises, thus the term *local area network (LAN)*. In the past, if users or systems were required to connect to customers or clients to exchange information, they used a dedicated circuit provided by the telephone company and an agreed-upon information format such as *electronic data interchange (EDI)*.

Today, communication over the Internet is so common that little regard or concern is given to the methods required behind the scenes to make it happen. Yet a number of different signaling and communication techniques are required between the two entities in order to facilitate basic communications.

Encapsulation

Throughout the history of the early personal computer industry there were very few standards. Each company that designed and manufactured computer equipment not only designed its own operating systems but even used completely different CPU technologies. Communication between devices was very difficult. It was so confusing that even the format of specific data characters was different, with some equipment manufacturers such as IBM using *Extended Binary Coded Decimal Interchange Code (EBCDIC)* and other manufacturers adopting the *American Standard Code for Information Interchange (ASCII)* as well as many other code formats. It was the wild west of information transmission and communication.

In 1991, Adobe Systems' co-founder John Warnock created a system called "Camelot," which eventually became known as the *Portable Document Format (PDF)*, as a way to share documents and images, including any special formatting required for the files, among computer users of completely different computer platforms who may not have access to mutually compatible application software.

In practice, the user encapsulates their original document utilizing the PDF file format. This encapsulation technique creates a file that completely describes the original document and includes text, fonts, graphics, and any other information required to display it. The PDF file is then transmitted to another host machine. The only requirement for the system to work is that the receiving host must be able to execute a PDF reader application. Through the use of the PDF reader application, the individual at the receiving host is able to open and view the file. This technique enabled users on totally disparate hosts with no similarity in operating systems, CPUs, or application software to open and view files received from another host.

This is an illustration of encapsulation in which a data payload is encapsulated using a technique specified by a protocol. The protocol includes instructions and other information required by the receiving host concerning the disposition of the data payload. This is also an illustration of the methodology used today in encapsulating any data transmitted between two different hosts and two different networks.

Each PDF file encapsulates a complete description of a fixed-layout flat document, including the payload information needed to display it. This allows two completely different host systems that utilize different operating systems, hardware technology, and underlying software applications to use a set of protocols to establish and control transmission and ultimately allow the receiving host to open the document.

TCP/IP and OSI Reference Models

Data encapsulation is the foundation of both the TCP/IP and OSI models. In essence, when a document is to be sent from one user to another, the entire document must be reduced into bite-sized chunks that can ultimately be transmitted over wires. To accomplish, this the data must proceed through a number of permutations, which establishes not only the communication path between the two host computers but also the agreed-upon signaling technology using copper wires, fiber optics, or wireless radio systems.

OSI Reference Model

The *Open Systems Interconnection (OSI) model* is a conceptual model that characterizes and standardizes the internal functions of a communication system by segmenting it into layers. The OSI model is not a protocol; it is a model used for understanding and designing a communication architecture that allows any two systems to communicate regardless of the underlying hardware or software infrastructure.

The model consists of seven logical layers, numbered 1 through 7. A layer responds to or is served by the layer above it and similarly serves the layer below it. For example, one layer establishes a connection between two host machines and accepts the data to be transmitted from the layers above it. Once the connection is established by this layer, the layer below it is responsible for actually sending and receiving the packets.

Figure 8.1 shows all seven layers and illustrates the relationships between them.

FIGURE 8.1   The Open Systems Interconnection model

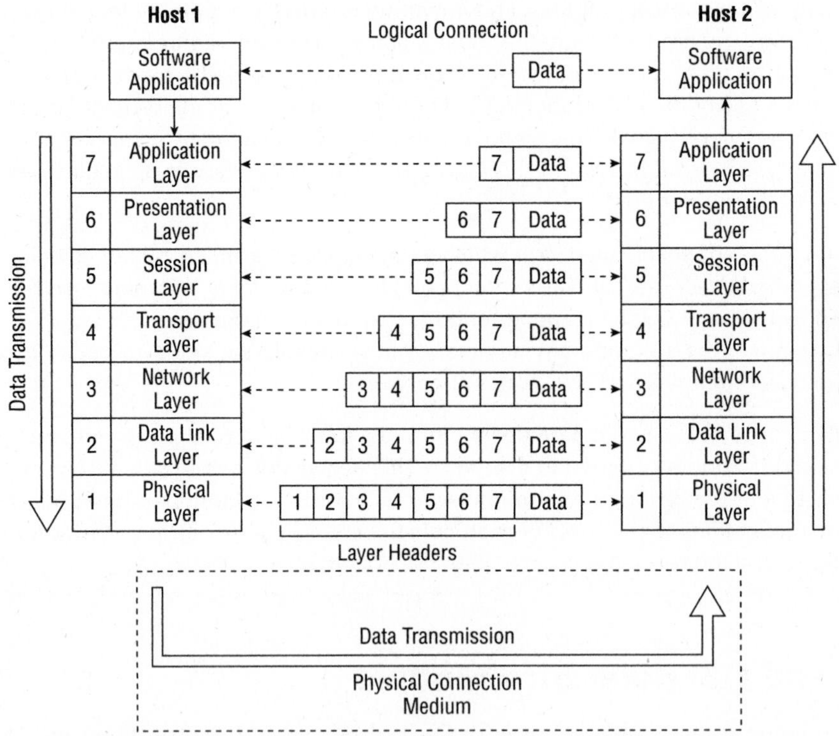

Host 1   Logical Connection   Host 2

Software Application ◀----- Data -----▶ Software Application

Data Transmission | Data Reception

	Host 1	Headers / Data	Host 2
7	Application Layer	7 Data	7 Application Layer
6	Presentation Layer	6 7 Data	6 Presentation Layer
5	Session Layer	5 6 7 Data	5 Session Layer
4	Transport Layer	4 5 6 7 Data	4 Transport Layer
3	Network Layer	3 4 5 6 7 Data	3 Network Layer
2	Data Link Layer	2 3 4 5 6 7 Data	2 Data Link Layer
1	Physical Layer	1 2 3 4 5 6 7 Data	1 Physical Layer

Layer Headers

Data Transmission

Physical Connection Medium

The OSI model groups data encapsulation functions into seven layers of logical progression. Each layer communicates only with the layer above it and the layer below as the information flows through the model. For instance, every layer serves a specific purpose. Each layer will add an appropriate header to the data, which will be interpreted at the exact same layer on the receiving host.

It is important to understand the operation of this model. It's only natural to understand that the transmitted data between two machines must flow over some sort of wire or media that connects the two computers. The actual physical connection is illustrated at the bottom of Figure 8.1. The original application data to be exchanged is illustrated between the software applications at the top of the diagram. This is the same data that might be saved to a USB drive as a data file and then reopened by the same application on a different computer.

To transmit the data over a wire connecting two computers, it is important to accomplish several functions, such as defining the type of data to be transmitted, beginning and maintaining the connection, checking for errors during the communication, determining the logical and physical addresses of the machine to receive the information, and finally, converting the data into electrical pulses on a copper wire, fiber-optic cable, or Wi-Fi radio signal.

All of this is accomplished at different layers of the OSI model. At each layer, a set of instructions is appended to the data that informs the other computer what to do and the operations to be performed at that specific layer. This information is embedded in a header created at each layer of the model and is attached in layer order to the data. Upon receiving the data, with all of the headers attached, the receiving computer processes the data up the OSI model, taking the appropriate actions at each layer and then stripping off that layer's header. Ultimately, the receiving computer, having completely processed the transmitted data, passes the data to the appropriate application.

 The individual layers in the OSI and TCP/IP models are numbered, beginning with 1 as the lowest layer. The total number of layers is referred to as a "stack."

TCP/IP Reference Model

The U.S. Department of Defense, through the *Defense Advanced Research Projects Agency (DARPA)*, created the TCP/IP model. The TCP/IP model is usually depicted with four layers that include Application layer, Transport layer, Internet layer, and Network access layer. It is a much simpler model and predates the OSI reference model. Figure 8.2 illustrates the mapping between the seven-layer OSI model and the four-layer TCP/IP model.

OSI vs. TCP/IP Models

When discussing networking, most refer to the seven-layer OSI model—long considered the foundation for how networking protocols should operate. This model is the most commonly used model, and the division between layers is well defined.

TCP/IP precedes the creation of the OSI model. While it carries out the same operations, it does so with four layers instead of seven. Those four layers are discussed in the following section, but it is important to know that while TCP/IP is the most commonly used protocol suite, OSI is the most commonly referenced networking model.

FIGURE 8.2   The OSI model mapped to the TCP/IP model

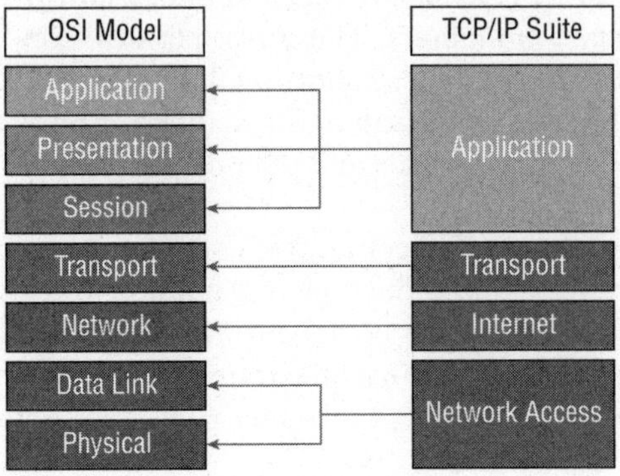

OSI Model Layer 1: The Physical Layer

All of the physical connections to the network are found at this layer. It is at this layer where 1s (ones) and 0s (zeros) become a voltage or flash of light or maybe even a modulated radio signal. All of the cables, connectors, interface cards, network taps, hubs, fiber-optic cables, and repeaters operate at this level. The physical layer is where we connect everything together using wires, radio signals, or fiber optics. All data at the Physical layer is represented by bits (1s and 0s).

There are many different types of media used for data transmissions, as explained in the following sections.

Wireless Radio Transmissions

Wireless radio transmissions utilize radio receivers and transmitters set at a certain frequency to both transmit and receive data communications. Because of the limited bandwidth available, several *radio frequency modulation techniques* are used to place more data within a limited *bandwidth*. A layer 1 wireless device would take the form of a *wireless access point* or a transceiver embedded in the circuitry of the cell phone. For instance, a cellular telephone may have two or more MAC addresses, one for each radio, such as the cellular radio and the Bluetooth radio.

Fiber-Optic Transmissions

Fiber-optic data transmission offers some of the highest bandwidth transmission rates and is least likely to be tapped into by an intruder. Fiber cable comes in various specifications:

Single-Mode   This type of fiber-optic cable has a small-diameter glass core that decreases the number of light reflections. This allows for greater transmission distances, up to 80 kilometers (km). *Single-mode fiber-optic cable* is much more expensive than any other cable and is used primarily in long-distance-transmission backbone environments. The standard color coding of the outer jacket for single-mode fiber-optic cable is yellow.

Multimode   This type of fiber-optic cable uses a much larger-diameter core than single mode. Light is allowed to refract and reflect, subsequently increasing the light degradation of signal loss. *Multimode fiber-optic cable* is used for shorter distances, up to approximately 400 meters (m). This cable is ideal for use in a local facility or building. The standard color coding of the outer jacket for multimode optical fiber cable is orange.

Plastic Optical Fiber   This type of fiber-optic cable uses a plastic core that allows for larger-diameter fibers. *Plastic optical fiber* is less capable of transmitting light over distances; therefore, this cable is restricted to 100 m or less but is the least expensive of any optical transmission cable.

Exam Point

Single-mode fiber-optic cable is created by a smaller glass fiber, is more extensive, and can transmit light large distances. Multimode fiber-optic cable uses a much larger glass fiber, is less expensive, and is used primarily within a facility or short-distance run.

Fiber-optic cable functions as a light conduit guiding the light introduced by a laser or *light emitting diode (LED)* light source at one end to a light-sensitive receiver at the other end. The light beams may be modulated to increase the number of communication channels on each fiber.

Fiber optics utilize a principle known as *total internal reflection* in which light is reflected back into the cable rather than exiting the glass. Using this technique, light beams in the form of modulated pulses transmit information down fiber lines. To minimize the loss of light and reduction of cable length, the fiber-optic cables must be made of very pure silica glass. Fiber-optic cables may be made of other types of glass based upon the shorter wavelength of ultraviolet or longer wavelength of infrared lasers.

Fiber-optic cable is subject to loss of lumen strength primarily through dispersion, which is the scattering of the light beam. For longer-length transmissions, repeaters may be utilized to strengthen the beam of light and to refresh the signal. A type of semi-flexible plastic conduit or subduct that is designed to both protect the bundle of fiber-optic cables from environmental elements and provide low friction through which to pull easily breakable, low-tensile-strength fiber-optic cables is called an *innerduct. Innerduct interior tube design* may include smooth walls, corrugated walls, and ridged walls to promote the lowest coefficient of friction when delicate fiber-optic cable is pulled.

Copper Cable/Twisted-Pair

Copper cable is the most common method of communicating signals from one point to another. Sometimes just referred to as "copper," twisted-pair wire has always been the transmission medium of choice. Easy to use and inexpensive, it also affords the easiest transmission method.

Copper cable is subject to *electromagnetic interference* from nearby radiating sources, which include lights, fans, motors, and other cables. When the cable is twisted, effective electromagnetic interference is weakened as well as the emissions from the cable itself.

Various types of copper cables may be used within a network environment:

Twisted Pair   This cable features pairs of twisted copper wires, referred to as *twisted-pair cable* TP, that are encased in a plastic outer casing. It's sometimes referred to as plenum wire because this cable is normally run within the plenum area above the ceiling or inside walls. The plastic casing in plenum wire is both resistant to burning and resistant to emitting toxic fumes during a fire.

Unshielded Twisted-Pair   This cable features numerous individual copper cable strands twisted together. In most network situations, these strands are encased in a plastic outer insulation. *Unshielded twisted-pair cable* is referred to as UTP.

Shielded Twisted-Pair   This type of cable, generically referred to as *shielded twisted-pair cable (STP)*, utilizes a common ground shield encasing the twisted strands.

Screened Shielded Twisted-Pair   This type of cable features shielding encasing each of the twisted pairs as well as the outer bundle of twisted pairs. This eliminates EMI between the twisted-pair sets and prevents EMI from entering or exiting the cable bundle.

Screened shielded twisted-pair is a cable description that specifies both an internal twisted-pair shielding as well as an overall cable bundle shield. This shielding may take the form of either metallic foil or metallic wire braiding. Using this nomenclature, *F* stands for foil-based shields, while *S* refers to metallic braided shields. For instance, F/FTP indicates a foil shield encasing the wire pairs as well as a foil shield encasing the wire bundle. The S/FTP designation would refer to a foil shield encasing the wire pairs with a braided metallic shield encasing the wire bundle.

This technique of shielding offers greater isolation from external *electromagnetic interference* signals and from internal signals being emitted between conductors. *Shielded twisted-pair cable* always utilizes a type of grounded metal shielding to encase the twisted-pair copper cables. There are three types of shielded twisted-pair cable for high-bandwidth applications such as CAT6a, CAT7, and CAT8 cables.

STP   Designates shielded twisted-pair, which is a twisted-pair cable with braided metallic shielding that encases all of the twisted pairs.

F/UTP   Designates a twisted-pair cable with foil shielding that encases all of the twisted pairs.

F/FTP and S/FTP   Designates a fully shielded twisted-pair cable where internal twisted pairs are individually shielded and the entire cable bundle is encased by an external shield. The *F* designates foil, while the *S* indicates a braided shield.

Figure 8.3 depicts various categories of shielded twisted pair cable and the relative transmission speeds.

FIGURE 8.3   Categories of twisted-pair cable

IT Industry Category Designation	Cabling Bandwidth	Cable Shielding and Design Construction	Network Applications	Notes
CAT5	100 MHz	UTP	Ethernet 100BaseTX and 1000BaseT	General Commercial LAN usage.
CAT5e	100 MHz	UTP	Ethernet 100BaseTX and 1000BaseT	A higher-quality cable referred to as enhanced CAT5.
CAT6	250 MHz	UTP	Ethernet 10GBaseT	Currently specified by many building codes.
CAT6e	500 MHz	U/FTP, F/UTP	Ethernet 10GBaseT	Extra shielding provides better EMI protection.
CAT7	600 MHz	F/FTP, S/FTP	Multimode and Ethernet in the same cable using 1000BaseTX or 10GBaseT	Much better shielding. Twisted pairs are individually shielded, and the cable bundle is encased in an outer shield.
CAT7a	1000 MHz	F/FTP, S/FTP	Includes VoIP, CCTV, multimedia, and Ethernet in the same cable using 1000Base TX and 10GBaseT	Twisted pairs are individually shielded. The cable bundle is encased in an outer shield. Uses four twisted pairs for increased bandwidth and isolation.

Coaxial Cable

Coaxial cable, or coax, is constructed as a large copper central conductor encased in a nonconductive dielectric material that is then encased within a braided copper shield. The entire assembly is then covered with a plastic casing. Coaxial cable is much less resistant to interference and cross talk. Also, due to the size of the central conductor, coaxial cable is capable of handling much greater current loads and is therefore ideal for radio antenna lead cables. Coaxial cable is much more expensive than twisted pair and requires a much wider bend radius.

Plenum Cable

Plenum cable is a specifically jacketed cable with a fire retardant plastic jacket. Most local building codes adopted cable specifications for any cabling or wires that are routed through the plenum spaces within a building. Plenum spaces include areas above all ceilings, interior walls, riser areas, and control cabinets and closets. Plenum cables not only offer fire resistance, they are constructed of low-smoke and low-toxic-fume-emitting polymers such as *polyvinyl chloride (PVC)*.

Data Transmission Methods

Data may be transmitted on media using two different methods:

Baseband   Data transmitted using baseband transmission occupies the entire frequency range of the media. No other data is transmitted concurrently.

Broadband   Broadband transmission, which is popular with cable television and networking providers, is used to multiplex a very large number of signals on a single media.

OSI Model Layer 2: The Data Link Layer

Layer 2 addresses traffic to a physical link address. Every network interface card contains a *Media Access Control (MAC)* address. A MAC address is the physical address of the directly connected device and consists of a manufacturer's identification as well as a unique number identifying the device.

Layer 2 *switches*, sometimes referred to as L2 switches, operate at this layer. As traffic comes into a switch on a specific switch port, the switch creates a map table identifying the device with the MAC address in the specific switch port. When data is received by the switch and is destined for a specific MAC address, it is forwarded out that specific port. Digital information received or sent at the Data Link layer is formatted as *frames*. The Data Link layer is concerned with directing data to the next physically connected device.

OSI Model Layer 3: The Network Layer

The Network layer determines the routing of data across a network utilizing a logical address referred to as an Internet Protocol (IP) address. An IP address such as 192.168.40.10 represents the logical address of node 10 on network number 40. Through the use of the *Dynamic Host Configuration Protocol (DHCP)*, a different logical address is given to a host at each logon.

The Network layer moves data along the network between two hosts that are not physically connected. Layer 3 devices such as routers read the destination layer 3 IP address and make use of a routing table on the router to determine the next device in the network to send the packet.

IPv4 and IPv6

The early designers of the Internet required a method of moving information between networks, hosts, and servers that were not physically connected. The design included using a protocol now in its fourth version and referred to as *IPv4* to route packets of information to a final destination address. IP is a routable protocol whose job is to make a best effort at delivery of the information. The header is normally 20 bytes long, but it can be as long as 60 bytes when options are included. Most businesses and organizations use IPv4 with *Network Address Translation (NAT)* to provide internal private IP addresses.

Unfortunately, with only IPv4 32-bit address, all total available addresses were exhausted by April 2011. By that time, many organizations have resorted to NAT in an effort to increase the total number of addresses available for their internal hosts and servers. NAT is a very normal environment for most internal local area networks and does provide a measure of security by obscuring the internal address structure to the outside world.

With knowledge of the very limited availability of IPv4 addresses, computer engineers have developed a much more robust IP routing system called IPv6. IPv6 offers a greatly expanded addressing structure of 128 bits. Along with the increase in address size come other improvements. *IPv6* offers an internal option to support IPsec-based security, which will offer end-to-end authentication, privacy, and integrity. NAT will no longer be required due to the incredible number of addresses available. *Address Resolution Protocol (ARP)* will no longer be required and will be replaced by a new protocol called *Network Discovery Protocol (NDP)*.

Challenges will exist during the adoption. Time and money will be a central issue in the conversion to IPv6. With millions of hosts, servers, and network devices currently operating using IPv4 for addressing, the conversion to IPv6 will be painful to say the least. In the short term, IPv6-to-IPv4 translation devices may be used as a temporary solution for organizations during the transition. Europe and most notably Asian countries far exceed the United States in the adoption rate of IPv6 and will seemingly drive the market for IPv6-compatible networking equipment.

The first illustration below depicts an IPv4 packet header with a 32-bit address space. The second illustration shows an IPv6 packet header with a 128-bit address space. Notice that the IPv6 packet header has fewer items prior to the address space.

IPv4 Packet Header

IP Version Number (4)	IHL (4 Bits)	Type of Service (8 Bits)	Total Length (16 Bits)
Identification (16 Bits)	Flags (4 Bits)		Fragment Offset (12 Bits)
Time to Live (8 Bits)	Protocol (8 Bits)		Header Checksum (16 Bits)
Source Address (32 Bits)			
Destination Address (32 Bits)			
Options (variable)		Padding (variable)	

IPv6 Packet Header

IP Version Number (6)	Traffic Class (8 Bits)	Flow Label (20 Bits)
Payload Length (16 Bits)	Next Header (8 Bits)	Hop Limit (8 Bits)
Source Address (128 Bits)		
Destination Address (128 Bits)		

Exam Point

IPv4 has an address space of 32 bits while IPv6 has an address space of 128 bits.

OSI Model Layer 4: The Transport Layer

The Transport layer moves data packaged in segments. This layer provides end-to-end and reliable communications services and includes error detection and recovery methods. Two primary protocols are utilized at this layer.

User Datagram Protocol   The *User Datagram Protocol (UDP)* is referred to as a connectionless protocol. *Connectionless* refers to sending information without first verifying that the connection exists between the hosts. The sending host has no expectation of receiving a reply or confirmation that the data has been received. Should an error occur or should data not be received, it is incumbent upon the receiving host to request a retransmission. UDP is ideal for transmission of voice or media.

Transmission Control Protocol   The *Transmission Control Protocol (TCP)* is referred to as connection-oriented because it provides guaranteed and reliable communication between devices on the network. TCP requires that the receiving host acknowledge every packet that it receives. Packets may be received out of order and may be re-sequenced by the receiving host.

Figure 8.4 illustrates the three-way handshake used to begin a TCP session. The first step of the handshake is where the host sends the server a packet with the SYN, or synchronize, flag turned on or "set." The server responds with a packet that has both the acknowledgment ACK and SYN flags set. Finally, the host responds with a packet that has the ACK flag set. At this point, the TCP session has been established.

FIGURE 8.4   TCP three-way handshake

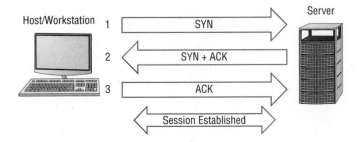

Other protocols that require guaranteed delivery may be paired up with TCP. Probably the most famous pairing is TCP/IP, where the IP address provides the packet routing information and TCP provides the guaranteed delivery and request for resend for error correction.

OSI Model Layer 5: The Session Layer

The Session layer establishes and maintains sessions between peer hosts. A session is similar to a connected phone line between two parties. The two parties in this case are logically connected without regard to the type or nature of information that is transferred between them.

Exam Point

Layer 5, the Session layer, maintains an open logical communication line between the two host machines. The analogy may be similar to maintaining an open telephone line.

Layer 4, the Transport layer, handles the transmission and retransmission of data. For example, if one host machine receives a message that it does not understand, it can request for the information to be resent.

OSI Model Layer 6: The Presentation Layer

The Presentation layer is sometimes referred to as the translation layer because of the change in data at this layer. At this layer, data being sent from a host application may be required to be translated or changed before being presented to the receiving host application. For instance, an IBM application may provide data which is formatted using the *Extended Binary Coded Decimal Interchange Code (EBCDIC)*. The receiving application may require the data to be presented to it in *American Standard Code for Information Interchange (ASCII)* code. The Presentation layer also maintains the capability of providing some encryption and decryption as well as data compression and decompression.

OSI Model Layer 7: The Application Layer

The Application layer provides a variety of services so that the application data can be transmitted across the network. This layer may also provide access control methodology, such as identification, authentication, and availability of remote applications; hashing for integrity; and the checking of digital signatures.

Exam Point

The OSI model has seven layers, while the TCP/IP model has four. It is important to remember that the IPv4 address space is 32 bits and the IPv6 address space is 128 bits.

 Real World Scenario

Remembering the Layers

Some folks find it difficult to remember the order of all seven layers in the OSI model. From layer 1 to layer 7, the layers are named Physical, Data Link, Network, Transport, Session, Presentation, and Application. It's fairly easy to get these out of order. Just remember one of the following sentences:

"Please Do Not Throw Sausage Pizza Away" or "All People Seem to Need Data Processing"

Continues

Continued

These are some of the more common sayings used to remember the OSI layer order, but feel free to make up your own.

Network Design Topographies

A network topology is the design, or the physical layout, of the network. In other words, it is the layout of wires, cables, fiber optics, routers, switches, and all of the servers and host machines.

The design of early networks preceded the availability of the basic networking component equipment such as routers and switches of today and even the use of Ethernet. Numerous challenges greeted the network engineers of yesterday. Wiring required a reduced-run length due to the attenuation or fading of the data signals. There was the problem of who had priority on the network to send data and what would happen if two hosts transmitted at the same time. These and many more problems led to some of the early network designs.

Network Topology Models

Network topology has changed through the years. The following five models depict the most popular layouts:

Bus   The bus topology was one of the earliest and most commonsense designs for local area network layout and design. The central bus wire featured terminators at each end, and computer hosts as well servers were connected to the central bus wire through what was known as "drops." There were a couple of advantages to this system. Adding a node to the bus was very easy, and if an individual node failed, it would not affect other nodes on the central bus wire.

A disadvantage was that if the central bus wire failed, the entire network failed as well because the cable run lengths had to be short due to signal fading. Each of the drop cables connected to the central bus wire with a special connector. The connector not only reduced the amplitude of the signal, but if they were disconnected inappropriately, the entire network would fail. Figure 8.5 illustrates a common *bus topology*.

Tree   The tree topology is similar to several parallel bus structures, each containing networking items, one placed on top of the other. The top-level bus drops to a server. The server then connects below it to another bus, which contains hosts or workstations. This is a layered approach to a bus structure, but it still maintains the same problems as a bus topology. If the last centralized device fails, everything below it also fails. Figure 8.6 illustrates a *tree topology*.

FIGURE 8.5 A bus topology

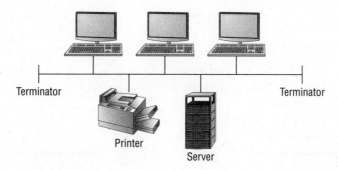

FIGURE 8.6 A tree topology

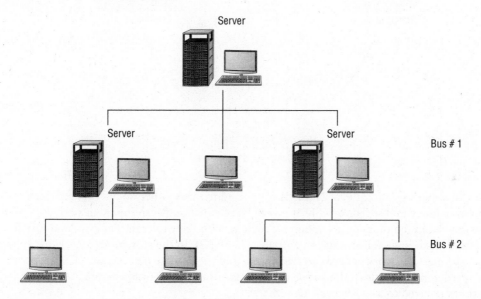

Ring   The ring topology is an older technology predating Ethernet networks and was made popular by IBM. It provided a solution to the problem of who talks next. When a token was circulated around a closed loop ring, each node could determine exactly when they could transmit next. This was referred to as a deterministic system. Typically, token ring networks consisted of coaxial cable or fiber-optic cable. Because the entire ring is a single point of failure, later technology such as Fiber Distributed Data Interface (FDDI) provided redundancy by using two rings for failover. Ring topology has been almost totally eliminated and replaced by Ethernet technology. Figure 8.7 illustrates a typical *ring topology.*

FIGURE 8.7   A ring topology

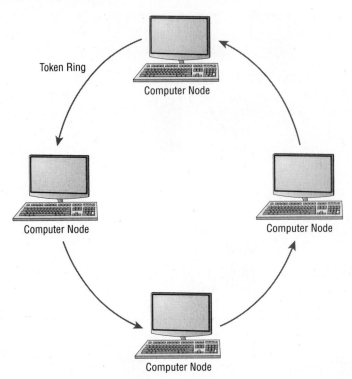

Mesh   In a mesh topology, every node is connected to every other node. This provides great redundancy and speed, usually at a very large expense. Mesh topologies are used where speed and redundancy are required, such as with fault-tolerant devices, load distribution server clustering, and storage area networks (SANs). In the storage area network application, the mesh network is between the servers and the storage devices, which allows for great speed and redundancy. This type of mesh usually consists of fiber-optic cables and is sometimes referred to as a *fiber fabric*.

The number of connections required in a mesh network can be illustrated through the equation $N * (N - 1) / 2$, where N equals the number of devices. For instance, if there were 10 devices on the mesh network, the equation would be $10 * 9 / 2 = 45$ connections. If 2 more devices were added to the network, the equation would be $12 * 11 / 2 = 66$ connections. So as you can see, when just two additional devices were added, the number of connections jumped by 21. Figure 8.8 illustrates a *mesh topology*.

Star   Present-day networks generally take the form of a star topology. In this type of layout design, each node is connected to a central device such as a switch or router. Although the use of a centralized connection devices inserts a single point of failure, the flexibility of this type of network design allows for shorter cable runs and ease of network deployment. Figure 8.9 illustrates a *star topology*.

FIGURE 8.8   A mesh topology

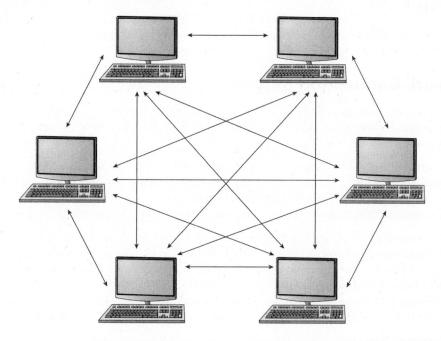

FIGURE 8.9   A star topology

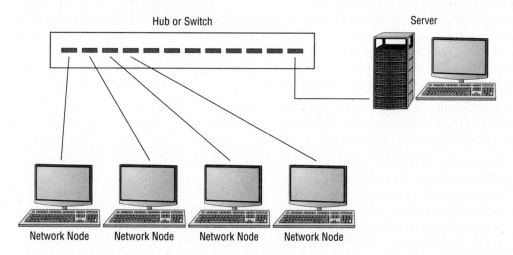

Exam Point

The star network topology is most frequently used in modern networks.

Network Connection Models

Various types of networks are required to transmit data across town or across the country. The design of these networks spans the period of wires hanging on telephone poles to today, when the very latest technologies are available.

Circuit-Switched Networks   *Circuit-switched networks* are created by physically connecting to endpoints through a series of wires and mechanical switches where the signal voltage generated at one endpoint is received by the other endpoint. A disadvantage of this early network communication was both lack of available bandwidth and poor line quality.

A typical example of a circuit-switched network was known as *plain old telephone service (POTS)*. Telephone companies grappled with digital technology as they made every attempt to transmit data over relatively low-quality standard telephone lines. One of the outgrowths of this was *Integrated Services Digital Network (ISDN)*, and other techniques were also used in the quest for higher speed and greater reliability. In these later data network offerings, carriers offered dedicated networks to clients and billed only for time of use.

Packet-Switched Networks   Typical of most wide area networks today, a *packet-switched network* makes use of a large number of devices with nondedicated connections. Information is subdivided into packets that feature an address of the ultimate destination. Devices such as routers use the destination address and forward the packet to the next router until the packet eventually arrives at its destination. Since the packet-switching network is dynamic and ever changing, packets within one conversation may take numerous routes. Because of this, packets may arrive out of order, and it is up to the receiving device to resequence the packets in the correct order.

Virtual Circuit Networks   Some organizations require high-bandwidth connections between offices, clients, or other endpoints. In such cases, they may contract with a carrier for a special type of data network.

Permanent Virtual Circuit   A *permanent virtual circuit (PVC)* is a connection between endpoints where the carrier configures the circuit routes to provide the requested speed and bandwidth through their equipment. This provisioning is usually accomplished when the permanent virtual circuit is initially contracted and when the dedicated hardware and contracted bandwidth is determined. Typically, once a permanent virtual circuit is established, it remains connected.

Switched Virtual Circuit   A *switched virtual circuit (SVC)* dynamically configures the circuit routes each time the circuit is used by the end user. A switched virtual circuit is less expensive and is billed for only time of use.

Media Access Models

Through the years network engineers have struggled with the concept of trying to get more users to communicate on a single piece of wire. Various techniques, some better than others, have been designed to eliminate congestion in an attempt to provide an orderly flow of data through a network.

Carrier Sense Multiple Access   *Carrier sense multiple access (CSMA)* is a media access control protocol used to communicate on the media such as a wire, fiber-optic cable, or modulated radio signal. *Carrier sense* refers to the fact that the device is listening to the media at all times. It is specifically listening for the transmission of other devices. *Multiple access* means that all of the devices on the wire or network are transmitted the same time. Of course, if they are, the transmitted data would be unrecognizable. This type of communication has no mediating controller and therefore is called contention-based access and nondeterministic. It is the least effective of any of the transmission protocols because none of the devices have any means of determining when to transmit data.

Carrier Sense Multiple Access/Collision Detection   *Carrier sense multiple access/collision detection (CSMA/CD)* is a media access control protocol used to communicate in an organized fashion on a type of media. As in CSMA, a device may begin transmitting at the same time another device transmits. When this happens, two frames will be transmitted simultaneously and a "collision" will occur. Each of the two devices will wait a random period of time and then retransmit. The random timer prohibits each of the two devices from immediately retransmitting and causing a collision once again. This is the most-often-used technique to reduce transmission contention on modern local area networks.

Carrier Sense Multiple Access/Collision Avoidance   *Carrier sense multiple access/collision avoidance (CSMA/CA)* is a media access control protocol used to announce that a device is wishing to transmit on the media. The device will transmit or broadcast a tone prior to transmission. The tone is referred to as a jamming signal and will be received by all other devices connected to the media. After waiting a brief interval to ensure that all other devices are aware of the device's desire to transmit, the device begins transmitting.

Ethernet   *Ethernet* is an IEEE 802.3 standard that supports a number of different media standards such as coaxial, fiber-optic, and shielded and unshielded twisted-pair cable. Ethernet speeds include 100 megabits per second (Mbit/s) to 1,000 Mbit/s over both unshielded twisted-pair and fiber-optic cables. Through the use of CSMA/CD, most collisions are dealt with on smaller networks or limited-broadcast domains. On larger networks, there may be major network media contention due to retransmission volume.

Exam Point

Ethernet is referred to as a "best effort" communication method.

Ports and Protocols

Ports and protocols are utilized within both hosts and servers to facilitate the connection between received and transmitted information. A port is a special type of memory address to which an application or service on the system listens and transmits. This is its access to the outside world and method of receiving data.

Ports

Ports are special addresses in memory that allow communication between hosts and applications or services running on a host. A port number is added to the address from the originator, indicating which port to communicate with on a server. If a server has a port defined and available for use, it will send back a message accepting the request. A server is instructed to refuse to connect if the port isn't valid. The *Internet Assigned Numbers Authority (IANA)* has defined and maintains a list of ports called *well-known ports*.

Ports may also prove to be a source of security weakness. An intruder may perform a port scan to determine which ports are open and may be penetrated to gain access into a system. Therefore, any unused ports should be blocked by a firewall to reduce the possibility of intrusion.

Port list

Ports are defined by the Internet Assigned Numbers Authority and may be viewed on the IANA website:

    www.iana.org/assignments/service-names-port-numbers/service-names-
    port-numbers.xhtml

Well-known ports are those ports that have been assigned to specific software applications, services, and protocols. For instance, port 80 is the common port for all Internet traffic. Ports are identified by the specific communication method they use. TCP ports expect to set up a three-way handshake, while UDP ports will transmit all of the information without expecting a confirmation of receipt. Table 8.1 lists well-known TCP ports, and Table 8.2 lists well-known UDP ports. Ports with an asterisk are important to know.

Exam point

It is important to know some of the well-known ports for the exam.

TABLE 8.1   Well-known TCP ports

TCP Port Number	Service
20	FTP (data channel)
*21	FTP (control channel)
*22	SSH and SCP
23	Telnet
*25	SMTP
*80	HTTP
*110	POP3
119	NNTP
*143	IMAP
389	LDAP
*443	HTTPS

TABLE 8.2   Well-known UDP ports

UDP Port Number	Service
*22	SSH and SCP
49	TACACS
*53	DNS
69	TFTP
*80	HTTP
*143	IMAP
161	SNMP
389	LDAP
989	FTPS (data channel)
990	FTPS (control channel)

There are total of 65,536 ports available. Note that there is a port number 0 (zero), which makes the range of port numbers 0 to 65,535. These ports are divided into three primary groups:

Well Known Ports: **Ports 0–1023**   Well-known ports are ports that are assigned and matched to specific protocols. The port number is embedded in a packet destined for a host or server machine.

Registered Ports: **1024–49151**   Registered ports are ports that are reserved to be used by third-party applications, services, and networking devices to communicate between machines.

Dynamic, or Private, Ports: **49152–65535**   The upper layer of the port range may be used by applications that begin a conversation at a port with a lower number and then switch the conversation to a port with a higher number. Using this technique releases the lower port to respond to additional communication requests.

Exam Point

There are 65,536 ports available, which are divided into three general groupings: well-known ports, registered ports, and dynamic, or private, ports.

Remembering the Port Number Ranges

Here is a trick used in the academic community for memorizing facts. To remember the three specific port ranges, only memorize the middle range, which are the registered ports, 1024–49151. From here you can interpolate the range above and below without having to memorize those numbers.

Common Protocols

There are hundreds of protocols. The difficulty is in determining how each protocol is used and whether it is secure. The following list details a number of common protocols.

File Transfer Protocol   *File Transfer Protocol (FTP)* is an older interconnect protocol that allows connections between machines for file uploads and downloads. FTP is among the original protocols developed for the Internet. Ports 20 and 21 are used by default by FTP to transfer information between hosts and the Internet. Due to its design, FTP is insecure.

Simple Mail Transfer Protocol   *Simple Mail Transfer Protocol (SMTP)* is the standard protocol for email communications. SMTP involves the use of email clients and servers to transmit messages. The default port is 25.

Domain Name System   *Domain Name System (DNS)* allows hosts to resolve hostnames to an Internet Protocol (IP) address. For instance, DNS would convert a fully qualified domain name into an IP address. The default port used by the domain name system when sending name queries for this service is 53.

Simple Network Management Protocol   *Simple Network Management Protocol (SNMP)* is a management tool that allows network devices to send selected parameter data to a management console. A software client runs on the network device and captures various parameters and performance data at the request of a central administrator. Most routers, bridges, and other network appliances can be monitored using SNMP.

Post Office Protocol   *Post Office Protocol* (POP) is a protocol used in many email systems. It is a standard communications interface in many email servers. Post Office Protocol is used for receiving email. The default port for version 3 (POP3) is 110. In its place, many systems now use the *Internet Message Access Protocol (IMAP)* to download email messages from a storage location upon request. IMAP is assigned to port 143.

Telnet   *Telnet* is a legacy protocol and performs as an interactive terminal emulation protocol. It allows a remote user to maintain an interactive session with a Telnet server. The Telnet session will appear to the client as if it were a local session.

Address Resolution Protocol   *Address Resolution Protocol (ARP)* provides a process for resolving IP addresses into Data Link layer MAC hardware addresses. ARP resolves an IP address to a *Media Access Control (MAC)* address. MAC addresses are used to identify hardware network devices and are assigned to the network interface card (NIC).

Internet Control Message Protocol   *Internet Control Message Protocol (ICMP)* provides reporting and maintenance functionality. ICMP includes a number of communication information commands, such as ping to test connectivity and traceroute to return the route used by packets to a destination. Routers and other network devices can report path information between hosts using ICMP.

It is important when securing any host or server that it is running the least number of protocols required for operations. Old or unused protocols that are no longer used should be removed. Leaving them on a system creates an opening for an attacker to access the system through weaknesses in unnecessary protocols.

Maintaining the security of ports is very important. One of the common procedures in hardening a system is to close unused ports and remove unused protocols. Closing unused ports is generally accomplished by blocking the port on a firewall. It is important to consider blocking not only popular specifically named ports but also a large range of ports that may be exploited by an intruder.

Secure Sockets Layer (SSL) is used to establish a secure communication session between two TCP-based machines. This protocol uses a handshake method that utilizes public key infrastructure (PKI) to establish a session and eventually symmetric encryption to maintain a session. SSL was originally developed by Netscape for e-commerce purposes, to connect servers to host browsers. SSL v3 has since been broken and is now depreciated.

Transport Layer Security (TLS) is a security protocol that expands upon SSL. The TLS standard was developed and supported by the *Internet Engineering Task Force (IETF)* and is not compatible with SSL.

Converged Network Communications

The convergence of network communications involves the combination of media transmission, including *Voice over Internet Protocol (VoIP)* as well as television, radio, and nontraditional data content that will be generated by the *Internet of Things (IoT)*. The basic type of network convergence is the combination of media files and data files and the physical connection across differing platforms and networks, which allows several types of networks to connect with each other within certain common standards and protocols.

Convergence involves new ways of communicating over a digital medium involving both existing and emerging content suppliers. Digital technology now allows both traditional and new communication services—whether voice, data, sound, or pictures—to be provided over many different types of digital transmission mediums that traditionally required separate networks. For instance, although broadcast television was an essential provider of both entertainment and news content through most of the 20th century, fewer and fewer homes will be equipped with broadcast receiver equipment. Television programming will soon evolve onto a digital communication medium where content may be provided across multiple platforms. Similarly, there has been a major decline within the newspaper industry as the majority of individuals are now seeking their news content digitally on multi-platform devices rather than reading print on paper.

Generational differences in the use of digital assets will drive the marketplace away from what was traditional mid-20th-century communication mediums such as wired telephones within the house, newspapers in the front yard, and a limited number of local broadcast television stations into a digitized world of information. Younger generations eagerly adopt new technology that offers the freedom of multi-platform, interactive information on demand.

Because the traditional communication methodology such as newspapers and broadcast media is no longer in demand, *digital convergence* will place all of the communication channels into a digital world. Whether at home, at the office, or in a classroom, the demand for convenience and entertainment will drive the marketplace into an expansive offering of digital services.

Network Monitoring and Control

Network monitoring and control is usually included in the job description of an SSCP. From monitoring the performance of devices to establish baselines and assure their continued security performance to monitoring network traffic to discover anomalies and possibly intruders, network monitoring and control provides an essential role in network security.

Continuous Monitoring

Continuous monitoring involves the policy, process, and technology used to detect risk issues within an organization's IT infrastructure. This monitoring may be in response to regulatory or contractual compliance mandates.

Continuous monitoring of network operations stems from a risk assessment program where it was required for financial transactions. During the financial transactions monitoring procedure, the disposition of all transactions is recorded and analyzed for risk and regulatory compliance.

The continuous monitoring of network operations is where security incident and event monitoring (SIEM) activities are maintained on a 24/7 basis. Logs must be maintained for specific time periods and analyzed as appropriate. Effectively, continuous monitoring requires that all users be monitored equally, that users be monitored from the moment they enter the physical or logical premises of an organization until they depart or disconnect, and that all activities of all types on any and all services and resources be tracked. This comprehensive approach to auditing, logging, and monitoring increases the likelihood of capturing evidence related to abuse or violations.

Network Monitors

Network monitoring devices are available with several different modes of operation, which include active and passive modes. Passive network monitors, otherwise called sniffers, were originally introduced to help troubleshoot network problems. Intrusion detection systems are also passive network monitoring devices.

A network monitoring system usually consists of a PC with a NIC (running in promiscuous mode) and monitoring or logging software. Promiscuous mode simply means that the network card is set in such a way that it accepts any packet that it sees on the network, even if that packet is not addressed to that network interface card.

The amount of information obtained from network traffic may be immense. Logical filtering to identify anomalies or items of interest must be undertaken due to the overwhelming amount of traffic.

Active network monitors, such as intrusion prevention systems, also monitor network traffic activity, but they are tuned to detect specific anomalies. In the event they discover traffic that should not be allowed on the network, an active monitor will take some predetermined action, such as dropping the packet or generating a firewall rule.

Managing Network Logs

Network logs are the lifeblood of a network monitoring operation. They can be set to record every event that happens on the network. This would create a large volume of information very quickly. There are several different types of logs, and the SSCP should be familiar each of them.

Event/Security Logs

*Event log*s are networking or system logs that record various events as they occur. Everything that happens on a network—an individual logging in, developing an application, accessing a database, and sending an email—can be recorded. When you combine the events caused by individuals with all of the events caused by applications accessing each other, the amount of event information can be huge.

Event logs is a broad category that includes some logs not relevant to security issues. But within that broad category are security and access logs that are clearly important to the security of the network. Microsoft Windows has a great amount of logging capability; the two most important logs for security purposes are listed here:

Application Log   This log contains various events logged in real time by applications, databases, or other programs. It is generated by many applications that will be recorded in the application log. This type of log is useful within an application such as SQL Server to determine problems within a database. An *application log* can be examined for evidence that an intruder has been attempting to compromise a database or application.

Security Log   The *security log* records events related to resource use, such as creating, opening, and deleting files or manipulating other objects. Among the many events the security log records, two of the most important are the successful and unsuccessful logon attempts by users. A security log can easily be fine-tuned so that a security administrator can audit events of interest.

Audit Logs

Audit logs offer crucial information about the actions and activities on an organization's network. Auditors that are internal to the organization review proper activities on servers and network devices while external auditors may be analyzing network operations for regulatory compliance.

The log files created by network services such as DNS need to be routinely examined. The DNS service, when running on Windows Server 2012 R2, for example, writes entries to the log file that can be examined using Event Viewer. Log size and overwrite options may be set by the operator for each security log object.

A firewall with event logging enabled will create log files the same as many other services. Since firewalls are extremely important to the network, administrators should regularly review the logs. Firewall logs may be generated in a central location or on the host's or client's firewall device.

Most *antivirus program*s also create log files that should be checked regularly by an administrator. The logs should verify not only that the antivirus program is running but also that the definition files being used are up to date and current. The administrator should pay attention to the viruses that are found and deleted/quarantine as well as any files that are being skipped.

Access Control Protocols and Standards

Every user must be authenticated when requesting entry into a computer network. As the number of network users increases, so does the complexity of the authentication mechanisms used to provide them with access to the network. Many users may be sitting at their desk or cubicle when logging into a computer network, but an ever-increasing number will be in a home office, at an airport, or at a client site when requesting access into the network. There are several techniques for both transporting information to a remote location and verifying the identity and authentication of the user.

A tunnel is created by encapsulating data into larger protected packets. These larger packets will have a separate IP address indicating the destination but not the original source of the data. Tunnels are usually called virtual private networks.

Remote Network Access Control

Users wishing access to an enterprise network may be across the street, across town, or around the world. In any event, they are normally transmitting data through an untrusted network, such as the Internet. It is important to place controls on the network to mitigate the risk of data interception, corruption, and a variety of other attacks that might occur when data is transmitted and receive across this type of network.

A *virtual private network (VPN)* is a private network connection that is established through a public network. Creating a tunnel, or VPN, is a method of encapsulating restricted or private data so that it may not be read or intercepted when traversing the Internet. Encapsulation is the act of placing restricted data inside a larger packet and placing a special destination address on the packet so that it may be routed to the intended receiver.

A virtual private network provides information security through encryption and encapsulation over an otherwise unsecure environment. VPNs can be used to connect LANs together across the Internet or through other public networks. When a VPN is used, both ends appear to be connected to the same network. A VPN requires a VPN software package to be running on servers and workstations. Figure 8.10 illustrates a virtual private network connecting two different networks.

FIGURE 8.10 A virtual private network

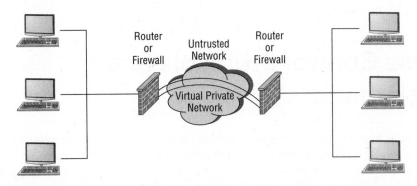

Tunneling protocols are used to encapsulate other packets that are sent across public networks. Once the packets are received, the *tunneling protocol* is discarded, leaving the original information for the receiver.

The most common protocols used for tunneling are as follows:

Point-to-Point Tunneling Protocol *Point-to-Point Tunneling Protocol (PPTP)* supports encapsulation in a single point-to-point environment. PPTP encapsulates and encrypts *point-to-point protocol (PPP)* packets. Although PPTP is a favorite protocol for network communications, one of its major weaknesses is that all channel negotiation is done in the clear. After the tunnel is created, the data is encrypted. Developed by Microsoft, PPTP is supported on most of the company's products. PPTP is assigned to port 1723 and uses TCP for connections.

Layer 2 Forwarding *Layer 2 Forwarding (L2F)* was created by Cisco as a method of creating tunnels that do not require encryption. Used primarily for dial-up connections, L2F provides authentication only. L2F uses port 1701 (a little Cisco humor; 1701 is the number of the *Starship Enterprise* while it "tunnels through space"). L2F uses TCP for connections.

Layer 2 Tunneling Protocol Due to the demands of the market, Microsoft and Cisco have reached an agreement to combine their respective tunneling protocols into one protocol, the *Layer 2 Tunneling Protocol (L2TP)*. L2TP can be used in many networks besides TCP/IP and will support multiple network protocols. Primarily a point-to-point protocol, L2TP is a combination of PPTP and L2F. Since it works equally well over such network protocols as IPX, SNA, and IP, it can be used as a bridge across many types of systems. L2TP does not provide security encryption, so it requires the use of such security protocols as IPsec to provide end-to-end or tunneling encryption. L2TP uses UDP and port 1701 for connections.

Secure Shell Originally designed for *Unix systems*, *Secure Shell (SSH)* is now available for use on Windows systems as well and is a tunneling protocol that uses encryption to establish a secure connection between two systems. SSH also provides an information exchange protocol for such standards as Telnet, FTP, and many other communications-oriented applications. This makes it the preferred method of security for Telnet and other cleartext-oriented programs in the Unix environment. SSH is assigned to port 22 and uses TCP for connections.

VPNs require special software running on both the network and the client PC or server in order to establish the connection. When the virtual private network is established, the connection logically appears to be part of the local network, and hosts may communicate with each other as if they are sitting in the same room. This is why a VPN established between two networks is considered a private connection and sometimes referred to as an extranet.

Exam Point

Tunneling protocols, usually referred to as virtual private networks (VPNs), create a tunnel by encapsulating the original packet and attaching a routing header to the new, encapsulated packet. Not all VPNs or tunneling protocols provide security. An encryption protocol such as IPsec may be added for encryption.

Internet Protocol Security   *Internet Protocol Security (IPsec)* is a versatile protocol. It has two primary modes of operation. Tunneling mode can be used between two routers or two firewalls to establish a tunnel connection, illustrated in Figure 8.11, between two local area networks. The IPsec transport mode, illustrated in Figure 8.12, can be used between two endpoints. The versatility stems from the fact that an *authentication header (AH)* is used, which provides authentication of the sender as well as an integrity hash of the packet.

FIGURE 8.11   IPsec in tunnel mode

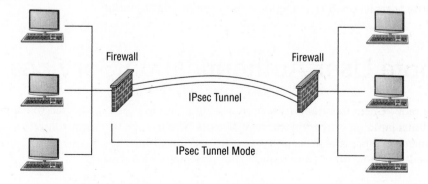

FIGURE 8.12   IPsec in transport mode

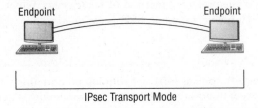

The *Encapsulating Security Protocol (ESP)* can be used to totally encapsulated and encrypt the original packet. *Security associations (SAs)* maintain the information concerning the symmetric encryption algorithm that has been agreed upon between the parties. Symmetric keys can be exchanged, either *out-of-band* or through a Diffie-Hellman key exchange. This key exchange is referred to as the *Internet Key Exchange (IKE)*. Due to its wide acceptance and versatility, IPsec was originally selected as the security protocol to be mandated in IPv6. Since this mandate was put into effect, it has been reduced to an optional security protocol in IPv6.

Exam Point

Since IPsec is the de facto standard for Internet security for IPv6, you might expect one or more questions concerning this topic.

IPsec Summary:

- Two modes of operation: tunneling mode and transport mode

- Internet Key Exchange (IKE): exchanging or deriving a symmetric key

- Authentication header (AH): provides sender authentication as well as integrity

- Encapsulating Security Protocol (ESP): encrypts the packet

- Security association (SA): the agreed-upon symmetric algorithm

---

Remote User Authentication Services

There is a requirement to authenticate users who are not physically connected to the network within a building or workplace, such as users who may be working from home, are on assignment in other locations, or are on the road traveling. There may be also users who are assigned to remote offices and request enterprise network access.

There are several means to centrally administer the authentication of remote users as they request access to the enterprise network. RADIUS and TACACS provide centralized authentication services for remote users.

RADIUS

Remote Authentication Dial-In User Service (RADIUS) is a protocol and system that allows user authentication of remote and other network connections. The RADIUS protocol is an IETF standard, and it has been implemented by most of the major operating system manufacturers. Once intended for use on dial-up modem connections, it now has many modern features.

A RADIUS server can be managed centrally, and the servers that allow access to a network can verify with a RADIUS server whether an incoming caller is authorized. In a large network with many users, RADIUS allows a single server to perform all authentications.

Since a RADIUS server may be used to centrally authenticate incoming connection requests, it poses a single point of failure. Many organizations provide multiple servers to increase system reliability. Of course, like all authentication mechanisms, the servers should be highly protected from attack.

TACACS/TACACS+/XTACACS

Terminal Access Controller Access Control System (TACACS) is a client-server environment that operates in a similar manner to RADIUS. It is a central point for user authentication. Extended TACACS (XTACACS) replaced the original TACACS and combined authentication and authorization along with logging, which enables communication auditing. The most current method or level of TACACS is TACACS+, and this replaces the previous versions. TACACS+ has been widely implemented by Cisco and possibly may become a viable alternative to RADIUS.

 **Real World Scenario**

Connecting Remote Network Users

John's organization wants to offer network connections for remote users. These users will use the Internet to access host systems and other resources in the organization's network. What should John advise the organization to use?

John should advise the organization to implement a tunneling protocol that supports security. He might explain that a virtual private network (VPN) can be set up to channel the packets through an insecure network such as the Internet while encrypting the data with an encryption protocol such as IPsec.

Local User Authentication Services

Identification and authentication are required of all users of the network. Every network must have a method of determining who has access and what rights they have once they are allowed access. Access control may be provided through a number of different methods.

LDAP

Lightweight Directory Access Protocol (LDAP) is a standardized directory protocol that allows queries to be made of a directory database, especially in the form of an *X.500* format directory. To retrieve information from the directory database, an LDAP directory is queried using an LDAP client. The Microsoft implementation of LDAP is *Active Directory (AD)*. LDAP is the main access protocol used by Microsoft's Active Directory. LDAP operates, by default, at port 389, and the syntax is a comma-delimited format.

Kerberos

Kerberos is an authentication, single sign-on protocol developed at MIT and is named after a mythical three-headed dog that stood at the gates of Hades. It allows single sign-on in a distributed environment. An attractive feature of Kerberos is that it does not pass passwords over the network. The design is also unique in that most of the work is provided by the host workstations and not the Kerberos server. Figure 8.13 illustrates a simplified version of the Kerberos process.

FIGURE 8.13   Kerberos diagram

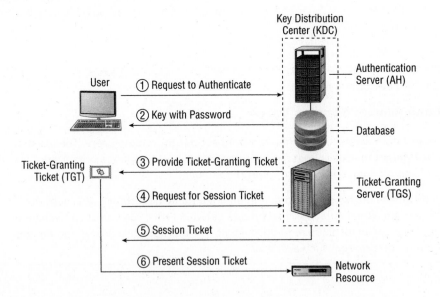

Kerberos authentication uses a *key distribution center* (KDC) to maintain the entire access process. As you can see in Figure 8.13, the KDC authentication server authenticates (steps 1 and 2) the principal (which can be a user, a program, or a system) and provides it with a *ticket-granting ticket,* or *TGT* (step 3).

After the ticket-granting ticket is issued, it can be presented to the *ticket-granting server,* or *TGS* (step 4) to obtain a session ticket to allow access to specific applications or network resources. The ticket-granting server sends the user the session ticket granting access to the requested resource (step 4). The user then presents the session ticket to the resource requesting access (step 6).

Through the use of a trust system, the resource authenticates the ticket as coming from the key distribution center and allows access for the user. Tickets are usually timed and will timeout after an eight-hour default unless set differently.

Kerberos is quickly becoming a common standard in network environments due to its adoption as a single sign-on methodology by Microsoft.

Kerberos Explained

One way to think of using Kerberos is to think of going to an amusement park. When you arrive at the park, you go to the main gate. You then proceed to the main ticket booth (the authentication server in the key distribution center) and purchase an all-day pass to the park (a ticket-granting ticket). You receive a purple wristband (because purple is the color for Wednesday) that indicates that you have paid your fee for that day and you have full access to the park. The colored wristband is good for all day.

While in the park, you must purchase additional tickets for the rides. You walk up to a ticket booth (ticket-granting server) and the attendant notices that you have a purple wristband. You tell her you are wanting to ride the roller coaster. She issues you a ticket (session ticket) for the roller coaster. When you get to the roller coaster, the roller coaster attendant sees your purple wristband and accepts the ticket issued to you by the ticket seller. The roller coaster attendant does not need to check with the ticket seller because that is the only place you could have obtained that ticket.

At the end of the day, when the park closes, the purple wristband for Wednesday no longer authenticates you. The wristband color for Thursday is orange. You also noticed that you did all the work. None of the ticket sellers or ride operators communicated with each other. It was up to you to procure tickets and walk around and distribute them. This is exactly the model as designed by MIT for Kerberos.

Exam Point

Kerberos makes use of two tickets. The ticket-granting ticket is issued to the user upon authentication. It is a timed ticket and generally expires in less than a day. The user presents the ticket-granting ticket to the ticket-granting server when requesting access to a network resource. The ticket-granting server then issues the second type of ticket, referred to as a session ticket, that is then presented by the user to the network resource.

Single Sign-On

On larger systems, users must access multiple systems and resources on a daily basis. A major problem exists for users if they are required to remember numerous passwords and usernames. The purpose of *single sign-on (SSO)* is to allow users to use one set of logon credentials to access all the applications and systems they are authorized to access when they log on.

 Single sign-on has both a positive and negative attribute. It is positive in that once the user is authenticated, they can access all the resources on the network and browse multiple directories. The negative aspect is that it removes the barriers that otherwise exist between the user and network resources.

With the Kerberos system, a single session ticket allows any "Kerberized" resource to accept a user as valid. It is important to remember in this process that each application you want to access using SSO must be able to accept and process the Kerberos ticket. Some legacy applications require a script that accepts a password or user credentials and then processes the information by inserting it into the correct places in the legacy application to log the user on.

Active Directory (AD), on the other hand, retains the information about all access rights for all users and groups in the network. When a user logs on to the network, Active Directory issues the user a *globally unique identifier (GUID)*. Access control is provided by the use of this GUID, and applications that support AD can use this *GUID* to allow access.

Using AD simplifies the support requirements for administrators. By using the assigned GUID, the user doesn't have to have separate sign-on credentials for Internet, email, and applications. Access can be assigned through groups such as role-based access control and can be enforced through group memberships.

SSO passwords are stored on each server in a decentralized network. Since a compromised single sign-on password would allow an attacker free reign on a network, it is important to enforce password changes and make sure certain passwords are updated throughout the organization on a frequent basis.

Although SSO offers a single point of failure in a potential security risk should a password be compromised, it is still better than having the user personally manage a large number of passwords for various applications and system resources. The tendency for an overwhelmed user is to write down usernames and passwords and place them in close proximity to the computer system. Single sign-on, despite all the possible headaches, can still be a substantial security benefit to an organization.

Federation

A *federation* is an association of nonrelated third-party organizations that share information based on a single sign-on and one-time authentication of a user. Figure 8.14 illustrates a travel booking site that would have a federated relationship with hotels, car rental agencies, and air carriers. Once the user signs on to the travel booking site, user inquiries and ultimately booking selections will be coordinated with the federated organizations without the individual having to log in to each organization's website.

FIGURE 8.14   Single sign-on with federated access

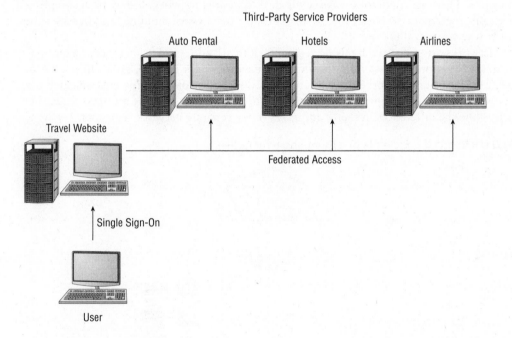

> **Exam Point**
>
> A federation is an association of nonrelated businesses or organizations that share user data based upon one-time authentication of a user.

Network Segmentation

On a LAN, hosts can communicate with each other through broadcasts, and forwarding devices such as routers are not needed. The number of broadcasts grows as the LAN grows. It stands to reason that with more hosts, more data collisions can be expected, and ultimately the performance of the network will be slower.

Shrinking the size of the local area network through segmenting it into smaller groups reduces the number of hosts in each group. This reduces the size of broadcast domains by reducing the total number of collisions possible in a segment. Advantages may be realized by subdividing a local area network into smaller segments, which will improve overall network performance and manageability.

Subnetting

One of the issues to consider when designing a network is how to subdivide it into usable domains. There are numerous ways to divide a local area network. It may be accomplished logically, topologically, physically, by workgroups, by physical building, and in almost any other way you can think of.

Networks are subnetted by using segments of the IP address. For instance, an internal local area network address for a specific host machine might be 38.8.210.2. In this example, 210 is the number of the network, and 2 is the number of a specific host machine on network number 210. Figure 8.15 illustrates a three-segment network set up as three subnets. Note the differences in the IP addresses of the separate network segments.

FIGURE 8.15   Example of a three-segment network

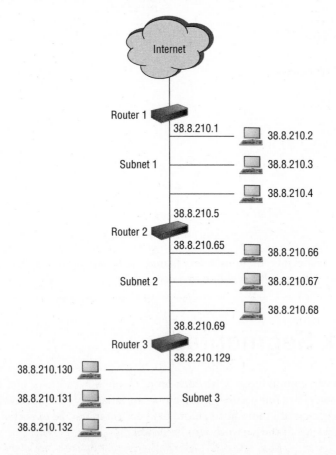

A special tool called a subnet mask value is used for *subnetting.* It covers up numbers in the address that are not required. When a network is subnetted, it is divided into smaller components, or subnets, with a smaller number of host machines available on each subnet.

The broadcast domain for a subnet is much smaller and has fewer hosts. The advantage to this is much better network performance because you are reducing overall network traffic while also making the network more secure and manageable.

Networks can be subnetted logically, topologically, physically within a building, by workgroups, or by a building within a campus. Subnetting is accomplished through the use of a *subnet mask,* which is used to identify the network number and the host number part of an IP address.

Virtual Local Area Networks

A virtual local area network (VLAN) is created by grouping hosts together. Hosts may be grouped by workgroups, departments, buildings, and so on. The hosts in a VLAN are connected to a network switch. The switch is responsible for controlling the traffic that is destined for each host based upon each hosts Mac address. Members of the VLAN do not necessarily need to be in the same area. They can be in another office or even in another building. The VLAN can be used to control the path data takes to get from one point to another and may constrain network traffic to a certain area of the network. VLANs differ from subnets in that they do not provide security.

A VLAN may be considered as a network of interconnected hosts that act as if they're connected physically even though there is no such connection between them.

Demilitarized Zones

A *demilitarized zone (DMZ)* is a network segment created between two firewalls, one of which faces an untrusted network such as the Internet, so that some servers on an enterprise network can be accessed by external communications. The purpose of a demilitarized zone is to allow people you might not trust otherwise to access a public server, database, or application without allowing them on to the internal local area network.

When a server is positioned in a DMZ, it may be accessed by both untrusted users such as those on the Internet, as well as users from the trusted internal network. Figure 8.16 illustrates three servers placed in a demilitarized zone formed by two firewalls. Note that the internal network is completely shielded from both the Internet and the demilitarized zone by a firewall.

FIGURE 8.16   Illustration of a demilitarized zone

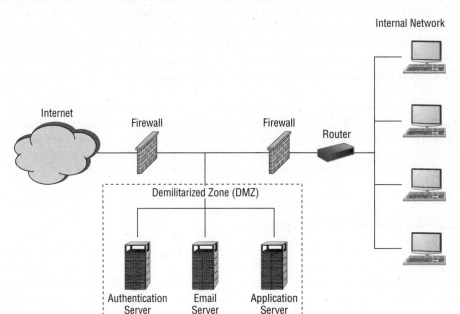

Devices placed in the DMZ are subject to attack. Routers, switches, servers, intrusion protection devices, and any other items that are exposed to the outside network must be hardened against attack. This means removing any unused services and protocols and closing all unused ports. After an attack, you might have to re-image or rebuild demilitarized zone network devices after an attack. Systems that allow public access and that are hardened against attack are usually referred to as *bastion hosts*. It is expected that bastion hosts may be sacrificed from time to time.

When establishing a DMZ, you assume that the person accessing the resources isn't necessarily someone you would trust with other information.

Exam Point

A demilitarized zone can be established between two firewalls. The first firewall, which is facing a untrusted network such as the Internet, screens unwanted traffic but allows desired traffic to access the demilitarized zone subnetwork. The second firewall protects the internal enterprise network.

Network Address Translation

Network address translation (NAT) is primarily used to extend the number of usable Internet addresses. IPv4 has since run out of unique network addresses. Therefore, organizations create their own IP addresses for their internal network using a translation methodology to convert from the internal IP addresses to the external IP address.

Network address translation allows an organization to exhibit a single unique IP address to the Internet for all hosts and servers on the internal network. The network address translation server provides internal IP addresses to the hosts and servers in the network and translates inbound and outbound traffic from the external IP address to the IP addressing system used internally. The only information that an intruder will be able to see is that the organization has a single IP address. The connection between the Internet and the internal network is usually through a NAT server or a router.

Exam Point

Network address translation (NAT) is used to extend the number of usable Internet addresses. NAT is primarily performed by a firewall or router at the boundary or outer parameter of the network. The firewall or router translates the extra traffic IP addresses to a nonroutable internal IP address.

Network address translation assigns internal hosts private IP addresses. These addresses are private and nonroutable across the Internet. The specific address ranges used for internal hosts IP addresses are as follows:

10.0.0.0–10.255.255.255

172.16.0.0–172.31.255.255

192.168.0.0–192.168.255.255

The NAT server operates as a firewall for the network by restricting access from outside hosts to internal network IP addresses. Through NAT, the internal network is effectively hidden from untrusted external networks. This makes it much more difficult for an attacker to determine what addresses exist on the internal network.

Port Address Translation

In addition to NAT, *port address translation (PAT)* may also be used to hide the internal network. Where NAT can use a number of public IP addresses, PAT uses a single external address and shares the port with the entire network. Because it uses only a single port, PAT is much more limited and typically used only on small and home-based networks. Microsoft's Internet Connection Sharing is an example of a PAT implementation.

Securing Devices

There are various methods used to secure devices. Devices can be prepared or hardened against attack and also set up in such a way as to communicate with each other securely.

MAC Filtering and Limiting

MAC filtering is a method whereby known MAC addresses are allowed and those that are not wanted are not allowed on the network. This is a type of white list/blacklist filtering. Even in small home networks, MAC filtering can be implemented because most routers typically give you the option of choosing to allow only computers with MAC addresses you list on an authorized access control list.

MAC filtering can also be used as a wireless identification access control. Most wireless devices offer the ability to turn on *MAC filtering,* but it is off by default. Although a user may wish to join with a network using the SSID of a wireless system, the wireless system may refuse a connection based upon the MAC address not being unauthorized. In various network access control implementations, the term *network lock* is used to describe MAC filtering, and the two are synonymous.

MAC limiting is specific to some brands of network switches and is used to enhance port security on the switch by setting the maximum number of MAC addresses that can be learned (added to the Ethernet switching table) on a specific access interface port or all of the interface ports.

Unfortunately, MAC addresses may be spoofed relatively easily. Therefore, MAC filtering and limiting are not always foolproof.

Exam Point

MAC filtering is sometimes used as a method of determining which Wi-Fi user may enter a network. Because Mac addresses can be spoofed, it is not 100 percent reliable.

Disabling Unused Ports

Part of system hardening is to disable all unused ports. Otherwise, they present an attack vector for an attacker to exploit. Any type of firewall implementation can be used to close or disable communication ports.

Security Posture

Many organizations are required to be in compliance with mandates such as HIPAA, PCI, and other relevant regulatory or contractual (industry) standards. Therefore, the security state of a network must be considered at all times.

It is important to establish a *security baseline* to document the network configuration. The baseline must represent a state in which you know the network is secure. Any future network or device audits will be compared to this state. A network or device baseline will also be referred to when conducting *regression analysis* after any changes have been made to the network or device to see if anything has changed from the original baseline. It is impossible to evaluate device or network security without having a baseline configuration documented.

The security baseline documents the current security configurations of network devices, which includes current patches, updates, sensitivity settings, and other configuration information. Network data flow and statistical information should also be included in the security baseline for later comparison and analysis.

Firewall and Proxy Implementation

From the early days of network design, firewalls have been the backbone of network security. They are used to separate a trusted network from an untrusted network and allow through traffic based on filtering rules. Firewalls are one of the primary methods for hardening host machines.

Firewalls

A *firewall* is an essential line of defense within a network system. They separate networks from each other and specifically separate interior networks from untrusted networks such as the Internet. A firewall is used as a border gate, usually depicted in drawings as a brick wall on the perimeter of the network.

There are many different types of firewalls, which can be either implemented as stand-alone appliances or embedded as an application within other devices, such as servers or routers. Operating systems such as Windows includes a host-based firewall.

 The purpose of the firewall is to *filter* traffic based upon various rulesets. Although firewalls are often associated with outside traffic, they can be placed anywhere. For example, one internal network may be isolated from another with the use of a firewall.

Packet Filter Firewalls

A *packet filter firewall* passes data based upon packet addressing information. It does not analyze the data included in a packet but simply forwards the packet based upon an application or port designation. For example, a packet filter firewall may block web traffic on port 80 and also block Telnet traffic on port 23. This is the standard filtering mechanism built into all firewalls. If a received packet specifies a port that isn't authorized, the filter will reject the request or simply ignore it. Most packet filter firewalls may also filter packets based on IP source address and allow or deny them based on the security settings of the firewall.

Building architects and designers regularly use the firewall concept when designing a building. To keep fires from spreading from one part of a building to another, fire doors in various corridors are designed to shut automatically upon the sound of a fire alarm. This minimizes the spread of a fire from one section of the building to another. Some modern apartment buildings are designed with a fireproof wall built to completely separate one section of the building from another in the event of fire. In times of old, large brick walls were built from the ground to above the roof of a house to separate different houses from each other. This brick wall is the inspiration for the illustration used in most network diagrams for a firewall.

Proxy Firewalls

A *proxy firewall* uses increased intelligence and packet inspection methodology to better protect the internal network. A proxy is always described as an intermediary between two systems, hosts, or networks. In effect, a proxy firewall isolates the internal network from the external untrusted network by intercepting communications. It does this by receiving a packet from an external untrusted source and repackages it for use by the internal protected network host. During this process, the untrusted source does not have direct access or even IP address knowledge of the internal host. Once the internal host decides to reply to the message, it sends the response message to the proxy firewall, which then repackages it, stripping off the internal IP address and sending it on to the external untrusted host.

A proxy firewall can provide additional services through its ability to cache information. Information such as frequently used web pages or documents is stored in memory and resent to the internal host should the request be made again.

Firewalls sometimes contain two *network interface cards (NICs)*, one connected to the external network and one connected to the internal network. When two network interface cards are used on a firewall, the firewall is referred to as a *dual-homed firewall*. The controlling software within a firewall effectively separates both network interface cards, thereby reducing the possibility that an attacker will bypass the firewall security.

Multi-homed always refers to the use of two or more network interface cards on a device such as a firewall or router.

Stateful Packet Inspection Firewall

*Stateful packet inspection (SPI) firewall*s analyze packets to determine the external originating source as well as the destination on the internal network. This type of firewall records this information as a continuity of conversation record. It keeps the record using a state table that tracks every communication channel.

A stateful firewall compares existing conversations with new packets entering the firewall connecting for the first time. The new packets are compared against rulesets for a decision about whether to allow or deny. Other firewalls that do not track the continuity of conversations and only make allow or deny decisions based upon simple rulesets are referred to as *stateless firewalls*.

 A *state* can be envisioned as a snapshot in time. For instance, a light switch has two states, on and off. Stateful inspection refers to an intelligent ability to inspect a packet to determine if it is one of a series of packets within a conversation. A stateful inspection rule may inspect two packet states. It either is or is not part of an existing conversation. If it is not, other rules should be applied to decide to allow or deny access.

Web Application Firewall

A *web application firewall (WAF)* is a specialized firewall used to regulate traffic to and from web servers and specialized web applications. It utilizes specialized rules such as content filtering, access control, and intelligent rulesets that are customized specifically for the web application.

A web application firewall operates at the highest layer of the OSI model, layer 7, and is dedicated to filtering traffic into and out of a web application or web server operating in real time. It operates as a very sophisticated intrusion protection system and protects against content-based attacks such as *cross site scripting (XSS)*, injection attacks, and *HTTP forgery* attacks.

Firewall Rules

Firewalls enforce various types of rulesets. The rules can be very specific, allowing or denying a specific IP or port address, or very general, allowing total access to a specific port such as HTTP port 80. Firewall and router rules may exist by default, meaning they are built into the system. These types of rules are referred to as *implicit rules*. *Explicit rules* are those specifically created to perform a certain function, like blocking a port or IP address.

Firewall rules is a list of statements used to determine how to filter traffic and what can pass between the internal and external networks. A firewall might have dozens if not hundreds of rules. There are three possible actions that can be specified in a firewall rule:

- Deny the connection.
- Allow the connection.
- Allow the connection if it is secure.

Firewall rules can be applied to both inbound traffic and outbound traffic. Firewalls may be placed anywhere within a local area network. For instance, firewalls can separate workgroups, filter inbound traffic from the wireless network, filter traffic to and from a virtual private network, and be dedicated to a specific server or application to filter content traffic.

Firewall rules may be constructed using various techniques. Some of these techniques are described in the following sections.

Access Control Lists

An *access control list (ACL)* is a list that specifies the actions that a user or system is granted to perform. An access control list allows a subject, which may be a user, system, or application, to access an object, which may also be a user, system, or application. The access control list usually specifies the rights and privileges allowed. For instance, at the root level, an access control list may specify allowing access to the object. At a higher level, the access control list may then specify what permissions the subject has, such as read, write, read/write, delete, create, or other permissions.

Access control lists can be used by both firewalls and routers to build rulesets that allow or deny access to various network resources.

Implicit Deny

Implicit deny is a type of access rule that states that if a subject is not listed on the access control list, access is denied. This type of rule is usually at the bottom of the rules list in either a router or a firewall. Its purpose is to act as a catchall. If entry has not been explicitly granted, it is implicitly denied. In other words, the implicit deny rule catches anything to which no other rule applies and denies access.

In an access control list, this is a type of white listing. In a *white list,* only entities such as a source address, a destination address, and a packet type may be allowed access. Anything not on the white list is denied. In a *blacklist*, everything you wish to deny must be listed. This would prove to be a huge list.

Exam Point

The implicit deny rule is a firewall or router rule that usually drops the connection if no other rule applies. It almost always is the last rule in the stack. An explicit rule is a rule that has been written to provide a specific purpose, such as to allow or deny access to a certain port number.

Exam Point

There are two types of lists, white lists and blacklists. A white list contains all of the entities that may be allowed into a network or accessed by users, while blacklists are just the opposite. It is much easier to create a white list of authorized entities and prohibit access to everything else. It is virtually impossible for you to create a blacklist that includes everything you could possibly want to deny.

Network Routers and Switches

Routers and switches are the primary network devices used for connectivity and local area networks. Relying on different addressing schemes, these devices forward data on the network based on logical addresses or physical addresses. They may also be used to divide a network into segments.

Routers

A *router* is a networking device used for connectivity between two or more networks. They operate by enabling a path between the networks based on packet addresses. Routers perform a traffic-directing operation within a LAN and over a network such as the Internet. Reading the destination address on a packet, the router, based on a routing table or internal rule, will forward the packet to the next network and router. This forwarding will continue until one of two events occur. Either the packet reaches its end destination or the counter on the packet, referred to as a "hop" counter, reaches zero, meaning it has exceeded the number of routers it has crossed and therefore the packet will be discarded.

Routers exchange information about destination addresses using a table listing the preferred routes between any two systems on an interconnected network. This *routing table* is created using a *dynamic routing protocol*.

The routing table contains information concerning destinations and local connections to which the router has immediate access. A routing table contains information about previous paths and where to send requests if the packet destination is not in the table. Tables expand as connections are made through the router.

Routers communicate with each other and share information using one of several standard protocols. These protocols include Routing Information Protocol (RIP), Open Shortest Path First (OSPF), and Border Gateway Protocol (BGP).

Exam Point

Routers provide routing based on IP addresses. Routers communicate with each other to determine the best path for packets. The *hop counter* on a packet begins at 15 and decrements each time it crosses a router. If the hop counter gets to 0, the packet is dropped. This prevents *packet loops*.

Routers can be configured in a number of ways, including as a packet filtering firewall and as an endpoint device for a virtual private network. Routers may also have different types of interfaces that accommodate various types of transmission media. This media includes fiber-optic cables, twisted-pair copper wire, and wireless transmission using modulated radio waves.

Local area networks can be subdivided into segments by routers based on IP addresses, effectively creating zones that operate autonomously. Each segment will have a unique subnet address. Subnets may be a logical group, a workgroup, a building, or any other subjective grouping of hosts or servers. Within a network, routers can be connected to other routers.

Routers do not pass network broadcasts. Therefore, they are ideal when creating subnets to reduce the traffic on the network.

Data Plane and Control Plane

A router has two operational stages called planes. Each plane is part of the architecture of the router and has an individual responsibility when receiving and forwarding packets.

Control Plane   The *control plane* is the part of the router that is concerned with determining the path that should be used to forward a data packet. It maintains a *routing database* and also determines the proper router interface port to use. Packet routes are established either through the use of preprogramming *static routes*, which can be edited manually, or through the router control plane learning *dynamic routes* from other routers around it through using one of several dynamic routing protocols.

Forwarding Plane   The *forwarding plane*, sometimes referred to as the *data plane*, is the part of the router that receives arriving packets and routes them through an output interface to the destination address. The forwarding plane utilizes destination addresses obtained by the control plane and maintained in routing tables.

Secure Router Configuration

A primary responsibility with many SSCPs is to work with and maintain router configurations. It is also important to make sure router configurations are secure. There are several simple steps that can be taken with every network device to ensure network security.

Keep the firmware upgraded.   Manufacturers quite often issue patches and upgrades in response to attacks or to resolve various problems that might occur with a piece of equipment. It is important to maintain an up-to-date patch level on each piece of equipment. Prior to installation, patches should always be tested in offline, nonproduction equipment. Installation of patches should be thoroughly documented and be in compliance with the change control methodology of your organization.

Change the default password.   A default password is loaded at the factory when every piece of equipment is built. Unfortunately, many organizations will put pieces of equipment into production without changing the default password. Passwords on networking equipment should be changed for initial installation and then updated in accordance with the password policy of the organization.

Use advanced configuration settings. Most pieces of networking equipment offer advanced configuration options for ICMP requests, MAC filtering, and various other specialized settings. Depending upon the router, options may differ, but by setting them correctly, network security can be enhanced.

Establish a baseline. A baseline is an established performance level or benchmark, for each piece of equipment. Once changes are made, such as adding patches or upgrades, the performance can be measured against the previous baseline.

Create configuration backups. Equipment settings should always be backed up prior to making any changes or upgrades. This allows for a fallback position should a patch or upgrade fail.

Switches

A *switch* is a network device that routes traffic based on physical MAC addresses. Most switches contain very little programming or intelligence. Previously, hosts on a network were connected by network hubs that forwarded the same information to each host. Modern switches are multi-port networking appliances that forward data to one or multiple devices.

Operating at the Data Link layer (layer 2) of the OSI model, switches switch information based on MAC addresses and are used to assemble virtual local area networks using a star network topology model. *Virtual local area networks (VLANs)* that are created through the use of a switch are not natively secure because the data within one virtual private network could possibly be exposed to other network segments. This is referred to as the VLAN "hopping."

More intelligent network switches combine the ability to switch MAC addresses as well as route IP addresses. Because IP addresses are at OSI layer 3, this type of switch is referred to as a *layer 3 switch.*

 Switches are used only on internal networks. This is because they switch only physical Mac addresses and must be connected directly to a host or server on the internal network.

Intrusion Detection and Prevention Devices

Intrusion detection and prevention is a method of monitoring data traffic through the network to determine, based upon some criteria, if the information flow is correct. Upon detection, certain actions may be taken to record the event, alert operators, or take actions that may involve blocking the intrusion.

Intrusion detection (ID) can be described as the passive process of monitoring various characteristics in a system or network to determine if an event is occurring. An *intrusion* is any activity, process, or action that attempts to circumvent or compromise the confidentiality, integrity, or availability of an organization's resources.

Intrusion Detection Systems

An *intrusion detection system (IDS)* is software that runs either on a host workstation or on a network appliance. Depending upon the location, the system may be referred to as a *host intrusion detection system (HIDS)* or *network intrusion detection system (NIDS)*. The primary role of a detection system is to monitor and analyze network traffic. This is a passive role, and no action is taken on the traffic itself.

There are two primary measurements of network activity used in setting up and fine-tuning an intrusion detection system:

Baseline   A baseline is a predetermined level of expected activity on a network segment or network component. It may vary by day or by the hour. An intrusion detection system may be tuned to expect a certain volume of traffic or a specific type of packet being sent over the network.

Clipping Level   A clipping level is an activity level established above the baseline that, when crossed, sets off an alarm or initiates some activity based upon an increased level of traffic on the network segment (Figure 8.17). A clipping level reduces noise and log entries.

FIGURE 8.17   Illustration of a baseline and a clipping level

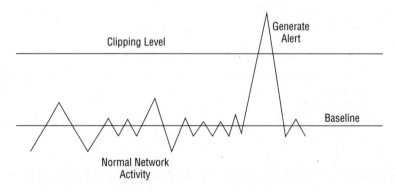

An intrusion detection system is a passive system that listens and alerts. The system is connected to the network through the use of a network tap or three-way connector that allows the device to monitor network traffic. An IDS is not inline in the network and does not provide a single point of failure.

Intrusion Prevention Systems

An *intrusion prevention system (IPS)* is software that runs either on a host system or on a network appliance. The IPS not only detects a potential attack, it takes a predetermined action to stop the attack. For example, if it appears as if an attack might be in progress, identified packets might be dropped, ignored, logged, or otherwise dealt with. Operators might be alerted, and other actions, such as changing of firewall rules to block a port or IP address, might be initiated. While an intrusion detection system is a passive device, an intrusion prevention system is an active device.

For an intrusion prevention system to work it must be in line with the network data stream. This is so it may take immediate action to drop or block packets or take any other action based upon its ruleset. It also creates the problem that the IPS may become a target for an attack and that by being in the data stream, it is a single point of failure.

Both IDSs and IPSs utilized four primary methods of network monitoring:

Behavior-Based Detection   A *behavior-based monitoring* system monitors network traffic behavior, such as unusually high traffic, high-volume traffic destined for a specific port, high-volume traffic destined for specific IP address, and unusual control or request packets. Behavior-based detection is monitoring deviations in behavior from established baseline standards.

Signature-Based Detection   A *signature-based monitoring* system monitors network traffic based on previously established signatures of typical attacks. Similar to an anti-malware identification system, this type of system might identify different types of attacks through the methods used during the attack. For instance, a SYN flood attack is characterized by an attacker sending a large number of SYN packets with no responding acknowledgment packets. This opens a very large number of communication sessions. Other types of attacks can be identified through a library of signatures, thus triggering a response or action against the attack. *Signature libraries* must be kept up-to-date for this type of detection to be effective.

Anomaly-Based Detection   An *anomaly-based monitoring* technique is very similar to a behavior-based monitoring system in that it looks for something completely outside of the ordinary. This type of device is usually more intelligent and learns what normal looks like from the typical traffic flow and activity on the network. Should anything out of the ordinary appear, the device would then take action. An anomaly-based device can be set within established baselines or be set to use automated processes to monitor traffic patterns to determine the baseline.

Heuristic-Based Detection   A heuristic-based monitoring technique produces a solution by monitoring network traffic and providing a result based on good enough information. A type of learning system, it uses just enough information to arrive at a solution. Thus, it is very fast, but it is also potentially inaccurate. A *heuristic* system uses algorithms to analyze traffic passing through a network; the algorithms can be used by themselves or in conjunction with other techniques and information to improve their efficiency and accuracy.

Many manufacturers are concentrating their efforts on the development of heuristics and intelligent sensing devices rather than signatures and baseline monitoring. The downside is that the systems are prone to errors if not adjusted correctly.

Wireless Intrusion Prevention Systems

A *wireless intrusion prevention system (WIPS)* is used to mitigate the possibility of rogue access points. These systems are typically implemented in an existing wireless LAN infrastructure and enforce wireless policies within an organization. They prevent unauthorized network access to local area networks through unauthorized access points.

A wireless intrusion prevention system might be simply a workstation with an antenna running a specialized sniffing application. A typical wireless intrusion detection system receives wireless transmitted packets, analyzes the packets, and then correlates against existing IT policy standards. Upon identification of a violation and classification of a threat, the *WIDS administrator* is alerted.

Several components work together to form a wireless intrusion prevention system:

WIPS Sensors   A wireless intrusion prevention system uses antennas and radio receivers that scan the 2.4 GHz and 5 GHz wireless spectrum and accumulate all packets transmitted. Such sensors may be installed throughout the internal perimeter of the organization. Packets are stored and forwarded to a centralized server for analysis.

WIPS Processing Server   A wireless intrusion prevention system uses a centralized server for analysis. The centralized server utilizes specialized wireless packet detection software that inspects packets against specific packet signatures as established by the policies of the organization. The WIPS processing server correlates the information, validates it against the defined rules, and notifies an administrator if it meets threat criteria.

WIPS Multi Network Controller   In very large organizations, a multiple-network controller is used, which is made up of several sensors and servers dispersed in geographic locations that coordinate a number of WIPS processing servers.

Comparing Intrusion Detection Systems and Intrusion Prevention Systems

While intrusion detection systems began the intrusion detection revolution, intrusion prevention systems have far surpassed them in popularity and integration into modern networks. NIST now classifies both IDS and IPS as one type of device, an intrusion detection and prevention system (IDPS).

Intrusion Detection Systems

Although older than intrusion prevention systems, intrusion detection systems served their purpose and are still in use in many networks today.

Advantages

- Offer offline monitoring. May easily be connected to a network tap.
- Not inline with network information.
- May easily be tuned to monitor for specific information.
- May trigger recording of logs.
- May alert operators.

Disadvantages

- Early versions may be hard to tune and adjust.
- No actions taken on other learning operators.
- Incredible amount of data captured if not filtered properly.

> ### Exam Point
>
> An intrusion detection system is passive; it only listens and alerts. An intrusion prevention system is active and is capable of taking some predetermined action.

Intrusion Prevention Systems

Intrusion prevention systems with advanced anomaly and heuristic sensing are the wave of the future. They take immediate action such as terminating a communication session based on triggering of various rulesets. In today's market, this product may be known as an IDS/IPS or just as an IPS. Since an intrusion detection system only alerts operators or initiates log files, the most popular device to purchase would be an intrusion prevention system that can take a predetermined action. This would potentially protect the network while it is logging and alerting.

Advantages

- Offer in-line monitoring. May easily be connected directly into the network data stream.
- Are directly inline, thus can take immediate action.
- May easily be tuned to monitor for specific information.
- Identify malicious activity, log information about this activity, attempt to block/stop it, and report it.
- Perform actions as sending an alarm, dropping the malicious packets, resetting the connection, and/or blocking the traffic from the offending IP address.

Disadvantages

- Hard to tune and adjust.
- May be complex for users to learn and understand.
- May provide a self-inflicted denial of service if not tuned correctly due to the fact they may drop packets indiscriminately.

 For several years, many manufacturers offered an intrusion detection system that was a passive device and only listened to the traffic on a network and alerted an analyst based on a ruleset. As the devices became more sophisticated, intrusion prevention systems came on the market. An intrusion prevention system has the ability to drop packets and even rewrite router or firewall rules based upon a ruleset.

The National Institute for Standards and Technology (NIST) has now combined both devices when referring to them in its documentation. It now refers to this family of devices as an IDPS, or intrusion detection prevention system.

Spam Filter to Prevent Email Spam

To prevent email spam, such as unsolicited email, various email systems use antispam techniques. Unfortunately, the techniques are not without the downside of sometimes eliminating legitimate emails or sending them to spam folders. Antispam techniques can be broken into four broad categories:

- Actions that must be taken by individuals
- Actions that may be taken by email administrators
- Actions that may be taken by those who send email
- Actions that may be utilized by data researchers and law enforcement officials

No technique is a complete solution that offers a trade-off between incorrectly rejecting legitimate email and rejecting all spam.

There are a number of appliances, services, and software systems that system administrators may use to combat spam within their network systems. Lists of known spam sites are available to administrators so they can blacklist known spammers from their networks. Another spam elimination and blocking technique uses specialized analysis of the message patterns to detect spam or typical spam behavior and then compare it to global databases of spam.

Telecommunications Remote Access

Network boundaries are becoming more obscure every day. Network administrators used to have full control over every device connected to the network. But with the advent of portable personal devices, there are more and more requests for network connectivity. Every individual has two or three personal devices they wish to bring to work and use on the job. Driving the revolution are the senior executives of the organization who need 24/7 connectivity with their personal devices. It is hard to say no when the tidal wave of public opinion is against you.

System administrators must grapple with the fact that *Bring Your Own Device (BYOD)* is very much a reality to be dealt with virtually immediately.

Network Access Control

Network access control (NAC) is a technology approach to control the wellness and hygiene of a device desiring connection to a network. NAC is a network access solution that uses a set of predefined protocols to define and implement a policy whereby devices must meet various standards prior to being allowed access to a network.

When a device attempts to connect to a network, it must first be checked by a network application accessing a preinstalled software agent on the device to retrieve various device parameters and to ensure that the device complies with a network access policy. The network access policy may include requirements for antivirus protection level, system update level, and app configuration. During this period, the device can only access resources that can remediate any issues. Upon being certified as compliant, the device is able to access network resources and the Internet within the policies defined by the NAC system. NAC might integrate automated remediation processes to bring the device into compliance. Network access control is described in the *802.1X standard.*

Network access control includes policies such as preadmission endpoint security checks and posted admission controls concerning the authorization of where users and devices can go on a network once access is granted.

 Network access control is a set of standards defined by an organization's information access policy for clients attempting to access a network. NAC is commonly adopted for issued devices such as laptops and cell phones and is slowly making its way into controlling access of personally owned devices. NAC enforces policies that require that devices meet established health and hygiene standards before being allowed on the network.

Wireless & Cellular Technologies

Wi-Fi and cellular technologies have become the mainstay of communication, not only at home but throughout the business community. Today it's hard to remember when any of us did not have a telephone in our pocket or purse. Portable devices such as cell phones and personal digital assistants (PDAs) as well as laptop computers and tablets have become commonplace in our lives. It is only natural that everyone wants to bring them to work and use them at their desk or job location.

There still is controversy among security professionals as to how to come to terms with increased worker productivity on the one hand and organizational asset security on the other. While it might be expected that some highly restricted government facilities and defense contractors have policies completely banning wireless cellular and other portable technologies in the workplace, it is becoming nearly impossible to enforce such restrictive policies in the business community.

It is important for the SSCP to understand the differences between wireless and cellular technologies as well as organizational policy and policy enforcement in the workplace.

⊕ **Real World Scenario**

Affecting Employee Behavior

Business policies cause interesting employee behaviors. Over the past few years, most businesses have banned smoking in the workplace. As a result, workers were required to go outside the building and in some cases down to the street corner off company property in order to smoke a cigarette.

What is interesting today is that in some of the companies that have banned or regulated the use of cellular telephones and personal devices, many employees are taking "cell phone breaks" and leaving the building to go to their car or down to the street corner to make a personal cell phone call.

IEEE 802.11x Wireless Protocols

IEEE 802.11 is a list of specifications for implementing wireless computer communications. Originally issued as a standard in 1997, the standard has received a number of amendments that are designated by a letter following the basic specification of 802.11 (Table 8.3). Various frequency bands have been allocated by the *Federal Communications Commission (FCC)* for implementing wireless local area networks. These frequencies include the 2.4, 3.6, 5, and 60 GHz frequency bands. *Wi-Fi* is a trademark of the *Wi-Fi Alliance*. It describes a local area wireless computer networking technology that allows electronic devices to communicate most commonly in the 2.4 GHz and 5 GHz bands.

Exam Point

802.11 is the IEEE standard for wireless communications. Through the years it has received a number of amendments. Although these amendments were originally intended as additional clarifications, each has become a standard in and of itself.

TABLE 8.3   802.11 Standards and amendments

Standard and Amendment	Description
802.11	The original IEEE 802.11 standard defines wireless local area networks that transmit at 1 Mbit/s or 2 Mbit/s using the 2.4 GHz frequency spectrum.
802.11a	Amendment a provides wireless bandwidth up to 54 Mbit/s using the 5 GHz frequency spectrum.

Standard and Amendment	Description
802.11b	Amendment b provides wireless bandwidth of up to 11 Mbit/s using the 2.4 GHz frequency spectrum. The specification also includes the ability to scale back to transmission rates of 5.5, and 2 Mbit/s for slower devices. Originally referred to as 802.11 high-rate, this was the original standard selected by the Wi-Fi alliance to be denoted as Wi-Fi.
802.11g	Amendment g provides wireless bandwidth of up to 54 Mbit/s using the 2.4 GHz frequency spectrum.
802.11i	Amendment i provides for security enhancements to the wireless standard and is referred to as WPA2 that uses the AES encryption algorithm.
802.11n	Amendment n provides for wireless bandwidth in a range from 54 Mbit/s to 600 Mbps and can operate at both 5 GHz and 2.4 GHz. This amendment offers the greatest flexibility with the least amount of interference.

Most commercially available wireless devices such as home routers offer flexible compatibility with several of the 802.11 amendments. Most commonly, all will have compatibility with 802.11n. The 802.11n standard also allows for the use of multiple antennas to maximize transmission bandwidth.

WEP/WPA/WPA2

Over a period of time there have been a series of wireless security implementations. Several wireless security protocols have been used, each replacing another after weaknesses were exposed. The following sections discuss the relative capabilities of the wireless security protocols.

Wired Equivalent Privacy (WEP) was intended to provide basic security for wireless networks, while wireless systems frequently use the Wireless Application Protocol (WAP) for network communications. Over time, WEP has been replaced in most implementations by *Wi-Fi Protected Access (WPA)* and WPA2. The following sections briefly discuss these terms and provide you with an understanding of their relative capabilities.

Wired Equivalent Privacy

In the early days of wireless communication, there was a need for a wireless protocol designed to provide data privacy through an encryption methodology that was equivalent to the encryption methodology used for wired networks. *Wired Equivalent Privacy (WEP)* was said to be just as good and "equivalent" to the type of encryption protection available on wired networks of the time and was therefore implemented on a wide number of wireless devices.

WEP was found to be vulnerable to attack due to the implementation of the *RC4* encryption algorithm. At the time, an initialization vector of only 24 bits was used in the implementation. This allowed for predictable key patterns, and thus RC4 proved to be easily cracked in as few as 30 seconds with a standard PC.

Wi-Fi Protected Access and WPA2

With the serious weakness and eventual cracking of WEP, the wireless industry required a more secure replacement to secure wireless communications. The Wi-Fi Alliance initially developed Wi-Fi Protected Access (WPA) in 2003 as a replacement for WEP. This was originally intended only as an intermediate step while a more complex and secure standard was developed.

A primary criteria for a WPA replacement was that it had to be backward compatible to existing WEP hardware currently in the field. *Temporal Key Integrity Protocol (TKIP)*, which utilizes a dynamically changing 128-bit key for every packet, was implemented along with the original RC4 encryption algorithm.

As of 2004, the Wi-Fi Alliance replaced WPA with *Wi-Fi Protected Access II* (WPA2). *WPA2* is a much stronger encryption product and uses Advanced Encryption Standard (AES) as the encryption algorithm. This encryption method is referred to as *Cipher Block Chaining Message Authentication Code Protocol (CCMP)*, which utilizes AES operating in *counter mode* with a 48-bit initialization vector. A significant cryptanalysis *Work Factor (WF)* is required to brute-force crack the algorithm password. This encryption method also minimizes the risk of a replay attack. WPA2 certification by the Wi-Fi Alliance is mandatory for all new devices that bear the Wi-Fi trademark.

Exam Point

802.11i refers to wireless security provided by the WPA2 encryption method.

WPA2 is the foundation encryption method adopted by the IEEE as specified in the *802.11i* standard.

 A *replay attack* involves the capture of portions of a message by an attacker who then plays the message back at a later time to convince the host receiver that it is still communicating with the original sender.

Exam Point

Here is a simplified summary of the encryption progression for wireless products: Wired Equivalent Privacy (WEP) came first and was ultimately broken by a bad implementation of RC4. The Wi-Fi Alliance introduced Wi-Fi Protected Access (WPA) as an intermediate measure, which uses the Temporal Key Integrity Protocol (TKIP) for security. Wi-Fi Protected Access II (WPA2) replaced WPA and has become the IEEE 802.11i standard, which consists of the AES algorithm operating in counter mode and is referred to as the Cipher Block Chaining Message Authentication Code Protocol (CCMP).

Wireless Networks

A wireless network includes network nodes connected by a radio. Two types of network topology are used for wireless networks.

Wireless Network   A network consisting totally of wireless devices.

Hybrid Wireless Network   This is the more common implementation of the wireless network and consists of wireless devices connecting to an access point that then interfaces with a standard wired network.

Wireless networks are designed to achieve a specific purpose. Two types of connection and authentication modes are used in wireless network:

Ad Hoc Mode   The IEEE 802.11 standard provides for communication between two or more endpoints where no centralized access point is involved. As illustrated in Figure 8.18, *ad hoc* refers to the ability to initiate or terminate wireless communications at will between individual devices. The access control model used is discretionary access control. Authentication is usually not a consideration.

Infrastructure Mode   The IEEE 802.11 standard also provides for the communication of numerous wireless devices connecting through network *access points (APs)*. Figure 8.19 illustrates devices connecting to a central access point. Access points are network nodes connected to a wired network. Formal access controls, including user authentication, are generally in place in infrastructure mode.

FIGURE 8.18   Illustration of an ad hoc mode wireless network

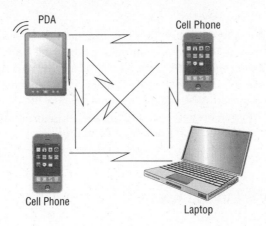

FIGURE 8.19   Illustration of the infrastructure mode wireless network zone

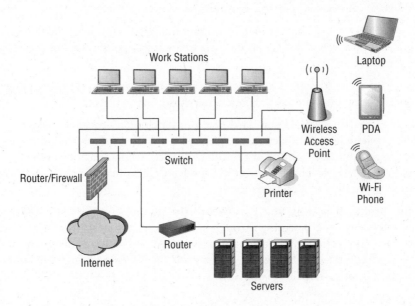

Several types of wireless networks exist to fill a specific purpose, topology, or user requirement. Figure 8.20 illustrates a small home network using a single wireless access point internal to a wireless router.

FIGURE 8.20   Illustration of a home network using a wireless router

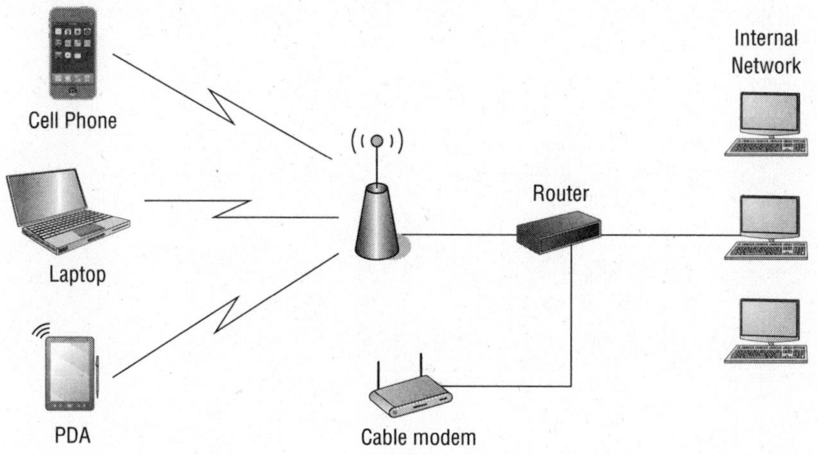

Cellular Network

A cellular network contains a system of radio towers referred to as a *cellular base stations* and featuring directional radio transceivers and antennas to form of geographic cell. Each cell borders other cells to maintain continuous coverage over a large geographic area. A cellular base station and its radio antennas transmit on different frequencies from the adjacent cell. As cellular devices such as cellular telephones traverse the geographic area, a handoff is made between cellular base stations, which is completely transparent to the user (Figure 8.21).

FIGURE 8.21   A cellular network illustrating geographical cells served by cellular base stations

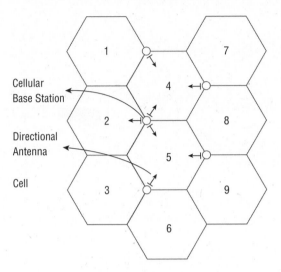

WiMAX

The name *WiMAX* is a trademark and was created by the *WiMAX Forum*. It is specified in the IEEE 802.16 standard.

The original concept of WiMAX was to replace Wi-Fi as a connection medium of choice. WiMAX is intended as a much stronger and robust geographically based system covering a much larger physical area than Wi-Fi covers. There are significant differences between WiMAX and Wi-Fi, and with Wi-Fi already embedded with many major manufacturers, it may be difficult for the WiMAX Forum to compete.

While the initial concept involved WiMAX competing in the commercial user marketplace, it has found a significant niche in corporate and government implementations. For instance, several cities have initiated WiMAX digital communication systems for their emergency services, such as police, fire, and ambulance communications. Also, large industrial complexes such as chemical plants, oil refineries, and major manufacturing plants have incorporated WiMAX communications over a large-scale physical area. A WiMAX connection is highly reliable and favorably replaces traditional *T1* or *T3* connections by completely bypassing the local telephone line service providers.

Wireless MAN

A *metropolitan area network (MAN)* is a very large geographic network that connects groups of smaller networks or connects directly to end users. Originally intended for a metropolitan areas such as cities, business parks, and college campuses, a MAN is connected physically by dedicated wireless links using microwave, radio, or infrared laser transmission. Many MAN providers rent or lease wired circuits from common carriers because laying long stretches of cable is expensive.

A *wireless MAN (WMAN)* utilizes radio transmitters and receivers to communicate to wired LANs through access points or directly to wireless endpoints. The WMAN eliminates the requirement for the leased lines of a MAN.

Wireless WAN

A wireless wide area network *(WWAN)* utilizes standard cellular radio transmitters, receivers, and transceivers (cellular telephones, laptops, and cellular-enabled devices) to communicate to wired LANs through access points or directly to wireless endpoints. The WWAN essentially describes the existing cellular telephone network, where any user can connect to a local area network using any current cellular service. Users and existing local area access points are already set up to use a WWAN.

Wireless LAN

A Wireless LAN (WLAN) utilizes standard short-distance cellular radio transmitters, receivers, and transceivers (cellular telephones, laptops, and cellular-enabled devices) to communicate to wired LANs through access points. A WLAN may be characterized as a local area network where several user workstations connect using Wi-Fi to an access point installed in the room.

Wireless Mesh Network

In a *mesh technology network*, each node communicates with all of the other nodes. Mesh networks are redundant and usually very fast. They are referred to as "self-healing" because if one communication path fails, another communication path is immediately available. In a *wireless mesh network*, each node is immediately available and can forward messages to other nodes. A wireless mesh network can be implemented in an ad hoc communication relationship.

Bluetooth

Bluetooth has become famous for connecting items such as keyboards, mice, headphones, speakers, and other devices to a user workstation. Bluetooth has also been a conduit for communication between two Bluetooth-enabled devices such as computers, tablets, and cell phones. Originally designed as a low-power transmission medium to replace wires and cables, it has been expanded to a number of other uses, including data synchronization between devices. Using a low-power, *Class II transmitter*, Bluetooth has a general range of approximately 10 meters, or 33 feet, and has a stated maximum range of 100 meters, or 333 feet. It has been proven through experimentation that with the use of sophisticated specialized "shotgun" antennas, it is possible to extend the range to 2 miles.

Bluetooth originally started as an IEEE 802.15 standard and has since been relinquished by IEEE and is currently managed by the *Bluetooth Special Interest Group*.

The original Bluetooth technology had several weaknesses, but newer versions continue to get more secure. A highly suggested way to secure Bluetooth devices is to not set their attribute to "discoverable."

Wireless Network Attacks

Because data is transmitted readily through the radio environment, it is subject to being captured either mistakenly or intentionally. There are a number of well-known attacks against wireless transmissions.

Parking Lot Attack   The parking lot attack is best characterized by a vehicle located within close proximity to a transmission source, such as in the parking lot of an organization. The attacker usually has sophisticated radio monitoring equipment.

Drive-By Attack   In a drive-by attack, attackers have already identified the target and either jam the target with powerful conflicting signals on the 2.4 GHz and 5.0 GHz bands, thus disrupting communications, or attempt to intercept communications.

Wardriving   The act of searching for wireless communications by driving through an area using antennas, software, and a portable computer. Wardriving may be also accomplished using smartphones or personal digital assistants.

Warchalking   The marking of symbols to advertise the availability of Wi-Fi networks and to indicate whether they are open. Similar to hobo symbols, warchalking symbols consist of a number of different hieroglyphs or icons that were usually more in shock on buildings with available Wi-Fi networks.

Bluesnarfing   The unauthorized use of Bluetooth to access information from a wireless device.

Bluejacking   Uses Bluetooth to send unsolicited messages to Bluetooth-enabled devices such as mobile phones, tablets, and laptop computers.

Bluebugging   A form of a Bluetooth attack in which the attacker accesses and uses all phone features.

Evil Twin   Referred to as an evil twin, a rogue Wi-Fi access point that appears to be a legitimate access point that is part of an enterprise network on the premises but has actually has been set up to eavesdrop on wireless communications.

Wireless Access Points

A *wireless access point (WAP)*, commonly called an access point, or AP, is a low-power directional transceiver (transmitter/receiver) that is connected to the local area network through a standard network connection. The wireless access point associates with wireless devices within its immediate vicinity and transmits packets from the wired network to the wireless device.

Wireless devices such as cell phones, personal digital assistants, and laptops will connect to the "loudest" (in transmission volume) or nearest access point to their location. This is an attack technique commonly used by nefarious individuals to establish an access point that appears to be authentic but in fact just monitors all of the wireless information sent from an unsuspecting user's wireless device.

Exam Point

An access point is a network node that converts wired network packets into wireless communications. They may be mounted on ceilings, on walls, or on desktop devices.

A typical method employed when spoofing an access point is for the attacker to use a secondary or *rogue access point*. This rogue access point will be under the control of the attacker and may be placed in closer proximity to the user machines that he wants to attack. In practice, the rogue access point will appear as the legitimate access point on the actual network to unsuspecting laptops and tablets and other digital devices. This rogue access point would then process or view all traffic destined for the original network and would appear to all users to actually be the access point of the original network. This is a typical attack method used in many public places, including airports and restaurants.

Captive Portals

A *captive portal* is a type of wireless implementation of a "guest logon page" used by many public wireless networks. Typically, a hotel guest would log in using a room number to obtain free Wi-Fi with the possibility of upgrading to a higher speed for an additional charge to their room. An airport, on the other hand, might display an initial logon page offering temporary Internet access for a small price.

A captive portal in a public place can be quite dangerous because it may actually be the front for a very devious individual who is running a rogue access point. The attacker can duplicate the hotel or business wireless guest login screen, thus appearing to be a legitimate site. Unsuspecting individuals mistakenly give up their credit card information in order to gain the services listed on the captive portal page.

Antenna Placement

Antenna placement can be a major factor in the successful implementation of a wireless network. Antennas radiate electromagnetic radio signals that are received by wireless devices. Generally, common sense dictates that the farther a radio signal must travel, the weaker it will become. Placing an antenna near a metal object will disrupt the radio signal, as will placing the antenna near the floor or near a major *electromagnetic frequency (EMF)* source such as a motor, florescent light ballast, or transformer. Various other building materials may easily absorb or block radio waves, such as concrete blocks, metal doors, rock and stone structures such as fireplaces, and sometimes even metallized glass.

The ideal antenna placement is within the center of the area served and high enough to get around most obstacles. Many access points include a transmission signal attenuator control (transmitter volume control or power level control) that may be used if the signal transmits outside of the space intended.

Real World Scenario

Estimating Signal Strength

Many building designs and floor plans offer challenges to the wireless network designer. Radio signals can be easily disrupted by large metal objects such as filing cabinets and cola machines. Cinderblock walls, metalized glass, large concrete items such as building support pillars, and metal doors will all block wireless radio transmissions.

A strangely unique occurrence happened in one company. When the door to the executive's office was open, she could get online. If it was closed, the connection would terminate. It was later found, through RF testing, that the wireless signal was so significantly weak that changing the position of the computer or closing the door reduced the signal just enough to drop the network connection.

When testing your environment, it is easy to download a free Wi-Fi strength meter application on a cell phone or laptop and walk around the building premises. You may find a location that requires an additional wireless access point or repeater.

Antenna Types

The selection of a wireless antenna is important to the success of a wireless access point. On most access points, the supplied antenna can be replaced by an alternate antenna. A replacement antenna may be selected to be more or less directional, allowing for the proper configuration within the work space. Some access points have antennas that are completely internal and thus are not accessible.

Other access points have one or more external pole antennas. The more sophisticated access points will have a radio assigned to each antenna and will select the strongest signal strength depending upon the location of the transmitter in relation to the antenna within the work space. Proper antenna selection can allow the signal to circumvent obstacles and minimize the effects of interference, thus increasing signal strength and focusing the transmission within the work space. This will ultimately increase the speed of data transmission.

There are several types of antenna to select from:

Omnidirectional Antenna Designed to provide a 360° pattern and provide an even signal in all directions. An omnidirectional antenna may be typically found on home as well as commercial wireless access points. When this type of antenna is used, the desired AP location is in the center of the work area.

Directional Antenna Designed to force or direct a radio signal in one direction. This allows the radio signal to cover a greater distance or to avoid obstacles. A directional antenna might be used to project a Wi-Fi signal down a hallway.

Yagi Antenna A directional antenna consisting of multiple parallel metal rods called dipole elements in a line. As opposed to a simple dipole antenna, this design achieves a high degree of directionality and gain.

An antenna's power gain, or simply *gain*, is a major design feature that combines the antenna's beam focus and transmission efficiency. For instance, an antenna advertised with a 10 dBi would be 10 times stronger than a basic antenna of 0 dBi. Theoretically, every increase of 3 dBi effectively doubles the power output.

Cloaking is a technique of hiding a wireless network in plain sight. This is accomplished by disabling or turning off the *service set identifier (SSID)* broadcast at the access point. An SSID is usually the name of the wireless network in clear text. Every service set has an associated identifier, which consists of 32 octets that frequently contains the name of the network. If the SSID is turned off, the access point is still broadcasting and may be easily accessed by those who know or have already associated with the SSID. This simply prevents other individuals from scanning for networks to readily see the network name. Cloaking is considered a very weak form of security.

Traffic Shaping Techniques and Devices

Many companies struggle with limited bandwidth as applications, data transmission, and *VoIP* traffic seemingly clog up their networks. More and more data is transferred, and corporate network users transfer files, make phone calls, and analyze data to make corporate decisions. Network engineers and architects must ensure that business-oriented traffic gets priority over best-effort traffic. *Traffic shaping* has become the term used to manage the priority of traffic on corporate LANs.

Traffic shaping, which is also known as shaping, is a network traffic management technique that prioritizes packets in accordance with a network traffic profile. It is used to optimize or guarantee the delivery of some packets prior to others. This is accomplished by delaying some packets while accelerating others, thus improving network latency and increasingly the usable bandwidth.

Traffic shaping is also a method of controlling the volume of network traffic through the use of *bandwidth throttling*. The maximum rate at which the traffic is sent is controlled by *rate limiting*. Traffic shaping can be accomplished using a number of different methods, but in each case it is always achieved by prioritizing and delaying packets.

Quality of Service

Quality of service (QoS) is a measure of satisfaction of the overall user experience of the computer network or transmission medium. Some applications, such as multimedia, VoIP, and other streaming media, require a fixed-rate data flow and are sensitive to delays. If the network has excessive congestion or limited resources, excessive packet dropping and bit error rate may increase. If this happens, the *quality of experience (QoE)*, which is a subjective business concept, will be markedly lower and very noticeable to users and may be measured by "user-perceived performance," the required "degree of satisfaction of the user," or the targeted "number of happy customers" with regard to a service-level agreement (SLA).

As business networks become more congested with both data and multimedia traffic, quality of service and maintaining user satisfaction are growing in importance.

Exam Point

Quality of service refers to the prioritization of some packets over others. This affects the quality and user experience with regard to VoIP and multimedia on a congested network.

Summary

As a security practitioner, you will be closely involved with various aspects of managing and controlling networks, providing security, working with wireless applications, installing and administering updates and patches, and many other hands-on activities. As such, it is important to understand the basic concepts of each practice.

In this chapter, you studied the OSI reference model as well as the TCP/IP reference model. Both models are used to illustrate the encapsulation of data when it's transported over media to a different address. The OSI model features seven layers, while the TCP/IP model has only four layers. Copper wires, radio transmission, and fiber-optic cable are all forms of media. IPv4 and IPv6 describe the IP protocols that are used to route packets between devices. It is important to remember that the IPv4 address space is 32 bits while the IPv6 address space is 128 bits. There are numerous ways for a device to access the media. Carrier sense is the process when a device is listening for signals on the media, while multiple access is the ability for all devices to speak at the same time. This was referred to as carrier sense multiple access. In the event of two devices transmitting at the same time, there are two different techniques, collision detection and collision avoidance, that are used to resolve the contention.

In this chapter we covered various types of data traveling over networks, including streaming media, such as VoIP and multimedia files that include audio and video files. Continuous network monitoring and management of network logs is very important to mitigate problems that may arise on the network as well as to be in compliance with various regulations.

Handling data in transit as well as authenticating users sending data or requesting access to the network is important. Knowledge of IPsec is useful because it will become a standard with the implementation of IPv6. Single sign-on techniques allow users to use one set of credentials to access network resources. Kerberos is a popular single sign-on authentication application. Network segmentation reduces the amount of congestion on a network by dividing the network into virtual local area networks, or subnets. Special networks called demilitarized zones are exposed to the trusted network and maintain servers and devices that require public access from the untrusted network or Internet.

Numerous network devices provide security services throughout the network. Firewalls filter data packets based on established criteria, such as sending or receiving IP addresses, port addresses, applications, and other information. Switches operate at layer 2 of the OSI model and switch information based on physical MAC addresses. Routers operate at layer 3 of the OSI model and route information based on logical IP addresses. A proxy refers to any device that is in between two networks and intercepts, translates, and forwards data. Intrusion prevention and detection systems monitor and analyze network traffic and either record or take action based on preset rules.

Wireless technology has become a central communication standard within modern networks. The IEEE 802.11 standard, along with its amendments, is central to understanding the available frequencies and data flow rates as well as security on wireless networks.

Many different types of traffic are now transmitted over networks. Some of this traffic, such as VoIP and streaming media, is very sensitive to congestion, and the dropping and delaying of packets may be quite noticeable to users. Quality of service involves techniques to prioritize packets on a network, thus improving user satisfaction.

Exam Essentials

Network Models   Be able to describe both the TCP/IP model and the OSI model.

Network Cabling   Understand different types of network cables, including twisted-pair and unshielded twisted-pair, fiber-optic cables, and coaxial cables.

Fiber-optic Cables   Know the difference between single-mode, multimode, and plastic optical fiber, including the benefits and uses of each.

IPv4 and IPv6   Understand the differences between IPv4 and IPv6, including the address space allocation.

TCP/IP   Understand that IP is a connectionless transmission method and that TCP offers a three-way handshake. Be able to describe the three-way handshake.

Typical Network Topologies   Be able to describe the bus, tree, ring, mesh, and star network designs. Know the benefits of each.

Network Connection Models   Understand circuit-switched networks, packet-switched networks, and virtual circuit networks.

Media Access Models   Be able to describe carrier sense multiple access, Carrier Sense Multiple Access/Collision Detection and Carrier Sense Multiple Access/Collision Avoidance technologies.

Ports   Know that reports are special addresses that allow communication between hosts and applications or services running on a host. Be able to recognize well-known ports.

Continuous Monitoring   Understand the reasons behind continuous monitoring and the methods that might be used, including capturing and reviewing logs files.

Remote Access Control   Understand the methods involved in remote access control, including the use of RADIUS.

Kerberos   Know the authentication technique used in Kerberos as well as all of the terms associated with the Kerberos system.

Network Segmentation   Be able to describe subnetting in the creation of virtual local area networks.

Firewalls, Routers, and Switches   Understand and be able to describe the roles of firewalls, routers, and switches, and know how they work and what addresses they block, route, or switch.

Wireless Cellular Technologies   Be able to describe Wi-Fi and cellular technologies. Understand the IEEE 802.11 standard and the amendments. Be able to explain the difference between ad hoc mode and infrastructure mode.

Wireless Security Protocols   Understand WEP, WPA, and WPA2 and when they should be applied.

Traffic Shaping Technology   Describe the reasons for and the methods of shaping traffic and the implications in a data/multimedia network.

Written Lab

You can find the answers in Appendix A.

1.   Write a paragraph explaining the importance of and use of IPsec.

2.   Describe the single sign-on technique of Kerberos.

3.   Briefly explain the differences between routers and switches.

4.   List the layers in the OSI model in the proper order.

Review Questions

You can find the answers in Appendix B.

1. Encapsulation provides what type of action?

    A. Ensures perfect forward secrecy with IPsec

    B. Places one type of packet inside another

    C. Provides for data integrity

    D. Provides encryption and VPNs

2. The OSI model features how many layers?

    A. Six

    B. Seven

    C. Four

    D. Five

3. Which of the following offers the highest bandwidth and fiber-optic transmissions?

    A. Single-mode

    B. Dual-mode

    C. Multimode

    D. Plastic optical fiber

4. The address space for IPv6 is how many bits?

    A. 144 bits

    B. 132 bits

    C. 32 bits

    D. 128 bits

5. Switches operate at layer 2 on the OSI model and route what type of information?

    A. HMAC addresses

    B. IP addresses

    C. MAC addresses

    D. Secure packets

6. Which of the following protocols is referred to as connection oriented?

    A. TCP

    B. UDP

    C. SYN

    D. NAT

7. The *most* redundancy and connection speed is offered by which of the following network typology?

    A. Ring

    B. Tree

    C. Mesh

    D. Star

8. In a private enterprise environment, which of the following is *most* secure?

    A. Decentralized key management

    B. Centralized key management

    C. Individual key management

    D. Distributed key management

9. Which of the following media access methods features a node broadcasting a tone prior to transmitting?

    A. CSMA/CT

    B. CSMA/CD

    C. CSMA/CA

    D. CSMA/CS

10. Which of the following *best* describes converged network communications?

    A. The combination of two types of media such as copper and fiber-optic

    B. The use of Ethernet when communicating on a wireless network

    C. Transmission of voice and media files over a network

    D. The combination of SMS and chat capability on business networks

11. Continuous monitoring is *best* defined by which of the following?

    A. An automated system that regulates the flow of traffic on a network

    B. An automated system used to detect humidity and condensation in a data center

    C. A method of monitoring that is used to detect risk issues within an organization

    D. A manual system for monitoring a hot site in the event of a requirement immediate use

12. Which of the following *best* describes Kerberos?

    A. A federation of third-party suppliers that use a single sign-on

    B. An authentication, single sign-on protocol

    C. A method of maintaining network usage integrity

    D. A method of sharing information between network resources

13. Which type of network device is used to create a virtual local area network?

    A. A router

    B. NIC cards in promiscuous mode

   C. A switch

   D. A network concentrator

14. Which choice *best* describes a federation?

   A. Organizations that may rely on each other in the event of a disaster event

   B. An association of nonrelated third-party organizations that share information based upon a single sign-on

   C. Group organizations that share immediate information concerning zero day attacks

   D. A single sign-on technique that allows nonrelated third-party organizations access to network resources

15. Which answer is *most* accurate regarding firewalls?

   A. They route traffic based upon inspecting packets.

   B. They filter traffic based upon inspecting packets.

   C. They switch packets based upon inspecting packets.

   D. They forward packets to the Internet based upon inspecting packets.

16. Which answer is *most* accurate regarding a wireless intrusion prevention system?

   A. It is used to fine-tune the traffic on a wireless network.

   B. Rogue access points are detected.

   C. It broadcasts a jamming tone at a potential intruder.

   D. It monitors all traffic arriving at a wireless access point for proper ID fields.

17. Which answer is *most* accurate regarding IEEE 802.11i?

   A. Provides 54 Mbit/s using the 2.4 GHz frequency spectrum

   B. Provides security enhancements using WPA2

   C. Provide security enhancements using WEP

   D. Provides both 5 GHz and 2.4 GHz compatibility

18. Which choice *best* describes Bluetooth?

   A. A secure transmission methodology

   B. A transmission tool used to back up hard disks

   C. A method of data synchronization between devices

   D. A method of converting data from one type of media to another

19. Which of the following is a term used for a rogue Wi-Fi access point that appears to be legitimate but actually has been set up to intercept wireless communications?

   A. Captive access point

   B. Evil twin

   C. Deception twin

   D. Hidden access point

20. For optimal signal quality, which of the following is correct concerning wireless antenna placement?

   A.   Always use a Yagi antenna for 360° broadcasts.

   B.   Place the antenna near a doorway facing into a room.

   C.   Place the antenna as high as possible in the center of the service area.

   D.   Wireless antennas must always be placed in the line of sight.

Chapter

9

Domain 7: Systems and Application Security

SSCP EXAM OBJECTIVES COVERED IN THIS CHAPTER:

✓ Understand Malicious Code and Apply Countermeasures

✓ User threats and Endpoint Device Security

✓ Understand and Apply Cloud Security

✓ Secure Data Warehouse and Big Data Environments

✓ Secure Software Defined Networks and Virtual Environments

As an SSCP, you may be called upon to be a member of an incident response team and take an active part in security investigations with regard to intrusion of malware, malicious code, as well as the exfiltration of information from corporate and enterprise networks. It is important for the SSCP candidate to understand the vocabulary used to describe the creation, distribution, and countermeasures related to malicious code.

As a security professional, your job description will undoubtedly include endpoint as well as network security in both working with network equipment and providing assistance in security investigations. Endpoints include any end of network connection that does not pass on or through information to another device. Endpoints include user workstations, network nodes such as printers or scanners or even point-of-sale devices, and portable devices such as tablets, cell phones, and other devices that contain data or are used to communicate between the end-user and the network. Each of these devices requires its own set of security controls that may require the security professional to install, calibrate, update, and monitor.

Big data and data warehouses, as well as virtual environments, each present challenges to the security professional. As an SSCP, you should be familiar with not only the terminology but also the type of attacks and mitigation techniques required in each environment.

Understand Malicious Code and Apply Countermeasures

Malicious code software is designed and intended to do some harm. You know from the discussion of risk analysis in Chapter 5 that risk is a threat that exploits a vulnerability. *NISP Special Publication 800-30 revision 1*, as illustrated in Figure 9.1, identified both a *threat source* and a *threat action. Malicious code* may be the result of any one of several threat sources:

FIGURE 9.1 Threat source and threat action as illustrated in *NIST SP 800-30 revision 1*

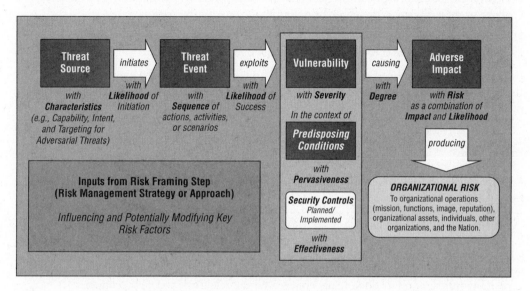

Reprinted courtesy of the National Institute of Standards and Technology, U.S. Department of Commerce. Not copyrightable in the United States.

Hacker *Hacker* is a broad term that can refer to individuals who only want to disrupt normal operations to terrorists waging a type of cyber war against a target and anything in between. A hacker may be a highly skilled individual with a personal agenda to exfiltrate data such as credit card information for their own personal gain.

Commercial Hacker (Comhacker) This is a type of hacker who may be hired by a third party to infiltrate a target for a specific agenda. This purpose of a *commercial hacker* may include stealing intellectual property, exfiltration of documents, changing information, and engaging in targeted disruption activities.

Certified Ethical Hacker (CEH) A *certified ethical hacker,* also referred to as a white hat hacker, is paid to infiltrate systems, break applications, and create reports concerning their activities. These individuals conduct penetration tests under strict guidelines and contractual relationships for the benefit of their employer.

Script Kiddie Usually an unskilled, inexperienced, immature hacker who utilizes hacking tools and scripts (thus, the term *script kiddie*) to generally attack sites or break into computer systems for fun and amusement.

Cracker The controversial name claimed by both black hat and white hat computer system intruders. White hat intruders, generally known as certified ethical hackers, claim that only a black hat hacker should be referred to as a *cracker.*

Nation State   Countries around the world that sponsor cyber terrorism are known as nation states. A nation state may promote a well-organized and well-funded hacking and infiltration organization that may plant *advanced persistent threats* (APTs) in foreign government or foreign commercial enterprises for intelligence gathering purposes. *Cyberwarfare* is a term to describe the activities carried out by nation states.

Hacktivist   A *hacktivist* is a person or group that exploits a weakness in technology in order to draw attention to a personal message or agenda.

Insider Attack   An *insider attack* may be performed by a disgruntled employee, third-party contractor, or anyone with direct inside access to an organization's network or host workstations.

Exam Point

Know the difference between the different types of intruders, such as hackers, script kiddies, crackers, and hacktivists.

Each threat source may create a threat action. The *threat action* is the actual attack or threat that exploits a vulnerability of the target. For instance, a threat action used by a commercial hacker may be to infiltrate the chief executive officer's personal computer and access any information or documents concerning the release of the new product.

Another example of threat sources creating threat actions may be that of a hurricane as a threat source. A hurricane may provide a number of threats such as high winds, flooding, lightning strikes, creation of debris that blocks roads, and disruption of utilities. Each of these threat actions may exploit a vulnerability. High winds may exploit the weak construction of the roof of the building.

Each threat action requires some sort of vehicle and means of delivering the payload to the target. The pathway into a target that is used by an attacker is referred to as a *vector*. For instance, a hacktivist creates Trojan horse malware that is loaded onto a host computer and installs a key logger as well as a means of dialing home and reporting collecting information. The attack vector was that the Trojan horse was included on a USB drive that was intentionally left on the ground near an individual's parking place and viewed as a freebie by the finder. The finder then plugged the USB drive into their computer, and it immediately uploaded the Trojan horse malware. The hacktivist may have selected several other vectors of attack, which might include network penetration attempts, a watering hole attack, a phishing attack, an insider attack, and a botnet exploitation.

Exam Point

A vector is the pathway to a target or the method used by the attacker to infect a target.

Malicious Code Terms and Concepts

It is important to understand a number of concepts and technical terms relating to malware. The following list includes technical terms and concepts relating to attacks, hacker tools, and types of malware.

Spoofing Attack   A *spoofing attack* is where the attacker appears to be someone or something else in order to mislead another person or device. Through this impersonation, the attacker may successfully launch a malicious attack.

Spyware   *Spyware* is software that is placed on the host computer and monitors actions and activities and often creates log of some sort. Spyware might also have some technique of sending the log to an external retrieval site.

Illegal Botnet   A network of compromised computers is called a *botnet*. Each infected computer is referred to as a bot. Computers can be infected through the use of malware. Users may be tricked into clicking links in emails, which may immediately insert the malware bot payload. A *bot herder* or *bot master* is usually the originator of the botnet or at the very least the current controller and operator. The most prevalent use of a botnet is for forwarding spam mail. The spam mail sender contracts with the bot herder and pays for the use of thousands of forwarding computers to send out spam.

Legal Botnet   Original botnets were linked by *Internet relay chat* (IRC), which was a number of Internet-connected computers communicating with other similar machines.

Zombie   A *zombie* is generally described as a compromised computer that may be controlled under remote control. A zombie could be a stand-alone computer or part of a much larger group, numbering in the hundreds or thousands of computers. Zombies are sometimes referred to as bots.

Cache Poisoning   Throughout a computer network there are a number of cache locations. Domain Name System (DNS) name servers and Address Resolution Protocol (ARP) make use of cache memory locations for short-term storage of information. Anytime erroneous information is placed into the cache or if the cache is corrupted, the term used is *cache poisoning*.

Computer Worm   A *computer worm* is a type of software that replicates itself without assistance. It may be installed by simply clicking a link in an email. A worm infects host computers as well as networks by leaving a copy of itself in each location or host machine. The primary use for a worm is to create a denial of service (DOS) attack.

Keylogger   A *keylogger*, also called a keystroke logger, is a malware program that records keystrokes. The program usually incorporates a method of transmitting the keystroke file to a remote location. The term *keylogger* also refers to a mechanical device that is inserted between the keyboard and the computer and performs the same keystroke interception activities.

Malware   Malware, sometimes referred to as *malcode*, is software specifically intended to cause harm. *Malware* is short for malicious software, while *malcode* refers to malicious code.

Privilege Escalation   *Privilege escalation* means a user or attacker acquires privileges they are not entitled to. Privileges are capabilities assigned to a system user. The higher the privileges, the more capabilities and more activities a user can perform within a system. For instance, system administrators have much higher privileges than end users. The goal of any attacker is privileged escalation. They may successfully intrude into a network and then progressively increase their privileges. The highest privilege level is generally called a "root privilege level." This originated in the days of the Unix operating system when the root level was the highest level assessable within the operating system.

Man in the Middle   In a *man in the middle* attack, a malicious actor is inserted into a conversation. At least one side of the conversation believes that they are talking to the appropriate or original party. In some cases, both sides of the conversation are being intercepted by the man in the middle. In this case, each side believes they are talking to the other. Man in the middle attacks are as common as rogue access points at a coffee shop or airport intercepting wireless communications.

Proof of Concept   A test case, or prototype, is used to prove the veracity of an idea. In the case of malware, *proof of concept* would be used to illustrate that a specific attack works. It may also be used in reverse engineering to test concepts.

Rootkit   A *rootkit* is a very old attack where malicious software allows the attacker to take root control of an operating system. This type of malware disguises itself by appearing as authentic operating system software to hide from antivirus/anti-malware software. The rootkit grants the attacker high-level authority with the ability to change system parameters and may remotely execute files.

Advanced Persistent Threat   An *advanced persistent threat* refers to continuous hacking processes often carried out by rogue governments or nation states against other nations, organizations, or large businesses. In practice, malicious code or malware is placed on various end-user workstations, personal devices, hosts, and servers to provide long-term surveillance and exfiltration of information. Typically, this malware is quiet and may be hidden for long periods of time, sending information out only infrequently. An advance persistent threat is stealthy malware primarily used for the discovery and exfiltration of state or corporate confidential information and is rarely if ever used for disruptive purposes.

Exam Point

Understand the differences between a worm and a virus. Be able to describe how they replicate themselves within the system.

Buffer Overflow   A *buffer overflow* attack occurs when more data is placed into a memory location, referred to as a buffer, than the memory location can accept. In such cases, the data overflows onto adjacent memory storage, thus corrupting the other storage or causing a failure in the application.

Pointer Overflow   A *pointer overflow* attack is similar to a buffer overflow attack. The pointer is used to index the process within a process stack. The attacker attacks the pointer through buffer overflow techniques to change it to point at the malicious code.

Cross-Site Request Forgery   *Cross-Site Request Forgery (CSRF)* is a malicious attack that tricks the user's web browser, by issuing unauthorized commands, to perform undesired actions so that they appear as if an authorized user is performing them.

Cross-Site Scripting   *Cross Site Scripting (XSS)* is based on inserting a client-side script into a genuine website. This is possible due to poor application or website design, such as limited data validation in websites. Scripts are then executed on other hosts that access the same website.

Directory Traversal   *Directory transversal* is a type of web attack using HTTP in which the attacker escalates their privileges to climb to a parent directory, or higher-level directory, out of the original website directory. *Transversal* refers to crossing the boundary between the website directory and higher directories, referred to as root directories.

Back Door   Originally the term *back door*, also called a *maintenance hook*, referred to an access device used by a program developer to access the application during the development stage. If it was not removed, at the very least it would allow the programmer access to the application around the normal access controls. Another use for back doors is for hackers to access applications and databases. Usually delivered by Trojan malware, a Trojan payload installs a malware application that creates a back door, or access port, for the attacker.

Reverse Engineering   The act of decomposing an item to determine its construction and method of operation is *reverse engineering*. For instance, malware is often reverse engineered to determine its construction, components, and the effect of the components upon the attacked system.

Adware   *Adware* is a type of spyware that, while making an advertising statement or showing a banner, solicits clicks from the end user. When the user clicks the adware banner, a Trojan or virus is be downloaded immediately, infecting the user's machine. This could be as simple as a keylogger, or it might convert the machine into a bot. Adware may also be used to create a revenue stream for the creator through a pay-per-click program. In this type of exploit, each time a user clicks a digital ad, the advertiser must pay several cents to several dollars. This revenue may also be paid as commissions if the ad is placed on a user's website. In an adware exploitation campaign, tens of thousands of users may be directed to high-paying advertising as bogus clicks. The hacker is then paid sometimes thousands of dollars for their effort.

Ransomware   *Ransomware* is malware often delivered through a Trojan attack that disables a system and advises the user to pay ransom to release the system. The ransom might be paid simply by purchasing a software application purported to be a virus scanner. The individual must expose their credit card information to the attacker. Ransomware is much more serious when entire organizations and companies have been attacked and held for hundreds of thousands of dollars' worth of ransom to release their systems.

Covert Channel   Any means of communication other than the standard channel of communication is referred to as using a *covert channel*, such as, for instance, sending messages on a control channel of a device.

Out-of-Band Transmission   Out-of-band is transmitting a message or date by any means other than through a normal channel of communication. *Out of band* is normally used to describe a method of exchanging passwords by not sending them over the same channel as the encrypted message.

Payload   A payload is the harmful code contained within any malware.

SQL Injection   *Structured Query Language (SQL)* is a communication system used to access databases. With a SQL injection, an attacker inserts a *SQL escape character*, a combination of SQL characters, or part of the SQL script into a website form field. If the form field offers limited data validation, the insertion may return database information or an error code, which may be useful to the attacker.

Virus   A *virus* is malicious code software that requires an action to reproduce. Viruses usually attach themselves to executable programs and thereby reproduce and spread every time the executable is launched. There are a number of terms associated with viruses:

   Virus *Payload*   The harmful component of a virus. Some payloads include devastating properties that can erase entire hard drives or permanently harm hardware equipment.

   Virus Hoax   Typically email warnings concerning potential virus attacks. The spread of the email warnings actually creates a denial-of-service attack among many users. *Virus hoax* notifications should always be referred to help desk or IT departments for verification prior to distribution.

   Macro Virus   A virus created through the use of macro programs usually found in Microsoft Office applications. Microsoft has since taken steps to request approval prior to executing macros in Microsoft Office Suite applications.

   Virus Signature   A specific identifiable string of characters that characterizes it as a virus or family of viruses. Anti-malware software as well as intrusion prevention and detection systems attempt to identify viruses based upon specific signatures.

   File Infecting Virus   A type of virus that specifically infects executable files to make them unusable or permanently damaged. By overwriting code or permanently inserting code, the virus changes the original files to perform differently.

   Boot Sector Virus   This type of virus infects the storage device's master boot record. This was a popular attack in the days of floppy disks. All modern operating systems contain boot sector safeguards and anti-boot sector virus controls.

Polymorphic Virus   A *polymorphic virus* changes slightly as it replicates throughout the system. This makes it difficult for scanners to detect this type of virus because of different variations. This type of virus most often attacks data types and data functions used in many programming languages. The virus will usually manage to hide from your antivirus software. Very often a polymorphic virus will encrypt parts of itself to avoid detection. When the virus does this, it's referred to as a mutation virus.

Stealth Virus   A *stealth virus* masks itself as another type of program to avoid detection, usually by changing the filename extension or modifying the filename. The stealth virus may also attempt to avoid detection by antivirus applications. When the system utility or program runs, the virus may redirect commands around itself in order to avoid detection. Stealth viruses modify file information by reporting a file size different from what the actual file size presently is in order to avoid detection.

Retrovirus   A *retrovirus* directly attacks the antivirus program, potentially destroying the virus definition database file. The virus disables the antivirus program yet makes it appear as if it is working, thus providing a false sense of security.

Multipartite Virus   A *multipartite virus* attacks different parts of the host system, such as a boot sector, executable files, and application files. This type of virus will insert itself into so many places that, even if one instance of the virus is removed, many still remain.

Armored Virus   An *armored virus* is constructed in such a manner as to be highly resistant to removal by anti-malware software.

Exam Point

Many attackers seek *privilege escalation*. This allows them to gain more rights to a system and thereby change operations or delete files.

Logic Bomb   A logic bomb is a script or malware usually installed by a disgruntled employee or insider to cause harm based on a certain event occurring. For instance, if the employee is fired and does not reset the script, the script executes, causing some harm to the network, host, or data.

 Real World Scenario

A Surprising Find

A midwestern manufacturing company had contracted a pen testing firm to test a brand-new application it had designed that was in the final test phase just before deployment. As usual, the contract was signed, authorizing the testing firm to make various penetration attacks using a variety of tools and methods. Unknown to the testing firm were some of the behind-the-scenes politics happening in the company at the same time. Evidently,

Continues

Continued

a senior contract programmer had a major disagreement with the firm and some of his superiors concerning the direction or implementation of some application designs and specific code. He had been released from his responsibilities and escorted off the premises prior to the employment of the pen testing firm.

As the penetration testers investigated the target application, they ran across a surprising find. Buried on an obscure server was a small, innocuous file with a name that did not mean anything to anyone. Upon further investigation, it was found that if this file had executed, it would have deleted major sections of the application code from production servers as well as from preproduction servers. It later was found that this was a type of logic bomb that was left by the disgruntled senior contract programmer with access to the servers. The trigger was Active Directory. The script was designed to check the directory for a specific person's name. If the name was not present in AD, the script would execute, assuming that the programmer no longer worked at the firm. Thanks to the coincidence that a penetration testing firm was employed to analyze the application, the script was found. As can be imagined, the information was then turned over to the authorities.

File Extension Attack The Windows *New Technology File System (*NTFS) allows filenames to extend up to 235 characters. These extremely long filenames are usually abbreviated on directory displays and in other presentations, thus hiding the fact that there may be a double file extension or other hidden filenames.

Double File Extension Attack The *double file extension* attack features two extensions within a filename, but only the final file extension is operative. The previous file extensions will appear to the system as part of the filename. For instance, .../.../.jpg.exe could be a double extension filename.

VM Escape *VM escape* is the result of an attack upon a virtual machine whereby the attacker is successful in bouncing out of or escaping the virtual environment and controlling the hypervisor. Within the hypervisor, the attacker may then successfully control any other virtual machine as well as attack the underlying hardware infrastructure.

Phishing *Phishing* is an attack that attempts to obtain personal information, credit card information, or login information by masquerading as a legitimate entity. Often the attack involves an email sent to an unsuspecting target, requesting confidential information. The email may appear legitimate and possibly direct the target to a fake website, which may appear to be identical to an authentic website.

Spear Phishing *Spear phishing* is a directed attack on an individual or group of individuals with the goal of gathering personal or corporate information. For instance, the CEO of an organization that is engaged in a merger or acquisition process may be targeted by individuals wishing to sell valuable financial information to unscrupulous investors.

Whaling *Whaling* is the targeting of senior executives within an organization, usually through officially appearing emails. Some of these emails may appear as legal documents or subpoenas and may appear to be generated by the U.S. Securities and Exchange Commission, the FBI, or a reputable law firm. In most cases, the senior executive is instructed to click a link in the email, which immediately infects the executive's PC.

 Real World Scenario

Marketable Information

Board members, the chief executive officer, as well as other C-level corporate officers and senior executives have detailed knowledge of important corporate activities all of the time. Details may be stored on or transmitted through many devices such as laptops and tablets as well as cell phones.

It is not unusual for non-security-oriented individuals to dismiss the importance of information protection. The terms *whaling* and *spearfishing* may not be taken that seriously, to the point that some of the senior individuals involved do not consider that they may be the direct and specific target of an attack.

Any significant event such as a merger or acquisition, corporate divestiture, introduction of a new product, or a major failure or success of something all may move the financial markets up or down if the information were to be made public. Once acquired, any of this information is marketable to the right financial parties. Aggressive, unscrupulous investors, nefarious money managers, and other individuals might pay top dollar to take advantage of "tips" before the information is made public.

Senior executives, board members, and other individuals may not realize the significance or possible monetary value of data they possess. Of course, the data may be held in confidence due to regulatory environments, but specific information, such as product release dates, investment amount, market impact, and data related to timing may well be worth paying for as black market financial information.

Security awareness sessions should be orchestrated specifically for board members, C-level corporate officers, and even senior executives to make them aware of the probability of being directly targeted for important information concerning a major corporate transaction. The security awareness training should also involve any administrative assistants, secretaries, or other staff who have access to the same information. Any of these people may be specifically targeted by spearfishing or whaling penetration techniques.

Vishing   *Vishing* (voice phishing) is usually carried out by sending a fake email that instructs the target to call a specific phone number. The recording at the fake phone number usually prompts users to enter an account number or PIN, thus allowing the attacker to obtain personal information.

Pharming   *Pharming* is a type of social engineering attack to obtain access credentials, such as usernames and passwords. In practice, it's a type of attack that redirects the user to an unexpected website destination. Pharming can be conducted either by changing the hosts file on a victim's computer or by exploiting a vulnerability in DNS server software.

Exam Point

Be able to explain social engineering attacks such as phishing, vishing, and pharming and know who may be a likely target, such as in the whaling and spearfishing.

Trojan Malware   Trojan malware is malware that is disguised as a usable program. For instance, malware may be inserted and hidden inside a program such as Microsoft Paint. Once the user executes the Microsoft Paint application, *Trojan malware* is immediately inserted into the system. Quite often, downloadable software, such as hardware drivers, software upgrades, and even software claiming to be free malware and virus scanners include Trojan malware.

Rogue Software   This type of Trojan software is loaded by the user, either willingly or through other practices, and once installed, functions as *ransomware*. Functionality is typified by frequent pop-ups, changing of desktop or application appearance, or difficult-to-remove screens.

In the Wild   *In the wild* refers to anti-malware that has been released onto the Internet. Imagine that this malware is roaming free and is being exchanged through unsuspecting host relationships, indiscriminate clicking email links, and other types of actions that spread the malware through the Internet.

Air Gap   *Air gap* is a networking term that describes how an internal network can be totally isolated from the outside world. With no connections in or out of it, the network is said to be air gaped, meaning that there is a complete isolation zone around the network perimeter.

Air Gap Centrifuges

Anyone familiar with the *Stuxnet virus* story will remember that June 2010 was the first appearance of Stuxnet, a computer worm that infected the software of at least 14 industrial sites in Iran, including a uranium-enrichment plant. The targets were industrial control systems produced by *Siemens* that were reportedly managed on an air-gaped network and were thus not able to be attacked from the outside world. The only way to deliver the virus and bridge the air gap was to load it on engineering PCs of third-party contractors. USB-infected drives were left for the employees of the contractor firms to find. The virus had no visible effect on the contractors' Windows PCs, so it wasn't detected. When the PCs infected with the Stuxnet virus were eventually connected to the industrial control system network, the Stuxnet virus identified the *Siemens Step 7 software* running on the Siemens programmable logic controllers as the target. Upon execution, it took control of the centrifuges, making them spin to failure, while providing the monitoring controllers with erroneous information indicating everything was fine. This is a prime example of bridging an air gap.

Zero-Day Attack   A *zero-day attack* is a type of attack in which the attacker uses a previously unknown attack technique or exploits a previously unknown vulnerability. The zero-day attack usually exploits a vulnerability but also exploits the time differential between the discovery of the zero-day attack and the time the manufacturer or developer issues a patch to correct the vulnerability. Many zero-day attacks are unreported and thus remain unpatched.

Managing Spam to Avoid Malware

Spam is the receipt of unwanted or unsolicited emails. It's not truly a virus or a hoax. It's one of the most annoying things that users encounter. Spam may also create larger problems for the user and a network administrator. Spam might contain links that automatically download malware on a mouse click, or it could contain a link that takes the user to an infected website.

There are many anti-spam applications available, and they can be run by network administrators as well as by end users. As with any filter mechanism, false positives and false negatives are always possible. On occasion, a spam filter will block important messages.

Although *spam* is a popular term to describe unwanted emails, similar terms have evolved to describe unwanted messages in other mediums. For instance, *SPIM (Spam over Instant Messaging)* and *SPIT (Spam over Internet Telephony)* describe specific unwanted messages.

Email identification

SPAM detection and prevention software as well as data loss prevention (DLP) applications seek to identify specific types of messages both entering and exiting the network. Many large firms have established a policy whereby individuals must specifically mark email messages for separate processing techniques. For instance, some defense

Continues

Continued

contractors require all individuals to put at the beginning of every subject line the words *External* or *Internal* to denote whether the ultimate destination is internal to the plant or external to the plant. When the applications detect these words, they route the email for further content processing based upon the ultimate destination.

Cookies and Attachments

To provide a customized web experience for each visit, a website may insert a *cookie* in a file on the user's browser. This text file typically contains information about the user, such as client's browsing history, browsing preferences, purchasing preferences, and other personal information. For instance, Amazon.com utilizes cookies placed on a user's computer to record user preferences and browsing habits. When the user returns to *Amazon.com*, the site reads the cookies and dynamically generates web pages illustrating products that may be of interest to the user.

Cookies are considered a risk because they have the ability to contain personal information about the user that might be exploited by an attacker. Passwords, account numbers, PINs, and other information may be inserted into a cookie.

Although cookies can be turned off or not accepted by a browser, websites have an ability to write a type of cookie that creates persistent data on a user's computer. An *Evercookie*, created by Samy Kamkar, stores cookie data in several locations the website client can access. Should cookies be cleared by the end user, the data can still be recovered and reused by the website client. Evercookies are written in JavaScript code and are intentionally difficult to delete. They actively "resist" deletion by copying themselves in different forms on the user's machine and resurrect themselves if they notice that some of the copies are missing or expired.

Similar to user preferences recorded in cookies, a device *fingerprint* (sometimes referred to as a machine fingerprint or browser fingerprint) is a single string of information collected from a remote computing device for the purpose of identification. With the use of client-side scripting languages such as JavaScript, the collection of device parameters is possible. Normally, a script is run on the client machine by a legitimate website or by an attacker wishing to enumerate the device.

If security is of utmost concern, the best protection is to not allow cookies to be accepted. Cookies may be enabled or disabled using any browser options menu. Most browsers allow you to accept or reject all cookies or only those from a specified server. Figure 9.2 illustrates a typical cookie. This screen shows that there are 12 cookies from Google.com. Notice that the selected cookie has various metadata as well as a content field. Applications may read or rewrite any of the information as required. Every browser allows the user to access the cookie file. Notice the X to the right of the cookie. Clicking this allows you to erase the cookie. All cookies can be bulk erased by clicking the Remove All button at the top.

FIGURE 9.2   The APISID cookie from Google.com

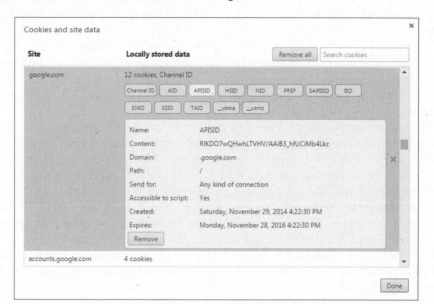

NSA Tracking

In 2013, a top-secret *National Security Agency (NSA)* document was leaked by Edward Snowden citing a method of tracking *Tor network* users. The document made reference to two types of cookies. The first referred to a *Quantumcookie*, which is claimed to be a device that forces clients to divulge stored cookies. Another reference was made to a type of cookie that would store cookie-type information in numerous locations so cookie information could be reconstructed when messages exit a Tor network. The second reference almost exactly described an Evercookie. Attacks using cookies or evercookies have long been recognized as a risk, but their success relies upon the existence of various client-side vulnerabilities. The release of the documents has prompted *The Onion Router (Tor)* network users to run current software versions and follow best-practice advice repeatedly offered by Tor volunteers.

Most of the time the word *attachment* refers to the file attached to an email document. Attachments may also be included in instant messages (referred to as IMs), text messages, and other types of communication. Attachments offer challenges for the security professional because they can harbor malicious code.

When someone is sending a message with an attachment, their email client marks the attachment with two different labels. These include the data type known as the content type or *MIME* type and the original filename. The labels instruct the receiver's email client as to what application to use to open the attachment. For instance, graphics data would be displayed as a photograph or picture, an audio or video file would be played in the appropriate media player, and a document such as a Microsoft Word document would be shown as a link that must be clicked to open the document.

Attachments can be dangerous. They can contain an executable program. The executable is interpreted directly by the computer and can possibly install a virus, covertly transfer data to a remote host computer, or even destroy host data entirely. However, executables must be written for a specific type of computer. For instance, an executable written for the *Linux operating system* will not operate on Windows-based computers. Another risk is an attachment containing a script. A script is an executable file that may be downloaded and may be executed directly by the browser or host computer. Scripts usually are interpreted by other programs such as Adobe Flash Player and Internet Explorer. An example of a malicious scripting virus is the *Melissa virus*. It was a Visual Basic script that infected the host computer and then mailed itself to the contacts in the host's email address book.

Not all attachments contain dangerous scripts or malicious software. Some attachments contain audio files, media files, static picture files, or other files that might be malformed and, when interpreted by the email client, cause the client or the entire host system to crash.

The following methods can be used to protect against threats contained in attachments:

- Keep all software up-to-date with current versions and patches.
- Create a white list of approved or safe email sources.
- Set an antivirus program to scan all attachments.
- If a link is present, save the contents in a file rather than clicking the link directly.

Malware Power Supplies

It has long been reported through numerous articles that malware code has been embedded in a number of power supply devices. One such report claimed that malware was inserted into a PC USB port through an *E-cigarette* USB power cord. In another report, it was claimed that malware was successfully installed on a wall wart power supply for Apple devices and infected the *Apple IOS* operating system in less than a minute. Federal investigative agencies suspect that a broad range of business and consumer devices flood the U.S. market with preinstalled malware from the factory.

Malicious Code Countermeasures

Numerous techniques are available to detect malicious code and to take corrective and recovery actions upon discovery. These techniques involve software applications as well as hardware appliances that may be used as controls to mitigate the risk of malicious code and malware affecting a network or network node device.

Anti-malware and Anti-spyware   *Anti-malware* and *anti-spyware* software must be installed on every network node, including host computers, mail servers, file servers, and detection and prevention devices. The software must be updated regularly and enabled to automatically receive the latest virus and spyware definitions. Anti-malware software should be tested regularly to ensure that a retrovirus has not corrected the application or deleted signature library files. The application should be set to automatically scan the following:

> **Scheduled Scan**   All anti-malware and anti-spyware software can be scheduled to auto-matically scan at a certain time, and in many cases the default is in the middle of the night. Care must be taken to ensure that the scans are properly accomplished. In some cases, the PC is turned off during the scheduled scan time or the scan will not occur. It is advisable to reference log files of the anti-malware software to ensure that scheduled scans were accomplished as expected.

> **Real-Time Scan**   Most anti-malware and anti-spyware software can be enabled to scan files as they are opened, emails as they are received, and devices such as USB drives as they are attached. The downside is that real-time scan can add latency when software is opened and files are loaded.

> **On-Demand Scan**   All anti-malware and anti-spyware software allow you to perform a file scan at any time. It is standard for these applications to have both an extensive scan, which may require several hours to complete, and an expedited or targeted scan, which scans either a set group of previously selected files or files that have recently changed.

Protocol Analyzers   The terms *protocol analyzer* and *packet sniffer* generally refer to the same technique or software application used to intercept packets flowing along the network. Data that is transmitted across the network may be intercepted by a per-sonal computer with a network interface card set in *promiscuous mode*. Normally, network interface cards listen for only the traffic destined to them. Promiscuous mode allows the software to receive and monitor all traffic. Protocol analyzers may be simply attached to a network using a network tap. This is simply a three-way splitter that routes the traffic to the network interface card. Protocol analyzers can display real-time network traffic and feature various filtering capabilities to better visualize the vast amounts of traffic being received. These devices usually keep all of the created recordings or log files of network traffic analysis for a later time. Some well-known protocol analyzers are *Wireshark*, *SAINT*, *SATIN*, and *Snort*. Figure 9.3

depicts a typical Wireshark packet capture. This capture collected 23 packets of a SSL handshake.

FIGURE 9.3   A Wireshark packet capture

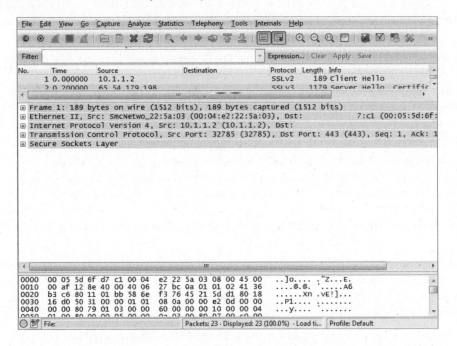

Exam Point

Protocol analyzers capture traffic on a network but do not take overt action to drop packets or rewrite firewall rules. They capture traffic by placing a network interface card (NIC) in promiscuous mode.

Vulnerability Scanners   Vulnerability scanners provide the ability to scan a network and search for weaknesses that may be exploited by an attacker. The vulnerability scanner software application looks for weaknesses in networks, computers, or even software applications. Vulnerability scanners can include port scanners and network enumerators, which conduct a series of tests on a target and search against an extensive list of known vulnerabilities. Some vulnerability scanning applications are listed here:

   Nmap   *Nmap* is a software application for probing computer networks, providing detection and discovery of hosts and services running on ports, and determining operating systems. In operation, Nmap sends special packets to target nodes and analyzes the response.

Nessus *Nessus* is a popular vulnerability scanner that checks for misconfigurations, default passwords, and the possibility of hidden denials of service. In operation, Nessus determines which ports are open on the target and then tries various exploits on the open ports.

Retina *Retina* is a commercially available network security scanner that provides advanced vulnerability scanning across the network, the Web, and virtual and database environments. Used to continually monitor the network environment, it may be used to detect vulnerabilities on a real-time basis and recommend remediation based on risk analysis of critical assets.

Microsoft Baseline Security Analyzer The *Microsoft Baseline Security Analyzer (MBSA)* is a tool that can scan a system and find missing updates and security misconfigurations. It can be used to determine the security state of a PC in accordance with Microsoft security recommendations and offers specific remediation guidance. It can be used to scan one or more computers at the same time and can use a computer's name or IP address to schedule a scan. Figure 9.4 illustrates a typical scan using the MBSA. The scan was enabled to scan only one machine and to rank the problems found from top-down.

FIGURE 9.4 A Microsoft Baseline Security Analyzer scan showing several problems that were found

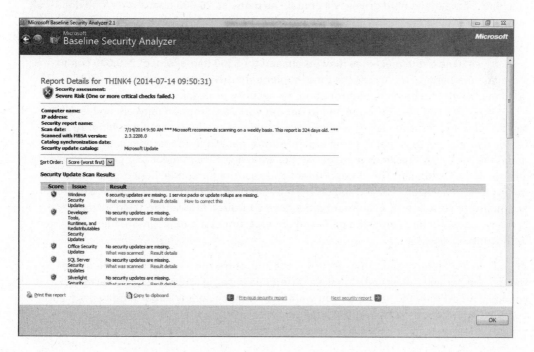

 **Real World Scenario**

Data Is Where You Least Expect It

It's a little-known fact in most corporate circles, but data can be hiding in some of the least suspected places. As security professionals, it is our job to protect corporate information assets. The first thing most of us think of is our networks, servers, host PCs, cloud, and other "information technology" devices. We live in a stratosphere of high-tech gizmos that transfer data at the speed of light. Who would suspect that the office filing cabinets, complete with hanging green folders and stapled copies of forms, could be a very substantial security risk to an organization? Sometimes we forget, in our world of flashing lights and colored wires, that in most of the corporate world, information storage is still as it was in the middle of the last century. Many people still feel a need to touch, feel, write on, and file paper. (Some information must be actually typed on a typewriter in triplicate!) Of course, the first thing security professionals might think of is physical security. This might easily be accomplished by locking cabinets or placing sensitive printed material in restricted access locations. But this is far from the correct answer. Look to the common office copier.

Armen Keteyian, in a CBS News investigation documentary, `https://youtu.be/iC38D5am7go`, reports that nearly every office copier built since 2002 includes a hard drive that contains a copy of every document copied, scanned, or emailed by the machine. Some of the hard drives will contain as many as 20,000 documents, and documents are added every day by unsuspecting office workers throughout the organization.

In the documentary, the investigation team purchased three copiers and extracted the hard drives. One of the machines they purchased for $300 had a total of 249,000 copies stored on the hard drive. Across the three copier hard drives, they found thousands of documents with incriminating information. As security professionals, we know that these everyday office copiers are connected to our networks as common network nodes. Users can forward and retrieve files as well as email and fax directly from the machine. What makes matters worse is that in some organizations, decisions concerning copiers fall under the purview of facilities management or even an office manager. Copiers are usually not in the IT domain. The IT department and security personnel in particular may not be involved in decisions concerning drive encryption, drive destruction, the installation of anti-malware software, or even routing the device through firewalls to the outside world. In many cases, copiers come and go based on departmental budgets more than concerns for document security.

At your next general organization security meeting, show the five-minute video at the URL shown earlier. This may just make a difference in some attitudes. It will certainly change your attitude the next time you walk into an office supply superstore to copy your personal information on their public copiers.

Dynamic Threat Analysis Appliance   *Threat analysis appliances* have recently come on the market that dynamically detect malware and are described as an anti-malware protection system. A threat analysis appliance is used to monitor and protect network, email, endpoint, mobile, and content assets. A major benefit is the ability of the threat analysis appliance. To dynamically monitor the environment for recently changed malware signatures or previously unknown malware attacks referred to as zero-day exploits. Upon finding a zero day, exploit, or changed malware signature, the client may send information to the manufacturer's investigation laboratory. A sandbox is usually tested and studied to determine the harm that it could cause. This information is then shared with a global network of similar devices, thus immediately protecting those environments from the recently discovered attack.

Intrusion Prevention Systems   Intrusion prevention systems are network appliances that monitor networks at various locations for malicious activity. They are placed in line and are able to execute rule-based actions based on attack detection. Such actions may include dropping packets, changing firewall rules, alerting operators, resetting connections, and blocking activity.

Malicious Add-Ons

Add-ons are small applications that are downloaded to the client computer during a web session. Because these are executable programs, they have the potential of doing harm to the client computer. Some of these apps, add-ons, or included scripts do harm unintentionally due to poor programming or poor design, while others are *malicious add-ons* that are designed with the intent of doing harm to the client computer. The following sections describe two general types of web-based add-ons: Java applets and ActiveX controls.

Java Applets

A *Java applet* is a small, self-contained JavaScript program that is downloaded from the server to a client and then runs in the browser of the client computer. For a Java applet to execute, Java must be enabled on the client browser.

Java applets are small programs that control certain aspects of the client web page environment. They are used extensively in web servers today, and they're becoming one of the most popular tools for website development. They greatly enhance the user experience by controlling various kinds of functionality and visuals presented to the end user. Java-enabled websites running Java web pages accept preprogrammed instructions in the form of *JavaScript* as they are downloaded from the server and control the actions and presentation in the user environment.

The Java applets must be able to run in a virtual machine on the client browser. By design, Java applets run in a restricted area of memory called a *Java sandbox*, or *sandbox* for short. A sandbox is set up anytime it is desired to restrict an application from accessing user areas or system resources. A Java applet that runs in a sandbox is considered safe, meaning it will not attempt to gain access the system resources or interfere with other applications. Potential attacks or programming errors in a Java virtual machine might allow an applet to run outside the sandbox. In this case, the applet is deemed unsafe and may perform malicious operations. The creators of Java applets understood the potential harm that running unchecked scripts on a client computer could cause, which is why they required the Java applets to always execute the Java sandbox.

ActiveX

ActiveX is a technology that was implemented by Microsoft to customize controls, icons, and other features to increases the usability of web-enabled systems. An ActiveX control is similar in operation to a Java applet. ActiveX controls have full access to the Windows operating system unlike Java applets. This gives ActiveX controls much more power than Java applets because they don't have the restriction or requirement of running in a sandbox. ActiveX runs on the client web browser and utilizes an author validation technology using Authenticode certificates. The *Authenticode certificates* are used by the client as a type of proprietary code-signing methodology. Web browsers are usually configured so that they require confirmation by the user prior to downloading an ActiveX control. Security professionals must be careful to fully train end users in allowing the use of ActiveX on their personal computers. Authenticode certificates that are invalid will provide a pop-up message for the user providing the options as accept and continue or reject the ActiveX plug-in. By choosing the accept option, the installation of malware or other harmful actions may be taken by an ActiveX plug-in.

Exam Point

Java applets download into a sandbox and execute in a protected environment where they cannot affect the underlying applications or hardware environment. Active X controls are prescreened prior to downloading using Authenticode certificates to identify and authenticate the author. The user may then opt out of downloading ActiveX controls.

User Threats and Endpoint Device Security

An organization's endpoint devices, such as desktop workstations, printers, scanners, and servers, as well as personally owned devices such as tablets and laptops, must be configured and used in a secure manner for several reasons. First, it is very likely that sensitive, confidential, or even proprietary information is stored or processed on the workstation.

Regulatory agencies or contractual relationships may expose the organization to liability and possibly substantial fines if information is not protected using generally accepted protection methods. The concept of due care dictates that appropriate controls are put into place to adequately protect information and ensure that it is not improperly disclosed. Second, system integrity is critical. End-user workstations must operate as expected, be available for use, utilize applications that are not compromised, and provide processed data that is complete and accurate. If a user's workstation has been compromised, lost, or altered, data may lead to wrong decisions. Loss of workstation availability will most certainly lead to lost productivity.

The security practitioner is absolutely essential in ensuring that the organization's end-user workstations meet minimum standards for connecting to the network as well as incorporating the health and hygiene to provide reliable computing services.

Since the security practitioner is the first line of defense, it is quite common for them to be involved in end-user training and communicating best practices relating to a variety of site work tasks, including protecting passwords, serving websites, and opening email attachments. Users must be made aware of the hazards of downloading software, clicking on phishing links, and performing tasks and activities that place the user workstation as well as the network in jeopardy.

General Workstation Security

Workstation security may be mandated through IT security policy. Typically, such a policy encompasses other policies, such as workstation policies. Workstation policies may include the activities that are carried out on a workstation, such as file sharing, making backups, managing software patch updates, and other general activities that involve the management of an organization's workstations.

Passwords

Workstation and application passwords should be changed routinely. A standard within the IT industry specifies an interval for password changes as 60 to 90 days. A number of organizations use a multi-tier password policy that involves changing passwords more frequently for sensitive or confidential information. In some instances, the changing of passwords may be more frequent based upon job roles such as power users or system administrators. General password policy administration should include the following:

Utilize the system key utility.   The *system key utility (Syskey)* provides an extra defense within a Windows-based system against password-cracking software. User account password information is stored in the *Security Accounts Manager (SAM)* database of the Registry on workstations in a Microsoft Windows environment. Often, the attackers target the SAM database or Active Directory services with password-cracking software to access user account passwords. The system key utility makes use of strong encryption techniques that make cracking encrypted account passwords more difficult and time-consuming than cracking non-encrypted account passwords. There are three levels of security offered by the system key utility depending upon how or where the system key is stored.

Password best practices.   There are numerous articles on the Internet outlining best practices for passwords. Any or all of these practices should be incorporated into security awareness courses for end users. Here are some suggestions:

- Create unique passwords using combinations of words, numbers, and symbols with both upper- and lowercase letters.

- Do not use easily guessed passwords such as your first name, *password*, *12345678*, or *user*.

- Do not use personal information as a password such as Social Security number, birth date, spouse's name, street name, names of family members, or other easily identifiable information.

- Do not use personal names or any word that may appear in a dictionary. Password cracking tools are available for English and most foreign languages and can easily test tens of thousands of words against your password.

- Using password phrases such as *IgraduatedfromtheUniversityofTexasin1977* will make it difficult for an attacker to use a brute-force cracking method. Complexity and length are the key strengths of a password phrase.

- Of course, remind users that they should not write passwords on sticky notes.

Figure 9.5 is a typical Microsoft warning screen advising users of a password change policy. The wording on these types of screens may easily be changed to fit the policy.

FIGURE 9.5   A typical password change policy advisory pop-up

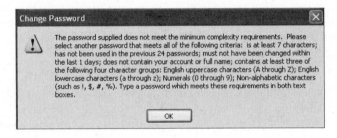

Password Lockout Policy

A password attack known as a brute-force attack can be automated to attempt thousands or even millions of password combinations. Account lockout is a feature of password security Microsoft has built into Windows 2000 and later versions of the operating system. The feature disables a user account after a preset number of wrong passwords. The number of failed login attempts as well as the period of time to wait before logins may resume may be set by the administrator. The three policy settings are as follows:

Account Lockout Threshold   The number of failed logins after which the account becomes locked out. The range is 1 to 999 login attempts.

Account Lockout Duration   The number of minutes a locked-out account remains locked out. The range is 1 to 99,999 minutes.

Reset Account Lockout Counter After   The number of minutes it takes after a preset number of failed logon attempts before the counter tracking available logons is reset to zero. The range is 1 to 99,999 minutes.

The account lockout feature is enabled through the *Group Policy Object Editor* and uses the relevant Group Policy settings. There are two other special settings:

Account Lockout Duration = 0   Once an account is locked out, an administrator is required to unlock it.

Account Lockout Threshold = 0   This setting means that the account will never be locked out no matter how many failed logon attempt occur.

Exam Point

Password lockouts lock an account after a preset number of password logon attempts. Using this technique prohibits brute-force attacks.

Malware Protection

Malware software is a type of computer software used to prevent, detect, and remove malicious software. Originally named antivirus software because it was developed to control and remove computer viruses, it now has much broader use, providing protection from Trojan horses, worms, adware, and spyware, among many other kinds of malicious software.

The backbone of endpoint security rests upon the prevention, discovery, and remediation of the effects of malware. Every endpoint on the network should have anti-malware protection software installed. Software should be maintained automatically because updates for new viruses are generally made available every week. Anti-malware software should be configured to automatically scan emails, transferred files, and any type of portable USB drive (such as thumb drive or memory stick), CD/DVDs, and software on any other media. Anti-malware should be set to automatically scan the endpoint at least once a week if not more frequently.

Anti-malware software makes use of a number of different methods to identify unwanted software:

Signature-Based Detection   Signatures are patterns of known malware. By comparing signatures to software within a workstation, malware software can identify potentially harmful software.

Behavioral-Based Detection   A detection mechanism that recognizes various software behaviors and matches them to a library of expected behaviors of known harmful software.

Heuristic-Based Detection A learning and statistical assumption technique used in making very fast decisions with relatively little information.

The implementation of an antivirus/anti-malware software solution should include the following:

- Scheduled daily or weekly antivirus/anti-malware signature updates.
- Scheduled periodic scans of all files and file types maintained in any storage location.
- Real-time email and attached storage device scanning enabled.
- Real-time Internet page scans with automatic script blocking enabled.
- If malware is found, clean the threat first and then quarantine it.
- Antivirus/anti-malware software must be initiated upon system startup.
- Antivirus/anti-malware must be protected from unauthorized configuration changes or circumvention.

Through an organizational IT security policy, antivirus/anti-malware software must be up and running on all network endpoints, including personal computers, file servers, mail servers, and network attached personal devices.

Backups

Most workstations store files on a local hard drive. If a workstation stores files locally that contain critical or sensitive information, those files should be transferred to a server for storage and scheduled backup. The level and frequency of backup required depends on the criticality of the data. This data should be considered in the IT backup policy. To ensure adequate backups of files, they should be copied to a secure server location that is backed up on a regular schedule. Some information within a specific security category or risk level may be regulated by IT security policy and should never be written to local hard drives.

Normally, workstations can be created by using a standard workstation image. But over time, additional software applications and data are added to the system drives. Users should be made aware of techniques to back up applications and data to a central source in the event a workstation should ever be required to be reimaged. The imaging, of course, erases all user data.

If workstations are ever backed up to portable drives, optical DVRs, floppy disks, or any other portable media, security precautions should be considered for the protection of the backup media. Not only should the backup data be kept in a safe place, the backup data should be protected from possible theft and exfiltration.

Anonymous Access

Anonymous access control is an access control methodology in which the server or the workstation may ask for user identification (username) or authentication information (user password) but no verification is actually performed on the supplied data. In many cases, the user is asked for an email address to simply access the system.

An endpoint or workstation that provides a *File Transfer Protocol (FTP)* service may provide anonymous FTP access. Users typically log into the service with an *anonymous* account when prompted for a username. In some applications, such as updating software, downloading information, or sharing files between users, identification of the user is not required.

Anonymous access may also be provided to various wireless network subnets that host guest access, such as in lobbies of buildings. Persons joining this type of wireless network can usually access only a limited amount of information and are totally screened from the internal network.

It is suggested that you do not allow anonymous access of any kind. User authentication should always be used to protect file transfer for any foreign user access to either a workstation endpoint or a server. User access should always be monitored by a network logging mechanism.

Patches and Updates

Proper endpoint configuration is essential for the security of not only the system but the entire network. Poorly configured devices can cause more harm than a software defect. Every endpoint should be scanned to detect and eliminate inappropriate share permissions, unauthorized software, and excessive user privileges. Weak or missing passwords or services running with executive or administrative privileges may possibly expose the device to a variety of exploits.

Patch management is crucial for the security of the endpoint. Many organizations utilize a centralized patch management system. The system automates patch distribution and installation and logs and verifies that patches have been made and updates have been installed. Patches should always be tested on simulated production systems prior to installation in the network. Users should be advised to leave their workstations powered up on the evening that the patches will be pushed out to the workstations.

All mobile devices issued by the organization should have security patches applied in a timely manner. Users should be directed to make their systems available at a specific place and time so that updates and patches may be installed.

Provision should always be made to back up workstations as well as mobile devices prior to installation of any patches, updates, or system upgrades. And for updates and upgrades, the appropriate procedures should be followed as outlined in the organization's change management policy.

Exam Point

Patches should be applied regularly as available from the manufacturer. All patches should be tested on simulated production equipment prior to being distributed to production. Upgrading and patching equipment should be documented for an established change management program.

Physical Security

The physical security of valuable assets is always a concern to any organization. Theft of a laptop or PC is always top of mind at the mention of physical security, but theft of information from unprotected workstations and unauthorized access to network wiring cabinets are also possibilities with lax physical security.

Many organizations usually have personnel access layers of security. For example, public to restricted access layers include a public lobby area, restricted work areas, and highly restricted IT areas. Most buildings include restricted badge access or even more stringent policies featuring biometric authentication, security guards, *CCTV cameras*, and even mantraps.

End users can take various steps to protect the assets of a business, which include both the physical hardware and the data contained on it. During a security awareness class, users should be made aware of the following:

- Power off workstations or place standby power when not in use.

- Ensure that office doors are locked when not in use.

- Employ a clean desk policy so no information remains on a desk when it is unattended. This includes locking cabinets and desk drawers.

- Workstations should employ a wire cable and lock or other appropriate antitheft device. Devices should be securely locked to an immovable device. If a workstation or desk top employees a power button key lock, it should be used as additional desktop security.

- Removable devices such as thumb drives, stick memory, micro cards, USB storage devices as well as portable disk drives such as network attached storage, and all types of media containing data should be properly locked and secured before a user exits the area.

- Workstation should employ a password-protected screensaver thereby requiring a password to re-access it.

- Workstations involving sensitive or restricted data should be set to log off after a brief period of inactivity.

Physical security should be a continuous concern for an organization and should become part of the organization's security culture.

Exam Point

All network devices should be physically secure to prevent theft or unauthorized access.

Clean Screen/Clean Desktop

There are several aspects of both physical and logical security in relation to CRT and LCD workstation displays. Of course, the display is the eyes into the data, the application, and the entire network. Care should be taken with information that appears on a workstation display. A security practitioner can utilize the following when securing visual information:

Screensaver A *screensaver* should be used every time a user is not in front of the workstation display. The screensaver should either be triggered by the user upon exit of the area or be triggered by a brief period of inactivity. The screensaver should automatically lock the computer, thereby requiring a user to enter a password to re-access the workstation.

Automated Log Off Workstation settings should be established to automatically log off the user after a period of inactivity. This may be a brief period of time, such as 10 minutes, but usually not longer than 30 minutes. In the event highly restricted information is used on the workstation such PII, HIPAA, or classified information, the workstation should automatically log off immediately after a brief period of inactivity. *Token workstation access* requires a token such as a plastic identification card to be inserted directly into the workstation to allow workstation logon and access. In the event the individual leaves the immediate vicinity of the workstation and withdraws the card, the workstation immediately logs off.

Automated Power-Down Such as Hibernate, Sleep, or Power Off Modes Workstation settings should be established to automatically place the workstation into power saving mode after a period of inactivity.

Visual Security Filter A polarizing plastic filter is a *visual security filter* that may be placed over the screen to reduce the area of view to only the user sitting directly in front of the screen. This reduces the possibility of other individuals observing data or sensitive displayed information.

Physical Security Positioning Display screens should be placed in an office or cubicle area that provides the least amount of exposure to undesired viewers. For instance, workstation displays should not face into the room so others can view the information. This is sometimes difficult with personnel working in cubes, but, with the use of polarizing security filters some security may be achieved.

A clean screen/clean desktop policy is a security concept that limits or controls information shown on the display screen. *Clean desktop* is the display of a minimum number of desktop icons. When the number of icons displayed on the screen is limited, prying eyes are not able to view folder names, document names, or other content displayed on the workstation desktop. A simple layer of defense is created in that an unauthorized individual gaining access to the system would not be able to easily click the desktop icon to gain access to valuable information.

The *clean screen* concept is a security technique that can be used to immediately blank out a monitor display screen or display dummy information. This is used to immediately hide anything displayed on the screen. There are a number of techniques used to accomplish this that are described on the Internet. One technique is that you can just press the hotkey combination Win+D to immediately return to the desktop. A fake background may be applied to the desktop to appear as an actual working document. To accomplish this, take a screenshot of an application page such as a spreadsheet or word-processing document. Save it as a desktop background. Hide all of the icons on the desktop. Once you use the hotkey to switch, the fake document will appear.

Email Security

Malware might easily enter any user's workstation with a simple mouse click in an email. As a security practitioner, it may become your responsibility to make your organization's users aware of the following secure email practices and the downside of various email schemes:

Do not open unsolicited attachments.   If the attachment is not from a trusted source, do not click it. Some emails are forwarded after being hijacked from the email address list of a friend and may have a subject line such as "You'll love this cat." In fact, filenames may be spoofed and a GIF photo file may actually be an EXE file in disguise. Once you click, it automatically loads and executes.

Set your malware scanner to automatically scan emails.   This may take just a little extra time, but an email could contain a keylogger.

Avoid checking emails on public Wi-Fi systems.   With any free Internet hotspot lurks the possibility of a nefarious individual with a rogue sniffer. An attacker utilizing a rogue hotspot can appear to be a legitimate hotspot location. Utilizing a rogue hotspot this person may intercept Wi-Fi traffic in the form of passwords, bank accounts, logins, and other personal information and use it again at a later time after you're long gone from the location.

Use separate email accounts.   With separate accounts, not only can you kill one that is becoming saturated with spam, you can use different types of accounts for different types of email. For instance, you might have accounts set up for work email, social email, and family email.

Use strong email account passwords.   It is quite common for individuals to make use of the same password for all of their accounts, not only email accounts but sometimes bank accounts and credit card accounts as well as Amazon and eBay. If a hacker compromised the email account password, they might easily extend the use of the password on other accounts that they intercept.

Be aware of phishing scams.   This type of scam may impersonate known websites such as eBay, PayPal, or your favorite department store. The site may look totally legitimate and email may state that account information needs to be confirmed or records need to be updated and so your username, password, and other personal information is required.

Never click an email link.   Any link in an email, no matter how innocent it looks, could lead directly to an executable that may be immediately downloaded and infect your system.

Of course, the IT department administration of email can be enforced by IT policy, software settings, and other security controls. Spam filters, data loss protection devices, as well as other protective controls can be put in place to mitigate the problems with endpoint email.

A comprehensive user security awareness program should include a complete discussion concerning the proper handling of emails as well as email attachments.

Host PC Firewall

Firewall software should be engaged on all endpoint devices. Windows and Mac OS currently include *Host-based firewall* protection. Firewalls can be set to specifically block all unused ports on the endpoint device as well as to allow white-list inbound traffic.

A host-based firewall is a piece of software that runs on the endpoint device and restricts incoming and outgoing information for that one endpoint. While network firewalls have much more detailed rule sets, a host-based firewall might simply list items to allow or deny.

Many current antivirus software applications contain a built-in firewall as an added benefit. It is important to read instructions carefully because the operating system firewall, as well as a malware application firewall, might conflict and cause a self-inflicted denial of service. Some firewalls contained in an antivirus software application may suppress website pop-up windows, filter emails, scan USB devices, and provide a variety of other attractive options.

Encryption Full Disk, File, Server, Removable Storage

It is always recommended that sensitive or confidential data not be stored on a local workstation or endpoint but be retrieved from a secure server as required. In the event that *personally identifiable information (PII)*, HIPAA data, financial information, or other restricted data must be saved to the user's local hard disk, it should be heavily encrypted. We have all heard on news programs that laptops have been stolen, exposing tens of thousands of accounts with information that was stored locally on the laptop hard drive. In all cases, sensitive information must be encrypted when on a personal computer or personal storage device such as a USB drive or an external hard drive.

All versions of the Microsoft Windows operating system developed for business use feature the *Encrypting File System (EFS)*. The default setting for Windows operating systems is that no files are encrypted. ESF allows users to apply encryption to individual files, directories, or the entire drive. It may be invoked through the use of Group Policy in Windows domain environments. EFS is available only on hard drives and USB drives formatted with *Microsoft New Technology Filesystem (NTFS)* file format.

Consideration should be given to exactly how to manage encrypted data stored in files and folders on an endpoint system. In most instances, files inherit the security properties of the folder in which they reside. Care should be taken when processing data from encrypted files that the resulting processed data is not placed in a non-encrypted folder, thereby declassifying or unencrypting the information.

Users should never encrypt individual files but should always encrypt folders. Encrypting files consistently at the folder level ensures that files are not unexpectedly decrypted by an application. A best practice is to encrypt the My Documents folder on all endpoint devices so the user's personal folder, where most documents are stored, is encrypted by default.

Commercial software encryption products such as the open-source TruCrypt, Microsofts' BitLocker, or the commercial product Check Point PointSec can be used to encrypt sensitive or protected data.

Trusted Platform Module

A *Trusted Platform Module (TPM)* is dedicated microprocessor that is mounted on a device's main circuit board and serves as a *cryptoprocessor*. The TPM offers many advantages, such as offloading cryptographic processing of the main CPU to a dedicated microprocessor. TPMs offer many services, such as providing a random number generator and the generation and storage of cryptographic keys. Beginning in 2006, most laptop computers targeted at the business market have been produced with a TPM chip. Use of a Trusted Platform Module has spread to other devices such as cellular phones, personal digital assistants, and even dedicated gaming devices.

The *Trusted Computing Group (TGC)*, an international consortium of approximately 120 companies, has written the original TPM specification and maintains revisions and updates to the standard. The current revision is TPM 2.0, which was released in the fall of 2014.

Trusted Platform modules provide numerous services, some of which are listed here:

Trusted Boot Protection   Provides system integrity during system boot by storing specific system metrics such as operating system hash values to detect changes to a system from previous configurations such as a the installation of a root kit malware. This ensures platform integrity.

Encryption Key Storage   Full disk encryption software applications use the TPM technology to store and protect keys that may be used to encrypt the host hard disks.

Password Protection   Users authenticate by presenting a password to access encrypted data or systems. The password is quite often used to generate or access keys used in the encryption process. The TPM offers an authentication mechanism that is implemented on the hardware rather than the system software. Software key encryption is prone to dictionary attacks. A hardware implementation offers dictionary attack prevention.

Device Identification   All TPMs feature an identification key that is burned in during the manufacturing process. This uniquely identifies the device, which can serve as the device integrity as well as authentication mechanism.

All server, desktop, laptop, thin client, tablet, smartphone, personal digital assistant, and mobile phone devices procured for use to support *United States Department of Defense (DoD)* applications and functions must include a Trusted Platform Module version 1.2 or higher (when available). The intended use for the device is for endpoint identification, authentication, encryption, monitoring and measurement, and device integrity.

Endpoint Data Sanitization

Local, non-network storage devices, such as USB flash drives, SD cards, hard disk drives, CDs, and other personal storage devices, are commonly used to store data within an organization. Users of these products are sometimes unaware of the need to ensure the privacy of the information stored on these devices.

Endpoint data sanitization is the process of taking a deliberate action to permanently remove or destroy the data stored on a storage device. A sanitized device has no usable residual data, and even advanced forensic tools should not ever be able recover the erased data. Sanitization makes use of two methods of data destruction:

Software Utilities   Utilities are available that overwrite the storage medium numerous times in an effort to totally erase the data, leaving no remnant or residual data on the device.

Hardware Destruction   You can physically destroy a device so the data cannot be recovered.

Users who routinely work with highly sensitive data or regulated data, such as HIPAA-protected data, credit card information, financial information, or other personally identifiable information, should be provided with a method to dispose of or least permanently erase storage devices. Many organizations provide users with a secure drop box into which they place printed materials, drives, CDs, and other media that contains sensitive information. The boxes are collected by a certified document destruction company and shredded to meet various specifications. Over the past several years, the National Institute for Standards and Technology's (NIST) *Special Publication 800-88 revision 1*, "Guidelines for Media Sanitization," has become the reference for data erasure compliance.

Application Security

Many software applications are available for distribution on the Internet, both freeware and commercially available software. Any software obtained through downloading or via DVDs or CDs, from any source, must be considered copyright protected. Even freeware and shareware often require a contractual agreement, which is mandated with commercial software and referred to as an *End-User License Agreement (EULA)*. Unauthorized use of copyrighted software may expose an organization and user to substantial monetary fines. An *Authorized Use Policy (AUP)* banner should advise end users of the consequences of indiscriminately downloading or installing software on a workstation. Endpoint devices such as end-user workstations should be regularly scanned for unauthorized installed software. Downloading unauthorized software may expose the endpoint device and provide vulnerabilities that attackers can take advantage of. Users should be made aware during security awareness classes that the Internet can be extremely dangerous when it comes to downloading software products; many products seem harmless but contain viruses that can wreak havoc on computers. Some of the most offensive sites are those offering hardware drivers for downloading. These sites appear to be legitimate representatives of the manufacturer and seem to offer authorized drivers and updates for manufacturers' hardware products. The design of these sites makes it easy for the unaware user to become confused and click links that immediately infect a workstation.

Exam Point

An End-User License Agreement (EULA) is a contractual agreement presented when a software application is installed. The user is presented with a choice of agreeing or not agreeing with the license agreement. If the user chooses to not agree, the software will not load. Users should be advised to completely read the EULA. Although it cannot be modified, it may stipulate various terms and conditions. For example, the user might be asked to agree that all user activity with the application be sent back to the manufacturer. This is quite common with video games, where all interaction is transmitted back to the manufacturer.

 ### Real World Scenario

Read before You Sign

Con games and shady practices can surface in any industry. There once was a software manufacturing company in the Southwest that produced, of all things, a security software suite. The con game and shady practice involved its sales and distribution program. Representatives of the company would attend large industry trade shows with a big show booth and plenty of "free sample software." People working the booth would aggressively hand out free sample CDs of the software. With each CD, they would ask the individual to fill out a short form and sign the bottom showing that they received the CD. The shady practice was that this form was the End-User License Agreement (EULA) that stipulated that the CD software received at the show was to be returned within 30 days if the recipient did not wish to purchase it for $1,000. The con game involved several different levels. First, the company would give out 300 CDs at a trade show. Then, with signed receipts in hand, they would book these as $300,000 in account receivables. At 30 days, they would send out invoices for $1,000 to the 300 software recipients. As you may imagine, a great many people balked at the invoice. Several firms just paid the invoice. The invoices that went past due were then "sold" at a discount to a bad debt collection company (which happened to be a subsidiary of the software company). Using this technique, the owner of the company was able to amass millions of dollars' worth of asset receivables, which were then used to obtain bank loans and investor backing. The con game worked well for a short period of time until the company owner took the money and fled, at which time local and federal authorities were close on his heels. This is an outlandish example of a software EULA being used for nefarious purposes.

Reputable manufacturers will offer a method of authenticating software applications as well as approved patches and upgrades offered for download by verifying the authenticity and integrity of the software files.

Code signing is a method through which the author is authenticated and confirmed as the original provider of the software. Code signing is accomplished by the software author using a cryptographic hash algorithm to process the software code to obtain a hash value or message digest. The hash value is then published on the author's website along with the name of the cryptographic hash algorithm that was used to produce a hash value.

The author then encrypts the hash value with their asymmetric private encryption key and includes the encrypted hash value with the software download. The encryption of the hash value is referred to as a digital signature. Through the use of public key infrastructure (PKI) and the application of digital certificates, it may be proven that the only person capable of signing the code was the owner of the private encryption key.

Once the software is downloaded, the user decrypts the hash value using the author's public key, which is found in the author's digital certificate, and then hashes the software code using the same hashing algorithm to obtain a second hash value. The second hash value is compared to the first hash value, and if they match, the user can be assured of the integrity and authenticity of the software code. Although this sounds like laborious work, it can be automated through most browsers.

Centralized Application Management

Centralized application management (CAM) is becoming popular with the advent of private and commercial cloud systems. *Virtual desktop* is a method of remotely implementing and administering operating systems as well as applications on a server rather than on the local endpoint device. When this type of client/server model is used, the data is not stored locally, and no applications are executing locally. All end-user keystrokes and mouse clicks are transmitted to the server, and the generated visual display is sent to the endpoint device. By incorporating client software that manages both the virtual desktop session and virtual private network communications onto a USB drive, you are not limiting end users to the location of the endpoint. They simply insert the USB drive into a workstation to log on and create their virtual desktop. The user is no longer constrained by the platform or device they wish to use. Using a virtual desktop data and applications may be made available across any device.

Cloud-based Software as a Service (SaaS) implementations will enhance the adoption rate of subscription-based software models. Subscription-based software models allow for the continuous update and maintenance of application software without the requirement to distribute patches and upgrades to the end-user endpoints. This provides an always up-to-date software application, which may be accessed at anytime and anywhere by the end user.

There are hundreds of cloud-based applications. *Microsoft Office 365* is an implementation of a popular business productivity online suite using a cloud-based subscription model. Coupled with the unlimited Microsoft OneDrive cloud storage, users are no longer required to have a software application or data stored locally on an endpoint device.

Stolen Devices

Lost or stolen devices possibly containing corporate data create a huge risk for an organization. Not only can the data on the device be compromised, but user passwords as well as confidential information might all be stolen and possibly sold. As end users use their personal mobile devices such as tablets, smartphones, and other devices for personal and work-based data storage, the harm to the organization should the device be stolen or lost is greatly increased.

The IT information security policy of an organization must address the use of both organization-issued devices and personal devices used for business. Here are some recommendations:

User Training   User awareness training must accentuate the risks and the policies and procedures involved in placing organizational information on a privately owned device.

Wiping Process   Stolen or lost personally owned devices should be subject to full or partial wiping to destroy the data contained on the device.

Device Recovery   All personal devices used for business purposes should have tracking and locating applications installed.

Device Registration   All personal devices used for business purposes should be registered with the IT department.

Device Seizure   Corporate policies may dictate, along with a signed acknowledgment of the individual, that any privately owned device used for business purposes must be turned over to the organization upon request without the requirement for a court order or search warrant.

Search and Seizure Training

It is highly recommended that in all security awareness training classes that involve managers, HR personnel, and specifically incident first responders, the topic of search and seizure of private and personal property be fully discussed and understood. With many companies offering Bring Your Own Device (BYOD) policies as a workplace benefit, everyone involved must understand the ownership of the device and the rights of the individual to personal property, according to the Fourth Amendment. Any corporate search and seizure policy should be completely vetted through the corporate legal department or local law enforcement authorities.

Along with the recommendations just cited, additional recommendations for organization-issued devices should be taken into consideration:

Personal Information   Personally identifiable information should not be maintained on an organization-issued device.

Dedicated Travel Device   Traveling executives or company personnel may be issued travel devices created with a clean device image. Personnel may load only the data required for travel on the device. The device is returned to the organization upon conclusion of travel and is wiped and reimaged. This is especially true with any travel to foreign countries.

All portable devices should invoke a locking screen requiring a PIN or fingerprint after a period of inactivity.

It is highly recommended that in the event of a device being stolen or lost, the authorities within the jurisdiction of the suspected theft be notified as soon as possible. Although device locator applications are available for most devices that pinpoint the current location of the device, it is highly recommended by most police organizations to not pursue the stolen item personally but to involve the local officials. This eliminates the likelihood of personal harm during a potential confrontation situation.

Thieves specifically target executive phones or portable devices for sensitive data and restricted information. Sensitive data, especially involving a new product release, merger, and acquisition information, and other organizational financial or proprietary information, may have a sizable street monetary value. Traveling executives should be made aware, through security awareness briefings, that they may be specifically targeted for device theft and to take special precautionary and protective measures.

Workstation Hardening

Endpoints can be hardened by deleting all of the nonrequired services and applications. All network services that are not needed or intended for use should be turned off. While all vulnerable applications should be patched or upgraded, other workstation hardening techniques include eliminating applications or processes that cause unnecessary security risks or are not used. File permissions, shares, passwords, and access rights should be reviewed.

It is very important that you have a good understanding of any service you intend to disable. Some services depend upon other services. Turning off one service could render others unusable. Fortunately, the *Microsoft Management Console (MMC)* features a Services snap-in for managing Windows services and will give you information on dependencies.

Host Intrusion Detection and Prevention System

A host-based intrusion detection/prevention system (HIDPS) is software that runs specifically on a host endpoint system. Operating similarly to a network-based NIPS, the software monitors activities internal to the endpoint system. Activities such as examining log files, monitoring program changes, checking data file checksums, and monitoring network connections are among several tasks managed by a HIDPS. Data integrity, logon activities, usage of data files, and any changes to system files can be monitored on a continuous basis.

Host-based intrusion detection prevention systems operate similarly to anti-malware software in that they use signature-based detection (rule based) and statistical anomaly–based detection as well as stateful protocol analysis detection to monitor activities within an endpoint. HIDPS software, similar to the network-based NIDPS, may take predetermined actions based upon the discovery of suspicious activity. This may involve terminating services, closing ports, and initiating log files.

Securing Mobile Devices and Mobile Device Management

Mobile devices should be protected at all times. It requires comprehensive measures regarding its physical security while also protecting all electronic data residing on it. Several major data breaches have been caused by simply leaving a laptop exposed in a parked car while running into a store.

Mobile Device Management

Mobile Device Management (MDM) is a corporate initiative that manages the growing use of *Bring Your Own Device (BYOD)* policies in the workplace. It addresses both the requirement of the organization for network security and the protection of corporate information as well as recognizing the desire for the organization's members to use their personal devices in the workplace. Although seen by some as highly restrictive and intrusive, MDM policies prevent the loss of control and impact to organizational assets through data leaks and information exfiltration as well as establishing a baseline for device patching, updates, and OS hygiene.

IT policies involving the security of mobile devices should include steps that may be taken by both the IT department and the end user and include user awareness training concerning risks involved with mobile devices. Mobile device security strategy for organization may involve the following:

Operating System Updates   Maintaining operating system patches and updates will safeguard against vulnerabilities and security risks.

Jail-Broken Phones   Any device that has been jail broken should be restricted from accessing a corporate network. They expose the organization to security risks and vulnerabilities.

Use of Strong Passwords   The device should have a strong password, and if any applications offer security features or passwords, they should be invoked. Applications should have a different password than the device password.

Encryption Technology   Make use of an encryption technology available for the device.

Wireless Encryption   Devices should connect only to encrypted access points using WPA2.

Bluetooth   Bluetooth should always be disabled when not in use. Disable Bluetooth "discoverable" when not required.

Email encryption   TLS or PGP utilized as encryption for all email.

Web Browser Security   Enable web browser security.

Exam Point

Mobile Device Management (MDM) is a corporate initiative that manages the growing use of Bring Your Own Device (BYOD) policies in the workplace.

Corporate Owned Personally Enabled (COPE) is a program whereby the organization owns and controls the device while the user may use the device for personal purposes as well as business activities. The IT department still maintains control over updates, upgrades, and software installation. This is ideal for network access control program that monitors the health and hygiene of devices connecting to the network.

Being almost the complete opposite of BYOB, the user is not bringing their device to the workplace but instead using a corporate-owned device for their purposes. To use this program, the organization purchases or subsidizes the purchase of a catalog selection of devices and makes them available to organization users. The organization usually participates in the monthly connection cost involving phone, data, and multimedia packages. Through this program, economies of scale can be realized by bulk purchasing devices for distribution while also negotiating connection packages with service providers.

COPE programs are not new. Many organizations have been issuing devices to employees and members for a number of years. COPE programs provide the organization with more oversight and policy enforcement capability, thus reducing some of the risk that comes with BYOD. It is now a viable economic means to take control of the BYOD environment.

Exam Point

Corporate Owned Personally Enabled (COPE) is a program whereby the organization owns and controls a device and the user can use the device for personal purposes as well business activities.

Understand and Apply Cloud Security

If one had to sit back and wonder where the world of computers will be in five years, the answer will emphatically be two words: *the cloud*. The truth of the matter is that the industry is there now. Cloud computing, as it was originally called, has since been shortened to just "the cloud." Without a doubt, there remain a fair number of old-school computer folks around who will jokingly point at a USB drive and proclaim to anyone listening, "That's my cloud right there." Unfortunately, they certainly do not grasp the significance and the magnitude of what currently exists and what is yet to come.

The cloud has appeared at a point in time that is nearly a perfect storm in the world of network computing. There are two major forces at work that together are forcing the adoption of cloud technology on the world stage faster than almost any other computer technology has been adopted in the past. On one hand, corporate and organization networks are growing at unprecedented rates. Corporate data centers are struggling with limited budgets, physical space, time, and manpower, among other factors, just to keep up with end-user demand from corporate departments. Applications and corporate databases are requiring terabytes and petabytes of storage, while the numbers of users requesting access are seemingly growing exponentially, all of the time requiring larger and larger amounts of network resources. On the other hand, financial forces are at work. IT department budgets have continuously been strapped. The saying in those departments has been "do more with less," while the C-level folks continuously struggle to provide greater returns to investors and shareholders. And, just when we need it, along comes a computing technology that addresses both needs.

The cloud offers a future that promises to address both the requirements of the IT department and the cash flow desires of corporate management. The IT department is thrilled because it no longer must expand and maintain massive amounts of corporate-owned networking resources. The cloud offers an ability to outsource all of the headaches involved with owning networking resources. The equipment no longer needs to be purchased, installed, configured, maintained, upgraded, and operated 24/7 by a small army of personal, all employed by the organization.

The cloud offers all of the resources required, including resources that can be virtually configured as well as expanded and collapsed on demand. No hardware ownership. The C-level folks are ecstatic about the arrangement.

The financial benefits of the cloud will make a substantial impact on the balance sheet as well as the bottom line of the organization. Simply put, purchasing servers, routers, switches, cooling equipment, and other hardware items are classified as a capital expenditure (or simply *CapEx*) for a business. For accounting purposes, a capital expenditure must be spread out over the useful life of the asset, and this is referred to as depreciation.

The outsourced cloud model is identical to that of a utility company for services such as telephone, electricity, and natural gas. The corporation pays on a regular basis, usually monthly, for the amount of service it uses. For financial purposes, this is referred to as an operational expense, or simply *OpEx*. And just as with any other utility, the organization pays for only the services that it uses at any given time. To add to the benefit, other expenses related to operating a large organization-owned data center will also be reduced.

So as you can see, the perfect storm is meeting the requirements from the IT department for additional flexible services that it can expand and contract on demand as well as satisfying the requirements from the finance department to switch from financing and depreciating an ever-increasing amount of fixed assets while converting the cost into a simple monthly payment out of operating expenses. Corporations and organizations large and small are rapidly adopting the cloud.

 Real World Scenario

Plastics?

Classic film fans may remember the 1967 movie *The Graduate* starring Dustin Hoffman, Ann Bancroft, and Katharine Ross. In the film, Dustin Hoffman portrays the character Benjamin Braddock, who is an awkward recent college graduate with no well-defined aim in life. During one scene, Benjamin is at a cocktail party. A well-meaning older gentleman wishing to offer Benjamin career advice pulls him aside and says, "Let me tell you just one word, *plastics*."

If this script was rewritten today, the word would obviously have to be *cloud*.

Cloud Concepts and Cloud Security

Many technology users today are quite familiar with storing data on individual public cloud systems. Google, Amazon, Microsoft, and Dropbox are just a few of the hundreds of service providers vying for the attention of the technology-savvy user community.

While millions of users have registered for free or subscription-based service accounts, hundreds of thousands of organizations, small and large, are already making use of cloud provider offerings.

Cloud computing may be readily accessed by any type of communication-enabled device or system. Traditional end-user devices such as smartphones, tablets, personal digital assistants (PDA), pagers, laptops, desktops, and mainframes are included on the top of the list of cloud access client devices. Although the first thing that comes to mind are those devices that we touch or type on, currently tens of thousands and in the near future millions of devices will directly access the cloud automatically.

For instance, some types of intrusion prevention systems and IT network appliances right now receive automatic updates from the cloud while transmitting information such as network attack signatures and profiles, including potential zero-day attacks. This attack data is automatically analyzed and immediately shared with other cloud-based devices within the same product group to inform and protect other networks with similar devices installed.

Cloud computing may be viewed as a huge data collection repository that monitors and collects information from sensors, industrial control devices, automobiles, and other mobile equipment such trucks, tractors, forklifts, boats, ships, and construction equipment as well as virtually any conceivable type of device with communication capability. Although the cloud may be a data collection repository, it may also be a collection of applications that download information, instructions, activity updates, and other operational reference data to connected devices.

Cloud Communication

By definition, the cloud is a collection of computer network hardware, such as servers, switches, routers, and other traditional networking equipment. These items operate in buildings that may be located across town, within the state, in several states away, or even in a totally different country. In the case of a private cloud, one that is privately owned and operated just for the organization, the cloud could actually be down the hall or within a data center in the same building.

Connecting to the cloud may be accomplished by a wide range of methods. Although most users communicate with the cloud through a personally owned device such as a laptop, tablet, or smartphone.

Although traditional methods of connecting to the Internet currently exist, other direct cloud connection methodologies are in place and used by a variety of products and devices. This includes satellite links directly to a cloud facility, hardwired packet-switching networks directly connected to a cloud facility, and other methods that may include radio transceivers.

Hybrid communication technology can aggregate communications within a geo-graphic location. For instance, consider that your house is a cloud-connected entity. Imagine that you have network attached sensing devices installed around your home. There is an embedded controller in each item referred to as a *dedicated computing device (DCD)*. Each device includes a processor, volatile and non-volatile memory, a variety of sensors and controllers, and a wireless transceiver, either Wi-Fi or Bluetooth. Each device may be specifically programmed to carry out a dedicated function, such as control something, report on something, or monitor something, and take a specific action upon an event occurring. Such items, as listed here, may be found around your home in the near future:

- Intelligent refrigerator
- Intelligent washer and dryer
- Intelligent kitchen appliances
- Household plant sensors
- Outdoor lawn and plant sensors
- Fish aquarium sensor
- Hot water sensor
- Hot tub and spa sensor
- Vehicle sensor
- Electrical power usage sensors

- Household water usage sensors
- Household air-conditioning system sensor
- Mailbox sensor
- Automated lighting control system
- Entertainment system control and sensors
- Automated air vent sensors and controllers
- Utilities-monitored sensors
- Intrusion detection sensors
- Fire detection sensors
- Flood detection sensors

And the list continues.

Each of the items in the preceding list represents both controllers and sensors dedicated to a specific purpose, with some of these devices being actually smaller than a key cap on a standard keyboard or possibly no larger than an aspirin. For instance, the vehicle sensor might report on the level of gas in the tank, air in the tires, or even a stored calendar of who's to use it next and their planned destination. The aquarium sensor may be a floating device that continually tests and reports on the temperature and quality of the water. The outdoor lawn and plant sensor may send continuous readings of soil moisture, nitrogen content, available sunlight, and other health and wellness parameters. Air-conditioning/heating unit sensors forward data on the outside compressor as well as the in-attic condenser and heating unit.

It is interesting to consider the future of "wearables." Such devices will include sensors and devices manufactured into your shoes and clothing, strapped onto your body, and perhaps embedded on your body that will provide various capabilities such as parameter monitoring and functional control. Yes, pacemakers today are embedded devices that may report on certain conditions and have their parameters adjusted wirelessly by medical professionals.

Imagine that in the near future your third-grade daughter comes home from school early and reports that she feels sick. You pop open a bottle of sensors and she swallows one with a little water. Virtually immediately, you begin receiving diagnostic information on your cell phone measuring dozens of parameters within her body. The cell phone application automatically downloads cloud-based data coinciding with the parameter measurements of the ingested pill and recommends health and remedy methods for you to take.

All of these devices must communicate by some method. Not all sensors and controllers have the power to communicate directly to the Internet. Imagine a home-based proxy device that communicates by Bluetooth over short distances within the house and then converts the signals into Wi-Fi or cellular radio format for forwarding to the Internet. This may be simply a dedicated black box device that simply plugs into a wall outlet.

As you can see, all of these devices and capabilities will be available in a very short period of time. The challenge will be securing these devices with cloud security and encryption methods to mitigate the problems of intrusion and attack. Although you might be able to live with an attack on your swimming pool sensor, you might not if the attack is on your pacemaker. This illustrates the seriousness and requirements concerning cloud security.

Cloud Characteristics

The computing industry continuously seeks a common source of reference for concepts and terminology to better understand and communicate technology concepts. The National Institute of Standards and Technology (NIST) through *NIST Special Publication 800-145*, "The NIST Definition of Cloud Computing," lays out some fundamental cloud-defining concepts.

The NIST special publication defines some broad categories that are characteristics of clouds:

Broad Network Access   Cloud services, whether private cloud offerings within an organization's IT department, non-fee-based free public clouds, or subscription-based services offered by large cloud providers, all include ease of access and use normal network connections. Cloud-based services may be easily accessed through the use of a standard Internet browser or client software downloaded to the user's device. For compatibility across a broad range of user-owned platforms, cloud access automatically transforms and reformats to the device requirements. This provides total access transparency to the user regardless of the device being used, be it a smartphone, smart watch, laptop, tablet, personal digital assistant, or intelligent entertainment center.

On-Demand Self-Service   Users can subscribe to services by simply selecting from cloud provider menus. Not only can they select cloud products, but during the process they can possibly engage a sharing and distribution system that, through the principle of discretionary access control, provides access rights to information and content. Various IT security publication articles are beginning to address the *Bring Your Own Cloud (BYOC)* concepts occurring in commercial businesses today and the possible security implications.

Rapid Elasticity   Elasticity allows the subscriber to purchase additional capability based on user requirements. For instance, a free cloud service might provide the user with 10 MB of storage space. Of course, this will be eclipsed fairly shortly. The user may then select a range of upgrades, usually for a small annual fee. In the event that the user commits to much larger storage than is required, they certainly have the ability to select a smaller volume of storage at a reduced annual fee.

Pooling of Resources   Cloud systems make use of virtualization to allow total hardware usage allocation. This means that rather than have one server with one client that uses the server 60 percent of the time, the same server might have several virtual machines running that use 95 percent of the hardware capability and can be adjusted for workloads very rapidly. For example, cloud hardware can immediately be reallocated to the demands of the client base. If the cloud-based client in Germany utilizes resources during this eight-hour workday and then shuts down in the evening, the same cloud-based hardware can be reallocated for another cloud-based client based in Atlanta, Georgia, as the workday begins. The expansion and contraction capability of cloud-based assets can be adjusted dynamically during the day or in relation to a holiday selling season where traffic volume is very high.

Measured Service   It's rare that in a standard corporate environment a department such as a finance or legal department may be directly billed and charged by the corporate IT department for the amount of assets, time, or space utilized. If this were true, there might not be such a contention over requesting IT budgets. Cloud providers, on the other hand, have determined charging methods that monetize the use of cloud services and assets. Not unsimilar to the charging methods utilized by utility companies, the cloud client pays for exactly what they use.

Exam Point

Clouds offer five major benefits: broad network access, on-demand self-service, rapid elasticity, pooling of resources, and measured service.

Security of the Five Cloud Characteristics

As a security practitioner, it will become abundantly clear that every benefit has a reciprocal potential of a security concern. The security practitioner should be concerned about the following initial broad cloud-based security issues:

Broad Network Access

Clouds may be accessed from a broad number of devices. This greatly expands the requirements for cloud-based access control as well as remote authentication techniques. Since clouds may be accessed from devices directly without them being connected to the organization's LAN, proper access and authentication controls must be provided at the cloud edge rather than in the business network. These controls must also be able to provide correct authentication across a number of personally owned devices and a variety of platforms.

On-Demand Self-Service

Cloud providers are in the business of selling services. They will gladly grant additional capabilities upon request. The organization must put into place corporate policies and organizational structures such as a change control board, a cloud services request control board, or a services request procedure that controls the allocation of cloud services to requesting corporate individuals, departments, and entities. This mitigates the risk of individual departments requesting additional services directly from the cloud service provider without prior authorization.

Rapid Elasticity

Any IT department that has managed a corporate "shared drive" knows how these can fill up very quickly. Also, it is usually very difficult to determine the owner of files and information stored on the shared drive. It's not unusual to find, for example, a series of PowerPoint presentations from 2002 with no information about whether they can be deleted or not. The same is absolutely true of cloud-based storage. Once storage space begins to expand, it is very difficult to contract it. Unlike the simple shared drive on an in-house network, cloud-based storage containing the same information will be incrementally more expensive.

Pooling of Resources

Cloud providers have an ability to pool resources as previously discussed. Some very serious security implications exist with this concept. First, cloud resources are shared among a huge number of tenants. This means that other users are on the same server equipment at the same time. The possibility that data may be written into another tenant's area exists. Second, in the event of another tenant conducting illegal activities, the entire server might be seized along with your data. Third, unscrupulous cloud provider personnel may access and exfiltrate your data. Fourth, investigations are complicated through the jurisdictional location of data on cloud service provider equipment. Five, information security is totally within the control of the service provider. If penetrated, corporate information, plus the information of many other clients, may be compromised. These are just a few of the security concerns for the security practitioner concerning cloud services.

Measured Service

It's not unusual in some countries to run a wire over to a neighbor's electrical meter. In fact, even in our country, theft of cable television services was quite a fad years ago. Theft of any measured service is possible if the attacker is determined. It is incumbent upon the cloud client to thoroughly check billing statements against authorized and requested services to mitigate the possibility of service theft.

Cloud Deployment Model Security

There are a variety of types of cloud services. Generally, they are classified by who owns the equipment upon which the cloud services are running and who are the potential clients that might use the services of the cloud provider. Again, NIST *Special Publication 800-145* offers a list of four cloud deployment models. These cloud models are described in the following sections.

Private Cloud

A *private cloud* is typically a cloud constructed as a part of the organization's existing network infrastructure. This allows an organization to provide cloud services complete with expansion and elasticity components for internal clients. This type of file is best utilized in the following cases:

- Data cannot be stored off-premises due to regulatory or contractual requirements.
- Cloud provider costs exceed the cost to build and own.
- Considerations exist regarding control over a location or jurisdictional, legal, or other proprietary information.

A private cloud may take the form of an intranet or an extranet with the added benefits of virtual allocation of assets and elasticity of storage.

Private clouds, having been created internally with organization-owned networking equipment, maintain the same security risks associated with any internal network. The organization must still provide the proper network safeguards, including intruder prevention controls and network access controls, as well as maintain all equipment with proper patching and updates.

Community Cloud

Community clouds can be established to provide cloud services to a group of users that can be defined as users requiring access to the same information to be used for a similar purpose. For instance, rather than set up an FTP site to transfer information between departments or external users, it is quite possible to set up a *community cloud* where everybody can access and share the same information. Using a specialized application, document versioning, access control, data file lockout, and user rights may be enforced. With a community cloud, it's easier to train inexperienced users in access control techniques based upon browser access rather than assign FTP accounts and educate users on the use of file transfer protocol techniques.

A community cloud may be as simple as a Dropbox location from which attendees to a family reunion may easily access all of the photographs that were taken. It's actually simpler to implement and explain the community cloud to inexperienced users than to explain the use of Facebook.

Security problems exist in a community cloud. Management of access control becomes a paramount interest. Authentication techniques as well as encryption key distribution become major factors between non-related third-party entities.

Public Cloud

The *public cloud* is probably the most common cloud platform. Public cloud services are offered by such providers as Microsoft, Google, Apple, and Amazon, among many others. The public cloud service is the easiest cloud offering for any individual to utilize. The most well-known have brand names such as SkyDrive, OneDrive, Amazon Web Services, iCloud, Google Drive, Carbonite, and Dropbox, and there are many others. The beginning monthly charge is usually less than $20, and they provide from 5GB to 500GB of storage. Most providers offer low-cost or no-cost entry-level services and escalate from there. Public clouds are easy to set up and easy to maintain.

Security problems exist in a public cloud environment. In the event that a public cloud is compromised, passwords, access control, and proprietary information may be exposed. The clients are purely at the mercy of the public cloud providers to provide adequate security.

Hybrid Cloud

Hybrid cloud structures consist of combining two forms of cloud deployments. Here are two examples:

Private Cloud/Public Cloud   This environment retains restricted or regulated information in-house in a flexible private cloud scenario. It provides the benefits of a public cloud to departments that require elasticity or cross-platform access.

Private Cloud/Community Cloud   This environment retains restricted or regulated information in-house in a flexible private cloud environment, while it provides extranet capability for suppliers or customers in a community cloud environment. This provides the flexibility of a community cloud with the continued elasticity and cross-platform access behind web browser functionality.

Hybrid clouds offer a great degree of flexibility to an organization that require cloud-based services but wish to capitalize on the cost savings afforded by cloud services providers. But, hybrid cloud security compounds the security threats that are of concern in a private cloud as well as the other cloud model that is included.

Exam Point

Clouds offer four deployment models: private cloud, community cloud, public cloud, and hybrid cloud.

Cloud Service Model Security

Although there appear to be a number of " _____ as a Service" offerings on the market, *NIST Special Publication 800-145* offers a list of three cloud service models, which are described in the following sections.

Software as a Service

The *Software as a Service (SaaS)* model only allows the user or client access to an application that is hosted in the cloud. Such applications run on a cloud provider's equipment, and the SaaS provider manages all hardware infrastructure and security. Access is usually provided by identification authentication and is based upon browser-based interfaces so that users can easily access and customize the services. Each organization serviced by the SaaS provider is referred to as a tenant. The user or customer is the individual or company licensed to access the application.

There are several delivery models currently in use within SaaS:

Hosted Application   In a hosted application delivery model, the application vendor does not own the cloud equipment and is hosting the application for a cloud service provider. The application vendor maintains the application with patches and updates and generally makes access to the application available on a subscription basis or through corporate entitlement contracts. Hosted applications in the cloud function identically to applications that may be loaded on a user's workstation and are transparent to the end user. Users usually utilize an Internet browser to access the hosted application from any location.

On-Demand Software   This type of software delivery model features a software application that is owned or created by an application vendor and is hosted on the application vendor's cloud infrastructure. The application supplier manages and maintains the application as well as the cloud infrastructure. Access to on-demand applications is provided by a subscription on a pay-as-you-go basis or for a flat monthly fee.

Cloud Provider Applications   This usually consists of a suite of applications hosted on a commercial cloud provider's infrastructure and owned and maintained by the cloud provider. The software suite usually includes application development tools, hosting tools, graphics tools, and other software applications that are of interest to client IT departments to facilitate interaction with the cloud provider or to create applications, APIs, or other items that may be hosted by the cloud provider.

> **Exam Point**
>
> Even though the cloud service provider supplies the infrastructure, maintenance services, security services, and other contractual requirements, the responsibility for the data in the cloud remains with the data owner at all times.

Platform as a Service

The *Platform as a Service (PaaS)* service delivery model allows a customer to rent virtualized servers and associated services used to run existing applications or to design, develop, test, deploy, and host applications. PaaS is delivered as an integrated computing platform, which may be used to develop software applications. Software development firms utilize PaaS providers to provide a number of application services such as source code control, software versioning tools, and application development process management tools. PaaS is used to build, test, and run applications on a cloud service provider's equipment rather than locally on user-owned servers.

Infrastructure as a Service

The *Infrastructure as a Service (IaaS)* service delivery model allows a customer to rent hardware, storage devices, servers, network components, and data center space on a pay-as-you-go basis. The cloud service provider maintains the facilities, infrastructure updates and maintenance, and network security controls. Although IaaS is the primary cloud service model, two types of specialized infrastructure service models exist:

Dedicated Hosting/Dedicated Server   Dedicated hosting is a type of hosting option in which the client leases an entire server, which is then dedicated solely to the client. The host provides the server equipment and usually provides administration services. This is an opposite application of the multitenant concept normally found in cloud service models. It may also be referred to as a dedicated server.

Managed Cloud Hosting   Managed cloud hosting is an IT networking process in which an organization extends its local network into a cloud-based environment. The organization may host critical applications extended over long periods or provide for rapid expansion to cloud-based equipment as required. The benefits include affordability, the ability to run both physical servers and virtual servers and thus provide consistent availability, and network security.

Exam Point

There are three types of cloud service models: Software as a Service, Infrastructure as a Service, and Platform as a Service.

Cloud Management Security

Cloud management security encompasses the policies, standards, and procedures involved with the transfer, storage, and retrieval of information to and from a cloud environment. As with any network, there are four primary activities:

- Executing applications

- Processing data, known as the compute function

- Transmitting and moving data, known as data in transit

- Storing and retrieving data, as data at rest

Specific threats and vulnerabilities may be identified and addressed with the proper use of security controls.

Executing Cloud-Based Applications

Executing cloud-based applications involves user interaction with an application through an application programming interface (API) or virtual desktop environment. The cloud-based application is stored in cloud storage and executes on remote cloud service provider equipment. Cloud-based application execution provides several concerns for the security professional:

Application Misconfiguration   Applications may be configured incorrectly through the lack of appropriate patches, ineffective patches and upgrades, or incorrect setup and monitoring.

Virtual Machine Attack   Similarly to any other item on the organization's network, virtual machines are capable of attacks. A successful attacker or network intruder may perform a VM escape, where a hacker breaks out of a virtual machine with the potential of attacking the host operating system. Should a hacker take control of the hypervisor environment, they can successfully attack all of the virtual machines under the hypervisor.

Access Control Violation   Application access control is a concern since the subjects requesting access may not be first authenticated into a physical network. They may request access through APIs or web-based applications that may not have access to the same LDAP or Active Directory credential libraries.

Software License Violation   Improperly supervised software license appropriation may lead to excessive license assignments with the possibility of fines or sanctions against the organization.

Application Design Vulnerabilities   Applications executing on a remote environment are subject to the same design vulnerabilities as an application executing on physical servers owned by the organization. Injection attacks, scripting attacks, buffer overflows, and denial of service are a few of the standard attacks against application design vulnerabilities.

Processing Data in the Cloud

Data processing in the cloud is referred to as the compute function. Transactional data processing represents computations performed on a continuous stream of data sourced from such devices as cash registers and point-of-sale devices and input from business operations.

Executing a compute function in the cloud as part of a cloud-based application is identical to executing the exact same data processing function using a local-based application in an organization-owned data center. A cloud-based application vulnerability is a flaw or weakness in an application. Application design vulnerabilities are primary weaknesses that can be experienced regardless of location. There are a wide variety of hacker tools and penetration techniques used for exploiting application vulnerabilities. Here are a handful that are much more common than others:

- Cross-Site Scripting (XSS)
- SQL injection
- Username enumeration
- Format string vulnerabilities
- Buffer overflow from multitenant clients
- Virtual machine escape
- Poor data validation

Security professionals should consider all aspects of application vulnerability mitigation when executing applications on cloud-based servers. A cloud-based application strategy should include the following:

- Clear data security strategies such as performing risk analysis that includes the Three Ps of data processing within an application:

  Preprocessing   The preparation process of data may involve sorting, screening, or normalization. This data is held in local storage and is queued for processing operations.

  Processing   Data is transformed, converted, or altered by an application.

  Post-processing   When data exits the application destined for a storage location, based on the usage and application, there may be several streams of data. This data may be further processed by other applications or sorted and stored using various techniques.

- Identification and mitigation of potential attacks against the application.

- Hardening of the application by controlling access.

- Applying patches and upgrades, as applicable, and utilizing regression testing to identify problems after change. Cloud-based patches and upgrades should always be tested in offline but similar cloud-based virtual machines prior to being put into production.

- Creating data protection policies and procedures for data being ported into and out of an application.

- Utilize application logging, database rollback, and database journal procedures to thoroughly document cloud-based application performance.

The Cloud—the Eighth Wonder of the World

It never ceases to amaze me how mankind has seemingly grasped upon the cloud as a panacea of all that's good. I recently read an article on how the cloud was going to cure cancer. Virtually every magazine everywhere uses the cloud as a go-to subject. Unfortunately, the article writers give little thought and explanation to the "how" part of their stories.

Transmitting and Moving Data in the Cloud

Businesses have ported data from one location to another for a long time. Bulk data transfer is as old as early mainframe computers. The foundation of data transfer has been the AIC security triad of integrity, availability, and confidentiality. Of interest to organizations that move large amounts of data are nonrepudiation, end-to-end security, and auditability as well as providing effective continuous monitoring that ensure accurate performance metrics.

Managed file transfer (MFT) is the transfer of data to, from, and between clouds securely and reliably regardless of data file size. It has recently found favor among cloud service providers as well as third-party data transmission providers. Managed file transfer is a technique of transferring data between sites or within an organization's networking environment utilizing best practices.

There are three specific areas of MFT:

File Size   Every organization requires data storage for files that must be retained to meet the business objectives of the enterprise. When it comes to big data, very large data sets, or data warehouses, large blocks of data can be moved at one time. On the other hand, continuously streaming data is constantly moving between locations.

Communication Reliability   Communication methodology is a decision point between the client and the cloud service provider. Service-level agreements are implemented between the user and provider to determine the type and capability of communication lines and equipment, transmission methodology, and the ability of the cloud provider to be ready to accept and process data when the client is ready to send it. Communication reliability will also provide nonrepudiation as well as performance metrics.

Data Security   Data security policies are put in place to support the requirements mandated by contractual or regulatory compliance issues or internal organizational policy. Most MFT data security is accomplished through encrypted tunnels. For instance, data in-transit security between a user and a cloud provider may be provided by IPsec. IPsec could be used to provide encryption, authentication, as well as integrity to form a secure connection between the cloud provider and client.

Exam Point

Managed file transfer (MFT) is the transfer of data to, from, and between clouds securely and reliably regardless of data file size.

Storing Data in the Cloud

Data stored in the cloud is stored on the cloud service provider's equipment. Data might be stored in large logical pools where the actual physical storage devices may span storage devices in several data centers, which are often geographically separated. Cloud storage devices range from traditional hard disks (HDDs) to *solid-state drives (SSDs)*, which are referred to as tiered storage. Cloud providers often mix different types of data storage technology usually tiered from slow to fast storage. For instance, a balance of performance may be accomplished by placing directories, cross-reference tables, and other data that must be processed extremely fast in solid-state drives and placing remaining data in high-capacity hard disk drives while data rarely used may be stored in less expensive slower hard disk drives.

Data redundancy is often provided by the cloud provider and refers to storing multiple copies of data across numerous servers in geographically separated locations. The cloud service provider is responsible for maintenance of equipment, integrity of the data in storage, and protection of data when moved between service provider locations.

Data stored in a cloud environment sometimes requires specialized handling due to the fact that they may be virtually stored in a number of different locations. A storage mechanism such as erasure coding may be employed to supply data redundancy in the event of error or loss, while cloud-based data encryption may be based upon the nature of the data or encryption services provided by the cloud service provider.

Erasure Coding   *Erasure coding (EC)* is a data storage and data identification technology used to provide high-availability and data reliability to cloud-stored data. Using erasure coding, a block of data may be divided into a number (represented by N) of blocks, or "fragments," and encoded with redundant data pieces. Each block may then be dispersed (a technique referred to as *data dispersion*) across the cloud provider's servers and, in many cases, geographic locations. If some of the data fragments are lost or corrupted for any reason, the entire data set may be reconstructed using a number (represented by M) of remaining fragments. In this technique *M of N* refers to the minimum required number of fragments required (*M*) to regenerate the data based on the total number of original fragments (*N*).

Erasure codes, in actual practice, may be compared to RAID data reconstruction technique because of the ability to reconstruct data using codes. Erasure codes can be more CPU intensive and require more processing overhead. But, this type of failsafe coding can be used with very large "data chunks" and works well with data warehousing as well as with big data applications.

Data Encryption   Various types of encryption are utilized for cloud-based data storage. Encryption in the cloud is dependent upon the cloud service provider's capability as well as the cloud delivery model requirements. The safety and protection a corporate policy may dictate data at rest in a storage location should always be encrypted. The downside is that encryption always inserts additional processor overhead and latency or delay into both the data writing and retrieval process. There are two major categories of cloud-based data encryption:

- *Storage-level encryption* is encryption performed at the storage device. Data entering the device is encrypted; data leaving the device is decrypted. Encryption keys are always maintained at the cloud service provider. Because the data is encrypted only on the device and the service provider has the keys, the benefit of storage-level encryption is realized only if the device is stolen.

- *Volume storage encryption* requires of the encrypted data recyclable and storage. Data encryption keys are maintained with the data administrator or data owner.

Exam Point

The two major categories of data encryption for data-at-rest in the cloud is storage-level encryption and volume storage encryption.

Cloud Legal and Privacy Concepts

As the growth of the cloud continues, several major concepts are on a collision course. The cloud is a seeming panacea of everything good about computing. The capability for expansion, simplicity of configuration, ease of virtualization, and the total demand-as-you-need mentality is extremely attractive to individual users as well as major organizations.

Although some cloud services seem expensive today, as with any competitive utility model, the marketplace will bring prices down to acceptable levels. The advantages of the use case models as well as the economics of the pricing models will only serve to drive more and more users to the cloud.

With all of these conveniences, the challenge and complexity of complying with legislation, regulations, and laws issued by countries worldwide will become an ever-increasing challenge for cloud providers as well as cloud users. Accomplishing adherence, compliance, or conformity to international laws on a global basis will become extremely important as the use of the cloud continues to expand.

As with any regulatory and legal environment, legislation, regulations, and laws will continue to change as legislators and regulators take actions. As always, when dealing with legal, compliance, and regulatory issues, the best advice to security professionals is to consult with relevant and knowledgeable professionals who specialize in legal cloud issues.

Borderless Computing

Borderless computing is defined as a globalized service that is widely assessable with no preconceived borders. The main concepts of data ownership and personal privacy are paramount when considering the transborder data storage and processing capability the cloud offers. Cloud provider offerings and the relevant contractual relationships will often refer to *availability zones*, usually on a global nature, which subjectively are areas of operation, data storage, data processing, and other activities carried out by a cloud provider. These availability zones define geographic areas such as North American zone/South American zone, which are sometimes combined and just referred to as "the Americas." Other zones include the Asia-Pacific zone and EMEA zone, which refers to Europe, the Middle East and Africa. Although these are somewhat standardized business operational territories, they become extremely large and unwieldy when you take into account transborder data flows, in-country data storage, and local data processing when related to complying with numerous country laws and regulations. Many cloud providers often segment the traditionally large business zones into smaller *cloud operational zones* based on geography or similarity of legislation, such as that of the *European Union* (EU).

Privacy Issues

Various international laws and regulations typically specify responsibility and accountability for the protection of information. Accountability for the adherence to these laws and regulations remains with the owner of the information. Therefore, corporate entities and organizations that utilize locally based services must impose the same accountability requirements upon the cloud service provider through contractual clauses specifying compliance requirements.

Personal data is defined as any data relating to a natural human being referred to as a *data subject*. An identifiable human being is a person who can be identified, directly or indirectly, by one or more factors specific to their physical, physiological, mental, economic, cultural, or social identity.

Legal Requirements

Numerous legal issues and requirements become relevant when personally identifiable data is collected, processed, transmitted, and stored in global-based cloud environments.

A number of legal requirements and compliance issues are of concern to data owners as well as cloud service providers.

International Regulations/Regional Regulations   International privacy regulations range from an unenforced to very strong depending upon the countries basic philosophy to ensure the personal privacy to its population. Countries that are bound by the European Union data protection laws, the OECD model sponsored by the *Organization for Economic Cooperation and Development (OECD)*, or the APEC model sponsored by the *Asia-Pacific Economic Cooperation (APEC)* are supporting very strict personal privacy requirements. The laws and regulations of these organizations generally state that the entity that originally obtains the personally identifiable information from an individual is responsible for ensuring that any users of this information comply with all applicable laws.

Restrictions of *Transborder Information Flow*   Globally, some national legislation, laws, and regulations enacted by various governments provide restrictions concerning the transfer of personally identifiable information to local jurisdictions where the level of privacy or data protection is considered weaker than the original storage location. This concept is similar to declassifying information by transferring the information to a lower-classified folder. This type of legislation is intended to enforce that whenever data transfer occurs, the data will maintain its integrity of privacy and protection.

Contractual Privacy Obligations   Many corporations and organizations are contractually bound to safeguard the privacy of personally identifiable information that is in their possession. Some of these contractual obligations may fill the gap created by the lack of specific laws and legislation. Typically, contractual privacy obligations are imposed by third-party contracts with information providers, industry consortiums, and other groups. For example, the *Payment Card Industry Data Security Standard (PCI DSS)*, which is a proprietary information security standard promoted by major credit card providers, establishes many standards for the protection of personal privacy and the handling of personally identifiable information.

Exploitation of Data Privacy   Individuals seeking the exploitation of restricted data, such as data that is confidential, consists of personally identifiable information, or is restricted by legal or regulatory dissemination prohibitions, make use of geographic or legal environments that are seemingly friendly to the concept of the computer network, which operate in this environment. A *data haven* is a location that is friendly to the concept of data storage regardless of the legal environment. Data havens may be geographic locations within country borders that have loose regulatory requirements, or they may be *onion networks* such as *The Onion Router (TOR)* network, which either stores or forwards information based upon anonymity.

Privacy Legislation and Regulations

Numerous laws and regulations have been enacted through the years to address requirements of personal privacy protection and accountability of the holders and processors of data and to provide transparency to operations.

Directive 95/46 EC   A highly developed area of law in Europe involves the right to privacy. In 1980, the *Organization for Economic Cooperation and Development (OECD)* issued guidelines governing the protection of privacy in transborder flows of personal data. The seven principles governing the OECD's recommendations providing privacy protection are as follows:

Notice   Notice should be provided to subjects when their personally identifiable data is being collected.

Purpose   Data should be used only for the purpose stated and not for any other purposes.

Consent   Personal information should not be disclosed without the data subject's consent.

Security   Collected data should be kept safe and secure.

Disclosure   Data subjects should be informed as to what entity is collecting their data.

Access   Data subjects should be allowed to access their personally identifiable data and make corrections to any inaccurate personal data.

Accountability   Data subjects should have a method available to them to hold data collectors, who are in charge of personally identifiable data, accountable for not following the preceding principles.

Unfortunately, the OECD guidelines were nonbinding and were viewed only as recommendations, while privacy laws remained mixed across European nations.

General Data Protection Regulation   The *General Data Protection Regulation (GDPR)* is an EU law that is the successor to *Directive 95/46 EC*. This legislation is intended to unify the data protection personal information rights within the 28 European Union member states. It is intended to address the ad hoc application of Directive 95/46 EC, which was only a directive and was viewed as optional by several countries. The General Data Protection Regulation will not require ratification of the member states but will bind them to a unified legal framework concerning information privacy. The law will introduce many significant changes for data processors and controllers, among which is a single set of rules with which EU member states must comply. The following may be considered some of the more important changes:

- Control of international data transfer
- Establishment of the role of a data protection officer
- Timely processing of access requests
- Single set of rules for all member states
- Definition of responsibility and accountability
- Increased sanctions for violations

The original term in the prior regulation was the so-called *right to be forgotten*. Although a noble concept and idea, it was vaguely worded, and it offered no means or methods for enforcement. It has been replaced in the GDPR by a better defined *right to erasure*, which provides the data subject with certain capabilities and means to request elimination of personal data based upon a number of explicit grounds. This allows for the exercise of the fundamental rights and freedoms of the data owner over the desires of the data controller.

Fundamental concepts such as *privacy by design* as well as *data protection impact assessments (PDIAs)* built in the requirements that privacy be a default operational scenario and impact assessments must be conducted identifying the specific risks that might occur to the rights and freedoms of data subjects.

A safe harbor provision is a provision of a statute or a regulation that specifies that certain conduct will be deemed not to violate a given rule. Applied to U.S. companies operating within the confines of the original EU Directive 95/46 EC, the *Safe Harbor Privacy Principles* allows U.S. companies to opt in to the EU privacy program and to register their certification if they meet the European Union requirements in the storage and transfer of data. The safe harbor program was developed by the U.S. Department of Commerce; it covers the U.S. organizations that transfer personal data out of the geographic territory of the 28 European Union member states referred to as a European Economic Area (EEA). Organizations utilizing safe harbor privacy principles may also incorporate information usage clauses within contractual agreements concerning the transfer of data.

Exam Point

Understand the relationship and differences between Directive 95/46 EC and the General Data Protection Regulation (GDPR).

Health Insurance Portability and Accountability Act of 1996   The *Health Insurance Portability and Accountability Act of 1996 (HIPAA)* legislation in the United States directed the Department of Health and Human Services to create and adopt national standards for electronic healthcare transactions and to identify and categorize national identifiers for providers, health plans, and employers. Protected healthcare information can be stored in the cloud under HIPAA regulations as HIPAA-protected data.

Gramm-Leach-Bliley Act   The *Gramm-Leach-Bliley Act (GLBA)* is United States federal law concerning banking regulations, banking mergers and acquisitions, and consumer privacy regulations. Major sections of the law put in place controls and governance over the collection, disclosure, and protection of consumers and nonpublic personal information, including personally identifiable information. This includes the protection of personal financial information as well as notification to the consumer of the collection and dissemination of information. Financial institutions are required to provide each consumer with the privacy notice stating the facts concerning where the information is shared, how the information is used, and how the information is stored. Through the *Safeguards Rule*, provisions very similar to the EU's General Data Protection Regulation were put into place, including a central point of contact and a data privacy risk analysis for each department handling nonpublic information. *Pretexting* provisions prohibit the practice of obtaining private information through false pretenses.

Exam Point

Be able to discuss the concept of "safe harbor" with regard to contracts or regulatory requirements.

Stored Communications Act   The *Stored Communications Act (SCA)* is a U.S. law that addresses the disclosure of electronic communications and data held by Internet service providers (ISPs) under various circumstances. It was enacted into law as Title II of the *Electronic Communications Privacy Act of 1986 (ECPA)*.

ECPA describes the conditions under which the government is able to access data and can help Internet service providers disclose private content stored by a customer.

Electronic Communication Service   This section stipulates that the government must obtain a search warrant to compel an ISP to turn over an open email that has been in storage for 180 days or less.

Remote Computing Service   This section of the law states that if data has been stored in excess of 180 days, the government can use various legal documents to require the disclosure of the information.

Patriot Act   The *Patriot Act* was enacted in direct response to the actions of terrorists on September 11, 2001. The act was instrumental in changing a large number of prior laws and strengthening the security of the United States against the threats of terrorism. Many privacy laws were greatly affected by the Patriot Act and remain to this day highly controversial. Titles under the act modified, reduced, or expanded the provisions of a large number of laws:

- Title I: Enhancing domestic security against terrorism
- Title II: Surveillance procedures
- Title III: Anti–money laundering to prevent terrorism
- Title IV: Border security
- Title V: Removing obstacles to investigating terrorism
- Title VI: Victims and families of victims of terrorism
- Title VII: Increased information sharing for critical infrastructure protection
- Title VIII: Terrorism criminal law
- Title IX: Improved intelligence
- Title X: Miscellaneous

eDiscovery

Discovery is a legal technique used to acquire knowledge required in the prosecution or defense of lawsuits or used in any part of litigation. *eDiscovery* specifically describes electronic information that is stored in or transferred over network storage devices, cloud systems, and other information repositories. The acquisition of such data is based on local rules and agreed-upon processes usually sanctioned by courts with jurisdiction; attorneys for either side request access to various data and are allowed access to data based upon court-established criteria. Attorneys may place a *legal hold* on data that is to be collected and analyzed as potential evidence in litigation processes. The *Federal Rules of Civil Procedure*, made effective in 2006 and 2007, substantially enhanced the proper retention and management of electronically stored information and compelled civil litigants to comply with proper handling techniques or be exposed to substantial sanctions. In the event of mishandling of electronically stored information, a finding of *spoliation of evidence* may be handed down by the court.

The following types of data are defined as electronically stored data:

Electronic Messages   In 2006, the U.S. Supreme Court recommended that a category be created under the Federal Rules of Civil Procedure that specifically included e-mails and instant message chat information.

Voicemail   Voicemail has been deemed data that is subject to eDiscovery and may be subject to *litigation hold*. A litigation hold is a legal requirement for participants of a lawsuit to retain and preserve records and evidence. Participants of lawsuits may have a duty to retain voicemail records that may be requested during legal proceedings.

Databases/Data in Repositories   Information that is subject to the discovery may be stored throughout the enterprise. It may be located in personnel notes and files, in databases and in stored communications. Structured databases referred to as relational database management systems (RDBMSs) store large amounts of data.

Exam Point

Understand the terms *spoliation of evidence* and *litigation hold*.

Cloud-based data storage provides challenges for the security professional as well as attorneys in identifying, locating, and obtaining information that may be subject to eDiscovery. Although the Federal Rules of Civil Procedure (FRCP) in the United States require parties to litigation to be able to produce requested electronically stored data that is in their custody, possession, and control, there is much debate concerning is the custody, possession, and control at the cloud provider or the information owner level.

Location is also an extraordinary problem in the production of requested electronically stored information in the cloud. Cloud information can be stored in a number of country jurisdictions and, due to failover or load-balancing activities, may be transferred between countries and jurisdictions frequently and at will. Obtaining specifically requested information from the cloud provider may be difficult under current laws, regulations, and contractual responsibilities.

Contracts with cloud service providers should also include that the service provider is required to inform the information owner in the event of any court-ordered legal action with regards to their data stored by the provider.

Cloud Virtualization Security

Virtualization is the essential technology provided for loud-based implementation of services. Through virtualization, virtual machines are separated from the underlying physical machines. In a virtual environment, the virtual machine is developed under a hypervisor and utilizes the underlying physical hardware. The virtual machine that was created is referred to as a guest machine while the physical server is referred to as the host machine. A hypervisor controls all of the interactions between the virtual machine and the host machine physical assets such as RAM, CPU, and secondary storage.

Virtual technology may be attacked just as with any the other technology. A benefit of a virtual machine is that it can be taken down and immediately re-created in the event of a penetration or attack. The virtual environment separates the attacker from the underlying hardware, although it is possible for a dedicated experienced hacker to successfully attack the root and attack the hypervisor. Once in the hypervisor, the attacker has access to all of the virtual machines controlled by that hypervisor.

Security, as applied to virtualization, includes a collection of controls, procedures, and processes that ensure the availability, integrity, and confidentiality of the virtualization environment. Security controls can be implemented at various levels within the virtual environment. Controls can be implemented directly on a virtual machine or address vulnerabilities in the underlying physical device.

Secure Data Warehouse and Big Data Environments

Big data refers to data sets that are so large and complex that through predictive analytics or other advanced methods to extract value from data, new correlations in an effort to spot business trends, prevent diseases, combat crime, promote solutions for complex physics simulations, and provide for biological and environmental research are made available. Data sets grow in size due to the ever-growing availability of cheap and numerous information sensing and gathering technology.

It is predicted that, as of 2014, in excess of 667 exabytes of data pass through the Internet annually. The retail, financial, government, and manufacturing sectors all maintain data repositories that are continuously analyzed to spot trends for the exploitation of marketing and other opportunities. For instance, it is reported that Walmart records in excess of 1 million customer transactions every hour, which are forwarded to databases estimated to contain more than 3.1 petabytes of data. This data is continuously analyzed to spot trends, outages, buying preferences, and other pertinent information on a worldwide basis. Big data is also used for climate change simulations, predicting financial markets as well as for military and science applications.

The data sets are so large that it is not possible to analyze the data on standard PCs or even mainframe computers. Standard relational database management systems, as well as predictive analytics and data visualization applications, are not robust enough to handle data analysis. The analysis instead requires hundreds or even thousands of servers running in parallel to perform the required processing. It is growing so fast that what was defined as big data only a few years ago is commonplace today. It is growing so large and so fast that analytic applications are having difficulty keeping up.

Big data has been described as having three vectors: the amount of data, the speed of data in and out of the database, and the range of data types and sources. In 2012, Gartner, Inc., updated a cloud definition as follows: "Big data is high volume, high velocity, and/or high variety information assets that require new forms of processing to enable enhanced decision making, insight discovery and process optimization." The data analysis requires new forms of integration to uncover large hidden values from large data sets that are diverse, complex, and of a massive scale.

Data Warehouse and Big Data Deployment and Operations

Big data requires exceptional technologies and the use of a virtual architecture as an option for dealing with the immense amount of data gathered and processed within a system. Multiple processing units designed as distributed parallel architecture frameworks distribute data across thousands of processors to provide much faster throughput and increased processing speeds.

MapReduce is a parallel processing model and application used to process huge amounts of data and is used as a method of distributing database queries across hundreds or thousands of machines, which then process the data in parallel. The results of these database queries are analyzed, gathered, and delivered. The *MapReduce framework* is an application that distributes the workload of processing the data across a large number of virtual machines. The Hadoop Framework is a big data file system that is referred to as the *Hadoop Distributed File System* that stores and maintains data in a very large format system. The MapReduce application uses the Hadoop Distributed File System.

A large number of companies, including eBay, Amazon, and Facebook, make use of the data and data warehouses to analyze consumer purchasing and merchandising trends. It is been estimated that the volume of business data worldwide doubles in just over 14 months.

Exam Point

The MapReduce and Hadoop frameworks are the methodologies of processing very large databases in parallel.

Securing the Data Warehouse and Data Environment

Big data makes use of a distributed processing architecture featuring tens of thousands of server clusters working in parallel. With the data volume, data velocity, and sheer magnitude of data storage and transport in a parallel processing environment that is web-based, securing the systems is much more difficult.

The immensity of the data and requirement for parallel processing increases the magnitude of encryption as well.

Encrypted search and cluster formation in big data was demonstrated in March 2014. Encryption speed and system resilience are the primary focus of the data encryption goals. Researchers are proposing an approach for identifying the encoding techniques to be used toward an expedited search without decoding and re-encoding data during the search process. This is leads to the advancement toward eventual security enhancements in data security.

Big Data Access Control and Security

The foundations of security are defined as availability, integrity, and confidentiality, and each is pushed to an absolute limit with the concepts of big data. Access control requires that a data owner classify data according to some criteria and provide access control decisions. The data represented in these monumental structures is so large and comes from such a variety of locations and sources that is very difficult to have one person or even a team of people assuming the traditional ownership role of the data when it is in the matrix.

The handling of big data creates challenges for many organizations. They must first determine data ownership and then determine the attributes that should be assigned to the data. One approach is to assign data ownership to the data outputs of search and analysis operations, which may be much more manageable than attempting to classify the entire database.

New terminology may appear where the data owner controls the data on the input side and the information owner assumes control of the data on the data output side. Two types of data ownership are surfacing out of this concept. The data owner places the data into the database, classifies the data, and determines access criteria. The information owner, on the other hand, owns and classifies information after a resulting process such as a search, sort, or analysis procedure.

Secure Software-Defined Networks and Virtual Environments

Virtual environments offer the capability of running numerous virtual machines on a single underlying server, thus taking advantage of economies of scale and enabling the most efficient use of the underlying hardware. Virtualization increases resource flexibility and utilization and reduces infrastructure costs and overhead.

Software-Defined Networks

As you saw in Chapter 8, to date, conventional network design has developed from a hierarchal structure such as tree, ring, star, and other network topologies built upon physical network connection devices such as servers, routers, and switches. In the world of client/server computing, the static design was suitable because once the client was connected to a server, the hardware routing did not change. With the dynamic computing requirements and increasing storage needs of today's enterprise data centers, designers have sought a much more flexible, dynamic means of interconnecting devices. These revolutionary design changes have been prompted by several environmental changes within the IT industry as well as resulting from business demand. Some of these changes are listed here:

Changing Data Traffic Patterns   Traditional data traffic featured client computers connected through a number of switches or routers and hardwired to a server. The job of the server was to acquire information from storage devices, process the information, and serve it to the client computer. The client computer, in this environment, was usually executing an application locally and was accessing the server environment purely as a communications method to the outside world of the Internet or two other servers that provided communications applications such as email and other services.

North/South is a classic data path in most enterprise networking environments. It refers to the standard data channel between a lower-level client computer and a higher-level server computer. As data centers have grown and the demand for higher-level applications that access multiple databases on many different servers has increased, a single request from a client computer may trigger a large amount of communications horizontally between a number of communicating servers containing databases and other components required for the communication. This data path is referred to as *East/West*, which describes a horizontal or machine-to-machine data path. Today's data processing environment requires a dynamic capability to set up data paths as required for the task at hand. Hardwired static data paths may no longer suffice.

Device-to-Machine Access Requirements   Users desire access to content and applications from multiple device formats. *Personally owned devices (PODs)* are quickly becoming the norm within most computing environments, which offer the ability to connect from anywhere at any time. In most organizations, users are employing mobile personal devices to access the organization's network. Network access must be established in such a manner as to provide flexibility in that the same user may be connecting using different devices and requiring different data formatting and different data presentation methods.

Virtualization and Cloud Services   Organization IT departments have wholeheartedly embraced all of the different types of cloud services, resulting in a substantial demand for virtualized networks. Network users now demand the capability to access applications, infrastructures, and other IT resources on demand from a wide variety of source devices.

The Demand for Dynamically Configured Network Environments   Big data, defined as mega data sets, is driving the requirement for the virtual configuration of massive processing capability, where thousands of servers are configured to parallel-process mega data sets well connected to each other. Virtualized networks will enable any connectivity required by massive cloud-based processing

Software-defined networking (SDN) is a virtualization methodology in which the actual data flow across the network is separated from the underlying hardware infrastructure. This allows networks to be defined almost instantaneously in response to consumer requirements. This is accomplished by combining common centralized IT policies into a centralized platform that can control the automation of provisioning and configuration across the entire IT infrastructure. Network configurations can be configured within minutes using virtualized technology rather than spending hours or days rewiring and reconfiguring hardware-based data centers.

Software-Defined Networks in Practice

There are a number of software-defined network application providers offering a wide selection of products. To date, no one standardized application is surfacing as a clear leader. There are several commonalities between all of the SDN models:

Southbound APIs   Information is sent to the underlying hardware infrastructure with provisioning and deployment instructions.

Northbound APIs   Information concerning network operation data volume and other considerations is communicated from the hardware layer to the applications and business logic. This allows operators to monitor network operations.

SDN Controller   The software-defined network controller is the central operational application that allows network administrators to design the virtualized network system using underlying hardware infrastructure.

Network administrators make use of preconfigured virtual machine images sometimes referred to as *snapshots* that are ready to deploy on a hypervisor. A *virtual appliance* is a virtual machine image that is preconfigured and includes preloaded software and is ready to run in a hypervisor environment. The virtual appliance is intended to eliminate the installation, configuration, and maintenance costs associated with running complex virtual environments by preconfiguring ready-to-use virtual machine images.

There is a difference between virtual machines and virtual appliances. A virtual machine is a generic, stand-alone virtualized platform that consists of a CPU, primary storage (RAM), secondary storage (hard disk), and network connectivity. A virtual appliance is in fact a virtual machine by definition, but it also contains the operating system as well as software applications that are preconfigured and ready to run as soon as the virtual appliance image is in place. The major difference between a virtual machine and a virtual appliance is the configuration of the operating system. Most virtual machines use a standard preconfigured image of an operating system that includes all of the latest patches and upgrades, whether it be Windows, Linux, or another OS. In a virtual appliance, the operating system may be customized for the specific application and environment in which the appliance will be performing. This stripped-down or specifically configured operating system is referred to as *just enough operating system (JeOS)*, which is pronounced "juice."

Host Clustering

A host machine provides the underlying hardware upon which virtual machines are running. A single host may run a very large number of virtual machines all sharing the same CPU, RAM, hard drive, and network communications capability. *Host clustering* is a method whereby numbers of host machines may be logically or physically connected so that all of their resources (such as CPU, RAM, hard drive, and network communications capability) can be shared among all of the hosted virtual machines. Host clustering provides the ability to expand and demand more attributes as a workload increases as well as provide the safety failover to another host in the event one host fails.

Within host clustering, all of the resources for all of the host computers are managed as if they were one large machine and are made available to the virtual machines that are members of the cluster. With a large number of cluster members (virtual machines) in contention for the limited resources of the host cluster, various resource sharing concepts are used to define the allocation of resources. The cluster administrator may define the requirements and allocations for each member of the cluster using the following techniques:

Reservations A virtual machine may be allocated a minimum amount of pooled resources, thus guaranteeing the availability of the resources for performing its application.

Maximum Limit A virtual machine may be restricted to a maximum amount of pooled resources, thus guaranteeing that a single virtual machine or application can demand excessive resources, thereby creating a denial of service for other virtual machines and applications.

Shares Allocation Shares allocation is a technique of prioritizing and distributing any remaining pooled resources among the cluster member virtual machines after all reservations have been fulfilled.

Storage Clustering

Storage clustering is the use of several storage servers managed and interconnected together to increase performance, capacity, or reliability. Storage clustering distributes workloads to each storage server and manages access to all files and data stores from any server regardless of the physical location of the files and data stores. Storage clustering should have the ability to meet the required service levels (specified in SLAs), keep all client data separate, and adequately safeguard and protect the stored data. The benefits of virtual storage clustering are as follows:

- One design of pooled storage devices is constructed of groups or arrays of inexpensive disks called *just a bunch of disks (JBOD)*. This array features a large number of inexpensive disks of varying sizes and capabilities attached with *Serial Attached SCSI (SAS)* host bus adapters.

- Pools of storage devices can be used to create large virtual disk storage. RAID-based storage methodologies such as simple, mirrored, and parity will be handled by the virtual storage controller, with parity being automatically striped across drives.

- *Data dispersion* will automatically copy data around the storage cluster, utilizing space efficiently and creating mirrored copies as requested. This will achieve space utilization load balancing to effectively utilize pool storage capability by storing data anywhere it will fit.

- Rules such as *anti-affinity* or affinity rules enforce hypervisor policies that keep some entities such as VMs together or separate depending upon requirements.

Two basic types of storage clustering architectures exist:

Loose Coupled Cluster   A *loose coupled cluster* is very typical of the use of JBOD technology in the hard drive array. It may start small and grow larger as disks are added. It is an informal assemblage of disks, all of which are virtualized into an apparent virtual single drive. The restriction on this type of disk clustering is the speed of the data interface. This may limit the accessibility to the entire drive stack. As more drives are added, access latency may increase.

Tight Coupled Cluster   A *tight coupled cluster* is a drive array that is usually provided by a single manufacturer and features a proprietary physical backplane, which maintains connectivity to both drives and controller nodes. This type of cluster usually has an initial fixed drive size and delivers very high-performance interconnect between servers for load-balanced performance. Tight coupled cluster products may be initially available in a variety of sizes and may growth through additions of both drives and controllers as space requirements dictate.

Security Benefits and Challenges of Virtualization

Attacks and countermeasures used in virtualized environments are very similar in nature to any attack and countermeasure utilized in a traditional hardwired network. Appropriate risk assessments should be made to identify probable threats and vulnerabilities within the environment. Organizations should conduct regular tests and assessments as well as provide for continuous monitoring and logging to identify the effectiveness of security controls and countermeasures.

Security Benefits of Virtualization

The virtualization of various network components offers many advantages over using static network devices:

Desktop Virtualization   *Virtual desktop infrastructure*, or *VDI*, is an implementation of a desktop display complete with running applications that is presented on the client computer or thin client device. The actual applications, stored data, and underlying computing infrastructure are operating in a central location, only the resulting images are sent to the client device. In a virtual desktop infrastructure (VDI) environment no applications or data is required to be loaded at the client location. This eliminates the risk of an attacker gaining access to applications or data stored on a client computer.

Virtual Machine Rollback   *Snapshots* may be made of a virtual machine at any time. A snapshot is an exact copy of a virtual machine at a point in time and may be used to reload or repair a virtual machine. In the event the virtual machine is successfully attacked, the machine can be easily rolled back to a state prior to the attack.

Virtual Machine Isolation   Virtual machines run in isolated VM environments under a hypervisor running on a host machine. Should the operating system or application running on a virtual machine be attacked, only one virtual machine and not the entire environment is affected.

Resource Pooling   Through host clustering techniques, resources are pooled and allocated among virtual machines. This allows for the economic use of resources as well as the expansion capability of any virtual machine or application. Clustering techniques also include clustered storage, which prevents loss of data should a single device fail or be compromised.

The benefits of *server virtualization* include better resource allocation as well as the ability to revert to an earlier snapshot or operating condition in the event of a problem or attack. *Desktop virtualization* referred to as virtual desktop infrastructure (VDI) allows more flexibility to push out the correct image to a user device depending upon the required format of the device.

Security Challenges of Virtualization

Substantial security challenges surface with the use of virtualization:

Hypervisor   The *Hypervisor* allows virtual machines to communicate between them. This creates a channel of communication that is no longer monitored by standard monitoring and threat mitigation methods. The data is virtually invisible to the standard hardwired network environment. If a hypervisor is compromised, the attached virtual machines will also be compromised.

Virtual Machine Theft   Extreme care must be taken to protect snapshot images of virtual machines. These copies of a virtual machine image can easily be stolen through the use of portable storage devices or may be exfiltrated from the company of a number of methods.

Snapshot Reverting   In the event of data corruption or a machine attack, a virtual machine can be rolled back to a previous *snapshot* or image of a virtual machine at a previous point in time. When this reversion takes place in a configuration, application changes or data updates may be lost.

Rogue Virtual Machines   Virtual machines can be created by users without the knowledge of the IT department. They may or may not conform to organizational security policies.

Insecure Trust Levels   Virtual machines operating a different trust levels should not be installed on the same host. Security of all of the virtual machines on a host or server is that of the lowest trust level of any one machine.

Virtual Machine Attack   Although virtual machines are isolated from each other, in the event of an attack or a compromise, a virtual machine may demand an inordinate amount of host resources. This demand for increased resources will create a denial of service for any other virtual machines on the same host.

Summary

As a security practitioner, you will be closely involved with various aspects of incident handling involving the penetration of malicious code and malicious software. It is important to have an understanding of the different types of malicious code and the factors upon which it may arrive at the network or host location. Knowledge of the various countermeasures, including both software and hardware appliances, is required. Proper maintenance, patching, and upgrading is required of all software and hardware. It is the responsibility of the security professional to upgrade anti-malware software and devices to maintain an adequate operational base level. All patches and upgrades should be tested in offline systems that are similar to production-grade systems prior to pushing out to production.

Endpoint devices include not only host computers but also portable devices and network nodes such as printers or scanners. Each device requires proper protection mechanisms and controls to ensure that it is adequately protected from attack.

The cloud is certainly a big buzzword in IT circles. But with the cloud comes extensive security requirements. Data must be secured in transit to and from the cloud servers and encrypted at rest in the cloud location. It is important to understand encryption mechanisms as well as storage and retrieval techniques used in cloud storage. Multi-tenancy refers to the practice of placing multiple tenants on cloud-based servers. This technique of dynamically sharing hardware can cause a number of security challenges.

Along with cloud comes the concept of big data. Big data and data warehousing are techniques of amassing huge amounts of data that may bridge across a number of storage locations. This amount of data is so large that specialized techniques of processing the data in parallel have been developed. Data ownership, classification, integrity, and confidentiality are all challenges facing the security practitioner.

The cloud is made up of virtual environments, which make the best use of hardware in an organization-owned data center. The software-defined network creates the concept of virtual machines and virtual storage that run on top of physical machines. These machines may be placed into operation and taken down very rapidly. Although a virtual server runs in a virtual environment, it is not without security concerns. Virtual machine escape is an attack whereby the attacker literally jumps out or "escapes" from the virtual machine and obtains control of the hypervisor or another virtual machine. With hypervisor privileges, the attacker has complete control of all of the other virtual machines as well as the underlying hardware infrastructure.

Of all of the ideas covered in this book, the concept of the cloud as well as virtual environments is among the most important for the SSCP to learn for the future. The cloud may definitely guide the future of information technology.

Exam Essentials

Hackers, Script Kiddies, Hacktivists Be able to describe all of the different types of attackers.

Viruses and Worms Understand the different types of malware, including viruses, worms, key loggers, spyware, and APTs.

Social Engineering Know the types of social engineering attacks, including phishing, vishing, and spoofing, among others.

Email Management Understand spam management as well as the hazards of clicking email links and opening attachments.

Cookies Understand that cookies may contain personal information that may be the target of an attacker. Persistent cookies offer a method of hiding this information in a number of locations on a PC.

Protocol Analyzers Be able to describe the methods protocol analyzers use to obtain data from the network and what the analyzers do with this information.

Vulnerability Scanners Understand the types of vulnerability scanners.

Physical Security Be able to describe securing endpoint devices using physical security.

Host Firewall Know the purpose of a host firewall and how it can be set to block or allow information.

Full Disk and File Encryption Understand the different techniques and tools used to encrypt folders or specific files.

Data Sanitization Understand the methods involved in data sanitization to meet various regulatory and contractual requirements.

Endpoint Hardening Know the reasons for and various methods of endpoint heartening.

Cloud Concepts Be able to describe the floor cloud deployment models as well as the three cloud service models.

Software-Defined Networks Understand the basics of network virtualization and the creation of data pathways that are separate from the underlying hardware infrastructure.

Host Clustering Know the reasons for and benefits of host clustering. Be able to describe failover as well as load-balancing techniques.

Storage Clustering Understand and be able to describe the reasons for storage clustering and the two major methods of drive coupling techniques.

Written Lab

You can find the answers in Appendix A.

1. Write a paragraph explaining the relationship between the hypervisor and a virtual machine.

2. Describe the difference between a hacker, a certified ethical hacker, and a script kiddie.

3. Briefly explain the EU General Data Protection Regulation.

4. Describe the four cloud deployment models and three cloud service models.

Review Questions

You can find the answers in Appendix B.

1. Which of the following is the most likely to attack using an advanced persistent threat?
   A. Hacker
   B. Nation state
   C. Cracker
   D. Script kiddie

2. Which of the following options best describes a hacker with an agenda?
   A. Cracker
   B. Nation state
   C. Anarchist
   D. Hacktivist

3. Which statement *most* accurately describes a virus?
   A. It divides itself into many small pieces inside a PC.
   B. It always attacks an email contacts list.
   C. It requires an outside action in order to replicate.
   D. It replicates without assistance.

4. Which option is *not* a commonly accepted definition for a script kiddie?
   A. A young unskilled hacker
   B. A young inexperienced hacker
   C. A hacker that uses scripts or tools to create a text
   D. A highly skilled attacker

5. Which choice describes the path of an attack?
   A. A threat vector
   B. A threat source location
   C. The threat action effect
   D. A threat vehicle

6. Which choice *best* describes a zombie?
   A. Malware that logs keystrokes
   B. A member of a botnet
   C. A tool used to achieve privilege escalation
   D. A type of root kit

7. Which answer *best* describes an advanced persistent threat?

   A. Advanced malware attack by a persistent hacker

   B. A malware attack by a nation state

   C. An advanced threat the continuously causes havoc

   D. Malware that persistently moves from one place to another

8. Which choice is the *most* accurate description of a retrovirus?

   A. A virus designed several years ago

   B. A virus that attacks anti-malware software

   C. A virus that uses tried-and-true older techniques to achieve a purpose

   D. A mobile virus that attacks older phones

9. Which choice is an attack on a senior executive?

   A. Phishing attack

   B. Whaling attack

   C. Watercooler attack

   D. Golf course attack

10. Which of the following is *most* often used as a term to describe an attack that makes use of a previously unknown vulnerability?

   A. Discovery attack

   B. First use attack

   C. Premier attack

   D. Zero-day attack

11. Which type of client-side program always runs in a sandbox?

   A. HTML4 control

   B. Visual Basic script

   C. Java applet

   D. Active X control

12. Which of the following would *best* describe the purpose of a trusted platform module?

   A. A module that verifies the authenticity of a guest host

   B. The part of the operating system that must be invoked all the time and is referred to as a security kernel

   C. A dedicated microprocessor that offloads cryptographic processing from the CPU while storing cryptographic keys

   D. A computer facility with cryptographic processing power

13. What is the prime objective of code signing?

   A. To verify the author and integrity of downloadable code that is signed using a private key

   B. To verify the author and integrity of downloadable code that is signed using a public key

    C. To verify the author and integrity of downloadable code that is signed using a symmetric key

    D. To verify the author and integrity of downloadable code that is signed using a master key

14. Which choice *least* describes a cloud implementation?

    A. Broadly assessable by numerous networking platforms

    B. Rapid elasticity

    C. On-demand self-service

    D. Inexpensive

15. Which option is *not* a cloud deployment model?

    A. Private cloud

    B. Corporate cloud

    C. Community cloud restoration

    D. Public cloud

16. Which of the following options is not a standard cloud service model?

    A. Help Desk as a Service

    B. Software as a Service

    C. Platform as a service

    D. Infrastructure as a service

17. Which of the following is the *most* accurate statement?

    A. Any corporation that has done business in the European Union in excess of five years may apply for the Safe Harbor amendment.

    B. Argentina and Brazil are members of the Asia-Pacific Privacy Pact.

    C. The United States leads the world in privacy legislation.

    D. The European Union's General Data Protection Regulation provides a single set of rules for all member states.

18. Which of the following most accurately describes eDiscovery:

    A. Any information put on legal hold

    B. A legal tool used to request suspected evidentiary information that may be used in litigation

    C. All information obtained through proper service of the search warrant

    D. Any information owned by an organization with the exception of trade secrets.

19. Which of the following is most accurate concerning virtualization security?

    A. Only hypervisors can be secured, not the underlying virtual machine.

    B. Virtual machines are only secured by securing the underlying hardware infrastructure.

    C. Virtual machines can be secured as well as the hypervisor and underlying hardware infrastructure.

    D. Virtual machines by nature are always insecure.

20. Which of the following is most accurate concerning data warehousing and big data architecture?

    A. Data warehouses are used for long-term storage of archive data.

    B. Data is processed using auto-synthesis to enhance processing speed.

    C. Big data is so large that standard relational database management systems do not work. Data must be processed by parallel processors.

    D. Data can never be processed in real time.

Appendix
A

Answers to Written Labs

The written labs are intended to give you an opportunity to either verbalize or put down in writing the concepts that you learned in each chapter. As a learning or memory tool, sometimes it's beneficial to rephrase terms, definitions, and ideas into your own words. The four questions at the end of every chapter are intended to prompt you to think about the chapter content.

Following are some brief answers for each of the written lab questions. These answers should steer you in the correct direction. For this to be beneficial, read the brief answers and elaborate on them in your own words. It's important that you know and understand the concepts and not just memorize facts, figures, and data.

Chapter 2

1. The implicit deny rule states that unless something (such as traffic on a network) is explicitly allowed, it is denied. It isn't used to deny all traffic but instead to deny all traffic that isn't explicitly granted or allowed. Implicit deny usually refers to the bottommost rule in a rule stack. Should no other rule explicitly allow the traffic, then the implicit rule would deny the traffic.

2. As a security concept, availability ensures that data, applications, and network access are available to users.

3. The security AAA triad consists of authentication, authorization, and auditing/accounting.

4. The three primary security categories are prevention, detection, and recovery. Prevention, of course, includes activities that may be used to prevent attacks or prevent the loss of or damage to an asset. Detection is the use of controls and devices that detect anomalies, signatures, or activity that trigger either an alarm or some course of action to control the event. Recovery is returning to normal or to a state just prior to an attack event.

Chapter 3

1. Federated access is a single sign-on technique that involves sharing properly authenticated user information with third-party entities that are grouped through contractual agreement. A typical illustration is a travel booking website. Once the user is logged in and authenticated, they can access hotel, flight, and car rental information and make reservations from other websites.

2. A primary vulnerability to single sign-on is that if an attacker can compromise an individual's credentials, they then have free access to all of the network resources that the individual has rights to. This is negated if the individual requires separate logins and passwords for each resource.

3. Mandatory access control (MAC) assigns labels to both the subject and the object. The subject would have a security clearance label, and the object would have a security classification label. Access by the subject to a secure object would be mediated typically by a device referred to as a trusted computing base. Mandatory access control is typically used in government and military organizations. Discretionary access control (DAC) is a default access control technique in Microsoft Windows. The owner/creator of the data has the capability of determining who has access to the data as well as what they can do when they access the data, such as read, read/write, or even create and delete actions.

4. Access controls are grouped under various categories. These categories include administrative, logical/technical, and physical.

Chapter 4

1. Anyone could write a policy within an organization. Unless the policy has executive-level endorsement, meaning that a senior executive has approved it, stands behind it, and indicates that it is the authorized or mandated statement from the organization, it will not be respected.

2. Standards, baselines, and procedures indicate the supporting details of a policy. Policies are created because of a standard that the organization must abide by. For instance, the requirement that an organization needs to meet HIPAA standards is a reason for a HIPAA policy. Baselines are a measure of the minimum amount of effort, compliance, or activity the organization must undertake to meet a certain standard. Procedures are steps or activities that should be taken in a sequential order to achieve a specific result.

3. During the interruption of regular organizational IT activity, such as during a disaster event, the business continuity plan (BCP) or the disaster recovery plan (DRP) may specify an alternate location for the continuation of IT activity. A hot site is a location that can be brought online within a number of hours. Typically, all required hardware, electrical power, HVAC, and communications capabilities are installed and ready to go. Current data is not installed on hot site equipment. A warm site may have some equipment and will take incrementally longer to bring online. A cold site is typically just a building location with no equipment installed. It will take the longest period of time to bring online.

4. Recovery time objective (RTO) is a component of the business continuity plan that indicates the period of time that the organization may be without a specific business function. It indicates the time that the business function must be up and running, even if at a reduced capacity. Recovery point objective is the point at which the last known good copy or backup copy of data can be restored to bring a specific business function back online.

Chapter 5

1. In the process of risk analysis, there are two types of asset valuation. Quantitative analysis is a method of determining asset value based upon various numerical values. These might include original purchased cost, depreciated cost, replacement cost, and a variety of additional costs such as installation, restoration, configuration, and other operational costs. *Quantitative* may be thought of as a "quantity" of money. Qualitative analysis does not make use of factual data such as monetary cost figures. It arrives at subjective values and impact values based upon the opinions of experts. The subjective value that is typically used in quantitative analysis might measure the impact of lost functionality as low, medium, and high.

2. A threat describes the action that a bad actor may take or cause to happen. A vulnerability describes a weakness in an asset or control. The traditional definition of risk is the probability that a threat will exploit a vulnerability, thus causing harm.

3. In risk analysis, various computations might be used to express the cost to the organization should an asset be lost or damaged due to the actions of a threat. Single loss expectancy (SLE) is the cost to the organization each time an asset is harmed due to the action of a threat. Annualized loss expectancy (ALE) represents the cost determined in a single loss expectancy multiplied by the number of times per year the loss may occur, which is described as the annualized rate of occurrence (ARO). The exposure factor (EF) is expressed as a percentage and represents the monetary loss of the value of an asset each time the asset is harmed due to the action of a threat. For instance, if an asset cost $10,000 and every time it was attacked by a threat it cost $5,000 to rebuild, the exposure factor would be 50 percent.

4. There are four acceptable methods of treating risk. They include accepting the risk, assigning risk, reducing risk, and risk avoidance. By default, ignoring risk means accepting the risk.

Chapter 6

1. Business continuity planning includes all of the actions required to develop a business continuity plan (BCP). A business continuity plan includes all of the requirements and procedures to maintain business operations after a disaster event. Business recovery planning includes all of the actions required to develop a disaster recovery plan (DRP). A disaster recovery plan includes all of the requirements and procedures that might be required to restore business operations to a point just prior to a disaster event. The recovery plan may include what is needed to restore facilities, equipment, and other assets.

2. *Triage* is typically a medical term. It refers to the prioritization of damages and the communication of this prioritization so that damaged entities can be addressed based on need, usually ranked high to low.

3. A business continuity plan will designate various time periods. The recovery time objective (RTO) is the period of time a particular business function may be nonfunctional and must be brought back online in some productive capacity. The recovery point objective (RPO) is the date and time of the last known good data for backup information that may be used to restore systems after a disaster event. The maximum tolerable downtime (MTD) represents the time period that a business activity may be unavailable, after which the business may begin to experience irreparable harm.

4. An incident response team is a team that responds with some set activities after the onset of an incident. The team determines the damage, takes actions, restores capabilities, and reports on findings or prepares after-action reports. Organizations will have different incident response activities depending upon the nature or severity of the event. The standard instruction to an incident response team is to follow the incident response plan.

Chapter 7

1. An asymmetric cryptography system makes use of two keys for each participant. These two keys include a public key and a private key. The private key must always be kept secret. The relationship between the keys is that the private key may be used to originate the public key, but it is mathematically infeasible for the person with the public key to determine the private key. Both keys can encrypt data, and either key can decrypt data but only the data encrypted by the opposite key. Asymmetric cryptography makes use of very large and intensive mathematical computations involving large prime numbers. Therefore, it is slow and cumbersome. Asymmetric cryptography is the basis for public key infrastructure (PKI), where certificates are used as a trusted means for verification of the ownership of a public key. Symmetric cryptography makes use of a single shared secret key between the participants. Symmetric cryptography is hardware based, and therefore encryption and decryption can be accomplished magnitudes of speed faster than with asymmetric cryptography. Generally, the drawback of symmetric cryptography involves key distribution. Sending a secret key to a previously unknown participant is difficult in symmetric cryptography. The strength of cryptographic algorithms is usually a function of key length.

2. The Diffie-Hellman key exchange is a method whereby two participants, who may be previously unknown to each other, can derive the same secret key utilizing a mathematical function. The two participants each create two numbers. One number is kept secret while the other number is exchanged in the clear with the other participant. These numbers are used in the mathematical function and will result in both participants arriving at the same final number. The final number will represent a shared secret key.

3. In public key infrastructure (PKI), the X.509 standard involves the use of digital certificates and various entities. The certificate authority (CA) is a respected and trusted organization that issues, maintains, and revokes digital certificates. The registration authority (RA) gathers information from users wishing to apply for digital certificates. The certificate revocation list (CRL) is a list of certificates that have either expired or been revoked due to compromise or other situations. Online Certificate Status Protocol (OCSP) is a protocol used by a web browser to automatically check the status of the protocol.

4. A digital signature is created by processing a plaintext message through a hashing algorithm to obtain a hash value or message digest. This hash value is then encrypted using the private key of the individual or entity providing a digital signature. Both the encrypted hash value and the plaintext message may then be sent to the receiving entity. The receiving entity will use the public key of the sender to decrypt the hash value. Upon rehashing the plaintext message, the receiving entity will compare the decrypted hash value in the derived hash value upon receipt to ensure that they are the same. A digital signature provides proof of origin and nonrepudiation. It does not provide confidentiality.

Chapter 8

1. IPsec is important because it is a popular method of protecting data while in transit and it has been adopted as a suggested encryption mechanism for use in IPv6. IPsec can be utilized in either tunnel mode or transport mode, depending upon the end connectivity. The end connectivity will also determine the type of header placed on each packet. The authentication header will provide both sender authentication and integrity to each packet. Encapsulating Security Payload (ESP) is a member of the IPsec protocol suite and provides authenticity, integrity, and confidentiality to packets. IPsec can be used to create tunnels between networks.

2. Kerberos is a popular technique that has been adopted by Microsoft as its single sign-on methodology. It makes use of tickets to grant user access to resources. The user logs in and is authenticated one time. The single sign-on provides a one-time user authentication and the assignment of a ticket-granting ticket (TGT) provided by a ticket-granting server (TGS). The ticket-granting ticket is utilized throughout a set period of time, typically one day, to request session tickets for each desired resource. Symmetric keys are utilized between the entities for authentication. The benefit of Kerberos is that the client provides most of the communication overhead.

3. Routers and switches are both network devices that provide directional control of packets on a network. Routers are OSI layer 3 devices that route packets based upon their IP address. Switches are OSI layer 2 devices that switch data packets between devices based upon Media Access Control (MAC) addresses. (Certain switches may be used at layer 3.)

4. The layers of the OSI model are numbered one through seven. In order, they are (beginning at layer 1) Application, Presentation, Session, Transport, Network, Data Link, and Physical.

Chapter 9

1. A hypervisor is a control program that runs on a PC or server and is referred to as a host because it will be used to host virtual machines. This control program interfaces with the underlying physical hardware of the host and controls the access to the resources for each virtual machine. This includes the CPU, RAM, and secondary storage such as hard disk drives. A Type I hypervisor interfaces directly with the physical hardware of the host and a Type II hypervisor interfaces with the operating system that is running on the host. The hypervisor is used to form and manage virtual machines. Each virtual machine is a separate instance of a computer system that shares the underlying hardware of the host.

2. The difference between a hacker, a certified hacker, and a script kiddie tends to be with the expertise and experience of each. The script kiddie is usually a young, inexperienced person who is utilizing readily available scripts to provide mischief on the Internet. A hacker, on the other hand, may be very experienced and is usually performing attacks for personal benefit or to exfiltrate data for financial gain. The certified ethical hacker is an experienced individual who has hacking skills and is generally employed by a commercial entity with particular assignments to penetrate networks, systems, and applications to determine weaknesses.

3. The European Commission has created a single law for the European Union, referred to as the EU General Data Protection Regulation (GDPR). This law will be replacing the EU Data Protection Directive 95/46 EC. The data protection directive was well intentioned and provided for concepts such as "data controllers" as well as the "right to be forgotten" idea. Unfortunately, the directive was not a law, and various European Union members could arbitrarily adopt it or not at their leisure. The difference between the two is that the EU Data Protection Directive 95/46 EC is only a directive, providing the effect as an advisory for the member states. The EU General Data Protection Regulation is a regulation, or law, that binds all 28 members of the European Union to a unified set of privacy standards.

4. The three cloud service modules include Software as a Service (SaaS), Infrastructure as a Service (IaaS), and Platform as a Service (PaaS). SaaS provides either third-party hosting of software in the cloud or the cloud provider hosting software for commercial use in the cloud. IaaS provides the user with various network components that may be assembled to duplicate or add to an existing data center. PaaS offers the user preconfigured computer platforms, which may be utilized for testing or application development purposes.

Appendix B

Answers to Review Questions

Chapter 2

1. C. The definition of the principle of least privilege is granting users only the minimum privileges needed to accomplish assigned work tasks.

2. B. Separation of duties is the process of assigning groups of tasks to different users to prevent collusion and to avoid conflicts of interest. The principle of least privilege is assigning users the minimal amount of access required to accomplish their work tasks. Mandatory access control is a means to control access by using classifications of subjects and objects. Integrity assurance is the process that ensures the controls put in place to maintain data integrity are operating properly.

3. B. Job rotation isn't appropriate because one person is still in charge of a particular position. M of N control, multiple key pairs, and separation of duties should be used to prevent a single person from compromising an entire system.

4. A. The correct answer is to reduce or mitigate risk to an acceptable level. It's virtually impossible to remove all risks from an environment. It may be a goal of upper management in general to minimize security cost. Assigning responsibilities to job roles might be accomplished by the department heads.

5. A. A PIN provides authentication. It is something you know.

6. C. When nonrepudiation is used as a security technique, a sender cannot deny sending a message.

7. B. Although encryption is security technique, it falls under the prevention security category.

8. C. User training is the best way to use nontechnical means to enforce security. The more the users know, the more secure the system will be.

9. D. Use of an alternate site after a disaster falls under the recovery primary security category.

10. D. Upon termination of any user, network access should immediately be prohibited by deactivating the user account.

11. A. No matter how hard you try, there is always some level of risk on everything that you attempt.

12. A. Vulnerabilities are weaknesses within a network. Mitigation reduces vulnerabilities and therefore risks. Risk is the probability that a threat will exploit vulnerability. Controls are tools and techniques for mitigating vulnerabilities.

13. B. Availability is the correct answer. Admission, auditing, and administration are all distractors.

14. B. Remuneration is not one of the security categories.

15. C. The correct answer is C, time of day restriction. The other answers are similar but not correct.

16. C. Implicit deny is built into most routers and the catchall that prohibits the passage of anything that has not been ethically or explicitly authorized. Explicit deny may be any one of dozens of router rules that the administrator creates to allow specific traffic. Deny any might be part of an explicit rule. Global deny is a distractor.

17. B. The correct answer is mandatory vacation, which in many security policies is stated as a mandatory one-week vacation once a year during which an investigation into ethics and job performance might occur. Ethical investigation is not the answer. Although we might like our company to send us on a mandatory cruise, that is not the correct answer either. M of N is a scheme requiring M number of people to agree to take action out of a possible universe of N number of people.

18. C. The correct answer is authentication, authorization, and accounting. It might be easy to picture this as a chain of access control steps. The first step is identification and then the authentication. It's important to get the words in the correct order. Option D is incorrect because the words administration and auditing are not part of the term. Option B is wrong because admission is not part of the term. Option A includes the correct words, but they are in the wrong order. Read the questions and options carefully.

19. C. The correct answer is time of day restriction. Time of week and time-based restrictions are similar, but they are distractors. Option A might be something out of a sci-fi movie.

20. B. Accounts that no longer belong to any active employees were called orphan accounts. Answer A, long-term accounts, and answer C, pseudo-active accounts, are obvious distractors. Answer D sounds plausible but is not the correct answer.

Chapter 3

1. C. The system is performing authentication. Option A is a distractor. Option B is incorrect because, in this case, the password is not used as identification. Option D is incorrect because the password does not provide authorization to the user.

2. B. The other answers are distractors.

3. A. Options B, C, and D are distractors.

4. D. Options A, B, and C are distractors.

5. B. Options A, C, and D are distractors.

6. C. The use of identification and authorization techniques best describes access control. Options A, B, and D are distractors.

7. D. Options A, B, and C are access controls, but they do not allow users to share files at their discretion.

8. B. Role-based access control (RBAC) permits authorization to be assigned according to an individual's role or title in the organization. Options A, C, and D are distractors.

9. C. Options A, B, and D are distractors.

10. A. Authentication is the method of verifying an individual's claim of identity. Options B, C, and D are distractors.

11. D. Options A, B, and C are distractors.

12. B. Options A, C, and D are distractors.

13. B. Privileged users are also known as super-users or administrators. Options A, C, and D are distractors.

14. B. Options A, C, and D are distractors.

15. C. Options A, B, and D are distractors.

16. C. Options A, B, and D refer to the same factor categories thus providing only one factor authentication.

17. D. The CER is where the false rejection rate (FRR) and false acceptance rate (FAR) crossover.

18. B. Options A, B, and D are distractors.

19. D. Options A, B, and C are distractors.

20. C. Option A, B, and D are distractors.

Chapter 4

1. C. Proper security administration policies, controls, and procedures enforce the AIC triad objectives, which are availability, integrity, and confidentiality.

2. B. Risk is the probability for likelihood that a threat will exploit the vulnerability. Options A, C, and D are distractors.

3. D. A security policy must be in alignment with the mission, objectives, nature, and culture of a business. Organizational policies are not based on best practices.

4. D. The Federation consists of third-party companies that share data based upon a one-time authentication of an individual.

5. B. A compensating control is a secondary control placed into use if the first or primary control is disabled or no longer usable. In this case, a hotel room door has a lock; the chain is a secondary or compensating control.

6. C. The policy will be doomed to failure if it does not have senior executive endorsement or a mandate from senior management. Options A, B, and D are distractors.

7. C. An acceptable use policy sets forth the acceptable behaviors that must be exhibited by all employees, contractors, and other personnel within the workplace or when accessing a network.

8. A. Acceptable behavior of individuals within any organization is put forth in the acceptable use policy. This includes the use of facilities and equipment as well as a large number of other behavioral considerations. The acceptable use policy is an administrative control.

9. B. An enforcement statement informs individuals of the potential penalties, fines, sanctions, or repercussions, which may result from the failure to abide by the policy.

10. B. Standards are the part of a policy that lists the criteria that must be met by the organization.

11. A. The organization's intranet is often the preferred method of communicating policy or policy changes. Social media and informal methods of communication such as including handouts and telephone calls should not be used to announce policy directives or policy changes.

12. D. Provide competent and diligent service to principles is the third canon of the $(ISC)^2$ Code of Ethics.

13. D. Service packs are issued by a manufacture to correct many software or hardware deficiencies and to upgrade the product. They may combine a large number of patches.

14. B. A sandbox environment, which resembles a production environment, is a location that patches and service packs should be tested prior to distribution to a production network.

15. C. Business information classification schemes generally do not include top-secret.

16. D. Objects within the U.S. military or government agencies may be issued a classification, classified top secret.

17. B. Any device that terminates a network connection may be classified as an endpoint device. In this case, a computer printer is an endpoint device because nothing follows it on the network.

18. C. The recovery point objective (RPO) is part of a business continuity plan.

19. C. A disaster recovery plan documents the procedures required to restore equipment and facilities back to the condition they were in prior to the disaster.

20. A. The maximum tolerable downtime is the point in time after which the survivability of the organization is in jeopardy.

Chapter 5

1. C. Option A is incorrect because eliminating risk is only part of a primary goal of security. Options B and D are incorrect because they are not primary goals of security.

2. A. Option A is correct because risk reduction alters elements throughout the enterprise to minimize the ability of a threat to exploit a vulnerability. Option B is incorrect. It is impossible to remove all risks. Option C is incorrect because it is one of four potential treatments for risk. Option D is incorrect because the organization accepts all the possible risks.

3. B. Option B is correct because the most likely source of an asset being lost is internal theft. Options A and C are external threats. Option D is also an external threat that might cause a denial of service attack.

4. D. Options A, B, and C are correct statements. Option D is wrong because risk cannot be completely eliminated.

5. D. Option A is incorrect because a weakness is a vulnerability. Option B is incorrect because a threat is not a protective control. Option C is incorrect because a threat is not a multilayer control.

6. B. Option A is incorrect because a safeguard does not exploit a vulnerability. Option C is incorrect because weaknesses are defined as a vulnerability. Option D is incorrect because safeguards do not warn of an attack.

7. B. Option A refers to a threat exploiting a vulnerability. Option C is a distractor. Option D is incorrect because it is the definition of asset.

8. B. Option A is incorrect because the words quantitative and qualitative are switched. Option C is incorrect because high, medium, and low are subjective results in qualitative analysis. Option D is incorrect because quantitative risk analysis can be automated.

9. D. Options A and B and C are correct answers. Option D is incorrect because a corrective control stops an existing attack.

10. A. Option A is correct because it involves talking to people and allows for immediate improvement. Option B is incorrect because it is a distractor. Option C is incorrect because a qualitative analysis does not deal with hard cost numbers. D is incorrect because a qualitative analysis does not deal with specific measurements.

11. C. The correct answer is option C because as interviewing terminated employees is not a common information-gathering technique for risk analysis. Options A, B, and D are common techniques.

12. B. Option A is incorrect because useful life has no relation to the classification. Options C and D are distractors.

13. A. Option B is incorrect because organizations cannot spend unlimited amounts of money to reduce all risks. C is incorrect; although it is treatment method of handling a risk, it is not the prime objective. Option D is incorrect because few individuals are prosecuted.

14. C. Option A is incorrect because it describes an incident that could negatively impact the organization. Option B is incorrect because procedures are not assets. Option D is incorrect because compensation and retirement programs are not assets.

15. C. Option C is the correct answer because risk assessment is not the final result of a risk management methodology; it is the first action taken. Options A, B, and D are accurate regarding the process of risk assessment.

16. C. Option C is the correct answer because a prudent company will spend only as much as the value of the item being protected. Options A, B, and D are part of a safeguard selection.

17. D. Option A is incorrect because it is part of continuity management planning. Option B is incorrect because it is impossible to achieve. Option C is incorrect because it refers to two concepts, neither of which is a primary goal of risk mitigation.

18. C. Subjective monitoring is not a type of monitoring. Options A, B, and D are all types of monitoring used within an organization.

19. B. Option B is the correct answer because it is not a risk treatment technique. If the risk is ignored, it is by default accepted. Options A, C, and D are typical risk treatment techniques.

20. C. Although there are preventative controls, it is not one of the three major categories. Options A, B, and D are the three major control categories.

Chapter 6

1. B. CPU cache is the closest memory to the CPU and the most volatile. Options A and D are long-term storage and not referred to as volatile memory. Option C is volatile memory, but it's not as volatile as CPU cache.

2. B. Always follow the procedures in a plan. Options A, C, and D are incorrect, although they may be included as a procedure in a plan.

3. C. Planned activities that enable the critical business functions to return to normal operations. Some critical business functions may resume operations at a reduced capacity. Option A is incorrect because it describes a function of risk assessment. Option B is incorrect because activities that are performed when a security-related incident occurs are a part of incident response. Option D describes a part of risk treatment.

4. A. This answer is very general and vague. Options B, C, and D are all commonly accepted definitions of a disaster.

5. C. Retaliation is not an acceptable incident response activity. Options A, B, and D are all part of an organization's incident handling response policy.

6. B. Stress reduction programs and other employee benefit programs is usually the responsibility of the human resources department. Options A, C, and D describe responsibilities of the person designated to manage the continuity planning process.

7. B. This plan is both cost effective and efficient. Option A is a very expensive test. Although they are types of tests, options C and D may be used to update information only.

8. A. A cold site does not have hardware. Options B, C, and D describe warm and hot sites.

9. D. Corrective controls stop an activity once it has begun. Options A, B, and C describe types of controls.

10. D. A full irruption test provides the most risk for the enterprise. Options A, B, and C are other types of test scenarios.

11. C. Hardware, software, and data must be installed in a cold site prior to it becoming operational. Options A, B, and D are other types of alternate recovery sites that include varying amounts of hardware and software.

12. D. A hot backup site may be brought online within minutes or hours. Options A, B, and C describe alternate sites, but they're not called hot backup sites.

13. C. Continuity is the act of keeping existing business functions operating. Options A, B, and D are distractors.

14. B. An incremental backup stores only the current day's data in a file. Options A, C, and D are backup techniques but are not defined as incremental backups.

15. B. The RPO is the location of the most accurate backup data prior to a disaster event. Options A, C, and D are distractors.

16. B. The functional incident response team should consist of a broad range of talents from across the organization. Options A, C, and D, although types of incident response teams, usually featured experts, dedicated personnel, or third-party contractors.

17. B. The chain of custody involves logging the location and handling of evidence. Options A, C, and D are items that may be used during investigation.

18. C. Data should be copied from a hard disk using bit-by-bit copy software. Options A, B, and D are distractors.

19. B. First responders should always follow the procedures as specified in the incident response plan. Options A, C, and D may be procedures included in an incident response plan but are incorrect because they might not be the correct procedures in this organization's incident response plan.

20. C. It is a level at which an operator is alerted. Options A, B, and D are distractors.

Chapter 7

1. D. The purpose of a hashing algorithm is to provide integrity. The message is hashed at each end of the transmission, and if the hash is equal, the message did not change. Options A, B, and C are incorrect because they have nothing to do with a hashing algorithm.

2. B. The only person who would have access to the sender's private key is the sender. Option A is incorrect. Anyone could encrypt a message using the sender's public key. Option C is incorrect; although anyone could encrypt a message using the receiver's public key, it would not provide proof of origin. Option D is incorrect because the only person who has access to the receiver's private key is the receiver.

3. D. Option D is correct because a set number of multiple persons (M) out of a group of persons (N) may be able to take the required action. Option A is incorrect because separation of duties has nothing to do with multiple-person key recovery. Option B is incorrect because there is no such thing as a multiple-man rule. Option C is incorrect because staged multiple interaction does not exist.

4. A. Symmetric keys are kept secret and are never publicly exchanged. Options B, C, and D are incorrect because they are all characteristics of a symmetric key.

5. C. Data encrypted with a user's public key can be encrypted only by the user's private key. This would not normally be in an organization's encryption policy. Options A, C, and D are all reasonable items to include in an organization's encryption policy.

6. D. Keys are never reused by different departments. Options A, B, and C are all activities that represent appropriate methods to manage keys.

7. B. Key clustering involves two different keys, resulting in the same ciphertext. Option A is incorrect because key clustering does not identify keys. Option C is incorrect because key clustering has nothing to do with timing. Option D is incorrect because key clustering has nothing to do with a keyed hash function.

8. C. A collision occurs when two plaintext documents result in the same hash value. Option A is incorrect. Symmetric keys do not corrupt plaintext documents. Option B is incorrect because collisions have nothing to do a ciphertext. Option D is incorrect. The decryption function has nothing to do with collisions.

9. B. Certificates always contain the owner's public key. Option A is incorrect because private keys are private. Option C is incorrect because certificates do not have anything to do with symmetric keys. D is incorrect because there is no such thing as a user's key.

10. C. The trust architecture does not include a certificate gateway. Options A, B, and D are part of the trust architecture.

11. A. The initialization vector adds to the power of a password or key so that the same text encrypted by the same key will not create the same ciphertext. Option B is incorrect. An initialization vector is not used with an owner's public key. Option C is incorrect. An initialization vector should create an environment where a code is not repetitive. Option D is incorrect because an initialization vector has nothing to do with speed.

12. B. Option B is the correct answer because a block cipher, by definition, encrypts one block at a time. Option A is incorrect because it describes a serial encryption. Option C is incorrect because it describes a serial encryption. Option D is incorrect because various types of keys may be utilized on a block cipher.

13. C. A hash function is a one-way function. Option A is incorrect because asymmetric functions are not one-way functions. Option B is incorrect because symmetric functions are not one-way functions. Option D is incorrect; a message authentication code may be decrypted using a symmetric key. It proves authentication because the sender possessed the same symmetric key as the receiver. Providing the receiver can decrypt the MAC with their symmetric key. The only other person who could have encrypted the message could be the sender.

14. D. The Caesar cipher is a substitution cipher. Options A, B, and C are incorrect because they do not describe the encryption technique of a Caesar cipher.

15. B. Steganography is the method of hiding data in a picture file, audio file, or movie file. This is referred to as hiding in plain sight. Options A, C, and D have nothing to do with hiding information in plain sight.

16. D. The keys in the key pair work together. When one encrypts, the other can decrypt. Options A, B, and C are incorrect usages of the key pair.

17. B. The message digest or hash value is encrypted by the sender's private key. Therefore, options A, C, and D are incorrect.

18. A. RSA is a widely used asymmetric algorithm. Options B, C, and D are symmetric algorithms.

19. C. With a digital signature, a hash value has been encrypted using the sender's private key. Only the sender's public key could decrypt it. Options A, B, and D are incorrect because they are not used by the receiver to verify integrity of a digital signature.

20. A. All symmetric key algorithms are faster than asymmetric algorithms. Options B, C, and D are incorrect because they are characteristics of a symmetric key algorithm.

Chapter 8

1. B. Encapsulation is a method of surrounding one packet with another packet. This technique completely encases the packet data. The outer packet does not have to provide encryption services. The other options are distractors.

2. B. The OSI model is a seven-layer model, with each layer responding to the layer directly above and directly below it. The TCP/IP model is a four-layer model. The other options are distractors.

3. A. Single-mode optical cable has the smallest diameter glass core, which decreases the number of light reflections. This allows for greater transmission distances of up to 80 km.

4. D. The address space for IPv6 is 128 bits. The address space for IPv4 is 32 bits. The other options are distractors.

5. C. Switches operate at layer 2 of the OSI model and route physical addresses, referred to as media access control addresses, which are unique to each node on a network. The other options are distractors.

6. A. TCP is a connection-oriented protocol because it establishes, through a three-way handshake, a communication path between two entities. A TCP connection allows for the receiving entity to request that a packet be resent in the event of an error condition. The other options are distractors.

7. C. Mesh topologies are used where speed and redundancy are required, such as with fault-tolerant devices, load distribution server clustering, and storage area networks (SANs). The other options are distractors.

8. B. Centralized key management is more secure, or at least more desirable, in a private enterprise environment. In a public or individual environment, decentralized key management is more secure. Individual key management and distributed key management are nonstandard terms that could be used to refer to decentralized key management.

9. C. Carrier Sense Multiple Access/Collision Avoidance describes a technique used to announce that a device is wishing to transmit on the media. The device will transmit or broadcast a tone prior to transmission. The tone is referred to as a jamming signal and will be heard by all other devices connected to the media.

10. C. The convergence of network communications involves the transmission of multimedia and data on the same network.

11. C. Continuous monitoring involves the policy, process, and technology used to detect risk issues within an organization's IT infrastructure. This monitoring may be in response to regulatory or contractual compliance mandates.

12. B. Kerberos is an authentication, single sign-on protocol developed at MIT and is named after a mythical three-headed dog that stood at the gates of Hades. Kerberos allows single sign-on in a distributed environment.

13. C. The hosts in a VLAN are connected to a network switch. The switch is responsible for controlling the traffic that is destined for each host.

14. B. A federation is an association of nonrelated third-party organizations that share information based upon single sign-on and one-time authentication of a user.

15. B. The purpose of the firewall is to filter traffic based upon various rulesets. Although firewalls are often associated with outside traffic, they can be placed anywhere. For example, one internal network may be isolated from another with the use of a firewall.

16. B. A wireless intrusion prevention system (WIPS) is used to mitigate the possibility of rogue access points. These systems are typically implemented in an existing wireless LAN infrastructure and enforce wireless policies within an organization. Typically, they prevent unauthorized network access to local area networks through unauthorized access points.

17. B. Amendment i provides for security enhancements to the wireless standard, is referred to as WPA2, and uses the AES encryption algorithm.

18. C. Originally designed as low-power transmission media to replace wires and cables, Bluetooth has been expanded to a number of uses, including data synchronization between devices. Using a low-power, Class II transmitter, Bluetooth has a general range of approximately 10 meters, or 33 feet, and has a stated maximum range of 100 meters, or 333 feet.

19. B. A rogue Wi-Fi access point that appears to be legitimate is referred to as an evil twin.

20. C. The ideal antenna placement is within the center of the area served and is high enough to get around most obstacles.

Chapter 9

1. B. An advanced persistent threat is a type of cyber terrorism malware usually placed by a well-funded, country-sponsored cyber-attack group.

2. D. A hacktivist has a political, social, or personal agenda.

3. C. A virus always requires an outside action in order to replicate.

4. D. All of the other options describe a typical script kiddie.

5. A. A threat vector describes the path of an attack.

6. B. A member of a botnet is referred to as a bot or a zombie computer.

7. B. An APT is malware usually put in place by a nation state.

8. B. A retrovirus attacks anti-malware software and sometimes disables a signature library or simply turns off the detection mechanism.

9. B. A whaling attack targets a senior executive to get them to click a link in an email in order to infect their computer.

10. D. A zero-day attack refers to a type of attack in which the attacker uses a previously unknown attack technique or exploits a previously unknown vulnerability.

11. C. By design, Java always creates a sandbox in which to execute an applet on a client machine. This prohibits the applet from being able to attack either the host machine or an application.

12. C. The trusted platform module is a crypto processor that performs as a dedicated micro-processor of cryptographic algorithms.

13. A. A private key is owned by the author and is used to encrypt the message digest or hash value of the code. The hash value provides the integrity, and the private key provides a digital signature and nonrepudiation by the author. The author's public key, usually provided in a digital certificate, is the only key that will decrypt the hash value.

14. D. The cloud is a metering, measured service similar to a utility, sometimes referred to as a "pay as you go" model. At this point, cloud services are still fairly expensive compared to installing one more disk drive in an organization's server.

15. B. According to NIST *Special Publication 800-145*, "The NIST Definition of Cloud Computing," a corporate cloud is not a cloud deployment model. *Corporate cloud* and *private cloud* refer to the same thing.

16. A. Help Desk as a Service is not one of the NIST-listed cloud service models, although it is a service that might be offered over the cloud.

17. D. The General Data Protection Regulation, which superseded Directive 95/46 BC, requires that all member states abide by the legal principles in the regulation and that these principles are not arbitrary.

18. B. eDiscovery is a legal tool used by opposing counsel to obtain requested information that may contain evidence or other useful information for a lawsuit. eDiscovery is not the information itself. It is the process of obtaining the information.

19. C. Security controls may be placed anywhere in a virtual environment. Security in depth is always the best practice when securing any environment.

20. C. Several big data processing models exist that illustrate how big data can be processed by parallel processors reaching into the thousands of servers.

Appendix C

Diagnostic Tools

As a Systems Security Certified Practitioner, you may be expected to use various tools when evaluating situations or solving problems. For example, analysis tools such as the Microsoft Password Checker are very handy to use during a user awareness training presentation. This tool drives home the point concerning the use of adequate passwords.

Although the use of these tools is not covered on the SSCP examination, it is advisable to review all of the tools available from Microsoft and other sources that may assist you in everyday problem analysis.

Microsoft Baseline Security Analyzer

Microsoft Baseline Security Analyzer (MBSA) lets administrators scan local and remote systems for missing security updates as well as common security misconfigurations. It offers a way for security administrators to form a vulnerability analysis on Windows-based PCs. It is a free tool that must be downloaded from Microsoft. It may be used to scan a single computer or several computers, and the administrator can choose to scan remote computers.

Using the Tool

In this exercise, you will download the Microsoft Security Baseline Analyzer and use it to scan your workstation.

1. Click the Download button on this page at

    www.microsoft.com/en-us/download/details.aspx?id=7558

2. Select the version by placing a check mark in the box to the left (Figure C.1). Then click the Next button.

    To enable the Microsoft Security Baseline Analyzer to scan a workstation once it has been downloaded, proceed with the following steps.

3. Start the Microsoft Security Baseline Analyzer.

4. Depending on your version of Windows, you may be prompted to confirm that you want to really run this. Choose Yes to continue Figure C-2. (You must have administrator rights on your PC to run MBSA.)

FIGURE C.1   Select an MBSA download version

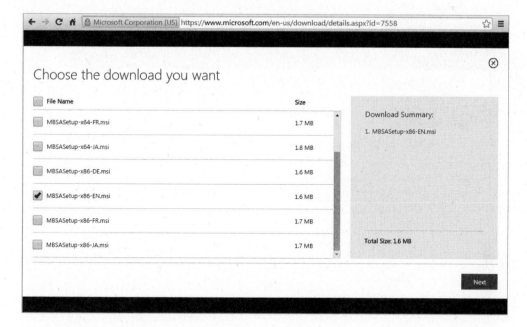

5. Click Scan A Computer (Figure C.2).

FIGURE C.2   MBSA selection choices

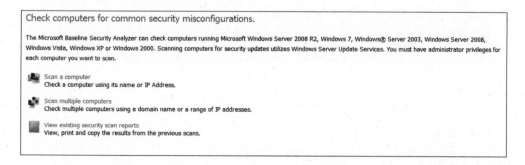

Notice that the computer's name will be inserted into the top box. You may also select the computer of your choice by inputting an IP address (Figure C.3).

6. To begin the scan, click the Start Scan button.

At the end of the scan, you will be presented with a report. The default will be to display the worst score first. Figure C.4 illustrates a saved report showing a number of security updates missing.

FIGURE C.3   Select a device to scan.

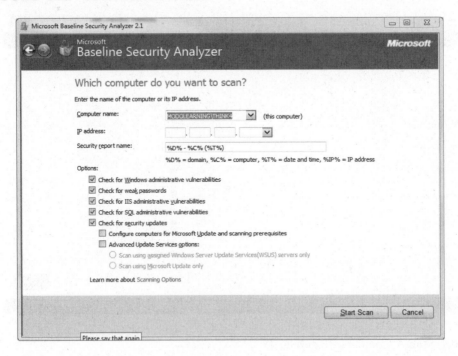

FIGURE C.4   Scanning report with errors

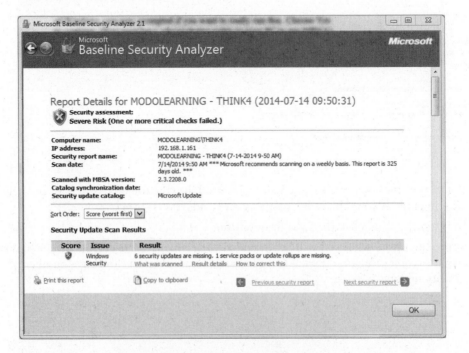

7. View the report details. Items identified are classified in the various sections.

8. Experiment by scanning other computers to view the report details (Figure C.4). If an item has a link titled How To Correct This, click it and examine the issue, solution, and instructions.

9. Exit Microsoft Security Baseline Analyzer.

Microsoft Password Checker

Passwords are usually used as the first choice as an authentication mechanism during a logon procedure. They represent the "something you know" authentication factor. Many organizations have a password policy that specifies the criteria to be used to create a password. Many of these policies indicate that passwords should be at least eight characters long, and the longer the better. The strongest passwords include uppercase and lowercase letters, numerals, punctuation marks, and special symbols.

Users should be advised that the best passwords are actually passphrases. For instance, the phrase Igrewupat1604Sylvandrive is a personal passphrase I might remember. It also provides enough characters that it would take in excess of 20 million years for current computers to determine it through brute force.

Using the Tool

In this exercise, you will navigate to the Microsoft Safety & Security Center web page and use the Microsoft password Checker.

1. Access the Microsoft Safety & Security Center page at

    `www.microsoft.com/security/pc-security/password-checker.aspx`

2. Enter your password in the password box. The strength meter below the box will indicate the relative strength of the password (Figure C.5).

This is an excellent tool to use during user awareness training classes. You will illustrate to your users how to gauge the effectiveness of their passwords. Not only will this apply to passwords used in the workplace, but it will also instruct them on how to construct safe passwords for their personal accounts.

FIGURE C.5   Using Microsoft Password Checker

Internet Explorer Phishing and Malicious Software Filter

Internet Explorer's SmartScreen Filter analyzes web pages as you browse the Internet. It searches for characteristics that might be suspicious. It does this by checking sites that you visit against a dynamic list of reported phishing and malicious software sites. SmartScreen

Filter will also check files that are downloaded against the list of reported software and programs that are known to be unsafe. If the filter detects the signature of a suspicious website or malicious software, it will display a message giving you the opportunity to comment and will advise you to proceed to the site using caution.

Using the Tool

In this exercise, you will enable the Internet Explorer SmartScreen Filter to analyze web sites that you visit.

1. Start Internet Explorer, click Tools ➤ Internet Options, and choose the Advanced tab on the top right.

2. Scroll down to the Security section (Figure C.6).

3. Under this section, find Enable SmartScreen Filter and place a check mark in the box. Click OK.

FIGURE C.6 Internet Options advanced settings

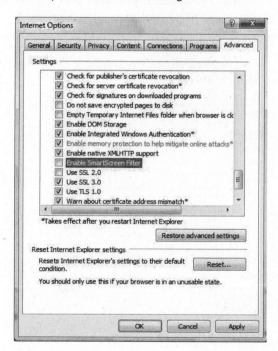

Manage Internet Cookies

Cookies are small text files that websites and advertisers placed on your computer. They used to contain your browsing patterns, shopping history, identification information, and other specific information about your preferences. The advantage of cookies is that websites will know your preferences based upon your last visit. For instance, forms might be pre-filled with information so you may not have to sign on every time you visit a site. Cookies specifically from advertisers, referred to as third-party cookies, allow the advertisers to obtain a tremendous amount of your information. Besides tracking your purchasing preferences on their site, they could monitor your search habits, web site navigation, purchasing activities and many other items such as product returns or typical amounts spent on other web sites. This is information that you may not want them to know.

Using the Tool

In this exercise, you will establish privacy settings in Internet Explorer to manage both first-party as well as advertiser third-party cookies.

1. Within Internet Explorer, click Tools ➢ Internet Options and choose the Privacy tab (Figure C.7).

FIGURE C.7   Internet Options Privacy tab

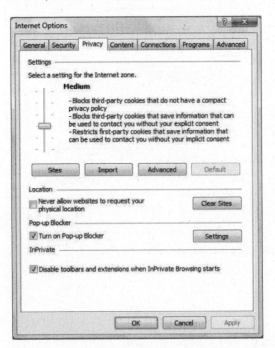

2. Click the Advanced button to open the Advanced Privacy Settings dialog (Figure C.8).

FIGURE C.8   Advanced Privacy Settings dialog

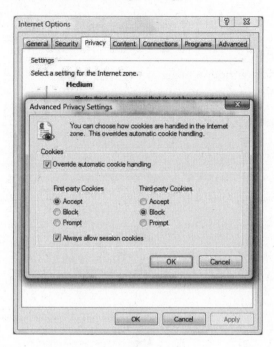

3. Check the Override Automatic Cookie Handling box.

4. Choose Accept for First-Party Cookies.

5. Choose Block for Third-Party Cookies.

6. Check the Always Allow Session Cookies box.

7. Click OK.

8. Click OK again to exit Internet Options.

Observing Logs with Event Viewer

Windows workstations automatically record many events and log files. Event Viewer is a Windows tool that you can use to view these log files. It can be useful when troubleshooting system problems and errors such as programs failing to start as expected or updates failing to download automatically.

Using the Tool

In this exercise, you use the Event Viewer in Windows to observe Windows log files.

1. Click the Start button and choose Control Panel ➤ System and Security (Figure C.9).

2. Under Administrative Tools, click View Event Logs. The Event Viewer window is shown in Figure C.10.

3. In the left panel, select Windows Logs.

4. In the pop-up window, double-click Application.

FIGURE C.9   Windows Control Panel

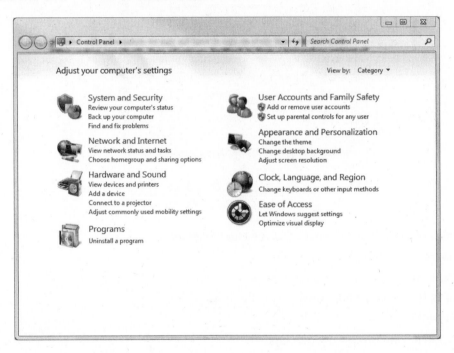

FIGURE C.10   Event Viewer

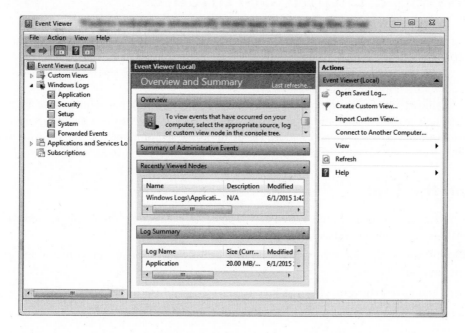

You'll see a list of events and errors (Figure C.11). You can click any event or error for detailed information.

FIGURE C.11   Event Viewer showing events and errors

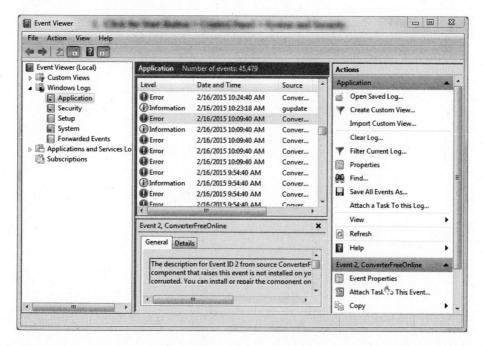

Viewing a Digital Certificate

You learned in Chapter 7, "Domain 5: Cryptography," that certificates are issued by third-party trusted certificate authorities and contain the owner's public key and other information about the owner. The certificate authority digitally signs the certificate to prove authenticity and nonrepudiation.

The certificate authority also provides a hash value, referred to on the certificate as a fingerprint, that can be used to validate certificate integrity. A typical web browser maintains dozens of certificates, and certificates can be added either automatically or manually when you are visiting other websites for the first time. Certificates can be easily viewed, installed, or deleted.

Using the Tool

There are two methods that can be used access certificates. To view the certificate associated with an e-commerce website, follow these steps:

1. Within Internet Explorer 9 or above, go to a website such as Amazon.com and log in if you have an account.

2. Once you have logged in, click the lock icon to the right of the URL.

3. Then click View Certificates to open the dialog shown in Figure C.12.

FIGURE C.12   Certificate properties

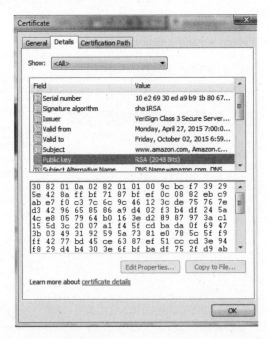

4. On the dialog, choose the Details tab on the top menu.

5. Scroll down to and click Public Key.

    All of the hexadecimal characters in the text box represent the public key contained on this certificate.

6. Click other fields within the Details tab.

    Notice that the issuer for the Amazon.com site is VeriSign. VeriSign is therefore the certificate authority. Clicking Subject will present the information concerning the public key owner, in this case Amazon.com, Inc.

    To view all of the certificates that are on your PC, do the following:

1. To open Certificate Manager, click the Start button.

2. In the search box, enter `certmgr.msc` to open the Windows Certificate Manager (Figure C.13).

FIGURE C.13   Windows Certificate Manager

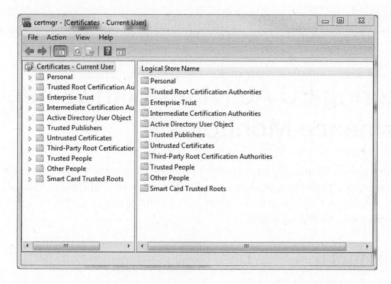

3. Click Trusted Root Certification Authorities ➤ Certificates (Figure C.14).

FIGURE C.14   Certificates of trusted root certification authorities

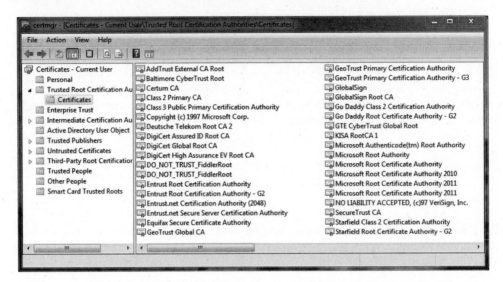

Monitoring PC Activities with Windows Performance Monitor

Windows Performance Monitor is used to examine how programs and applications you run affect your computer's performance. You can view activities in real time or collect logs for later analysis. Windows Performance Monitor uses performance counters that can be used to create custom views of PC activities.

Using the Tool

In this exercise, you will use the Performance Monitor in Windows to observe the current PC activity.

1. Open Performance Monitor by pressing the Windows button on the keyboard and typing **R**.

2. Type **perfmon.msc** into the Run box. Figure C.15 shows the Performance Monitor window.

FIGURE C.15   Performance Monitor

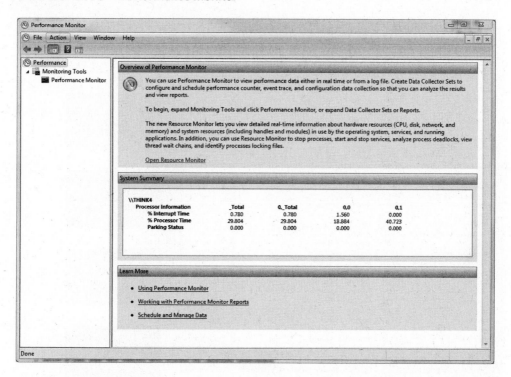

3. Click the blue Open Resource Monitor link in the center of the Performance Monitor Window.

   Resource Manager is shown in Figure C.16.

FIGURE C.16   Resource Monitor indicating usage levels

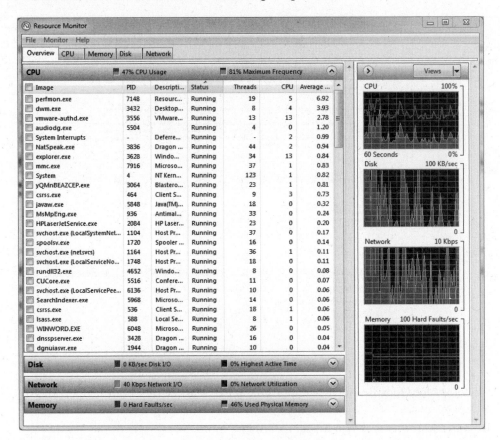

4. Notice the graphs of the current PC activity. Click across the tabs at the top to see different views.

   The listing under CPU is a list of currently running services. You can see that it is dynamic and changing all of the time.

5. Click the down arrow on each of the three tabs below the CPU listing to expand them (Figure C.17).

   This will provide a report on disk, network, and memory usage.

FIGURE C.17   Performance Monitor expanded view

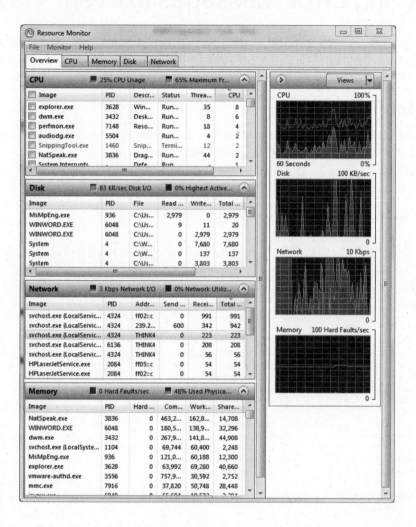

Windows Performance Monitor may also be used to monitor specific applications and activities. You can track errors and watch the real-time performance of events as they transpire on the PC.

Analyzing Error Messages in Event Viewer

Analyzing log files has been a central method of determining problems within a system. Event Viewer is a Windows tool that allows you to view a number of log files and drill down to specific entries to identify potential problems.

Using the Tool

In this exercise, you will access Windows log files using Event Viewer. You will be able to observe events and sort critical errors in descending order.

1. Click Start ➤ Control Panel ➤ System and Security ➤ Administrative Tools ➤ Event Viewer (Figure C.18).

FIGURE C.18 Selecting Event Viewer from Control Panel

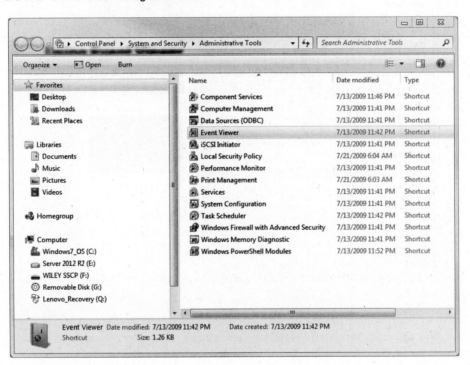

2. Double-click Event Viewer. Figure C.19 shows the Overview and Summary page.

FIGURE C.19   Event Viewer Overview and Summary

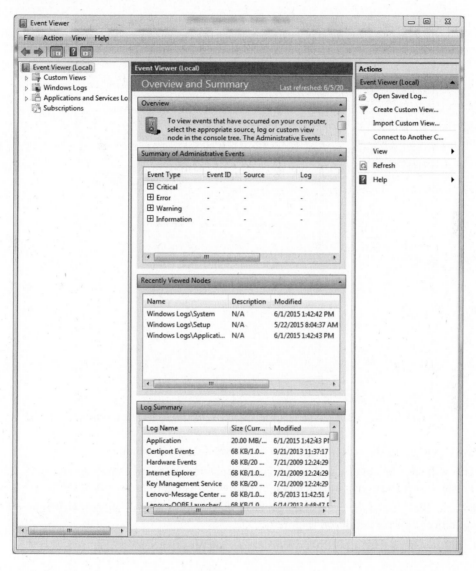

3. Expand Windows Logs in the left pane to open the panel shown in Figure C.20.

FIGURE C.20 Windows Logs

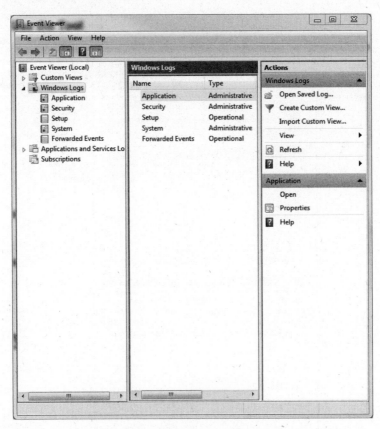

4. Click System. In the center pane, click the Level column heading.

This will sort the column and may take a couple of minutes to complete (Figure C.21). This will sort the events into descending order according to how critical they are.

5. Double-click one of the events. An Event Properties pop-up will appear with an explanation of the error condition (Figure C.22).

6. Click the Details tab and expand System to view the error details (Figure C.23).

FIGURE C.21   Summary of the system event errors

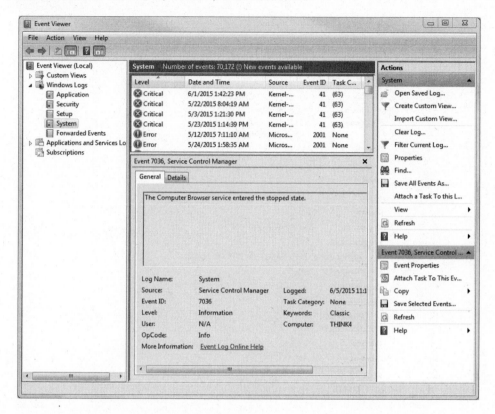

FIGURE C.22   Event properties

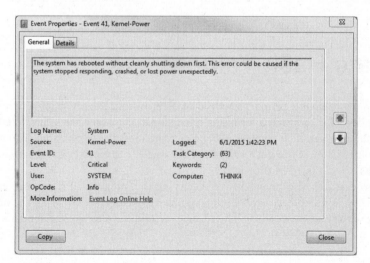

FIGURE C.23   Event details

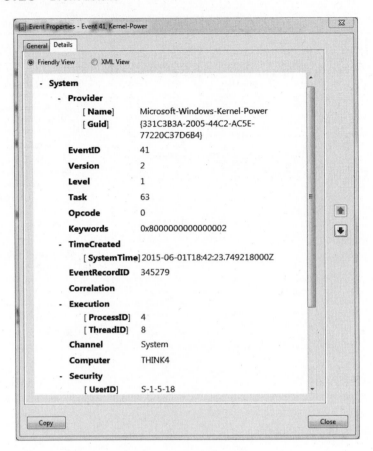

Calculate Hash Values

Calculating a hash value is a primary method of determining the integrity of a message. The sender hashes their message to obtain a hash value. Messages are sent along with the hash value to the receiver. The receiver also hashes the message to obtain a second hash value. Upon comparison, if the hash values are the same, the receiver can be assured that the message has not changed in transit.

The same process can also be used when verifying the integrity of a message signed with a digital signature. When preparing a digital signature, the sender encrypts the hash value of the message with their private key. The receiver would have to use the sender's public key to decrypt the hash value. This would provide proof of origin as well as nonrepudiation, and at the same time the hash value would provide message integrity.

There are a number of different hash calculators on the Internet for free download.

Using the Tool

In this exercise, you will download a typical free calculator and explore processing a message to obtain a hash value.

1. Download the free hash calculator from the following location:

   `http://sourceforge.net/projects/hash-calculator/`

   Figure C.24 shows the calculator in text mode.

FIGURE C.24   The MD2 Hash Calculator in text mode

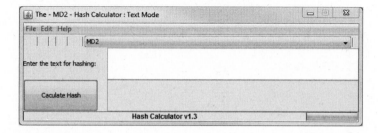

2. Expand the drop-down list to view the available hash algorithms (Figure C.25).

   Notice that the SHA-*XXX* algorithms will produce a hash value with the corresponding number of bits. For instance, SHA-256 will produce a hash value of 256 bits.

FIGURE C.25   Choosing a hash algorithm

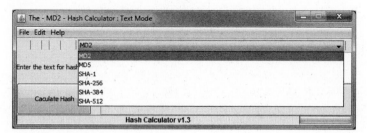

3. Select a hash algorithm.

4. Enter a message into the message box and click the Calculate Hash button.

Notice the resulting hash. Change the message by one character and view the new resulting hash. This proves that even if one character changes, the entire hash value changes, and therefore when compared with the sender's original hash value, it will be quite obvious that the hash values are not equal and therefore the message has changed (Figure C.26).

FIGURE C.26   Hash Calculator creating a hash value from a message

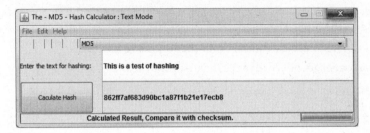

Index

Note to the Reader: Throughout this index **boldfaced** page numbers indicate primary discussions of a topic. *Italicized* page numbers indicate illustrations.

E

N

Comprehensive Online Learning Environment

Register on Sybex.com to gain access to the online interactive learning environment and test bank to help you study for your (ISC)² SSCP certification - included with your purchase of this book!

The online tool includes:

- Assessment Test to help you focus your study to specific objectives
- Chapter Tests to reinforce what you learned
- Practice Exams to test your knowledge of the material
- Electronic Flashcards to reinforce your learning and provide last-minute test prep before the exam
- Searchable Glossary gives you instant access to the key terms you'll need to know for the exam

Go to `http://sybextestbanks.wiley.com` to register and gain access to this comprehensive study tool package.